I0891092

Routledge Revivals

Making People Pay

First published in 1973, this book offers a fascinating and systematic description of the debt-collection process in 1970s England. Basing his research on the words of creditors, debtors, solicitors and debt-collectors, Paul Rock's research was conducted when imprisonment for debt was still in existence. The book covers the major stages in a defaulter's career, from enforcement by his creditors and the work of the debt-collector, through the various processes of the law, often to a period of imprisonment. Particular attention is given to the attempts made by debt-collectors to manage an unusual form of deviance and the consequences of their actions.

Making People Pay

Paul Rock

Routledge
Taylor & Francis Group
ROUTLEDGE REVIVALS

First published in 1973
by Routledge & Kegan Paul

This edition first published in 2013 by Routledge
2 Park Square, Milton Park, Abingdon, Oxon, OX14 4RN

Simultaneously published in the USA and Canada
by Routledge
711 Third Avenue, New York, NY 10017

Routledge is an imprint of the Taylor & Francis Group, an informa business

Publisher's Note
The publisher has gone to great lengths to ensure the quality of this reprint but points out that some imperfections in the original copies may be apparent.

Disclaimer
The publisher has made every effort to trace copyright holders and welcomes correspondence from those they have been unable to contact.

A Library of Congress record exists under ISBN: 73083121

ISBN 13: 978-0-415-82831-4 (hbk)
ISBN 13: 978-0-203-52152-6 (ebk)

Making people pay

Paul Rock

Department of Sociology,
London School of Economics

Routledge & Kegan Paul

London and Boston

First published in 1973
by Routledge & Kegan Paul Ltd
Broadway House, 68–74 Carter Lane,
London EC4V 5EL and
9 Park Street,
Boston, Mass. 02108, U.S.A.
Printed in Great Britain by
Unwin Brothers Limited,
The Gresham Press,
Old Woking, Surrey.
A member of the Staples Printing Group

ISBN 0 7100 7684 3

Library of Congress Catalog Card Number: 73–83121

Contents

Tables and figures

Tables

Figures

Preface

This book is a piece of descriptive sociology which attempts to lay bare the basic structure of the English debt collection process. I believe that it can serve two main purposes: it offers information about a central but almost totally neglected area of social control; and, more important, it documents the manner in which social deviancy is managed so that few defaulters undergo significant transformations of identity. In Lemert's terminology, it is a study of 'primary deviation', deviation that is slight in its implications for the rule-breaker's beliefs about himself and his place in the social world. Debt collection is a system of artful control which is quite unlike any other that has received formal analysis. It represents a deliberately constructed moral career whose effects and organization contain remarkable features.

Some major changes have taken place in the collection system since the study was completed. The report of the Payne Committee on the Enforcement of Judgment Debts generated new legislation which led, in particular, to the substitution of the attachment of earnings for the older sanction of imprisonment under the 1869 Debtors Act.[1] Those changes have not really robbed my study of its interest. The sociological significance of a work does not disappear when the practices that are described themselves disappear. Moreover, although the procedures which were introduced in 1971 by the Administration of Justice Act have not yet brought about a completely stable system, it is unlikely that they will deny debt collection its integrated character or its propensity to protect debtors' conceptions of themselves. Enforcement will remain a bureaucratically-ordered career which rests on an intricate manipulation

[1] The legislation was contained in the Administration of Justice Act, 1970, which came into effect in August 1971.

of symbols. Again, legislation has now rendered a whole field of study inaccessible to anyone but the social historian. When the new control structures crystallize, they should present interesting contrasts whose evolution deserves attention.

Although some of the phenomena described in this book are now extinct, I shall continue to describe them in the present tense. Any other practice would lead only to convoluted language and an unnecessarily complicated style.

Making People Pay is a truncated and revised version of the doctoral dissertation which I prepared at Oxford. Terence Morris was extremely kind to me when I was unsure whether I could pursue graduate work. Officials of the County Courts Branch and the Prison Department were most patient with me, being generous with their advice. In particular, I would like to acknowledge the assistance of the staffs of the Lambeth, Westminster and Willesden county courts and of the Registrar of Bow county court. I would also like to thank the creditors, debtors, debt-collectors and solicitors who gave me their time and expertise with little or no obvious gain to themselves. Above all, I am deeply grateful to Nigel Walker whose supervision and interest were most stimulating. I was extremely fortunate to be placed in his care.

1 Organizing perspectives

Debt collection is a most complex process whose ramifications extend into many areas of social life. It is distinguished by an internal intricacy, being made up of ordered stages. Each stage is a different kind of activity guided by different ideas and governed by different sentiments. Each stage is organized by a particular grouping of institutions which have their own functions, conceptions of collection, relations with one another and links with institutions in adjoining stages. Enforcement itself is but a part of a larger economic, political and legal system of credit, consumption and market behaviour. It is patently impossible to present all the faces of so complicated an entity in one coherent model. Any manageable analysis must neglect or obscure vast tracts of potentially interesting terrain.[1] I shall thus try to make my description more intelligible by dwelling on a few major substantive and formal themes. These themes will lend order to discussion and permit a detailed focus.

Making People Pay is mainly a study of enforcement as a type of status passage. I shall ignore those features which have comparatively little influence on the shape of the enforcement career and on the assumptions that dictate how far and how fast a defaulter will be propelled through the sequence of unpleasant experiences prepared for him. Debt collection can be pursued over long periods of time. Its structure and style are carefully devised to impart an impression of significant change and development. It fosters the belief that the defaulter's intransigence is becoming ever more consequential for him. In order to promote this belief, those who collect debts work with an elaborate symbolism based upon the timing, spacing, pacing and contents of their approaches. Enforcement is represented as an

1 The Report of the Committee on Consumer Credit (Crowther, 1971) provides a most useful introduction to understanding the larger context of debt collection.

unambiguous progression towards an unpalatable fate. As debtors near that fate, they are encouraged to review the meanings of their actions and their relations to the collection system. The bureaucratic control of default is therefore organized around the managed transformation of debtors' identities. It routinely prepares status passages for hundreds of thousands of people. *Making People Pay* will focus on this preparation and on the perspectives that lend it coherence.

My concentration on enforcement as a career mirrors not only a central quality of debt collection but also an intellectual concern of the sociology of deviance. That concern may be traced back to a dialectical tradition which was established by Simmel and furthered by the Chicago school of sociology. The Chicago sociologists linked a formalist interest in ideas of 'succession' and the 'natural history' (Park, 1967, 1927, 1936 and 1937) with a substantive interest in the sociology of education and the sociology of occupations.[2] In turn, the sociology of deviance and the Symbolic Interactionist paradigm which fathered it have conceived of social life as an orderly process of 'becoming'. Social phenomena undergo a regular and intelligible evolution whose emergent properties cannot be explained simply by some 'fixed set of determining events' (Davis, 1963, p. 10). In its most rigid and organized form, that evolution exhibits all the character of a career—a patterned series of connected stages leading to a discernible goal.

At each phase of the collection career, new influences appear and are transformed in systematic fashion. For the defaulter passing through the phases, these influences become materials for the construction of an emerging self. It is this fusion of deviance and social control that has also preoccupied the sociology of deviance. Social control is not taken to be a mere context of deviation. Instead, it defines, shapes and infuses rule-breaking. Control plays an unusually critical role in the regulation of debtors' identities because there is relatively little autonomous development within default itself. The debtor is typically a passive deviant. His deviancy resides in his refusal or inability to perform desired acts. Process is *imposed* on default by the career which is organized for the debtor. A defaulter who does not repay a debt is *made* to undergo a series of forced changes of experience. The moral career of the debtor is so arranged that his passivity is interpreted as 'becoming'. Without the effort of debt-collecting institutions, there would be no process.

[2] An early example is Cressey (1932), in which the 'moral career of the taxi dancer' is discussed. More recent works on the career include Hughes, 'Cycles, Turning Points and Careers' in Hughes (1958); Strauss, 'Transformations of Identity' in Rose (1962); Roth (1963); and Glaser and Strauss (1971).

A third strand will be a stress upon the interpretative procedures that debt collectors employ to make sense of their work. It is these procedures that animate the enforcement machinery and give structure to the routine treatment of defaulters. Debtors are continually subjected to a system of classification, testing, typing and prediction. Bureaucratic collection is an exercise in mechanical decision-making, and its practices are as much involved with the production of information as with coercion or cajolery. Indeed, collectors treat every part of their activity as pregnant with significant knowledge about the past, present and future of defaulters. *Making People Pay* will examine the manner in which the organizations involved in enforcement generate and apply such knowledge. Unless recourse is made to these practices, much enforcement simply becomes unintelligible. Collection must be analysed as an enterprise devoted largely to the nurturing of a particular version of social reality. That reality explains, predicts and justifies enforcement work.

My argument will be simplified in this and following chapters by elementary models of the Creditor, the Defaulter, the Debt-collector and so on. They will portray how significant figures employ 'occasional rationality' to evaluate and act upon the limited information which they have before them. The trajectory and outcome of any default are 'necessary' products of the way in which enforcers define important areas of the world. The models will be stylized representations of the perspectives that are brought to bear on enforcement. Some ideal type construction must be performed in order to capture and reproduce the contents of social life. I shall attempt to use my ideal types for the purpose of providing what Scott (1968, p. 6) calls 'adequate description':

> An adequate description should be sufficiently detailed so that one could write a set of instructions enabling a stranger to reproduce the scenes described. If, for instance, one describes the interaction of a mental patient with other role partners, such as a psychiatrist, a nurse, and so forth, one should write a set of instructions so that a stranger acting them out would be identified by the psychiatrist and nurse as a mental patient—and they should behave in a manner that the scenes described would be recreated. To meet this criterion, one must construct 'personal ideal types'. The personal ideal type refers to the construction of a 'puppet' endowed 'with just that kind of knowledge he needs to perform the job for the sake of which he was brought into the scientific world'.

It is clear that there will always be some variation within types of institution, and I shall amplify these differences as each model is developed. Nevertheless, it is useful to refer to the Creditor or the Debt-collector as if each were a homogeneous entity. Creditors, for instance, share much in common. Every institution rests upon a system of beliefs about its role and its relations with outsiders. These systems resemble mythologies because they simplify the world, people it with symbolic beings who serve to explain events, and provide rules for assessing causes and effects. Institutional mythologies are moulded by the structure of an organization and by the routine and exceptional situations which it encounters. Bureaucratic creditors confront the same universe of consumers, dealers, competitors, defaulters, debt-collectors, solicitors and courts. They are often bound by identical legal restraints and face common problems. The perspectives provided by the mythologies are thus frequently dominated by common themes.

The low visibility of enforcement

Perhaps the most significant feature of debt collection is its cultivation of low visibility. It is this, and the consequences that flow from it, that explain most of the principal qualities of enforcement as a status passage. A discussion of the inconspicuous nature of enforcement serves as a useful introduction to a general analysis of collection.

The visibility of a social problem is dependent, in part, on the political context of deviation. Few problems are immediately and unambiguously regarded as demanding attention. Instead, their perturbing qualities must receive definition. It is the manner in which issues are presented by interested groups that affects the evolution of deviance. Fuller and Myers (1941, p. 321), for instance, argue that deviation cannot be explained solely in terms of its autonomous development:

> Social problems do not arise full-blown, commanding community attention and evoking adequate policies and machinery for their solution. On the contrary, we believe that social problems exhibit a temporal course of development in which different phases or stages may be distinguished. Each stage anticipates its successor and each succeeding stage contains new elements which mark it off from its predecessor. A social problem thus conceived as always being in a dynamic stage of 'becoming' passes through the natural history stages of awareness, policy determination and reform.

Debt collection is so organized that it contains very few of the mechanisms which can attract and hold the attention of people towards a social problem. Indeed, when there *is* anxiety publicly expressed about enforcement, it is often an anxiety about the nature of the social control procedures that are applied. Default is one of those instances of deviance that exist and are policed in a context of popular unawareness.

Cressey (1967, p. xii) has remarked that the usefulness of Sutherland's book, *White Collar Crime*, lies in:

> Its demonstration that a pattern of crime can be found to exist outside both the focus of popular preoccupations with crime and the forms of scientific investigations of crime and criminality. Explanations of why such a pattern could remain for so long outside both popular and scientific purview is a sociological question of first-rate importance. . . . What is needed, in effect, is a 'sociology of crime reporting'. . . . Why does a society report the crimes it reports, why does it overlook what it overlooks, and how does it go about deciding that it has, in fact, overlooked something?

Implicitly, at least, this book will be just such a sociology of deviance reporting. I shall put forward the argument that debt collection is organized around a number of concerns that preclude public excitement and encourage a lack of interest. These concerns are maintained by the authorities who provide dominant interpretations of social control and by the debt-collectors who find it expedient to support such interpretations.

Lawyers, sociologists and others appear to have been given a mandate to provide authoritative definitions of social reality. They conventionally portray default as a form of private deviance which is not a proper subject for massive state intervention. Debt collection has thus been allowed to remain a most unusual form of social control which is largely entrusted to the victims of the deviance. Such a portrayal flows from legal, philosophical and sociological definitions of society as a dual entity. Society is represented as a phenomenon which is qualitatively different from the aggregated attributes of its members. It has its own discrete purposes and interests which must not be confounded with those of individual persons. Offences against society are vastly more significant than offences against separate members of the community. Such offences constitute an attack on society as a moral, political and collective enterprise. The harm they inflict is more potent because it can impair the moral fabric which unites men.

Default causes no such harm in this interpretation. Rather, it provokes discomfort or unhappiness in individuals. The organized response to default is consequently milder and less symbolically laden. Gregory (1962, p. 1), in the official handbook for county court staff, expresses this interpretation most clearly:

> The object of criminal justice is to punish an offender for the wrong he has committed; the object of civil justice is to enforce a right at the suit of the person in whom it is vested. Certain acts, such as murder, arson and theft, are regarded by the law as so harmful to the general community that they are treated as crimes and forbidden under pain of punishment. . . . Certain other acts, while recognised as wrongful are not regarded by the law as crimes but merely as infringements of private rights. In such cases the law does not punish the offender but merely lends its machinery to the injured person to enable him to recover the money, land or goods which are due to him.

Thus conceived, enforcement has no place in the ritual life of society. It does not centre on the defence of the sacred. It is in radical contrast to the procedures of the criminal law. Whereas the criminal law is based on the notion of a conflict between the state (or society, conveniently reified) and the individual, civil law is based on the notion of a conflict between individuals. This is signified by the different structures, ceremonies and consequences of the systems which control criminal and civil deviance. Criminal law is upheld by agents of the state; prosecuted by representatives of the state; adorned, in many cases, with ritual and status-degradation work; and leads to the imputation of *guilt*. Civil law is prosecuted by private individuals; divested of ritual (in most county court cases); and leads to no imputation of guilt until the state, personified by the court, is thought to be harmed.[3] Moreover, part of the cost of civil law enforcement is met by private individuals.

The unceremoniousness of debt collection has important consequences for the defaulter's experience of enforcement as a status passage. Most systems of social control revolve around *rites de passage* which serve declaratory and isolating functions. Thus Erikson (1964, p. 16) argues:

> The community's decision to bring deviant sanctions against an individual is not a simple act of censure. It is a sharp rite of transition, at once moving him out of his normal position in society and transferring him into a distinct deviant role. The ceremonies which accomplish this change of status . . . perform an act of social *placement*, assigning him to a special role . . . which redefines his position in society. These ceremonies tend to be events of wide public interest and usually take place in a dramatic, ritualized setting. Now an important feature of

[3] When, for instance, there is a contempt of court.

> these ceremonies in our society is that they are almost irreversible. Most provisional roles conferred by society . . . include some kind of terminal ceremony to mark the individual's movement back out of the role once its temporary advantages have been exhausted. But the roles allotted to the deviant seldom make allowance for this type of passage.

The official regulation of default makes no provision for such ritual. Debt collection is not thought to be consequential enough to deserve the dramatization which would render it highly visible. It is this treatment of enforcement which marries well with a peculiarity of default itself. Debtors are redeemable deviants who are held to require management because they have *failed* to perform certain acts. Those acts can be performed at almost any time in the enforcement career. Defaulters are thus conditionally deviant. Their deviance can be attributed neither to an immutable inner state nor to the commission of a completed act. Debtors can always repay their debts and, having done so, instantly cease to be defaulters.

Conditional deviance requires special handling. Debtors cannot be exposed to overt denunciation which might bring about an irreversible status passage. Instead, they must be carefully protected against degradation and ostracism. Debt collectors seek to provide only one route from the role which defaulters temporarily occupy. That route is a return to the normal, moral community. The debtor's ability to make good his default places him in a strong position from which to negotiate a career for himself. The weakly-armed collector can ill afford to estrange him.

Most systems of control generate possibilities of deviance-amplification (Wilkins, 1964, p. 85) or a transition from primary deviation to secondary deviation (Lemert, 1951, pp. 40–64). That is, the deviant experiences an organized response to his rule-breaking and is then constrained to evolve a satisfactory method of coping with this response.

Lemert (1951, p. 75) states, 'when a person begins to employ his deviant behavior or a role based upon it as a means of defense, attack, or adjustment to the overt and covert problems created by the consequent societal reaction to him, his deviation is secondary.' A conditional deviant undergoing secondary deviation is likely to be confirmed in his alienated status. His chances of redemption are considerably reduced. Thus, dramatized enforcement processes are most dysfunctional to the debt collection system. The dualistic conception of society eases the work of enforcement. It limits the number of defaulters who organize their roles around defence or attack.

Much of the organized reaction to default is sustained by hostile definitions of the debtor, but these definitions remain covert and no clear deviant role-styles are offered.[4] Because collectors do not engineer status degradation ceremonies or publicize their work, enforcement is never as overtly spectacular as other types of control. It contains the minimum of ritual. The rhetoric which is routinely employed in the debt-collecting courts is mild and neutral. No county court judge could call debtors 'hordes of hooligans . . . long-haired mentally unstable petty little hoodlums . . . sawdust Caesars who can only find courage like rats hunting in packs'. (A magistrate quoted in Cohen, 1967, p. 128.) Debtors can be manipulated because they are kept apart and without significant support. In London, at least, there does not appear to be a viable subculture of default.[5]

Although the public face of debt collection discourages passion, the system's hidden anatomy has many of the features of a conventional enforcement machine. It is a mistake to assume that the public face disguises nothing and it is equally naïve to assume that the system exactly corresponds to its formal blueprint. As Lemert (1951, p. 68) argues, 'agencies and institutions have a private as well as a public history; but the former, thanks to careful attention to public relations and publicity, seldom become common knowledge.'

Not only do moral authorities and enforcers promote the low visibility of collection, professional communicators also deflect public attention away from default and its regulation. They appear to endorse the dominant interpretation of collection as a dull and uneventful process. One of the most central areas of social control in Britain therefore remains virtually unreported.[6] Those who are active in it expect anonymity and invisibility as a matter of course. They voice surprise when their practices are described by the mass media. For instance, an official at a new county court remarked on

[4] *Micawber* might represent a viable social type, so might the creditors' *Professional Debtor*, but neither is offered to the debtor and they do not seem to be as significant as, say, the *dope-fiend*, the *tart*, the *Teddy Boy* or the *hooligan*. What distinguishes defaulting roles is the fact that there are no implicit or explicit rewards attached to them. By contrast, deviant roles are frequently encouraged (cf. Scheff, 1966 A, p. 84).

[5] By a 'subculture of default', I mean a system of beliefs which focus on default, encourage predatory behaviour, and instruct their adherents in the arts of deceit and evasion. Any substantial community in Britain does, of course, contain some who are versed in these arts; but they are comparatively ill-organized and unselfconscious.

[6] It is significant that the only incident which did receive wide coverage in the period of my research was based on a misapprehension. A large number of newspapers reported the remarks of a Minister without Portfolio who stated, 'it was not generally recognized that at any one time there were 7,000 people in prison for non-payment of debt'. The Minister had mistaken the annual number of receptions into prison for the 'daily average population'.

the unusual publicity which some of his court's proceedings had attracted (Roberts, 1961, p. 31):

> The first courts, both Judges' and Registrars', held in one of the two new modern buildings which we share with the magistrates, were given quite a splash in the local press. We have been startled to find the reporters taking a keen interest even in the judgment summons and Registrars' courts. Many regular debtors, shielded up to now by a decent obscurity, are being shocked to find their names and addresses in the local paper.

The newspaper is one of the most influential agents in the structuring of a public awareness of deviance and deviants. With the exception of a few manuals written by enforcement personnel for enforcement personnel, the mass media are the only commonly available source of information about debt collection. But the media do not treat enforcement as newsworthy.

When newspapers refrain from attending to enforcement, public ignorance is further increased. Such reticence appears to stem from the two roles which newspapers play in deviance reporting. One role focuses on deviance as a significant departure from everyday life. Rule-breaking receives attention because it falls outside the mundane experience of most readers. Deviation is routine, but it is not thought to be routinely encountered. Park (1967, p. 110) suggests that the metropolitan press offers a 'flight from reality' by its 'persistent search in the drab episodes of city life for the romantic and picturesque, its dramatic accounts of vice and crime . . .'. It is evident that most enforcement cannot provide much material for flights from reality. When it does become newsworthy, debt collection has either taken a bizarre form or else routine has gone awry. Newspapers sporadically sport such headlines as: 'Stolen: A List of "Shame" ' (*Daily Mirror*, 24 May 1965); 'Vicar's Bad Debts Plan Under Fire' (*Evening News*, 7 September 1966); 'My Eviction—By Cripple of 95' (*Daily Mirror*, 6 April 1966); 'Debtors, Beware of the Dog' (*Observer*, 21 November 1965); 'Acid Threat Over a Debt' (*Daily Mirror*, 17 June 1965); 'Bingo! It's the Rent Van' (*Daily Mirror*, 19 July 1965); or 'The Bailiff Bit Me, says Widow' (*Daily Mirror*, 5 August 1965). These incidents are not likely to illuminate the nature of the typical enforcement processes which I shall describe.

There is another account of the newspaper's function in the reporting of deviation. Erikson (1964, p. 14) argues:

> Transactions between deviant persons and agents of control have always attracted a good deal of attention in this and other cultures. . . . An enormous amount of modern 'news' is

> devoted to reports about deviant behavior and its punishment. . . . In a figurative sense, at least, morality and immorality meet at the public scaffold, and it is during this meeting that the community declares where the line between them should be drawn.

Issues revolving around the resolution of morally problematic behaviour are held to be capable of generating news. Areas of moral ambiguity and official measures to dispel that ambiguity have always attracted newspaper interest. Reports of deviance and its containment define the normative contours of society and establish its frontiers. According to the dualistic perspective, default is not morally problematic because it does not bear on matters which affect the community. As an ethically neutral entity, default does not engender important encounters between the rule-breaker and the rule-enforcer. There can be no excitement in debt collection because it does not take place on the contested frontiers of society.

Authoritative understandings, then, conventionally depict society as a dual phenomenon. They cast debt collection into the role of adjusting relations between individuals, relations which have no implications for the moral map of society. As a result, enforcement cannot assign societally significant roles to its deviants because it is not a societally significant process. It is not the subject of press concern because it does not manufacture issues appropriate to the deviance-defining function of the press.

Such legal and journalistic distinctions between the private and public worlds of social control appear to be critical. They organize the social reality of debt collection so that it becomes an inconsequential activity. Default and defaulters cannot be presented as interesting or dramatic. Rather, they are mildly sordid parts of a dull and uneventful process.

This distinction is vital to an understanding of the way in which defaulters are managed, classified and exposed to the view of outsiders. Those who are responsible for master interpretations of social life have dismissed enforcement as peripheral and defaulters as incompetents. Yet debt-collectors themselves do not necessarily subscribe to this definition. They are not always a party to the dualistic view of deviance, and their dissent provides another reason why there is an overt and a covert system of control. The social reality of the professional interpreters may not percolate through to the enforcers or it may not tally with the organized perspectives which are derived from a routine confrontation with default. Whilst the legal machinery of debt collection is largely restitutive, the grounded experiences of collectors generate a retributive posture towards debtors.

The public view of debt collection

If debt collection is kept as undramatic as possible, and if it is handled as a private system of control which merits no press commentary, public understandings of the process should be marked by some confusion and lack of interest. It is these understandings which provide the contexts for enforcement activity and the definitions which debtors apply to their own default. The uncertainty and anxiety which surround enforcement are important materials for exploitation by collectors. Public ignorance provides opportunities for the manipulation of threats to the person and social standing of the defaulter.

I attempted to assess the nature of public knowledge about default. A modest survey was conducted in London in order to tap Londoners' knowledge and interpretations of the enforcement system. In particular, I examined three of the relations which might exist between debt collection and the interviewed group: the extent of the group's involvement in enforcement; its knowledge of the enforcement system; and its understandings of the system. One hundred and nineteen Londoners were subjected to an interview which lasted, on average, for half an hour.[7] The sample is obviously too small to generate very meaningful results and they certainly cannot be confidently applied to many other people. Nevertheless, the results do bear out my argument.

It is important to stress the sheer numbers of people who are affected by debt collection. Enforcement is a career structure which filters debtors off at each stage. It may be represented by a pyramid whose apex is made up of the minute proportion of defaulters who are thought to merit legal coercion. In 1962 this 'recalcitrant' residue comprised the 1,200,000 judgments which were entered in the county

[7] The Centre for Urban Studies has compiled a thirty-fold classification of electoral enumeration districts based on socio-economic data culled from the 1961 census. A year's county court judgments were recorded against addresses of people who lived in electoral districts of the most common single type. I selected the district which had the highest frequency of judgments and matched it with a neighbouring district whose inhabitants had had no judgments registered against them. One in three of the people whose names appeared in these areas' electoral rolls were then interviewed. This was an arbitrary selection method, but it seems less arbitrary than any other. Some 'rational' means of choosing one hundred Londoners had to be devised. In fact, the interviewees were rather disproportionately middle class.

I have combined the two groups together here because comparisons were not especially illuminating. The social class composition of the areas is shown in Table A and their involvement in debt collection in Table B. (Area 2 was the district which had the greater number of judgments.)

courts of England and Wales. Several million more debtors are fed through the preceding stages.

The Londoners, however, knew very little about the workings of the enforcement machine. Although they were either prepared to express opinions about it, or at least persuaded by the interviewer to make a choice of replies, they were poorly informed. It was clear that they acknowledged the legitimacy and justice of the system even if they were unsure about what the system actually does. Tables 1.1 and 1.2 suggest that, whilst most of the Londoners had never heard of the county courts, they were satisfied that these institutions had a proper role to play and performed it impartially.

The Londoners thus believed that legal coercion was proper but they did not know when and where this coercion was applied. The evil of debtors is not dramatized (cf. Tannenbaum, 1938), it does not attract publicity, and the names of judgment debtors appear only in privately circulated lists of debtors' names.[8] In addition,

TABLE A *Social class composition of sample*

	Area 1	*Area 2*
Managerial-professional	3	6
Non-manual	11	16
Skilled manual	18	25
Semi-skilled manual	9	7
Unskilled manual	1	—
Self-employed	2	1
Other (refusals, pensioners, etc.)	12	8
	56	63

TABLE B *Involvement in debt collection of sample*

	Area 1	*Area 2*
People who had taken credit but stated that they had not experienced difficulty in replaying it	37	37
Debtors who were experiencing present difficulty	2	2
People who had never contracted a debt	16	18
People who had experienced past difficulties	1	6
	56	63

[8] *Stubbs Weekly Gazette* is an example. Almost all the attempts to advertise the names of debtors meet with some hostility. The Consumer Council was reported by the London *Evening Standard* (25 March 1968) to be concerned about orthodox black-lists: 'The Council reports: "If a person has accidentally failed to pay a bill, perhaps because he is out of the country, but pays immediately on his return, his name will still be on record. . . .' This Council is also worried that a trader who dislikes a customer for any reason could tell a credit information organization that he is a bad risk.

TABLE 1.1 *Londoners' knowledge of county courts*

Do you know the name of the type of court that is used in debt collection?	
High court	–
County court	26
Magistrates' court	15
Other	7
Don't know	71
Total	119
Do you know the name of your local county court?	
County court correctly named	13
Other county court	2
Other	47
Don't know	57
Total	119

TABLE 1.2 *Londoners' views on county courts and their use*

	Agree strongly	*Agree*	*Disagree*	*Disagree strongly*	*Don't know*
Courts should not be used for debt collection	5	18	67	15	14
Courts are always on the side of the creditor, not the debtor	4	15	61	15	24
Ordinary people do not understand what goes on in these courts, it is only the creditors and solicitors who do	22	70	20	1	6

'A malicious action of this sort could result in the innocent victim being denied facilities by finance companies,' says the report. Concludes the Council: 'How can you discover whether you have been blacklisted, fairly or unfairly? The disturbing answer is that this will become only known to you by accident—some friend in the trade tips you off or refusal to allow credit arouses your suspicions.' Unconventional methods tend to be labelled by such names as 'lists of shame' and their appearance is called a 'shock'. The *Daily Mirror* (25 March 1967), for instance, stated, under the headline of '"Shame List" Shock for Debtors', that 'debt dodgers may soon find their names going up outside a town hall for everyone to see'.

agents of control do not wear distinctive uniforms or possess distinctive props such as special motorcars. They may try to shield their dealings off from the curious gaze of bystanders. As a result, outsiders rarely recognize manifestations of the esoteric conflict which is waged between debt-collectors and debtors.[9] Interestingly, therefore, Table 1.3 shows that the interviewees were far more uncertain about the state of enforcement in their own area than

TABLE 1.3 *Londoners' views on levels of indebtedness*

	Do you think that it is common for people to get into trouble with payments?	*Would you say that it is common in this area?*
Very common	34	8
Quite common	60	12
Not common	17	38
Very uncommon	1	3
Other	1	1
Don't know	6	57
Total	119	119

elsewhere. The Londoners were sure that default was generally widespread but there were no visible signs which could enlighten the uninitiated about local activity.[10] Despite this, people were prepared to attempt to characterize the actors involved in the enforcement process. Their attempt could be a product of the interview situation; it could be a result of the desire to impose structure on uncertainty; or it could be an example of what Scheff calls the 'theme of simplicity'. Scheff confines his argument to the mentally ill but it could well apply to the defaulter. He argues (1967, pp. 2–3):

> The theme of simplicity, and even more, the attitude of detachment that characterize popular conceptions of mental illness provide a clue for locating the phenomenon within its social context. The casual assumption of simplicity is reminiscent of situations involving racial or class distinctions. The superordinate group often holds stereotypes about the members of the subordinate group: 'everybody knows' that

[9] It is, of course, true that the public may well be equally ignorant about other forms of social control. Such ignorance would not invalidate my specific argument about debt collection.

[10] It might also be true that they felt an acknowledgment of a high level of local indebtedness would cast a slur on their own respectability.

Negroes are inferior or that the lower classes are incapable of governing themselves.

That is, 'common knowledge' rids people of the necessity to know much about a group before they define it. Sixty-four per cent of the interviewees stated, for example, that they did not know how debt-collectors proper worked. Nevertheless, a significant number were able to assert that debt-collectors intimidated defaulters. I shall deal with conceptions of three statuses in turn: defaulters, debt-collectors and bailiffs.

TABLE 1.4 *Londoners' conceptions of debtors*

DEBTORS	*Agree strongly*	*Agree*	*Disagree*	*Disagree strongly*	*Don't know*
On the whole, people who are in trouble with debt are just those who have been unlucky	6	36	61	10	6
On the whole, people who are in trouble with debt are the poorest in the community	11	20	61	26	1
People who don't pay their debts are usually dishonest	3	31	61	18	6
People who don't pay their debts are not like the normal run of people	4	42	49	10	14
People who are in trouble with debt do not know how to run their lives properly	27	62	19	6	5

Londoners believed that debtors were incompetents and did not, in the main, associate default with poverty, dishonesty, or ill-fortune. However, there were substantial dissident minorities in each case. Few Londoners felt that they were unable to define defaulters. This combination of disagreement and confidence could be explained in a number of ways. I would like to propose *one* of these solutions because it is consistent with my previous argument. Table 1.4 suggests that there is a theme of simplicity which focuses on debt collection. It also suggests that the theme does not contain clear-cut and unambiguous stereotypes of the defaulter. Everybody *should* know what a defaulter 'is', but everybody does *not* know.

Table 1.4, then, reveals an important facet of enforcement. It reveals that enforcement is a marginally important control system which deals with marginal deviants (Rock, 1968). Lemert (1948, p. 24 f.) argues that the quality of deviance is a product of the quality of the reaction it evokes:

> Because some method must be found to distinguish that portion of differentiation which can be designated as appropriately falling within the field of social pathology, the . . . necessary postulate is that there is a space-time limited societal awareness and reaction to deviation, ranging from strong approval through indifference to strong disapproval. Thus, by further definition, sociopathic phenomena simply become differentiated behavior which at a given time and place is socially disapproved even though the same behavior may be socially approved at other times and in other places.

To the extent that enforcement institutions have an impact on public attitudes, default will remain marginally deviant. Debt-collectors discourage social disapproval of default, and the interaction (which is actually a *lack* of interaction) between the enforcement system and the wider social audience doubly reinforces such discouragement. Not only does the system eschew publicity, the staging of dramas and the awarding of deviant identities; it also receives little support or interest from the community. Disapproval may exist in embryo outside the system and it does secretly flourish inside the system, but it cannot provide the basis for an ongoing social organization. Ironically, too much public support for debt collection would have a disruptive effective. 'Villainous' stereotypes[11] of the defaulter are withheld by a system which refuses to offer up the debtor as a subject for labelling and identification.[12] However, the

[11] Cf. Klapp (1964, pp. 16–17), who believes that 'the hero, villain and fool represent three basic dimensions of social control in our society. Heroes are praised, set up as models, and given a central part in dramas. Villains and fools are negative models, respectively, of evil to be feared and hated, and absurdity to be ridiculed. Heroes, villains and fools represent three directions of deviation: (1) better than, (2) dangerous to, and (3) falling short of, norms applied to group members or status occupants. These basic kinds of models are used by all societies to maintain the social system, especially to control persons and put on significant dramas and rituals.'

[12] In Chapter 13, I shall deal more fully with this aspect of enforcement. I shall argue there that debt collection is necessarily assimilative in form, if not always in substance, and it attempts to woo the defaulter back into conformity. In consequence, the system eschews coercion because it might alienate an otherwise potentially compliant deviant.

interviewed Londoners tended to define the debtor as a person who lacked *moral* qualities rather than as a victim of fate or poverty. It is certainly significant that the largest minority dissent group held that 'people who don't pay their debts are not like the normal run of people'.

Tables 1.4 and 1.5 thus suggest that debtors *could* become villains. An appropriate deviant role-style is available which contains many

TABLE 1.5 *Londoners' views on causes of indebtedness*

What would you say is the main reason for people being in trouble over debt?	
Poverty	9
Other debts	3
The cost of living	2
Too easy to get credit	20
High-pressure salesmanship	6
Not enough self-control, etc.	61
Drink	2
Gambling	9
Illness	2
Unemployment	5
Don't know	0
Total	119

of the attributes which seem to be imputed to the defaulter. This might be best described as the 'dangerous sick-role' and it is played by such deviants as the drug addict, the alcoholic[13] and some of the mentally ill. Smiles (1877, p. 180) reflected:

> The courage of self-denial exhibits itself in many ways, but in none more clearly than in honest living. Men without the virtue of self-denial are not only subject to their own selfish desires, but they are usually in bondage to others who are likeminded with themselves. . . . They cannot resist the temptation of living high, though it may be at the expense of others; and they gradually become reckless of debt, until it enthrals them. In all this, there is great moral cowardice, pusillanimity, and want of manly independence of character.

Smiles' portrait of the debtor is similar to some popular conceptions of other occupants of the 'dangerous sick-role', and it is precisely

[13] Cf. Lemert's description of the societal reaction to the alcoholic, 'Drunkenness and the chronic alcoholic' (Lemert, 1951, pp. 353–6).

this identification that debt-collectors fear. For instance, marihuana use has been 'authoritatively' described by Anslinger and Tompkins (1953, pp. 21–2):

> In the earliest stages of the intoxication the willpower is destroyed and inhibitions and restraints are released; the moral barricades are broken down and often debauchery and sexuality result. . . . Dormant tendencies are released and while the subject may not know what is happening, he has become powerless to prevent it. Constant use produces an incapacity for work and a disorientation of purpose.

Smiles and Anslinger and Tompkins could be defining the same person—a fibreless, immoral individual who, through his lack of self-control, not only endangers himself but also flouts society. He is anomic, freed from social restraints and is a creature of selfishness and impulse. The Londoners are not yet in agreement with this stereotype, but they could share it, especially if debt-collection techniques allowed them to. They have already discerned several qualities in the defaulter which feature in this role.

Debt-collectors and bailiffs

The interviewees' reactions to debt-collectors and bailiffs are more complex than their reactions to defaulters and are, for this reason, more interesting. I believe that they may be explained in terms of culture lag and the invisibility of the control agents.

Table 1.6 demonstrates that, although most of the Londoners were unable to say how debt-collectors worked,[14] they were familiar with the two activities of bailiffs which are likely to attract public attention. Not only are eviction and execution spectacular procedures, they also proclaim that a bailiff is a person who is armed with extraordinary powers. They demonstrate the brutality of the warrant officer role.[15] Bailiffs do, however, play another role which is far more characteristic of their occupation, yet very few of the interviewees referred to the bailiff as Process Server.

Table 1.7 indicates that the theme of simplicity does not dominate statements about these agents of control: that the Londoners were

[14] It is possible that even the knowledge of a stigmatized phenomenon may confer stigma on the knower. Just as middle-class women of the nineteenth century were commonly supposed to know 'nothing' about prostitution or contraception, respectable Londoners may not know about debt-collectors. Knowledge about bailiffs is probably less taboo because it seems to be agreed that a bailiff is more akin to a policeman than a debt-collector. Seventy-four of the interviewees thought that this was so, thirty-one disagreed, and fourteen did not know.

[15] See Chapter 5 below.

TABLE 1.6 *Londoners' knowledge of debt collection*

Do you know what steps a debt-collector takes when he is asked to collect a debt?

Personal calls	23*
Letters	9
Telephone calls	0
Intimidation	1
Recovery of goods	3
Other	6
Don't know	77
	119

Do you know what bailiffs do?

Issue summonses, etc.	3
Eviction	22
Recovery of goods	1†
Arrest and imprison debtors	0
Routine collection of money	3
Execution on goods	53
Other	9
Don't know	28
Total	119

Have you ever met a bailiff?

Yes	10
No	109
Total	119

* Most debt collection is placed in the hands of large urban agencies who very rarely, in fact, make use of the personal call as a method.

† To an outsider, recovery of goods could resemble execution.

as prepared to describe debt-collectors as bailiffs, although they claimed that they knew less about them; that debt-collectors were seen as more menacing than bailiffs; and that the roles of the agents received legitimation although their occupants were treated with some suspicion. Scheff mentioned three groups which suffered from simplistic definitions: the mentally ill, ethnic minorities and subordinate social classes. Each of these groups is either visible or has been subject to prior stereotyping. Defaulters are not made known to outsiders in these ways and it must be assumed that statements about them have different bases. Debt collection does not force

TABLE 1.7 *Londoners' views on debt-collectors and bailiffs*

	Agree strongly	*Agree*	*Disagree*	*Disagree strongly*	*Don't know*
On the whole, debt-collectors often use intimidation in their job	6	50	30	3	30
On the whole, bailiffs often use intimidation in their job	5	32	38	6	38
On the whole, debt-collectors are often worse than the people with whom they deal	8	30	40	2	39
On the whole, bailiffs are often worse than the people with whom they deal	2	24	55	5	33
You have to be an unusual type of person to become a debt-collector	17	47	33	5	17
You have to be an unusual type of person to become a bailiff	16	38	49	3	13
On the whole, debt-collectors are just doing a job like anyone else	48	62	5	0	4
On the whole, bailiffs are just doing a job like anyone else	46	64	3	0	6

defaulters into publicized status positions. As a result, definitions of debtors can rest, in part, on empathy because default can be viewed as an extreme version of a familiar state, not an alien and unrelated state.[16] Control agents are not visible and they engage in little public drama. In addition, there is no empathetic basis for

[16] It may certainly be significant that debt is the most likely occasion of the ordinary man's being involved in litigation.

labelling unless that basis is an imaginative construction of what the defaulter feels about agents.

There are other reasons for the uncertainty which the Londoners felt about the agents. Most enforcement agencies cope with consensually defined social problems. The community is concerned about these problems and about the efforts which are made to control them. The agencies, on the other hand, need to justify their existence by proving that the problems are real and threatening. Debt-collectors and bailiffs, however, do not require this support and do not attempt to justify themselves. There is little interaction and communication between the enforcement system and the public. Moreover, to the extent that default may be called an embryo social problem, the community's attention is directed at the deviants-in-embryo and not the control system. As Cicourel (1968, p. 22) argues of juvenile delinquency, 'studies . . . seldom view such activities as products of the agencies of social control'. Sociological ideas are often rooted in lay ideas, and lay ideas seldom stress the importance of non-deviant actors in social problem areas. It is not surprising that the Londoners were less interested in debt-collectors and bailiffs.

Finally, as Mead (1963, esp. pp. 128–34) has shown, any individual has a dual involvement in his social environment. Social groups employ symbolic systems to translate themselves and their surroundings to themselves. These systems not only highlight certain phenomena: an individual will also seek out the phenomena which are defined as appropriate to his interests. I have suggested that debt collection and its agents are unlikely to present themselves as problematic or significant to an individual, and, if he does notice them, are liable to be reinterpreted as manifestations of more familiar processes.

The last statement in Table 1.7 was the only one with which very few people disagreed. The Londoners thought that the agents were not playing a deviant role. This is in accord with their opinion that courts should be used to coerce debtors (Table 1.2). The agents' role, then, was legitimate but the role-players were regarded as rather sinister. I believe that the unpleasant ideas which are associated with debt-collection techniques are fossilized and anachronistic, but I also believe that the agents cherish this fossilization. It is curious how debt collection is coloured by its heyday. In the late eighteenth and early nineteenth centuries, debt collection occupied a terrifying place in the social structure. In 1759, for example, a writer in the *Idler* estimated that there were some twenty thousand prisoners for debt in Great Britain and Ireland. At that time, three-quarters of London prisoners were debtors (Bayne-Powell, 1937, pp. 216–17). Not only were the debtors' prisons squalid and miserable institutions, it seemed that people could be sent to them on the flimsiest evidence or for the most trivial sums. A journalist (Grant, 1838, pp. 50–51) observed in 1838 that such was

> the faculty of the debtor and creditor law in consigning human beings to prison, that a person has only to go and swear a debt of a shilling or sixpence against any other party, before the City Court of Requests, to have that party, if unable or unwilling to pay the debt, shut up in this [the Queen's Bench] prison for twenty days.

The selection process could often be frighteningly indiscriminate (Anderton, 1831, p. 220):

> Almost every man's liberty is liable to be invaded, be his means what they may; clergyman, gentleman, merchants and tradesmen are all alike subject to be torn from their families, at almost any moment, and arrested for debts they do not owe.

It may well be that cultural lag has preserved some residual memory of these more terrible modes of enforcement.[17] Lag is encouraged by a process which has few dealings with the non-defaulting public. There are no mechanisms built into debt collection which can check the growth of misconceptions about the process or eradicate those which already exist. The presence of lag is suggested by the commentaries which are written on the subject of enforcement. Morris (1962), for instance, introduces an article by saying 'imprisonment for debt is one of the hidden facets of contemporary Britain. To the average man, the debtor's prison belongs to the pages of Dickens and seems curiously out of keeping with a Welfare State.' Similarly, an editorial in the London *Evening Standard* (24 May 1966) asserted, 'imprisonment for civil debt is still very much part of the British scene, even though it is often thought that, with the passing of the Debtors' Act 1869, the harsh days so graphically depicted by Dickens were gone forever.' Both writings bolster up my argument; they assume that enforcement is unknown and invisible, and they perceive it as an anachronistic and tainted system. Again, they both refer to Dickens, who may have been largely responsible for this ossification. As the Payne Committee (1969, p. 249) observed of enforcement's heyday, 'many thousands of debtors each year had been arrested by sheriffs' officers and detained in the Fleet, the Marshalsea and similar prisons all over the country. Descriptions of the plight of these prisoners have become part of the folk lore of the country portrayed by writers such as Dickens and Fielding.'

Control agents seem to welcome their stigmata. Creditors exploit all the distasteful meanings which are associated with enforcement.

[17] I shall discuss this kind of enforcement at greater length in Chapter 13.

Each stage of a debtor's career is a preparation for a succeeding stage, and the next stage is always presented as unpleasant. The sanctions offered a creditor are weak and they are expensive to enforce. Debt collection thus maximizes the value of threats which it can offer. A creditor would be loath to rid a defaulter of his fear of debt-collectors. In consequence, threatening letters will often suggest that debt-collectors are frightening and, in so doing, they preserve mistaken cultural ideas.[18] One mail order firm invented a debt-collector because the word 'debt-collector' flourishes a threat. It would routinely send out letters which stated:

> Having given you every reasonable opportunity we have now to inform you that unless your account is paid or some satisfactory arrangement made immediately, we shall be reluctantly compelled to place your account in the hands of a Debt Collector for settlement.
>
> It is in our mutual interests to avoid such unpleasant proceeding, so will you please make the necessary arrangements for payment of the balance outstanding.

If these letters brought about no results, they would be followed by others which stated:

> ADVICE OF PASSING TO DEBT COLLECTOR
>
> Your account is now prepared for passing to Mr. ——, Debt Collector.
>
> Arrangements have been made to hand it over in SEVEN DAYS TIME.
>
> A payment immediately and a promise to keep to regular payments would enable us to cancel these arrangements.
>
> **SO IF YOU WISH TO STOP US TAKING THIS STEP, REMIT BY RETURN**
>
> Once your account is in the Debt Collector's hands the matter

[18] Some debt-collectors seem to have added considerable embellishments to these ideas. The John Hilton Bureau (*News of the World*), for example, refer, in a memorandum to the Payne Committee, to 'The Van': 'This has a touch of genius about it. So far as we are aware, it does not actually exist. We have no record of a reader having received a visit from "The Van". It appears to be used as a psychological trick.'

The John Hilton Bureau (Payne Committee, p. 29) also condemn what they call 'the failure of communication' between the agents and *defaulters*. 'An important problem is the failure of communication between those responsible for the administration of the law and a large section of the public. . . . Impressive incomprehensibility may have its place. Some debt collectors design their circulars to look like legal documents but their object is to frighten the debtor into parting with his money: not to clarify his legal rights.'

> is beyond our control—he will take whatever steps he considers necessary.
>
> **PAYING AT ONCE IS YOUR ONLY REMEDY**

The debt-collector was, in fact, nothing more than a dummy firm which sent out further letters. It is clear that such a creditor encourages the stereotypes of debt-collectors which are held by the Londoners.

This survey shows that debt collection is an extremely unusual control system. Most writings on deviance assume that a social problem is surrounded by a very different set of circumstances. They argue that community concern sustains the definition of a social problem and that the deviants who pose the problem are pursued, labelled, segregated and subjected to coercion, reform or treatment. They also argue that the relevant control agencies have an interest in demonstrating that the problem exists, that it is threatening, and that it is being combatted. Moreover, in many cases, the agencies attempt to show that they are morally superior not only to their deviants but also to the community which they manage.

Default does not seem to be a social problem in this sense. Indeed, it seems that some aspects of credit lending and recovery are regarded as more deviant than the actions of the defaulters themselves.[19] A memorandum to the Payne Committee stated, for instance:

> We think it is important that the Courts try and recover control over debt collection: streamline their own methods and that the activities of private debt collectors should be severely restricted. It is most unsatisfactory to have individuals seeking a profit by frightening people into parting with money by despicable tricks . . . (John Hilton Bureau).

Debt collection turns many conventional theories of deviance on their heads. Debtors are candidates for a shaming role but the system does not allow them to assume that role. On the other hand, the agents who deal with them are somewhat marred by stigmata which they welcome. Control agents in collection oppose the formation of a societal reaction to their problem. Lemert (1967, pp. 31–9) has challenged the idea that there is a natural history of

[19] Caplovitz (1963), for example, is critical of the collectors and treats them as the problem group. Elsewhere (1968, pp. 647–8), he labels the provision of credit to the poor a 'deviant system' and remarks 'under present marketing arrangements in our society, unethical practices may be an inevitable consequence of serving the wants of the poorest risks. Society now virtually presents the very poor risks with twin options: of foregoing major purchases or of being exploited.' See also Crowther, 1971, vol. 1, p. 309.

social problems. He argues that one cannot assume that a social problem will necessarily pass through a series of predictable stages simply because it *is* a social problem.[20] Similarly, it cannot be assumed that deviance always takes the same forms, evokes the same reaction, and has the same consequences for its participants. The role alternatives offered to a defaulter are unusually generous and debt collection seeks to emphasize choice. This indeterminacy has profound structural effects on enforcement and makes it a unique process. The study of debt collection must encourage some modification of statements which are made about the general nature of social control and deviance. At the very least, it must impress upon the observer how varied and ramified are the deviant processes of a complex society.

20 Lemert's argument, which is directed against Fuller and Myers, does not completely undermine the 'natural history' approach. It may well be true that discernible, coherent stages can be traced when a social problem's development is studied *retrospectively*. Such a view of development does not necessarily involve successful *prediction* in all cases. Yet sociologists *must* assume that prediction is a desirable, if not always accessible goal. They must strive to produce natural histories of phenomena. If there is no logic in the growth of deviant behaviour, and if deviant behaviour cannot be classified according to the kinds of transformations which it will undergo, the sociological study of deviance would become an impossible exercise. One must assume (if only for heuristic purposes) that changes in social problems are intelligible and orderly

2 Entering the career

Making People Pay is an analysis of the way in which the processing of credit and default in London is made bureaucratically manageable. Routine strategies must be evolved to impose order on the vast enterprise of financing consumer credit. In 1966 £3,692,000,000 of credit was extended in Britain (Crowther, 1971, vol. 1, pp. 52–3). In that year, a fifth of the money spent on clothing, 41 per cent of that spent on furnishings, and 45 per cent of that spent on motor cars, took the form of credit (Crowther, 1971, vol. 1, p. 111). Such a system cannot but receive a high degree of organization and routinization. Mail-order firms, hire purchase companies and money-lenders are constrained to transform immensely complex judgments into a series of mechanical acts which can be delegated to junior employees.

A crucial decision is whether to grant credit to an applicant at all. Firms generally subject all applications to a set of probes before deciding to lend money. These probes are collectively known to creditors as 'credit sanctioning', and they prepare the basis for any subsequent transactions with the debtor.[1] Sanctioning determines whether a person will be allowed to adopt the status of debtor; it is informed by the rest of the collection system; and it is used both to predict future default and to guide enforcement strategy should enforcement prove necessary.

Credit sanctioners occupy a gate-keeping role, and their activity is far from simple. It is made to reconcile competing goals and it is directed by discrepant information. It represents an attempt to regulate an unpredictable and dimly understood world which continually threatens the creditor's organization. Although they attach importance to sanctioning, creditors seem unsure of their

[1] For a comparative description of credit sanctioning in the United States, see Caplovitz, 1968.

ability to exercise rational control over the selection of worthy customers.

The financing and management of small debts is governed by institutionalized definitions of the debtor. Creditors operate with master typifications of defaulters. These typifications emerge out of the everyday work of collection, and they are endowed with life-histories, motives and plans.[2] At the credit sanctioning stage, effort is given to the detection of the three defaulters in the creditor's pandemonium; the Professional Debtor, the Feckless Debtor and the Unfortunate Debtor. These defaulters are a part of the social reality of collection, and they are described by creditors who may never collaborate in their construction. They appear to arise out of day-to-day experience:

> There are two types: there is the man you might call the sort of professional defaulter, the man who just defaults. He's got a, well, a twisted mentality and his object is to catch everyone. And the other one is the man who is improvident and just doesn't think, he takes on far too heavy commitments—perhaps because he's been oversold. And then, of course (I'm just thinking as I go along), there is the defaulter who's been unfortunate, who might start off one day with every intention, with every possibility of carrying out his commitments, and then something happens and he just cannot do it. (Creditor 19, a large hire purchase company.)

> There's a very small number who've no intention of paying. They make a living out of it. They're gamblers, people to whom bankruptcy means nothing. This is fair game providing you can get mugs to give you credit. There're people who've genuinely fallen on hard times and have the will and the wish to get out of it and come and make an arrangement. And the third category—people who've no intention of letting you down but are so weak in character that they let you down. (Creditor 7, a large department store.)

Professional debtors are often considered to be too expert at deception to be detected. They are 'determined villains which every finance company does, unfortunately get; and they will get through all sort of checks' (Creditor 16, a small hire purchase financier). They are the confidence tricksters of the creditor's world. They are sophisticated, knowledgeable, persistent and, above all, plausible candidates. 'I've seen smooth operators work who you'd 've trusted with anything' (Creditor 18, a medium-sized hire purchase company). Creditors feel that they might be able to devise means to

[2] For a description of the origins and nature of these typifications see Ch. 12.

check the professional, but this would entail an expensive and lengthy procedure designed to ward off only a minute fraction of applicants. The credit manager of one mail order company argued, 'we try to detect it, but we are not prepared to slow down our service on the other 95 to 97% to pick out this other 5%' (Creditor 4, a medium-sized mail order company).

Credit sanctioning can, at best, inform a creditor about a person's past default or predict future default on the basis of present data. It cannot foretell the misfortunes of the unfortunate debtor who is regarded as a 'stable man' afflicted by the vagaries of a malevolent fate. There is nothing in the applicant's profile that can warn the creditor. Indeed, even the feckless debtor may be identified only when he has received a loan. His past behaviour may have been exemplary. The abrupt movement of a debtor from a 'good' status to one of the poor ones may be quite disconcerting to a creditor:

> We can make investigations of these people within limits but, obviously, there's no guarantee that the information we're given is correct and there's no guarantee that a good customer won't suddenly develop into a bad customer. It happens in many cases. We've had clients where we get the report 'has an account with so-and-so, paid out perfectly'. We accept them and they don't even bother to make their first payment! They just don't bother to pay! (Creditor 16.)

Three subsidiary functions are served by credit sanctioning. Information about a customer may be useful later as an aid to a company's enforcement strategy. It may be employed as a weapon against the defaulter. If, for instance, 'anything goes sour in court, the more you can prove that you've gone into your underwriting very carefully, the better you are' (Creditor 20, a medium-sized hire purchase company). Sanctioning might also deter the professional defaulter who attacks the unvigilant creditor. There is a fear that 'if you let up, the villains move in' (Creditor 21, a large hire purchase company). In addition, it is probable that the very activity of sanctioning reassures the uncertain creditor that he is in control and that he is wielding some influence over his company's losses.

Credit sanctioning revolves around the quest to identify and retain the desirable candidate. Whilst the creditor shuns the feckless, unfortunate and professional debtors, he seeks out the 'stable man' who is incapable of default. The stable man is firmly entrenched in a network of supporting relationships. He owns his home, is married, middle-aged and sure of continuing employment. A moneylender observed that 'we place quite a large store on stability to the extent that a person who's been working at a factory for ten years and makes fifteen pounds a week is a better credit risk than a man who's been changing his job every year as a representative and *can* earn up to thirty pounds a week'. (Creditor 29, a large moneylender.) Above all, the stable man is unlikely to detach himself from his network and decamp. Creditors are beset by anxiety about the debtor who 'skips' or 'flits' and the stable man 'doesn't pack up overnight'. (Creditor 17, a large hire purchase company.) Yet even this appearance of stability and immobility can be feigned by an astute professional:

> If they're intending to move, and they've got a furnished flat, they will be quite prepared to borrow money from us today knowing that they'll move tomorrow and we can't trace them. You even get to pay a visit to their home and they've got a *nice* home and they're paying their rent up to date; but they've decided they're going to move the next day and, when they decide that, they don't leave any traces at all. They get a van in the middle of the night and leave then. (Creditor 27, a small moneylender.)

The act of credit sanctioning is complicated by numerous difficulties and restraints. The creditor must construct a portrait of an unknown and often unseen applicant in sufficient detail and clarity to permit a rational decision. Mistakes will make him lose money, and serious mistakes will make his losses irrecoverable. He may be required to deal with thousands of applications each week and the way in which he handles them is inevitably shaped by the sheer volume of judgments which he must make. The impatience of potential customers, the demands of dealers and the competition of rivals threaten his ability to survive as a viable company and can be offset only by extremely rapid evaluation. The very knowledge that sanctioning is taking place may jeopardize transactions with offended applicants and delays cannot be attributed to its existence.

These pressures for speed and organization are applied to a bureaucratic procedure which is structurally predisposed towards the performance of simple, standardized and repetitive acts. Sanctioning is delegated to the junior staff in a creditor's organization and it is controlled by elementary rules laid down from above. An extremely complex decision is thus translated into a series of routine and inflexible judgments which is bypassed only when a quite exceptional case is considered.

Decisions necessarily depend on simplistic ideas about the relations between 'social' facts and on the invariable and immediate significance of these facts (cf. Caplovitz, 1968, p. 650). Thus, doctors are considered good risks, Negroes bad risks, and milkmen indifferent risks. Substantial sections of the community are thereby classed as embryo defaulters on the basis of very meagre information. The characteristics of candidates cannot generate ambivalent or unclear meanings. They must indicate that a person is *obviously* eligible for the status of an honest, professional, feckless or unfortunate borrower. The application of a West Indian, for instance, might be judged on the assumption that 'all West Indians always default'. Once such a rule is established, it can permit no exceptions. When these characteristics do not cluster together to form an unambiguous indicator for social placement, the applicant is rejected or referred to an official with greater authority and discretion. The creditor's chief aim is not justice but profit and he is not unduly concerned about the unfairness of refusing credit in ambiguous cases. His rules are crude and frequently unjust, but more skilled enquiries would add excessive costs to his overheads.

The organization of this process must inevitably impress itself on any information injected into it. A procedure which performs rapid acts of social placement cannot easily digest cumbersome material whose collection takes time. Credit sanctioning thus feeds on specially tailored information, and this further narrows a creditor's range of responses to applicants. This sort of information is necessarily accessible, simple and phrased in a relevant style. Each of these qualities may be discovered in a number of dimensions. Accessibility has temporal, financial and relational dimensions. There is also what might be named the dimension of the unsolicited detail. These dimensions tend to overlap. Details provided by 'status enquiry agents',[3] for example, are usually transmitted within a few hours, they are cheap and part of a well-regulated exchange between organizations. A creditor does not seek information which is not readily available to him at little cost.

As a result, specific demands are placed on the institutions whose business is the provision of information, and they shape the manner in which it is recorded. One such institution has 'six million recorded items of information and this is being increased by 15–20,000 weekly'.[4] It reports that 'our national index gives a 24-hour service by post to clients all over the country, handling 30,000–40,000 enquiries weekly . . .' (Taylor and Bentham, 1965) and that it can 'give you by telephone information, recorded, of any known defaulter within two minutes'. Accessibility can be secured only by establishing close links between the creditor and reporting agent. The agent therefore becomes an essential part of the sanctioning system and interacts with his neighbours. Although he is largely the arbiter of the information he stores, he is also subject to the demands

[3] Also variously called 'trade protection societies', 'credit default registers', and so on.

[4] Advertisement for British Debt Services. See also Crowther, 1971, vol. 1, pp. 101–3.

of the credit sanctioner. A large agent, for instance, offered to increase the scope of his services and 'when we did a survey with the trade . . . we found that people were enthusiastic about it, but were not prepared to pay the increased charge'. (Debt-collector 1, a large, status enquiry agent and debt-collector.) The demand for financial accessibility may therefore preclude comprehensive information.

The charges made by a credit status reporter will depend on his efficiency and the complexity of the data he supplies. Whilst a simple enquiry could cost as little as 10p, a detailed report based on a personal visit to the applicant's home could cost £1. Most enquiries entail a routine search in the reporter's files and are inexpensive. Yet even a charge of a few pence may be defined as a barrier by some creditors. Their profit-margins may not allow them to spend money on sanctioning. Thus, the proprietor of a small mail order company (which deals in items costing up to £3·50), felt that he could not afford credit sanctioning. Nevertheless, he *did* have access to fortuitous information in the dimension of the unsolicited detail. The following quotation demonstrates how economic inaccessibility and selectivity can co-exist:

> I don't delve for information. I'm not concerned. If my losses were to creep up, I'd probably do something about it. But to take out an investigation, it costs about five bob, one has to take into consideration your actual losses against your overall margin and then reckon if half my customers are credit customers, and assuming that I have to pay X pounds to find out if their credit rating was good, it's offset in my method whereby I say, if you like, 'right, I will insure myself'. Mind you, if I find a letter comes in from someone and he looks pretty dicey . . . You can tell by looking at the letter. [Prompt] Literacy, the sort of letter they write. Some people will send in five bob and say 'alright, send me two of these'. I don't refuse to send it. All I do is point out they haven't sent a sufficient deposit, would they please send a further deposit of X number of shillings. Now, that kind of customer invariably waxes indignant. She sends me back a snotty letter saying 'don't you trust me?' and all that nonsense. Well, I'm better off sending her back her five bob. So after a period of time (I've been doing this for a long time) you begin to see the type of customer you've got to deal with. And as I say, once my percentage is down to 1%, I'm perfectly happy to leave it that way and I save a lot of money by not insuring. . . . Parts of Ireland, Glasgow, Liverpool are bad. One again has to rely on past experience. You come across a thing where a whole street is bad. Now, it happens once, it happens twice, you won't let it

happen again. And particular parts of Glasgow or Liverpool, it's a duff street, you daren't send them anything. (Creditor 3, a small mail order firm.)

The proprietor was given a number of pieces of gratuitous information and he read meanings into all of them. Although his credit sanctioning was based on the provenance and appearance of letters alone, it *did* exist. His attribution of considerable significance to these details reveals another important feature of sanctioning and enforcement. Creditors tend to impose a structure on their uncertainty by transforming all data into significant symbols. Every little item of information becomes pregnant with meaning. The criterion of relevance or utility does not really exist. Credit sanctioning has an almost omnivorous appetite for material and treats very little as insignificant or meaningless.

A major restraint on the type of information used is the way in which the creditor visualizes his enquiries will affect the applicant. The very search for information should not endanger the ends to which the information will be put. The act of collecting data should not jeopardize the projected transaction. Some companies harbour the belief that certain areas of enquiry are taboo and imagine that they will be rebuffed if they probe there. 'We prefer to keep away from the chap's private life as much as possible' (Creditor 14, a medium-sized hire purchase company). Similarly, an exhaustive application form could tire and annoy a candidate. As a result, few creditors will ever know the exact size of an applicant's income and other details may be equally obscure. Ideas about what might antagonize a potential customer vary. The companies that *do* ask reputedly unpopular questions do not seem to feel penalized. Indeed, they often argue that an applicant's willingness to answer such questions is itself a test of eligibility for credit.

Just as the mechanics of credit sanctioning shape the information which it can receive, so they limit and affect the sources of that information. The needs of simplicity, accessibility and phrasing must also be met by the seven major sources which a creditor can draw on.[5] The first of these is an institution which performs a multiplicity

[5] I do not propose to discuss one of these sources—circulated black-lists. Some reporters (Debt-collector 12, for instance) publish regular lists of the defaulters whom they have encountered in their work. The lists are distributed to the reporter's subscribers and can act as fairly effective screens if the creditor-reporter group operates within a small area. A more important blacklist is based on the official register of county court judgments which the County Courts Branch must maintain under Section 101 of the County Courts Act, 1959. The register contains records of all judgments entered for £10 or more which have not been paid or reduced within a month of their being signed. The 'blacklist', *Stubbs Weekly Gazette*, circulates the names and addresses of the judgment debtors together with

of functions; the status reporter typically advises creditors, collects their debts, traces their defaulters and supplies them with data. Status reporters carry out their tasks with different degrees of skill and they vary enormously in size. Whilst one small reporter (Debt-collector 2, a small status reporter and collector) answers some six hundred credit enquiries a year, British Debt Services deals with well over a million and a half. Their records also vary in number. Yet even one of the smallest reporters (Debt-collector 13, a small status reporter and collector) claimed to possess half a million names on his files.

A status reporter is capable of providing a creditor with comprehensive data which stem from diverse sources. His files are primarily the fruits of his encounters with the defaulting population. He records the names and addresses of all the debtors he is asked to pursue, trace, report on, or enquire about. Many reporters control a system of 'mutual communication' between subscribing member creditors. Members forward accounts of their unfortunate experiences of debtors and these experiences become available as warnings to other credit sanctioners. The files are also based on other published and unpublished information about default. A status reporter may record cases of bankruptcy; county court and High Court judgments; abortive executions; repossessions; compositions; bills of sale; liquidations; dishonoured cheques; husbands who disclaim responsibility for their wives' debts; and debtors who use impersonation as a device to acquire credit. He may check an applicant's name on an electoral roll or in a telephone directory. He may construct ecological indices of a person's propensity to default. Towns, streets and even houses may acquire functional significance:

> You only got to mention the word H—— O—— Estate and you're out! B—— G——, P—— —nobody wants to know it! You might be a *decent-living* citizen, A—— W—— Estate—now there's some very nice people living on A—— W—— Estate—but it's got a bad name, L—— Street,— . . . You've only got to mention L—— Street! Pouff, they've gone! Or, if you take the—— —— Buildings, any one of those buildings anywhere in London . . . ! (Debt-collector 4, a medium-sized status reporter and collector.)

the judgment debt. The *Gazette* also publishes details of judgments obtained in the High Court, bankruptcies, and so on. It seems to be used for two main purposes: as the basis of status reporters' own files; and as an independent check available to creditors. Various banks, for example, refer to the *Gazette* when they decide whether to extend credit. In areas where default is common (Brixton, for instance), a bank manager may note the names of all the judgment debtors who reside in his district and then refer to this list each time a new customer approaches the bank.

There is an extensive network of 'sub-agents' who receive work from these status reporters. One medium-sized reporter, for example, claimed to have liaison with fifty thousand agents throughout Britain who were prepared to investigate the local reputation of applicants (Debt-collector 5). The agents question tradesmen and others who might have knowledge about an application. The canons of enquiry laid down by creditors also govern these actions:

> We make enquiries locally as *discreetly* as possible. We never make a direct call. We never call at the next door neighbour so that they can find out. We do make a few enquiries from the local tradespeople—if possible, the people he buys the papers from. (Debt-collector 5.)

Agents' reports tend to focus on the qualities of the applicant's neighbourhood, his employment and his 'stability'. The agents themselves appear to be either small independent firms of debt-collectors or laymen who treat investigation as an additional source of income. Their usefulness to the reporter lies in their contacts with significant figures in local communities, and reporters cite the extraordinary links, especially with policemen and milkmen, which they manage to acquire in this way.

These data serve to advise a creditor about the truthfulness of an applicant's statements, about the applicant's history of default and his reputation as a consumer. Despite the apparent scope of the reporting service, most creditors tend to view it with distrust. Their distrust forces them to turn back to their own understanding of what usefully predicts default. They feel compelled to manipulate their information into a form which has some predictive power:

> I think you're very much in the crystal ball stage here. This seems to be a fundamental weakness in British credit reporting. I think that, apart from the existence of one or two major entities which are beginning to get very large recording systems, our experience has been that the quality of reporting you get back is not good. Very often we're guided. Certain trades become known to you as doubtful cases and we endeavour to protect the company by calling for a guarantor. . . . (Creditor 13, a medium-sized hire purchase company.)

There are inherent weaknesses in the status reporting system. The chief limitation is the parochialism of each institution. Status reporters tend to attach themselves to specific types of creditor and their files reflect the default patterns of that type alone. A debtor who has defaulted on an agreement with another type of creditor will remain unknown. Reporters who are more catholic in their membership are still restricted to recording the experience of a very partial group of creditors. There is also a regional parochialism. A status reporter is largely dependent on the default incurred by his client creditors and his records will directly reflect the geographical scale of their business activity. If that activity is confined to one area, his records will also be confined. A small reporter typically abstracts and stores details of the county court judgments registered against defaulters in his area. A London reporter may thus know nothing of defaulters outside London. Parochialism is further fostered by competition. A reporter's commodity is information and it is a commodity which he jealously guards. He is most reluctant to improve the efficiency of his rivals.[6] 'There's no connections between any of us at all.' (Debt-collector 13.)

Parochialism is not the only weakness. Few reporters manage to cover all the types of information which might stigmatize an applicant. Some specialize in the provision of relatively recondite data at the expense of more mundane material. One creditor told me:

> We seek normally if he's a householder, or the tenant of a flat; what his family are, what his commitments are in other words; whether he's ever been in trouble with the county courts; whether he's been in any trouble with the police, whether he's got a criminal record. [Prompt] Well, the latter is obtained only by ourselves. This is a system which no other company operates. We have access to our own methods of obtaining whether he has a criminal record or not. (Creditor 24, a medium-sized hire purchase company.)

A creditor who sought comprehensive information might have to approach a number of small reporters. Other firms tend to concentrate on their function as debt-collector or enquiry agent to the detriment of their role as status reporter. Both sorts of lacunae may be increased by the physical problem of storing hundreds of thousands or millions of files. Many reporters are forced to destroy files which have reached a certain age in order to house incoming information. To some this may not represent a loss in efficiency. Those who define default as an unalterable component of personality bemoan the missing records whilst those who believe that their files lose value with age are undisturbed. Whatever the case may be, material which is five, ten or fifteen years old is unavailable to many credit sanctioners. This storage problem may be aggravated by the limited quantity of recent information which a reporter can cope with. Some may be unable to report county court judgments because the addition of nearly two million items a year is unmanageable and expensive. Such lacunae may necessitate more than one status

[6] One solution adopted in the early 1960s was the resort to mergers and takeovers as a means of acquiring access to records.

report and prevent the cheap, rapid and simple transmission which most creditors seek.

The final difficulty facing a creditor is the guile of the professional debtor. A status reporter may simply be incapable of identifying a candidate who changes his name or address. 'Now there's the type that'll give false names, literally tell every lie under the sun to obtain them goods *knowing* that he's going to defraud that company.' (Debt-collector 4, a medium-sized reporter and collector.) Reports may offer a dual service, providing information about both a name and an address, but the professional debtor may still remain unchecked.

These weaknesses are mirrored in the proportions of applicants who are branded as poor risks by various reporters. The small agencies appear to have damaging information about three to five per cent of the candidates they examine. The largest firms claim to identify about twenty per cent as possible defaulters.[7] These differences may be a result of the types of creditor which agents act for but, more often, they demonstrate the poorness of the coverage of any one small reporter.

A credit sanctioner will have seen a candidate's application form before any status reporting takes place. Application forms are usually the first contact which a creditor has with a debtor and they are a basis of a number of significant decisions. They typically ask an applicant about items of information which then become coloured and judged by the institutional experience and mythology of the creditor. Collectively, the items are used to form a manipulable image of a candidate:

> If you talk about the customer specifically, well then, of course, his general standing in life, I think, is important. One looks at his age. One looks if the chap is married. One looks to see how long he's been at his address, if he's the tenant of it, or the owner, or what-have-you. . . . All of these things are necessary. You can't, it's not the practice of hire purchase companies at the moment to ask how many dependants he's got, or what his mortgage repayment is, or what his salary is and that sort of thing. I mean, it's not done in normal hire purchase. But I think you want a general picture of the man. As I say, his general stability, employment. . . . I mean, if the chap is a lodger, for instance, it's far easier for him to pack a bag and get away, than it is if he owns his house. (Creditor 20.)

[7] British Debt Services, for instance, states that it provides 'an overall average notification of registered information of 20 to 25 per cent with some trades as high as 40 to 50 per cent' (Taylor and Bentham, 1965).

People in certain occupations are reputed to be 'unstable'. Dockers, small builders and others enjoy a notoriety amongst creditors which leads to rejection or cautious acceptance:

> You assess a man by how he describes himself . . . if a man's a labourer, you know who he works for. Say it's ——, you know he's a floating chappy. It's bound to be a furnished flat, rooms perhaps, and he goes on contracts all over the country. We would go for a guarantor of a householder. (Creditor 7.)

The stable man is found in a profession or a secure job which ensures that he is anchored to an area and has 'a reasonable amount of integrity because of his following in life' (Creditor 31, a large moneylender). He is not a minor or a woman. He certainly does not live in any of the districts which a creditor defines as prone to default. 'If somebody comes from a certain street in my area, he'd be turned down before he starts' (Creditor 32, a small moneylender). He owns his home and should not have a Cypriot or other recognizably foreign name. If his surname is patently Jewish or Polish, however, his stability may be even more pronounced.

The application form is more than a simple attempt to subject a candidate to scrutiny. It also indicates further action. If a form suggests that an applicant is 'obviously' stable or unstable, a creditor may decide that he knows enough about the person to accept or reject him without seeking confirmation from a status reporter. A wary creditor will peremptorily dismiss the applications of people he identifies as unstable, and ask for reports on the seemingly stable applicants only. The form may additionally be read as a guide to the scope of a creditor's status enquiry:

> We take up bank reports, we check ——.[8] We use outside status reporting agencies such as —— . We check, if given, completed accounts or current accounts with other finance companies. You know, we don't do all these things for everybody. It depends largely on the size of the deposit and the general appearance of the man. If he's putting down a large deposit, if he's been at his address twelve years and at his job twenty, and we get a good status and a good bank or something, we probably wouldn't involve ourselves in making comprehensive checks. If we've got somebody who's putting down a small deposit, who's only lived in his address a shortish while, on paper doesn't look all that good, we'll probably exhaust all those sources. (Creditor 18.)

8 A subsidiary of Debt-collector 3, a member of one of the mergers referred to on p. 35. This illustrates the effects of the lacunae in status reporting. Creditor 18 was forced to take a report from one agency and an enquiry from another.

The substance of the application is not the only basis for making a judgment. The style in which it is completed contributes to the creditor's image of the applicant. The willingness with which it is completed furnishes another perspective. 'If he's not prepared to give us adequate information, well, we prefer not to deal with him anyway' (Creditor 15, a small hire purchase company). The form lends itself to further test. An applicant's statements can be verified by an enquiry agent and inconsistencies between the two versions will make a creditor suspect the honesty of a candidate. An application form can also provide a cover for an elementary sanctioning device.

> We take notice of the address itself. If the address looks to be an accommodation address, or the address of a caravan site, or an hotel, or something like that, we write to the customer. And we have a letter which we call an electoral letter, which simply tells the customer that we've been unable to trace the customer on the electoral roll. We don't in fact look at the electoral roll. So in these circumstances, and also where we read a letter which is asking for goods and there is something about the letter that makes you wonder, there is often a letter comes to you which appears to be in a child's handwriting, what we're trying to do is open some correspondence between us. (Creditor 4.)

The application form and status report may be reinforced by other minor probes. Most creditors maintain their own records which cover the past agreements they have entered into. Although a gas or electricity board is likely to encounter all the adult consumers in its area, the internal files of a normal creditor can provide only a slight check on the reputability of a candidate. Equally weak is the system of reference between creditors. Bank references are thought to be too fulsome in their descriptions of customers and require liberal interpretation:

> You have to read into bank references quite a bit. We all know that you can ask for a bank reference for a certain figure and a bank will reply 'undoubted, good for that figure'. And then there are various other terms which of course one gets to understand and has to read into. (Creditor 11, a credit card firm).

The reluctance of banks to condemn an applicant has led creditors to look upon the bank reference as an insufficiently discriminating instrument of selection.[9] Other references are exchanged between

[9] One creditor (25), a medium-sized hire purchase financier, even alleged 'it's not a good policy to take bank reports because the banks will try and snatch the business off us.'

firms but they are occasionally marred by suspicions of duplicity. Suspicion is rife amongst mail order firms and has led to a breakdown of communication between them:

> There was a gentleman's agreement before the war on this sort of interchange. Mail-order companies for a long time used to interchange. Then somebody had a naughty idea and put the names of their good agents into this blacklist so that they knew that no competitor would ever take their agents away. So it broke down because of deception and chicanery. . . . We were very upset about this . . . but nobody trusts anybody else in this game. (Creditor 5, a large mail order firm.)

Similar pressures encourage mistrust amongst hire purchase companies:

> If you get a hirer who's been a bad or a difficult hirer, and another finance company ring you up and this hirer has gone to sell the car, and the second dealer can't do his finance by another finance company; the other finance company will ring you up and ask you 'what is your experience of this man?' Well, if you say 'our experience has been good', you'll get rid of him. If you say he's been bad, you're left with him. The other finance company won't take him. And this puts you in a very difficult position about whether you should tell the truth and still have the bad hirer, or tell a lie and get rid of him. . . . And we often wonder when another finance company, when we ring them, whether they're telling the truth or are they not?! (Creditor 24.)

Most creditors are perfectly scrupulous with one another but such distrust is not the sole failing of the method. There are other uncertainties which limit its usefulness. One problem is an applicant's frankness in his disclosure of other contracts. He may conceal his liabilities or present ones which are more creditable. An impeccable reference may not reassure a creditor who believes that professional debtors establish attractive biographies to foil him. Communication between firms is not therefore treated as a sure defence against default.

These modes of sanctioning entail no personal confrontation between creditor and applicant. In certain cases, however, selection is buttressed by a face-to-face meeting in which a creditor may be able to read non-verbal clues and use flexible techniques of questioning. The large bureaucratic creditor cannot interview thousands of applicants who are dispersed throughout Britain. If he were to do so, it would be at the cost of the economic and structural advantages of centralization. There are other creditors whose location, architecture and organization lend themselves to the use of interviewing as a routine stage in sanctioning. Shops are designed for frequent and easy encounters between staff and customers. Banks are especially prone to base their lending and enforcement policies on personal exchanges between manager and customer. Interviewing may also be a critical part of sanctioning when a creditor feels that his business is exceptionally hazardous. Moneylenders insist on interviewing an applicant before they consider offering him a loan. Some firms, especially department stores, may engineer meetings only when there is doubt about an applicant.

Most interviewing seems to rest on three foundations. The substance of the answers received by a questioner is of subsidiary importance. Apart from increased versatility, the interview is little superior to an application form. The significant difference lies in the areas which are untapped by a form. The first area is 'obvious' non-verbal information. A creditor may believe that it is indelicate to ask an unseen candidate named Smith or Jones about his race although he could be a West Indian. A Goldsmith or a Gordon might be a disguised Jew. Inaccessible clues for assessing stability are effortlessly revealed in an interview. These normally hidden features are often considered to be important:

> It is no secret that eighty per cent of my hire purchase debts are coloured people. One tends to be influenced by the fact that these new countries are not sufficiently developed in character to manage their affairs. Indians are generally very honourable in their commitments. West Indians are not . . . The majority of Jews are very good payers but if the situation develops and you're going to be taken, you're going to be taken for a very *big* ride. (Creditor 7.)

Interviewers also feel that they can discredit the pretences of people who wrongfully claim such attributes as a desirable age, occupation or 'social position'. They match the customer's appearance with their own expectation of how a person entitled to that attribute should appear. Other cues inform an interviewer about what the applicant is 'really' like under his mask:

> Over the years one does get a certain amount of experience. One becomes quite a judge of character, but that is merely arrived at through experience and not by any set of rules or regulations. Very often you get a chap comes in here and he's probably the worse for drink, for instance. Well, straight away, you think, 'well, if a bloke's spending all his money on beer, he must obviously be neglecting his job, probably his family. Out!' (Creditor 30, a small moneylender.)

Honesty, integrity and sincerity are elusive social qualities which are conventionally recognized by corresponding body, facial and interactional styles. An interviewer will concentrate on interpreting these styles in an attempt to unmask the fraudulent candidate. The performance of an applicant may be irreparably damaged by brashness or other flaws:

> One can only say that if they look you in the eye; if they answer your questions without default, without getting round the questions; normally I think that's the kind of thing we go on. (Creditor 27.)

The interview not only provides an opportunity for examining the discernible and nameable properties of a performance, it also exposes a creditor to signals which are so imprecise or implicit a part of interaction that they cannot be defined:

> You get a third or sixth sense. Whenever I feel not inclined to do it, and against my better judgment have either been coerced or talked into it, it's usually been a bad one. (Creditor 32.)

The interview finally functions as a trap for the professional. One creditor who interviewed the marginal candidate would submit him to a simple interrogation about his income and expenditure. He would then

> sit back and give him three minutes—you don't need to time it—to get his indignation off his chest and to tell you how important and how affluent he is, that he doesn't really need your accommodation anyway. Before he's finished, he'll either put two feet completely into it or he'll put you in such a position where you'll feel, well, perhaps you have wasted this chap's time. . . . Talking—they're very garrulous people who're what I call trying it on. They are there to impress *you* and they're not going to give you a chance if they can help it. There'll be an aggressive opening stage of indignation, and all the other. Then they slip up by contradicting something they've said at the outset. They contradict themselves before they go out. They will always get caught because they must take calculated risks. (Creditor 7.)

The trap may be prepared either by precipitating this kind of 'flooding out' or by lulling an applicant into unwariness. Both methods rest on the belief that a professional's front is a difficult one to maintain with any consistency. It is not a widely shared belief and most creditors assume that they can be easily gulled by a professional debtor. Their assumption is coupled with disquiet about their inability to identify the cues which make them suspect a candidate will default:

> I don't personally feel that it is possible to look at a person and talk to them and know absolutely that they're honest. You may do this for many years and you still slip up on it. If they've decided that they're trying to get something for nothing . . . they will go to such lengths to make out their honesty that you can be fooled. (Creditor 27.)

Status reports, application forms, references and interviews are all contrived procedures aimed at the construction of an image which can direct a creditor's future actions. The last source of information which I shall consider is built into the very process of lending money. A credit transaction is a simple business activity but, when it is properly interpreted, it is also a bundle of facts which have esoteric meanings for the sanctioning system. I have described how a person's place of residence or name can acquire significance. A transaction is replete with such fortuitous detail and the rules for understanding it vary from one creditor to another. I shall illustrate how these rules are applied to two of a transaction's components; the goods which are bought on credit, and the link which originally brought a creditor and a customer together.

Creditors believe that the character of a person is reflected in the objects which he buys on credit. A pair of shoes or a house can suggest something about its consumer's propensity to default. Sanctioning and enforcement policies are therefore founded on a creditor's reading of the risks presented by his particular range of goods.[10] Not surprisingly, each creditor tends to define his own type of business as relatively safe and doubts the wisdom of lending money in another fashion. The goods are slotted into his mythology and become the centre of a system of meanings attributed to his customers:

> It's been our experience that while you can repossess a man's car without a great deal of difficulty, you attempt to repossess a wife's washing machine and you're in for trouble. She will see that her husband moves heaven and earth in order to see that the things which assist her in her work in the house stay where they are. Furthermore, of course, there is the point that the instalments are much smaller. . . . Now, if you're only in for a small amount . . . if you're regular in your follow-up of a debtor . . . no matter what happens, come hell or high water, those accounts are chased every seven days, if you're regularly calling for your money for the sake of three or four pound, they're not going to be troubled. They're going to *pay* you. But

10 Moneylenders, who feel that they encounter exceptional risks, place great stress on the purpose of a loan. They refuse to lend money for what they regard as a frivolous purpose.

> if it's a fifteen pound vehicle account, and perhaps it's got one month in arrears . . . quite a number of working men face difficulty in finding it. (Creditor 15.)

This conception of the place of the washing machine was formulated by a creditor who financed the sale of washing machines. It contrasts interestingly with the ideas of a creditor who specialized in vehicles:

> I think it's generally accepted that furniture is the worst. Washing machines, T.V.s, tape recorders—something like that which is a pure luxury item is very bad. Generally speaking, a bad payer in trouble will endeavour to pay for his T.V. and his motor car. See, there's a social stigma attached to his losing his car. The neighbours will know. 'He hasn't got a car. Why?' They won't know if a man comes round and retakes his refrigerator or his washing machine. (Creditor 18.)

Whilst a creditor may be sanguine about his overall range of business, he is less sanguine about specific goods within that range. His credit sanctioning will be more cautious when it concerns a vulnerable item. Any one of a number of relations between a debtor and his goods can engender default. For example, a creditor believes that a debtor's payments depend on a continuing satisfaction with the goods which he is buying. If a commodity does not survive the life of an agreement, a debtor's discontent may express itself in default. One mail order company suffered an abnormally high loss when it lent money on Christmas hampers (Creditor 4). Similarly, hire purchase firms distinguish certain makes of vehicle which age prematurely and thereby endanger transactions.

Other goods complicate enforcement because their low second-hand value undermines the efficacy of repossession. A creditor who finances carpets, television sets, or refrigerators may feel impelled to compensate for the weak collection stage by a more stringent sanctioning stage. He may also argue that a professional debtor has enough acumen to know that these goods may be defaulted on with comparative impunity. One solicitor remarked:

> A lot of these debtors know far more about the court workings than they're given credit for. Now, if it's a hire purchase transaction, they know that if they paid more than a third, you can't get it back unless you get an order of the court. . . . If it's linoleum or carpets, they know that once it's on the floor it's useless. Therefore they don't pay, and they're the most difficult people, because they *know* that the dealer is going to think hard and long as to whether he's going to recover items of that description. (Solicitor 1, a large agency solicitor.)

Greater caution may also be exercised when a commodity is associated with a nefarious use.[11] Unusual orders for goods which are easily disposed of and cannot be traced will trigger off an extremely suspicious response. Tape recorders, binoculars and so on can be sold by a professional debtor who will pay no more than a deposit. So organized do some defaulters seem that one debt-collector classified a type of call as a 'pawnshop visit':

> They go in for all heavy stuff like fridges, television, radiograms—anything that would sell at a reasonable price. Within *minutes*, I would say, there's a van round the corner. Somebody's bought it and it'll go for a tenner. . . . We've got calls what we annotate in our book what we deem 'pawnshop calls'. That is, we'll say you want a pair of sheets or shirts cheap, something like that, see. Right. Now, on a pawnshop call, when you go there you've only got to say 'have you got so-and-so and so-and-so?' and she says 'No. Why?' You say 'well, I'm looking for some' and she'll say 'come back next week'. (Debt-collector 4.)

A creditor tends to trace at least three relations between a consumer and the objects which he consumes. The first is the reluctance with which a debtor would part with a commodity if enforcement ensued. Creditors assume that things which occupy an important position in a household are eagerly protected and are not lightly defaulted on. A 'luxury' has a relatively marginal place in a debtor's scheme of affairs, however, and presents something of a risk to the sanctioner. This evaluation of the meaning of an object can take another form. A creditor seeks for congruence between a commodity and the person who will purchase it. This idea of the appropriateness of the transaction implies that types of people cannot responsibly desire certain types of goods. An incongruous relation suggests that the applicant's intention is frivolous, dishonest or so misplaced that it signifies instability. Hopkins (1964, p. 2), for example, argues 'a prosperous man may afford, and put to good use, a luxury automobile. Another of more modest means might like to own the same car and be induced to buy it. But a few months of enjoyable, but financially burdensome driving will soon reveal the folly of the purchase.'

Finally, there are connections between people and things which a creditor cannot explain. From experience, he will predict that defaulters are mysteriously attracted by one object but not by another:

> I've run several time checks on the types of vehicles people take, and you'll find that one particular make of car is the one most often times repossessed. You repossess more Fords than

[11] In the case of hire purchase credit, this tends to be 'larceny as bailee'.

> any other make. (Prompt) No idea at all (why). This is just a peculiar thing. There are other types you rarely repossess. A Morris 1000, for instance, you don't take 'em back—very, very rarely. Whether it's the type of person that buys that sort of merchandise, I don't know. (Creditor 24.)

A creditor can know an applicant by imputing motives to him. He can also embellish his knowledge by reconstructing something of the applicant's world. Each source of applications is responsible for introducing a particular population of consumers to a creditor, and differences between sources will lead to differences between populations. An applicant will be judged by the entrance he takes into an enforcement career. Some of the criteria employed to assess the manner of entry are based on reasoned accounts of relationships between an applicant and social forces. Others are empirically derived expectations of the effect which a source has on default. Dealers, advertisements and other sources are repeatedly examined and their reputations may be critical in a sanctioning decision:

> What we tend to do, and this is one of our best guides, from our past experience of the kinds of customers dealers introduce to us, we tend to judge the customers on the dealers. If there's a doubt in our mind for one reason or another, 'well, what's the dealer like?' (Creditor 13.)

Some creditors rely so heavily on a dealer that they believe it is unnecessary to take out a status report on a customer who has been recommended by a 'good' dealer. A good dealer carries on business with stable customers, refuses to forward applications which he is himself unsure of, and co-operates with a creditor in enforcement. A poor candidate from a good dealer may be more readily accepted than a good candidate from a poor dealer.

An unusual source is especially suspect. Links between dealers and finance houses tend to be so firmly established that a request from an unconnected dealer carries the implication that it has been already rejected by another creditor. A creditor can comprehend why a dealer in a 'bad' area contributes to his losses. He can also understand the actions of an unfamiliar dealer. They both obey the 'rational' rules of behaviour which govern his own conduct. Fortuitous detail, however, *is* fortuitous because it is available at no cost and without effort. All the other information used by a creditor is structured by the methods which elicit it. It must conform to some of a creditor's notions of rationality because these notions directed its collection. On the other hand, a creditor may be unable to explain why fortuitous details so often predict default, but he cannot ignore them or cease looking for them:

> This is a sort of ancillary thing, but you find that certain publications . . . incur a tremendous amount of bad debt. There are three well-known Sunday newspapers in terms of circulation and their use for mail order advertising. Two of these are not much good for mail order advertising because they incur such heavy bad debt unless you take special precautions. The third one, for some reason, has a very good bad debt ratio. . . . So you see the problems involved in this. Therefore your credit control exists right down to very sophisticated techniques that we use in assessing the pulling power and profitability of various publications. . . . It's not just a socio-economic readership either. That's the funny thing, this has no bearing on it at all. It must be some sort of psychological type of person. . . . You have to invest in these bad debt publications, but you have to be circumspect about it. And there are sizes of advertisements and types of advertisement which incur lower bad debt ratios than others. (Creditor 5.)

Credit sanctioning is thus an organized effort to assimilate disparate data of uneven weight and often contrary meanings. Creditors have little confidence in the reliability of individual items of information or in their ability to make a valid decision. A credit sanctioner must juggle with all the perspectives he is offered on an applicant and produce a satisfactory and clear answer. The 'folklore' of a company[12] provides an orientation but it also creates the conflicts which must be reconciled. Status reports, application forms and so on may all have different prognostications. The attempt to make sense of the process is not covered by explicit rules and cannot be formally taught:

> It's intangible. I was talking to two trainees this morning and I was trying to explain that it is not an exact science. (Creditor 7.)

The translation of sanctioning into a routine process means that these dilemmas are solved by rapid and impressionistic judgments. A sanctioning decision is a quick intuitive response to a complex whole. A creditor cannot formulate an interpretive scheme which will help him to balance dissonant information or impose order on data.[13] He resorts instead to intuition: 'a third or sixth sense'

[12] Creditor 6, a large mail order company, referred to the institutional wisdom of creditors as 'folklore'.

[13] Creditor 23, a medium-sized hire purchase company, has attempted to use a weighted questionnaire to rank applicants into four grades of 'credit-worthiness'. The weightings were acquired from the American experience of the creditor's parent company and the firm's credit manager was unsure about their applicability to Britain. This was the sole instance of a departure from intuitive judgment.

(Creditor 32), 'a seventh sense' (Creditor 5), or 'a matter of smell and experience' (Creditor 4).

Not all sanctioning is complicated. An applicant may be transparently 'good' or 'bad' or there may be some piece of evidence which overwhelmingly recommends or damns him. A county court judgment, for example, is so great a stigma that it can be offset only by exceptionally favourable data. The bad applicant is a known defaulter or an unstable man and a good one is his antithesis. Between these two poles there is a vast group of marginal cases who must be assessed intuitively.

Few creditors can reject all marginal candidates. Their decisions are formed in response to a set of pressures which force them to adopt a liberal definition of the acceptable customer. One major factor which makes the acceptance of a marginal person imperative is the simple absence of any other kind of applicant. Moneylenders, for instance, know themselves to be lenders of last resort:

> Let's face the fact, people don't come to a moneylender if they can get it elsewhere. If people go to a bank and get it for eight or ten per cent, you're not going to pay forty eight per cent to the moneylenders are you? The risk is colossal really. (Creditor 30.)

An awareness that ideal candidates do not present themselves to a firm may produce a shift towards less rigorous standards. There may, in any case, be an absolute scarcity of desirable customers. A creditor will be able to have a considerable business only if he accepts applicants who are not clearly good or stable. Indeed, he may welcome these marginal people:

> To me a business that does not have a certain amount of bad debt is just not a good business. I don't like to see our bad debt reduced. —— had this instance some time ago when they really started cracking down on bad debt, and their sales just went Chung like that! —— . . . tended to get hammered by this, and they had to pull back again on it because they found that their sales were plummetting down. (Creditor 5.)

The margin can be forcibly enlarged by the demands of dealers. A creditor may have to relax his criteria in order to retain his links with others in the credit system:

> We're open to the pressures that the dealer has on us. We may be persuaded to accept a person who, on paper, is less creditworthy than we would choose in order to protect a dealer's source of business. Because a dealer may give us a tremendous amount of good business, it would be silly for us to put our

> account with him in jeopardy for the sake of refusing to do a particular transaction with a weak hirer and then lose all the other good business from that dealer. (Creditor 18.)

Competitors may place similar restraints on a creditor's freedom of choice:

> The only thing is, you see, everyone at the present moment is afraid of losing business. There isn't really enough business to go round. And if, when a bloke comes round and says 'I want the set', well the salesman who is probably working on a commission is *dying* to sell it (a) to get the commission and (b) to stop any other bloke getting the sale. Now if, at that point, things don't run smoothly and you're apparently sort of saying 'well, you know, do you keep a car and are your father and mother married?' and all those sorts of questions, that bloke will just walk out of your shop and go somewhere else. So the position is that you really cannot afford to be intensely critical of your customers. (Creditor 2.)

Credit sanctioning cannot be a rigorous search for the unimpeachable consumer. It must be a subtle exercise in the definition of what is just tolerable as a risk. It must indicate when a dealer can be antagonized or a competitor successful. Sanctioning should suggest how the protective and deterrent functions of a creditor can be reconciled with the need to maintain and enlarge the volume of business.

The extension of credit to a marginal customer need not be an invitation to default. A creditor's disquiet produces a drive to improve the customer. In many cases, creditors will expand their search for 'good' data to counterbalance the customer's flaws or they may create these data themselves. A creditor can reduce a customer's marginality by demanding an abnormally high deposit or security. He may insist on one or more guarantors who will become responsible for the debt if default occurs. If he is a gas or electricity board, he is able to instal 'prepayment' rather than credit meters in a dangerous area,[14] or adjust meter charges so that a sizeable surplus is generated.

Not only is a creditor's discretion curtailed, there are also considerable restraints on the extent of his investigation. My description of a creditor's sources of information has mentioned few of the

[14] A consumer is entitled to choose between a credit and a cash meter but a board may stipulate that a credit meter cannot be had unless a sizeable deposit is first paid. There is considerable doubt about the wisdom of installing cash meters in bad districts. The costs of maintaining them are comparatively high and, in bad districts, default may be dwarfed by the problem of larceny.

factors which direct and restrict his use of them. Some of these factors are constraints resented by a credit sanctioner, others are imposed by his mythology or folklore.

Economy is the first determinant of any investigation. A creditor who lends small individual sums cannot afford expensive sanctioning on each transaction. The proportion of his receipts devoted to defence would be prohibitive and the sums themselves would not be worth defending. A hire purchase company, however, may lend several hundred pounds to each customer and rigorous checking becomes both relatively cheap and necessary. One creditor estimated that sanctioning led to a four per cent drop in bad debt. (Creditor 4.) He consequently checked an application only when the sanctioning cost was less than four per cent of the money which would be risked by a loan.

The second economic limitation is the size of a creditor's losses. If his experience of debtors has been fortunate, he will be reluctant to lavish money on vetting them:

> If this became a colossal problem for all the rental companies, then I think everyone would tighten up. You'd ask to see their birth certificate and things like that. I don't think it's reached that point—it certainly hasn't with us. (Creditor 2.)

There is no one definition of an acceptable loss, but all companies have some critical figure which cannot be exceeded without a drastic change in sanctioning policy. The size of bad debt is one of the indices which a creditor uses to infer how principled applicants are. This general attribution of honesty or dishonesty as a British trait is vital to how wary a creditor will be. A jaundiced sanctioner can devote an unusually large proportion of his resources to gather data:

> We worked on the assumption, possibly naïve, that the majority of people are honest and all the rest of it, which is fallacious reasoning. People are not. You've got to work on the assumption that people are out to catch you if they can. (Creditor 16.)

A creditor's caution is also determined by his beliefs about the types of people who approach *him* for credit. Various companies have deliberately sought middle-class customers, such as doctors and teachers, and their sanctioning has reflected their confidence in the status of their applicants. The third group which a creditor is forced to consider is the professional debtor. If he fears that he has attained a reputation for vulnerability, he may well initiate extravagant checks:

> At one time I had nightmares of Mrs Smith telling Mrs Jones, and Mrs Jones telling Mrs Brown, and Mrs Brown telling somebody else: 'Oh, they're alright! You don't have to worry

> about paying 'em.' And I was watching it terribly carefully but it never happened. Although it has always been a fear that it might, it never did. Whether it might happen in the future, I can't tell, but immediately I see the warning light . . . (Creditor 3.)

There is at least one other influence on the scope of sanctioning. The more a creditor believes that enforcement is efficient, the less will he stress the importance of vetting. Gas and electricity boards are haphazard in their selection of applicants but they are armed with a powerful combination of conventional and unconventional sanctions against default.[15] Their losses are slight in consequence:

> What happens now is, the consumer goes into the showroom and the agreement is completed there and then on the spot. So that any credit enquiry you make . . . Subsequently if it was found that this chap was a bad egg, in point of fact, you're faced with the fact that there it is! This sounds awful, but there again we're very, very big hire purchase people but the percentage that we lose through bad debts is absolutely negligible. (Creditor 9, a gas board.)

In addition to these general barriers to investigation, a creditor may make specific exceptions to his sanctioning policy. Few companies check previous customers who have had a good record, and some may even refrain from checking new applicants who are recommended by customers or favourably regarded dealers. Again, the high status of a person may colour an application so strongly that no other checks are necessary:

> Say if someone comes in who's a local headmaster of a school. We know he's been established for some time. It's pointless to put in a check on a man like that because he's obviously of undoubted character. So we go ahead. (Creditor 25.)

Credit sanctioning is thus a manipulation of stereotypes based on social characteristics which are seen as causally linked with default. A defaulter is thought to be a dishonourable or hapless person, and attributes which coincide with this image precipitate an applicant's rejection. Actual rejection rates depend on the type of creditor, the risk he faces and the quality of his sanctioning. The people I interviewed gave me the following rough estimates of the business they turned down: some mail order firms refuse 5 per cent of their applicants, most refuse 10 per cent; hire purchase companies appear to reject between 10 and 20 per cent; and moneylenders reject between 30 and 90 per cent.

[15] For example, the *Daily Express* (5 September 1968) reported that 23,000 families in the Midlands had their electricity supply cut off in 1967 for not paying their bills.

3 Enforcement by creditors

When a successful applicant passes the stage of credit sanctioning, he may take any one of a number of prepared routes before he becomes of no further interest to his creditor. From a creditor's point of view, the ideal route is a strict adherence to the norms established in the contract. A debtor who commits himself to paying eighteen monthly instalments will pay those instalments in eighteen months without any intervention from the creditor. The most common path, however, combines eventual repayment with minor forays into an enforcement career. Every time a person receives a notice from a gas board, a rating authority or a commercial concern, he enters a carefully contrived system of social control. Most creditors expect that the majority of their agreements will go into default on at least one occasion and, at any single time, their enforcement will be directed at some 10 per cent of their customers.

The organized response to default is superficially simple but analytically complex. It maps out alternative sequences of action which can be applied to different 'types' of default. The sequences are all variants of one basic model: a stream of ever more threatening letters; a personal confrontation between debtor and creditor; and, finally, enforcement prosecuted by debt-collectors or the courts. This process conforms to Roth's (1963, p. xviii) definition of the career as 'a series of related and definable stages or phases of a given sphere of activity that a person goes through on the way to a more or less definite and recognizable end-point or goal (or series of goals)'. Any career can be described in terms of its key structural characteristics; its complexity, duration, intensity of experience, direction, goal, spacing, pacing, tempo and prevailing rational and sentimental order (cf. Glaser and Strauss, 1971). These features are all interrelated and their interaction becomes especially complicated when a career is as protracted and devious as an enforcement sequence.

Any deliberately constructed career is shaped primarily by the purposes which it is supposed to serve. Enforcement has no single purpose. It is not only aimed at the rapid recovery of debts, it also performs ancillary functions and is subordinated to other institutional goals. It is evident that creditors are chiefly concerned with finance, and financial criteria dominate their handling of default. Enforcement cannot be conducted in a way which conflicts with a creditor's companion demand for economy. Creditors will be reluctant enforcers if the collection of debts costs more than the amounts which they can recover. They may even resort to a token display of vigilance and abandon any pretence of serious action:

> It usually takes about three months before they get a final letter from us saying we're going to do this, that and the other. In actual fact, we do *nothing*. I don't even take them to court because it's not worth it. (Creditor 3.)

Most firms establish an arbitrary 'write-off' figure which represents the minimum debt they are prepared actively to collect. The margin is based on the cost of enforcement and the extent to which a creditor imagines himself to be vulnerable to the predatory professional debtor. Present losses may be countenanced if they avert a larger future default:

> If the sum of money's smallish, we decide whether it's *worth* spending money to get less than we spend. Alternatively, we may take the option that things have been too lax and lenient. You're getting a reputation for an easy mark. Even if it cost you a few bob or a few pound, go ahead with a half dozen people who are obviously nasty cases and, even if you lose money, deal with them in the court. (Creditor 16.)

Above all, the margin reflects the autonomy of a creditor's enforcement department. External institutions may impose an unwelcome 'write-off' figure. Solicitors and debt-collectors may simply refuse to take action about certain sums. Relations within a creditor's organization may also bring about particular decisions which run counter to the department's conception of a suitable margin. A relatively powerless department may have to harass debtors for trifling sums:

> It's not worthwhile pursuing them but it's just as difficult for us to get thirteen bob written off on a month's schedule as it is for us to issue a summons. (Creditor 10, a gas board.)

Creditors must structure the whole enforcement system so that it is not unduly expensive. Although all enforcement agencies are troubled by economic restraints, debt-collecting institutions are uniquely restrained. Murder, drug addiction and other forms of deviance cannot be neatly measured in monetary terms and their prosecution is impelled by 'moral' pressures which resist such measurement. Collection, however, is peculiarly susceptible to costing. The ostensible aim of enforcement is the reduction of economic loss, and collection is governed by considerations of how cheaply an efficient system can be administered and how financially advantageous each step is likely to be. A creditor who is owed large individual sums will therefore tend to be more strenuous than a firm whose debts average a few pounds.

Enforcement is strongly influenced by economy because it almost always involves a creditor in loss. The Inland Revenue permits certain companies[1] to claim allowances in taxation for bad debt and the expenses incurred in enforcement (cf. Pinson, 1968, pp. 49–50). Such allowances are assessed at Corporation Tax Rate which, at present (1969), is 42½ per cent. Hence, for every £100 lost by a firm, £42·50 can be deducted from its taxable profits. A fortunate creditor might regain his county court costs in full but he cannot totally recover what he spent on debt-collectors, solicitors and his own enforcement machinery. In consequence, he will lose money even when his debtor repays the debt. When the debt has to be written off altogether, less than half can be recouped. The growth of consumer credit has transformed collection into an enterprise which deals with millions of pounds each year and the management of careers has therefore become extremely expensive.

There is no certainty that enforcement costs will be recovered from a recalcitrant debtor. Some debts are discharged by people who do not pay the costs of an action, whilst others are abandoned as irretrievable. Any large creditor stands to lose a substantial sum each year because he may have to pursue several thousand accounts. Enforcement leads to an inevitable diminution of profits and creditors try to make this loss as small as possible. Their search for inexpensive remedies affects all collection policies.

The ostensible aim of reducing loss may nevertheless permit enforcement to take the guise of punitive action against certain 'types' of defaulter. Punishment of the professional debtor may be of economic value but it sometimes appears to displace dispassionate monetary calculation:

> With the professional debtor, if you can lay your hands on him, we would go to all ends. This is the one exception where we'd

[1] Allowances are made when the company's trade consists of making loans (cf. Halsbury, 1957, p. 178).

> throw good money after bad because I feel that one has a certain amount of public duty in these things and it is the right thing to do, quite definitely. (Creditor 11.)

Other creditors believe that it is proper to punish all defaulters:

> There are two schools of thought. One is that you ought not to throw good money after bad. The second, which is far more important, is that you have a duty to ensure that these people are taught a lesson, are brought to book, because, if you don't, and you can afford to lose the money, they're going to do it to people who can't afford it. So we say it is a matter of principle that we take *all* cases to court. But we don't make a nonsense of it—if it's thirty bob or anything of that nature. (Creditor 7.)

Straightforward enforcement may also be upset by a perceived need to deter potential defaulters. In some cases, debt collection may simply become a gigantic exercise in deterrence. Most creditors budget for bad debt and they can claim allowances for it in taxation. They can also adjust their prices by gearing them to their expectation of default. Their main concern is to keep their losses within 'manageable' proportions and their chief fear is an increase in the numbers of their 'bad' accounts. Their losses may grow to a bankrupting size if they do not conspicuously collect debts. The money they lose is an inevitable consequence of their acceptance of marginal applicants, the duplicity of professional debtors and the poor luck of the unfortunate debtors. No creditor can avoid loss and some firms welcome it as a sign of their exhaustive exploitation of the consumer market:

> If we get caught, we get caught quite often by professional tricksters and by people who are just not too keen on paying. We collect and, to be quite frank . . . we write off this bad debt. Our only interest in collecting bad debt, or attempting to collect it, is *pour discourager* [sic] *les autres*. We just don't want it to escalate. It's not worth our while to chase it up. If I had my way, I'd say 'scrub the whole damn lot and write it off because it's far more trouble than it's worth'. (Creditor 5.)

Successful deterrence hinges on forcing harassed debtors to play a role in a drama enacted for an audience of professional and feckless defaulters. Enforcement must be visible, frightening and seemingly unavoidable. A creditor who stresses the deterrent function of collection commits himself to a special presentation of the institution he serves:

> We're very keen on publicity. If we prosecute a hirer, we're very

> keen that we should get publicity about it. We try and get it as much as we can, to get it as a deterrent. (Creditor 24.)

This search for publicity can pose an acute problem for an enforcer. A creditor plays a number of roles and these place disparate demands on the organization of his public face. The role of enforcement is what Hughes (1964, pp. 52–4) calls 'dirty work'; it is squalid, and does not confer prestige. It also conflicts with another image which a creditor hopes to promote. Firms usually want to represent themselves as the attractive and co-operative suppliers of a desired service:

> Let me put it this way. No person who has been a client of this company has ever gone to prison for debt. Our whole business is built up, and you'll find all moneylenders'll tell you the same, their business is really built up on a friendly atmosphere between lender and borrower. And, if you don't have that friendly atmosphere, you might as well get out of business altogether. (Creditor 30.)

The dirty work of collection cannot easily be disentangled from the other work of the creditor. He may achieve something of a solution by delegating the damaging part of enforcement to an outside agency with another name. One bank, for example, experimented with a debt-collector: its collection manager observed, 'I think some of their methods are a great deal more ruthless than the bank's, and one of the things that's exercising our minds is how closely the bank's name will be linked with whatever methods are being adopted.' (Creditor 1.) An enforcement career will be strongly influenced by the choice taken by a firm. A creditor who wants to impress his respectable aspect on the outside world may well curtail all collection that tarnishes it. Bad publicity may stem from a creditor's mistakes and the selection of inappropriate targets for tough enforcement will lead to sympathy for the debtors and criticism of the creditor. There are deficiencies in the creditor's system of acquiring information about defaulters and the task of differentiating between types of debtor is expensive and of limited utility. As a result, a creditor may be unable to avoid selecting debtors whose pursuit will harm him. In many cases, therefore, a creditor does not extend his information-acquiring mechanisms but restricts all vulnerable modes of enforcement:

> On the whole, the bank finds this [execution on goods] very, very unsavoury. It always attracts publicity. I mean, the average county court judgment and court order attract no publicity at all. But the bailiff going knocking on the door and working on investigating what's available for creditors, *always* attracts

> publicity and the last thing we want is publicity. And therefore in —— Bank, anyway, and particularly bearing in mind too—this has some effect on the position—the majority of our branches are in the North West in some of the smaller communities where it'd get even more publicity than in London. You see, London is a bit different. I mean, local influences are just about nil. You can probably get away with all sorts of things in London, doing things to people and threatening them, which people would never raise an eyebrow. (Creditor 12.)

The goals of deterrence and the avoidance of publicity may prove irreconcilable and one may have to give way to the other. Creditors who define both as desirable will have to tailor enforcement so that it permits the use of sanctions innocuous to them, the elaboration of their methods of differentiating between cases, and attack on unquestionably deviant debtors. These demands may impose economic and organizational stresses which can be resolved only by emasculating the potency of their collection system. Discreet enforcement is unlikely to be the most effective enforcement. Moreover, it is interesting that 'bad publicity' can be doubly bad for the creditor. Not only might such publicity deter potential customers, it can also justify the selection of the creditor as a victim by defaulters. The moral status of a vengeful creditor is even lower than that of a benign one. Impersonal organizations tend to be regarded as legitimate targets for predatory activity; the discredited organization becomes an even more vulnerable victim. In the case of crime, for instance (Smigel and Ross, 1970, p. 5):

> [The] failure of the public to stigmatize crimes against bureaucracies leads to [a] dilemma for the victims. Having apprehended a criminal, bureaucracies cannot routinely pass him on to official law enforcement agencies because the bureaucratic interest does not always coincide with a system of law enforcement based on the concept of a personal victim. The organization must retain a positive public image in order to avoid becoming an even more justifiable victim.

A creditor does not only confront an audience of external critics and potential consumers. There are many debtors among the larger population of defaulters whose reactions to tough collection techniques are as important as those of uninvolved outsiders. Most defaulters are 'normal' consumers whose payments have temporarily lapsed. They usually resume paying if they are tactfully dealt with. A creditor cannot therefore afford to estrange an unfortunate or feckless debtor and turn him into an embryo professional. All enforcement attempts to prevent the transformation of mere rule-breaking into secondary deviance and this applies particularly to the first stages of an enforcement career. Indeed, it is one of the reasons why enforcement is constructed around stages.

An important support for this check on immediate action is the failure of some creditors to understand the logic of the system which they man:

> The bulk of people with bad debts are just plain stupid or incompetent and we don't want to lose them as customers. We'll get the money off them eventually. It's very funny but we used to be very severe on this, we used to be very keen on pulling up bad payers. We pulled them up as soon as they missed one payment. We've been expanding at a fantastic rate. Our growth rate is fantastic even for a mail order organization, and we got behind with our work quite frankly. We said, 'right, we don't want to chase. We'll just leave them for two or three weeks because we haven't got enough staff to fill the orders even, and this is a minor point in our philosophy, so just leave them.' And we found at the end that most of the money came in. They're merely erratic payers, that's all. They're just slow in their payments so we don't chase them. (Creditor 5.)

The apparent lack of a relationship between the methods employed in a career's first stages and the recovery of money tends to cast doubt on the rationality of enforcement. A creditor has to be sure that vigorous enforcement is necessary before he actually applies sanctions. Estrangement can be risked only when he is certain that all defaulters are always dishonest. This assumption is fashioned by his use of credit sanctioning and his confidence in it. Thus, creditors who rely heavily on sanctioning may believe that they have filtered out most of the worst risks:

> We made a judgment in good faith, going on all the facts that were given and were asked for at the interview and the credit decision based on those facts. So when there's an inability to pay later on, we must assume that the facts that were given were correct, that there was no intent to defraud, otherwise *we're* lacking in our job. So we feel that a problem's cropped up and a customer, human nature being what it is, is just a little embarrassed about calling us up about it. (Creditor 29.)

On the other hand, a relaxed creditor may spend little time or money on sanctioning because he has a sanguine view of humanity and its economic behaviour, a view which is also applicable to the opening phases of the career he manipulates. Many enforcement systems are designed to open up negotiations between debtor and creditor because of this tendency to define the typical defaulter as honest, and because of the cost entailed in taking any real action. Collection may simply be directed at easing the burden of a contract which has become onerous:

> Things may go wrong and for various reasons he may not be able to repay you, but that would not be because he'd deliberately set out to mislead you. It is because something unforeseen has happened. And bad debts that arise through circumstances beyond lots of people's control or, even if it's not beyond their control, for reasons other than dishonesty, are sort of fairly easy to deal with, insofar as you know you're going to get your money back over the long period or you've just got to write the thing off because everything's gone wrong and you don't blame anybody in particular. (Creditor 1.)

There are other idiosyncratic goals pursued by individual creditors. Gas and electricity boards, for example, are primarily interested in the sale of power and their hire purchase departments feel diffident about repossessing the equipment which uses it. In all these ways, the aims of the career are turned away from the elementary collection of debts. This proliferation of ends complicates the construction of an enforcement system, and the choice of ends establishes its characteristics. Most of the available choices necessitate a multi-tiered process. A creditor can solve some of the problems of estrangement, publicity, deterrence, punishment and selection by setting up a serial system of tests. Each stage of a career encapsulates one or more tests of hypotheses about a debtor's situation. The results of the tests suggest actions in succeeding stages.

The results take the form of a reasonable or an unreasonable response from the harassed debtor. A reasonable response leads to a temporary abatement of enforcement whilst a debtor's behaviour is carefully monitored. The unreasonable response is most often no response at all, and it automatically suggests the need to pass the debtor on to a more severe stage. That is, if a desired response is not forthcoming, a creditor must assume that the debtor does not fall into the class of situations covered by the actions of that stage. The defaulter may be appropriately dealt with in a more unpleasant fashion and the apposite technique will eventually be found for him after sufficient tests have been applied. 'If you don't get any sense out of the debtor, you've got to put him into the machine.' (Creditor 31.)

In the main, therefore, a career generates its own understandings about default. The information which a creditor typically acts on is an absence of information. The default which receives the deviant label is often the sheer inaction of debtors. It is not solely the absence of a reaction that allows default to acquire an increasingly sinister meaning, it is also the growing magnitude of that absence. Time itself is a valuable measure of what a debtor is really like and what should be done to him. As consecutive instalments remain unpaid, the default increases and the debtor's deviance swells.

Roth (1963, p. xvii) argues, 'those who control the careers of others to some degree must decide upon appropriate times for making changes in those careers, and if they deal with many such careers, they are under pressure to regularize this process of definition'. The larger creditors are forced to organize their enforcement in minute detail. In most cases, a creditor has before him the information which he derived from the credit sanctioning stage and the knowledge that a debtor is not replying to his overtures. He might hazard guesses about the reasons for default, the risk presented by any default and the most successful method of dealing with it. A haphazard and individualized system is extraordinarily expensive and cumbersome to manage when there are several thousand cases to cope with. Above all, a debt cannot be neglected. Default must be countered immediately and without any initial enquiry:

> If you neglect somebody who hasn't paid, you can turn a good debt into bad debt. You can be the *cause* of bad debt. (Creditor 32.)

The collection system, if it is seriously intended to recoup loss, is made to cater for all possible contingencies, starting with the most sympathetic definition of the cause of default and ending with the least. The whole gamut of institutional conceptions of indebtedness is mechanically incorporated into the career. Problems of selection are reduced to a minimum. The process produces all the answers necessary for action.

As a result, a debtor's inaction is read as highly significant. It is a signpost to tougher enforcement. Institutional conceptions of indebtedness are not very numerous. They suggest that default can be engendered by fecklessness, deceit, misfortune or normal consumer behaviour. This last cause leads to default which can be cleared up at the beginning and without difficulty. Freidson (1968, p. 118) suggests:

> In the course of defining and classifying the universe which they claim needs their services, all control agencies in effect become responsible for drawing clearer lines than in fact exist in everyday life or in the processes by which people were originally led into their services, and agencies may come to define people as deviant who would not ordinarily have been so defined.

Stereotypes employed by an enforcement agency are thus artificially discrete and clear-cut. They are also distorted when an agency has little information about people, little contact with them and a limited body of professional or scientific knowledge about their behaviour (cf. Scheff, 1966B). Even if a creditor could expand his typology, he would be unlikely to use it fully because he cannot often afford to prepare a wider range of careers. Creditors who do select, map out routes for their four types of defaulter and all debtors must perforce fall into one or other of these categories. The first couple of letters dispose of an occasional defaulter who is not a risk to the creditor. There are contingencies which can explain default as a 'reasonable' act:

> You've got all these things to take into consideration before you start really bashing them, as it were. (Creditor 11.)

A debtor who does not reply to polite reminders cannot be anything but a potential control problem:

> The first thing you expect from a man of integrity, if he's not going to make payment, is to write and say why he's not. The fact that he's not done so is sufficient for us to consider we're on to a bad debt and to operate accordingly. (Creditor 31.)

It is possible that a seemingly recalcitrant debtor may 'really' be an honest person, and a collection system must be flexible enough to allow for reclassification. When an occasional debtor is discovered to be a professional, enforcement becomes both punitive and immediate:

> We write to them and ask them what the trouble is and if they can make some reasonable offer, to bring the account into line. Now, if they come back and say 'well, my husband's broken his legs' and so forth and produce a doctor's certificate to prove it, we say 'right, twenty five per cent of normal instalments for the next three months and review it then. Can you afford this?' And if they say that they can, right, that's a firm offer. Now, provided they comply with that arrangement, we know that we're on to a reasonable account. But, if we go a fortnight and hear nothing, then the red light occurs. We know jolly well that even though a man may have broken his leg, these people are out to catch us. (Collector 15.)

In the main, reclassification does not take place and a creditor is faced with the need to differentiate and act. His ability to label is shaped by the factors which affected credit sanctioning. A creditor who could not pay for elaborate sanctioning cannot pay for much information when default occurs. He must again rely on fortuitous detail. Sanctioning itself provides accessible biographies of those who default; the lavish sanctioner will be the informed pursuer. Risks presented by dealers, occupations, goods, age and geography all precipitate the labelling of a defaulter as a feckless, unfortunate or professional debtor.

Identification of a debtor precedes decisions about how the basic career should be applied. The whole process of differentiation is organized around the attempt to confront different types of defaulter with different career possibilities. The length and complexity of the basic career allows it to be accelerated or telescoped for the professional; expanded or suspended for the unfortunate; and abruptly terminated or exhaustively exploited for the feckless. Each of these models serves one or more of the goals of enforcement. It would be inappropriate or even dangerous to feed a debtor into the wrong career. The careers of those who cannot repay are designed to help debtors:

> The rock bottom basis of all our dealings is to help the client and keep him a good client, not to destroy him. (Creditor 30.)

The careers of those who will not repay exist to punish or provide salutary examples:

> Sometimes [Debt-collector 13] will write to us and say 'well, this woman's well known to us. She's doing this all over the place. You won't get any joy.' Well, then I see my colleague and he says 'yes, well, to hell with that. Someone's got to teach her a lesson!' (Creditor 8.)

These goals are completely at variance with one another, and no creditor would wish to give a professional latitude or antagonize a person who might pay. The task of placement is therefore of major importance. The search for information is built into the enforcement process, carried on as a parallel activity and pursued in the area of the fortuitous detail.

In addition to the meanings generated by a debtor's progress through a career, a creditor can make use of other sources of enquiry. The most significant one has already been partly discussed. A debtor may or may not reply to collection letters and overtures. The absence of a reply, especially when it is coupled with damaging information, will propel a debtor on to the next stage. A provocative response will suggest that a debtor is a professional who deserves coercion:

> It depends entirely on the reaction. If the bloke writes back and says we can go to hell, then, of course, the strong arm couple of ex-Scotland Yard blokes go along and try to get the money out of him. (Creditor 2.)

Such responses lead to a truncation of the career so that the defaulter is rudely faced with real action. Most letters, however, explain why default has occurred or supplicate the creditor. A beseeching letter will either be closely scrutinized or understood as a sign that a debtor is unfortunate or occasional because of his readiness to negotiate. The suspicious creditor will distrust almost any reply:

> You can be fairly easy-going, which we were in the past. People wrote in with what seemed to be a reasonable excuse. Alright, you let them go. But they find eventually that, whatever they say, you don't really press them too viciously. Consequently they take advantage of it. Give them an inch . . . (Creditor 16.)

Attempts to detect the untruthful debtor are framed in terms of intuition, 'hunch' and 'third sense':

> The genuine ones are the genuinely ill ones and they take trouble to write very early on. You can tell a genuine one from an excuse-maker straight away. You develop a knack for telling whether people are telling lies or telling the truth. (Creditor 24.)

Unless a creditor has a very jaundiced attitude towards his customers, deals in large individual sums, or feels that his risks are exceptional, he will accept the letters as pleas which are *prima facie* honest. The debtor who does not adhere to a negotiated agreement can be roughly dealt with whilst the one who does adhere will have been channelled out of the career.

Ideally, if not always in practice, a creditor has three separate histories of the defaulter which can be used to predict behaviour and direct enforcement policies. The first history was acquired at the sanctioning stage; the second is the debtor's profile as a consumer; and the third is provided by his reactions to approaches made in collection. There are thus three facets of the debtor: his performance before he became one of the firm's customers, his performance as a customer, and his performance as a defaulter. Most of a creditor's accounts will go into default at some time and they cannot be immediately labelled pathological or disturbing. The quality of the default must be assessed so that appropriate action can be taken. The degree of pathology can be gauged only by comparing the debtor's actions with normal payment patterns. When a firm regards default as both common and tolerable, it will be concerned only about the extraordinary case:

> The repayment period *ought* to be eight weeks but it's usually about three months. I think they've got problems, they're not bad payers in the main. (Creditor 3.)

Similarly, the creditor is unlikely to be alarmed if default occurs at certain times because this too is normal behaviour:

> It depends, you see. There are certain employments, obviously, where you have a seasonal trend. February is the worst month of the year when people are two months down following the Christmas stoppage of paying their instalments. Then September goes up because, while they're on holiday, they don't make a payment either because they've spent their holiday money or they've got the money with them. They've gone off on holiday, and they're just a fortnight late in paying. Whitsun, Easter and August bank holiday all give a kick to your graph as well. . . . You know it's going to happen. You don't rush out and repossess the car immediately. (Creditor 18.)

A debtor's history may be marred by a missing payment, but the seriousness of his omission is coloured by a creditor's conception of its significance. Seasonal default may be trivial, but other patterns may indicate that more than an occasional lapse has taken place. The most important warning signal is the stage in the agreement when default occurs:

> If he fails to pay the first two, you *are* going to have trouble with him. The majority of people who relapse at the end of the agreement do so because they're spending more money . . . realizing that they've almost completed the agreement and getting a bit more relaxed. I don't think it's an intentional step to avoid payment. If they fail in the beginning of the transaction, we would say that they're going to be a risk all the way through but, if they fail through the middle of the transaction, it's usually due to illness. (Creditor 14.)

Interpretations of the meaning of default at a particular stage vary from creditor to creditor. Some define default in the middle as a sign of the feckless debtor who cannot manage consistent payments, and default at the end as a mark of the unfortunate who has behaved well until he is struck by a catastrophe. Creditor 14 assigned different meanings, but his attribution of significance and consequent behaviour are typical of most creditors. All seem to agree that the professional pays as little as he can and that a contract broken right at the beginning is a sign of danger:

> A man who's going to be a completely bad debt, he'll default from the off. (Creditor 32.)

The other cue which suggests that a defaulter is more than an occasional debtor is a bizarre or sinister pattern of spending. This cue is available to stores who extend credit, credit card firms, mail order companies and other creditors who offer a certain licence to their consumers. A feckless debtor can be recognized by his irresponsible use of credit, and a professional is assumed to demand large quantities of marketable goods:

> We can tell very often when they're trying to do us. They buy watches, they buy jewellery, they buy negotiable items, consumer durables. If we get an agent who just starts ordering watches and typewriters, you put the clamps on them pretty quickly. (Creditor 5.)

A professional is also thought to exploit the facilities offered him and then vanish:

> All these duns are created automatically, then it goes to the credit team. He might decide 'I don't like the look of the account—large balance; quick build up; the type of charges, luxury charges, cameras, liquor. . . .' You expect to see hotels, rent-a-car, entertainment, but you don't expect to see clothing, shoes, things like that. (Creditor 12.)

The professional debtor is finally assumed to be completely predictable in his attempts to prey on creditors. It is consistent with his stereotype that he opens accounts with firms, defaults without any payment, and then moves on to other unwary firms. Creditors do not look for deviant debtors amongst their tried and familiar customers, but they do suspect their new ones. A recent contract may have been undertaken by a professional and the creditor's apprehension is reinforced by his ignorance of the customer. Ignorance can lead to delays and a misdirection of effort. Each new customer must also be taught that the creditor is not 'soft' and that default will not be countenanced.

A debtor's biography may reveal that he is prone to frequent default. If this is the case, the career will probably be accelerated in order to place him under some duress. Creditors surmise that such a defaulter must be feckless. He cannot be unfortunate because upsets should be spaced at decent intervals if they are to be credible. He is certainly not a professional because such a debtor 'skips' or is elusive and would not remain long enough to resume payment after the first default.

A creditor's knowledge of a debtor can be supported by other data. He may summon a debtor to interview or send a representative to his home. Personal confrontations are meant to coerce the debtor, guide enforcement and lead to negotiations. They are governed by the canons of enquiry which ruled a credit sanctioner's interview:

> It's an experience that comes about to try and pick who is genuine and who isn't. . . . It is how a person explains. . . .

> It's a *feeling* more than anything. If it *sounds* logical, there's a feeling of a person *and* an explanation. If a person is a bit too glib . . . (Creditor 17.)

Most creditors try to detect such underlying qualities as sincerity and honesty in debtors. Their detection is founded on common understandings about the meanings of verbal and non-verbal styles of expression (cf. Shibutani, 1966, pp. 19–20); on a heightened sensitivity which they believe they have developed over time; and on their peculiar definitions of significance.

Interviews are a useful means of classifying debtors because 'generally they fall into categories pretty quickly'. (Creditor 25.) Personal confrontations are, however, rare. Few firms have the inclination, money or organization to engineer face-to-face meetings. Their enforcement may be so routine and standardized that it proceeds automatically without much feedback from the defaulter. Some creditors believe that easily acquired data are all that is required to inform a viable collection system. On the whole, only those creditors who were able to interview debtors during the sanctioning stage are able to see them during the collection phase. The rest are not structurally equipped to interview. They may employ enquiry agents to trace a debtor who has flown but, in the main, enforcement is an interaction (or series of actions without reactions) based entirely on written communication between its participants. A detailed profile of a debtor is a luxury which most creditors cannot afford and would not be able to apply.

The nature of sanctions

Any enforcement career is built on three crucial foundations: the system of differentiation; the temporal structure of enforcement; and the nature of the sanctions which can be implemented. A collection sequence is a progress into controlled unpleasantness. The regulation of default, like other enforcement systems, rests ultimately on what an agency can do to the people it is supposed to control. A creditor's relations with his weapons mould a career.

A creditor can make a defaulter suffer a variety of pains: discomfort, stigma, repossession, intimidation, harassment by a debt-collector, and legal action. His choice and use of weapons are so circumscribed that any action is postponed as long as possible. Many of these restraints permeate all the dealings a creditor has with debtors. The fear of publicity and the risk of selecting inappropriate targets, for instance, rule out certain enforcement techniques altogether:

> We would write off a debt sooner than collect. It's just not

> worth our while. You see, mail order is desperately trying to become respectable. It is respectable, in fact, but there's a dodgy image sticking to it. (Creditor 5.)

Some creditors, mail order companies in particular, will abandon any court action which a debtor proposes to contest.[2] If their losses are tolerable and their individual debts small, creditors may refrain from acts which jar with the presentation of a clean front. Those who cannot divorce dirty work from their public image will abjure all dirty work. I have argued that county courts are the focus of little popular attention. Nevertheless, court proceedings always act as a threat because they *may* attract the hostility of the press. A creditor who refuses to employ these modes of enforcement may still try to exploit them. They will threaten the debtor with a sanction they have no intention of using.

By far the most important check on a creditor's ability to sanction is the financial cost of doing anything concrete. Unless the function of a career is punitive or deterrent, a creditor will be loath to lose money in his pursuit of a debtor. He may sham activity but he will usually shun it. Solicitors, debt-collectors and the creditor's own conception of urgency will establish a minimum debt worthy of the application of sanctions. All sums below this margin will be chased in a seemingly strenuous manner but no action will be taken. The fear caused by words and symbols becomes a substitute for the reactions evoked by a real confrontation with social control. Indeed, there appears to be a clear relationship between the belligerence of the sentiments expressed in the letter sequence and the creditor's reluctance to follow up the letters with activity of any sort. This relationship also resolves itself in the timing of the career. A small debt will be enforced with more strongly worded letters, and the letters themselves will be sent over a longer span of time. The cost of flourishing threats is the same whatever the size of the debt and, again, they will be offered when no action is planned. One mail order company, for instance, designed a standard letter which would be transmitted by its solicitors:

> If this does produce a certain amount of money, we've arranged with the solicitors that they should take 25 per cent. We'll probably use this for all debts under five pounds, where we

[2] Cf. S. Marsden-Smedley (1969), who states of her sample of 1,238 county court actions, 'the defendant filed a defence or counter claim in 50% of our sample of trader cases—which amounts to 7% of the summonses actually served by traders on consumers. We examined the case papers for each of these. The most striking thing that emerged was that in 32 cases (70%) the action was withdrawn after the defence was filed. We could not tell why from these case papers. The reason may have been that the firm thought the defence sound, or that they preferred, simply, not to fight.'

> have no real intentions of suing, and they have no intentions of suing, but the debtor doesn't know this. And it may be a means of picking up a certain amount of money. It costs us nothing to try it. (Creditor 4.)

Similarly, a bankruptcy notice may be sent to a debtor. The notice is cheap although the proceedings themselves are expensive and seldom undertaken:

> Invariably in this business you're coming across types that don't want bankruptcy, and therefore you come across quite a lot of response to a bankruptcy notice. (Creditor 11.)

Each creditor must decide how far and how actively he is prepared to pursue different sums of money. The firm that *is* prepared to act may still stay its sanctions. A creditor tends to reason that there is no need to use sanctions if a threat alone is effective. The threat should at least be made. However, there will be no staying when his money is in serious jeopardy or when a professional is identified:

> If it was a genuine fraud, he [a representative] would ring me no matter what hour of the day or night. He'd ring me at home and tell me so straight away. And I'd take action immediately. (Creditor 24.)

In all other cases, the fear of publicity, the cost of action, the disruptive alteration of routine and the attractiveness of serial tests recommend delay. Delay is additionally encouraged by the weakness of a creditor's sanctions. Physical intimidation is both uncommon and unusually dirty work. It may be resorted to by those who place an extraordinary stress on the value of deterrence:

> In this company you must not let the defaults rise. Defaults must be kept down by hook or by crook. By any method, whatever method you choose, you must keep them down. This is constant. From day to day, the staff are under pressure. . . . My own personal opinion is, when a hirer goes into default on the first occasion, he should be immediately visited. That's the time to stop him. I think it has a salutary effect on him if you have a rep standing on the doorstep and they are, after all, pretty big chaps you know, the two or three chaps who are calling on him, they know you're not fooling, you're not playing shop, you mean business. . . . You must work on collecting debts. You do intimidate a hirer. You have to, to get money from . . . A lot of other finance companies, and I know because I've been in other finance companies, they employ these debt-collectors. They're glorified debt-collectors—little men with a car and a bowler hat. They're not, they don't get anywhere at all. . . . (Creditor 24.)

It is uncommon for enforcers to express such enthusiasm. They are generally ill-disposed towards rigorous and visible collection and prefer 'little men with a car and a bowler hat'. They rely on a conventional use of conventional weapons and protract a career if they are not efficient. In many cases, the weapons are not regarded as efficient. The police, for instance, are defined as uninterested in the larcenies committed by debtors:

> They don't exhibit any interest. They take notes. They go through the motions. [On one occasion] we did take the trouble to go to —— police station. Well, the Sergeant did take the trouble of taking all the particulars and then showed us the crime book. Well, very quickly, so as we couldn't see the names. Well, my God, our little case was one in a million! I can quite understand the police point of view. (Creditor 2.)

The transfer of control from the creditor to another institution is always attended by risks. The creditor not only loses his ability to manipulate the debtor, the debtor himself may be reappraised. The enforcement career is manned by a number of institutions with often conflicting definitions of collection and the defaulter. One of the chief difficulties facing a creditor is this likelihood that a debtor will be redefined and consequently treated with what is thought to be excessive leniency. I shall discuss later the changes in pace that occur when a debtor is fed into the county courts and then into prison. These changes are all resented by a creditor who feels that his power and enforcement generally have been weakened as soon as legal action is taken. A creditor typically believes that court instalment orders are too small; that delays in court proceedings are too great; and that bailiffs are too lax in their prosecution of cases.

The repossession of goods on hire purchase may also have drawbacks. The rapid loss in value of most hired commodities and the difficulty of disposing of them induce a creditor to seek alternatives to the imposition of this sanction:

> We try and arrive at any sort of agreement whatsoever, and for him to go on paying and do what he can. The ultimate aim, the whole ambition . . . is to get the money and not the vehicle out of the person, of course, because a second-hand vehicle is really no use to us: we want the chap's money. (Creditor 25.)

Again, most debt-collectors act as an extension of the mechanical process of letter writing initiated by a creditor. Many are dummy firms set up by a creditor to embroider and enlarge the threats he can offer. They are not sanctioning agencies but a prolongation of the attempt to suggest that sanctions are imminent. There are, nevertheless, active debt-collectors who call on defaulters and these may be an exception to the general impotence of a creditor's armoury. When a collector of this sort is employed, delay becomes immediately unattractive:

> We don't expect any debt-collectors to write. We're not interested in writing. We've already written. (Creditor 4)

I shall analyse some of the relations between a creditor and his debt-collector below. The active collector is used when debts are relatively small. He is regarded as a forerunner to, or a substitute for, real action. He is not a final sanction when debts are sizeable and may hinder the imposition of that sanction. Even when trivial debts are involved, resort to a collector may be defined as incompatible with the creditor's goal of economy. 'In effect, we're buying money, our *own* money.' (Creditor 16.) Such resort can also endanger the creditor's public image because collectors might 'overstep the bounds'. (Creditor 29.) Outside agencies may be of little value to the creditors who have their own staff of representatives. The most important restraint on the use of the small collector is the network of supporting relations in which a creditor is enmeshed. Large collectors are institutionally linked with the creditor because of their status reporting function. The existence of such a connection predisposes a creditor to use their letter-writing services rather than establish new links with other external agencies. Ease of access to a large collector tends to preclude use of a small agency. As a result, the vigorous collector may not be seen as a satisfactory enforcement tool.

A creditor's reluctance to enforce sanctions is reinforced by his definition of the career as a serial testing system. A debtor who is unshaken by the threat of action must 'necessarily' be a person who will be unperturbed by the realization of that action. He has failed the test, passed a bench mark and become even more incorrigible. Failure increases a creditor's hestitation because such a debtor will be untouched by his weak and expensive techniques of coercion. The threat thus becomes of greater significance than the sanction itself:

> The threat of court is *efficient*. If a person's willing for it to go as far as there, then I don't think it really matters. The *hint* of taking someone to court is much better than having to take someone to court who's obviously, if it's gone as far as actually proceeding in court, then he *must* be a bad egg and he's not perturbed about it. (Creditor 32.)

Curiously, then, the need to use force implies that force will be useless. Courts, prisons, debt-collectors and so on exist to provide symbolic ammunition for a creditor. The threat of action at all times is more important than action itself. Action is impotent, expensive, a test of its own lack of value, and it might precipitate secondary deviation. Some creditors, moreover, are completely uninterested in action because collection is of little moment to them. Firms such as Creditors 3 and 5 are not prepared to make their enforcement systems anything more substantial than a transmission of letters and, perhaps, the sale of debts to a collector.

Enforcement thus relies on an extensive and continual manipulation of threats (Barnes, quoted in Black, 1962, p. 51):

> You can't get away from the use of fear in collecting bills. We can't offer the debtor anything positive like a nice frosty cake. We can only offer relief from anxiety, and, therefore, the collector has to make sure that a certain amount of anxiety is present.

Creditors try to create this controlled anxiety by building an abundance and variety of threats into the career. Creditor 7, for instance, devised a mild sequence of letters which are spaced at weekly intervals:

> *Letter 1:* We have recently sent you a statement of account showing an amount outstanding of . . .
>
> We hope you found our statement to be in order and that we may look forward to receiving your remittance in course of post.
>
> *Letter 2:* We wish to remind you that we have outstanding on our books an amount of £ . . .
>
> As this amount is overdue for payment we shall be grateful if you will let us have a cheque in settlement by return.
>
> *Letter 3:* When sending you a statement of your credit account with us earlier this month and also in the preceding month we asked if you would favour us with a settlement payment, but we cannot trace that this has been received.
>
> We are very anxious indeed to meet your wishes about this account, but the position is that our credit policy is based upon the expectation that all accounts will be paid monthly, and we therefore respectfully request that you will send us a settlement of the account within the next few days.
>
> *Letter 4:* Although we have addressed a number of applications to you for payment of your overdue account, we cannot trace that you have as yet made settlement.
>
> In order to avoid further difficulties arising we must ask you to be good enough to send us your payment for the full amount due.

> Failing receipt of such payment from you within the next few days we shall have to consider taking other steps for the collection of this debt.

The sequence is then taken over by a dummy debt-collector:[3]

> *Letter 5:* —— present their compliments and would point out that the instalment due under your Hire Purchase Agreement has not yet been received.

> *Letter 6:* —— regret that the instalment due under your Hire Purchase Agreement remains unpaid.
>
> If payment to cover this instalment in full is not received at once we shall have to take such steps as we feel to be best without further notice to you.

> *Letter 7:* We are unable to trace a reply to our previous applications to you for payment of instalments due under your Hire Purchase Agreement.
>
> In order that you shall continue to enjoy unhindered the benefits of this hiring, we must ask you to make immediate payment of the amount due.
>
> Failing receipt of such payment within the next few days we shall have to consider taking other action in this matter.

This enforcement programme clearly illustrates a number of critical aspects of the career system. First, tests are successively applied to ascertain what the most appropriate collection tone should be. By Letter 4, it is apparent to the creditor that the debtor must be somewhat recalcitrant. The first three letters completed one movement of the career and the fourth introduces the second movement. The idea of process is mechanically written into the sequence. Roth (1963, p. 115) argues that 'long stretches of time may be made more "psychologically manageable" by being broken up into smaller segments. When the markers used to divide periods of time into segments are also signposts of progress in a given direction, we have the foundation of a career timetable.' When a debtor refuses to respond to three letters he passes a marker and deserves some coercion.

The coercion to which he will be exposed in the second movement is unspecified; a threat is often more unpleasant if the sanction is unknown. Ambiguous threats are a second feature of collection. Enforcement would be discredited if it contained falsifiable pre-

[3] The creditor's sequence pursued a credit account debt whilst the debt-collector's letters refer to a hire purchase debt; they are parts of different careers. Nevertheless, the two movements are formally similar to a continuous career series.

dictions about action. Thus the threats offered by the debt-collector in Letters 7 and 8 are also vague. They hint at 'such steps as we feel to be best' and 'other action' but nothing more. The third movement will be based on a solicitor's threats, the fourth on a county court's threats and so on. No action may be taken for several months after the eighth letter but there is an impression continually being fostered that sanctions are in the offing.

A third feature, then, is a perpetual alteration of the tempo of the career by the introduction of artificial changes of mood and actor:

> If he's unco-operative, then, of course, you may do something more strong about it. A lot of people respond quite sharply to solicitor's letters where they don't respond to reminders and routine letters from us. You get something with a solicitor's name and address at the top stating this, that and the other in seven days, then they all of a sudden find the money. (Creditor 18.)

The symbolic value of names, words and tone are exploited to the full in an attempt to discover the level of anxiety which will make a debtor pay what he owes. In the main, the next stage is always depicted as the movement when action will be taken, and it usually turns out to be a means of foretelling the awfulness of the stage after that. This process may be embellished to a fine degree; letters will be followed by a dummy collector; the dummy will be followed by a real collector; the second collector will be succeeded by a solicitor and so on. The logic of threats prolongs and multiplies a career's movements; it is one of the chief reasons why collection *is* a career.

The last feature of the career timetable is its temporal basis. Like most commercial activity, collection is spaced out at standard intervals of time. Actions are taken every week, month or year. Such an arrangement seems perfectly rational because ordinary people and creditors both live in a world which regards these yardsticks as natural. Creditors use these intervals as the skeleton of the career; enforcement is likely to last for one or more years, its stages being separated into monthly periods. They also use these intervals as measures of the defaulters' deviance. A person who has not paid for three months is 'obviously' more deviant than one who has missed two payments. A debtor's deviance thus develops in a manner which is highly organized and calculable. To a large extent, the career imposes this kind of development of default. Not all deviance grows in this fashion. Becker's (1963) marihuana user, Cressey's (1932) taxi-dancer and Goffman's mental patient (1961) do not change in so uniform or neat a way. Instead, they are transformed by processes which are unevenly spaced out and have no minute connection with such conventional yardsticks as weeks or months. These careers are based on their own peculiar timetables. One short critical stage may be much more significant than any of its companions.

It is possible that default would be similarly organized were it not for the imposed career timetable. Thus, the initial refusal or inability to pay an instalment might be as important as the next three or four stages put together. Creditors themselves do not assign equal weights to all the career's stages. Some believe that an account which has become two or three months in arrears has acquired a dramatically new meaning. These numbers have a 'magical' (Sommer and Osmond, 1961, p. 261) property of great significance for the career manipulator who seeks suitable markers for altering policy.

An enforcement apparatus of this kind tends to create deviants through self-fulfilling prophecies. When the apparatus is in operation, a great variety of data assumes increasingly sinister meanings. The meanings lend momentum to enforcement and enforcement colours the meanings. The autonomy of the collection system leads to the production of deviants despite a paucity of information about debtors, their motives and their situations. Someone who is illiterate, perplexed or absent will be automatically treated as if he were a recalcitrant or elusive professional defaulter. Many creditors recognize that there is a disparity between the reality conveyed by their machine and the reality they are trying to organize. One large creditor stated, for instance:

> My assumption is that the majority of those [passed on to debt collectors] don't start out with the intention of defrauding. They have fallen on to bad times and they haven't been sufficiently well educated to discuss it to bridge the gap. It's resulted in them going in so deep, and these tougher and tougher letters coming in, they feel they can't face the collection. (Creditor 7.)

Nevertheless, very few creditors can respond to defaulters in these terms. They are offered nothing but the perspectives furnished by the enforcement system. Unless debtors negotiate, they are inevitably branded as deviant. Creditors who appreciate that this kind of disparity exists receive some reassurance from the fact that each movement of the career filters out a substantial proportion of debtors. The career, starting at default and ending with prison, resembles a pyramid. Such a structure persuades the creditor that each successive stage is occupied by debtors who are less and less typical of the general population of honest consumers. It is illustrated by Table 3.1 which shows the volume of letters sent by a large suburban store.

TABLE 3.1 *Enforcement letters sent by a large store**

	Amount sent monthly	*Success rate %*	
Printed (unsigned)	1,500	50	
1st letter	1,200	60	
2nd letter	800	50	
Strongly-worded letters	400	30	full payment / part payment
'Final' reminders (recorded delivery)	200	60	full or part payment, or offers of payment

* The table is an accurate copy of one sent to me by the store.

I found it extremely difficult to obtain any figures of the numbers of accounts that were involved at each stage of enforcement. This information was guarded so closely that it was inaccessible to me, or else it was not compiled at all. Thus, the solicitor of the store which featured in Table 3.1 said, 'quite frankly, we do not keep statistics which would provide indisputable answers to your queries. The keeping of such statistics would not greatly assist us in our day-to-day business, though I appreciate that they may well be of considerable interest to an outsider.' It was equally difficult to gain data about creditors' bad debts. Only one creditor was prepared to show me detailed figures of his losses. It is obvious that that type of information not only exposes a firm's failures but also might enlighten its rivals. It seems that a firm's accountants are the only outside body which has access to this dangerous material. Although I approached the Board of Trade, the Institute of Chartered Accountants, insurance companies and so on, no data were forthcoming.

I have reason to suspect the typical statistics which I was offered in interviews. When the rough verbal estimates made by creditors were checked against an independent source, gross discrepancies were revealed. Those verbal statistics suggested that between 50 and 90 per cent of a creditor's accounts went into default at some time; 5 to 10 per cent of accounts were in arrears at any one time; 2 per cent were defined as serious enough to merit action more severe than letter writing; and half of this last group was abandoned as irrecoverable. The latter sequence was therefore held to collect some 70 per cent of defaults successfully.

The few accurate figures which I did obtain (but cannot publish) show that there is a wide variation between firms and within the same firm over time. Whilst one giant retail store loses 25p on bad debt and its recovery for every £100 it extends in a year, a small hire purchase company lost £32 for every £100 it lent. The former concern estimated that 55p in every £100 was seriously at risk at the beginning of a particular financial year; it recovered 20p out of those 55p, wrote off 10p, and spent 15p in every £100 on enforcement purposes. The losses of the smaller firm fluctuated wildly. Over a period of ten years, it devoted 2½ per cent of its income to credit sanctioning and debt collection, and it wrote off 4 per cent of its income as bad debt. Within that period, however, its losses ranged from nil to 32 per cent, and they rose and fell quite dramatically. Another small hire purchase company lost 14 per cent of its income over a four-year period and allocated 1 per cent for legal charges. Within that period, its losses ranged from 5 to 20 per cent of its income. Default was clearly of little importance to the large store, but it was a matter of overriding concern to the two smaller creditors. One of them, indeed, appeared to be heading for financial collapse.

I have portrayed the enforcement career as an uninterrupted series of increasingly unpleasant threats. All firms have a blueprint for such a complete timetable, but few debtors run the whole gamut of sanctions. Most defaulters are exposed to one or two letters before they retire from the career. Creditors can juggle with these minor expeditions into enforcement. A debtor whose arrears are relatively large may be introduced at the end of the first movement and retreat when he receives a letter from a debt-collector. Petty, persistent defaulters may be sent a second letter every time their payments lapse. Thus the blueprint offers an inventive creditor many configurations of stages, sanctions and threats.

4 The debt-collector[1]

In this chapter, I shall describe the ways in which some collectors exploit widespread public ignorance and act as effective agents through the creation of anxiety. Outsiders seem to know so little about debt-collectors, and so fearsome is their reputation, that most collectors are able to recover debts without engaging in face-to-face enforcement. Even the very large collectors can operate with threatening letters as their sole weapon. Because collection is carried out mainly by written threats, the occupation covers an immense variety of organizations. At one extreme, a debt-collector could be an enormous concern employing dozens of staff in West End or City offices and, at the other, a solitary individual working from his suburban home. It requires almost no capital and very little expertise to establish an agency and, as a result, there is a considerable turnover of firms. In 1965, for instance, eighteen firms in London called themselves debt-collectors.[2] By 1968, five of these firms had vanished and another eight had appeared.

At the very margins of the occupation are firms which are set up by professional or experienced defaulters. Role-switching opportunities are quite common in the world of enforcement. A detailed knowledge of default, coupled with skills at 'conning' and manipulation, are shared by inveterate debtors and debt-collectors alike. For instance, a journalist reported that a man who was closely associated with two Scottish firms of debt-collectors had been sent to prison in the past for defrauding eight people and embezzling money from fifty others. At the time he was sentenced, he had been the head of

1 I have adopted the arbitrary convention of referring to the work of debt-collectors proper with the hyphenated word *debt-collection*. By using the hyphen only when agencies are described, I can distinguish their activities from more general enforcement.

2 Source: *London Classified Telephone Directory*.

another debt-collecting firm (*John Bull*, 16.7.1938). Marginal firms may be established with the sole intention of exploiting the creditors they purport to serve.[3] Such collectors typically offer a cheap service to local shopkeepers and, when they have secured a number of commissions, decamp with the money which they have recovered. An example of this kind of exploitation was related in the *People* (12 February 1961).

> J—— P—— D——, Irishman with a thick brogue and a slick line of sales-talk, made a big impression when he drove up in his gleaming car and offered to collect traders' bad debts. Many of them paid £4 4s. a year fee for his services. But now D——, partner in a flourishing debt-collection company, has quit the firm and vanished. Now some of his own creditors are anxious to see him. They claim he owes them more than £500.

The more grandiose collectors often label themselves 'trade protection societies'. Such societies typically serve a particular trade and they again vary in size. One society might claim an alliance with a trade without receiving any encouragement or interest from members of that trade. Thus, the Shoe Lace Manufacturers Protection Association might have only a nominal connection with the makers of shoe laces. Other societies, however, effectively represent the bulk of the traders they claim to protect. Thus, the National Pharmaceutical Union has a membership consisting of most of the smaller chemist shops and has 'for marketing purposes about 11,300 outlets' (Annual Report, 1963–4, p. 6). The functions of a society can also vary from simple debt-collection to the provision of a wide range of services. In the former case, the title of 'protection society' is adopted merely because it is a less stigmatized name than 'debt-collector'. In the latter case, enforcement plays only a minor part amongst the society's multifarious activities. The National Pharmaceutical Union, for example, negotiates with government bodies over such matters as Resale Price Maintenance; secures links between retailers and suppliers; advises about shop modernization; sponsors products; initiates staff training schemes; operates a

[3] See, for example, accounts in the following newspapers: *Daily Express* (Glasgow) (17 February 1931); *Daily Herald* (23 February 1934); *Daily Herald* (7 May 1936); *Sun* (1 November 1968). My references are fairly antique because the *Daily Express* library did not cover debt collection between 1940 and the 1960s. The librarian of this extraordinarily comprehensive collection of newspaper cuttings told me that no one had been interested in the subject. It is interesting that a library which covers the most recondite subjects should have ignored enforcement for twenty years. It reflects the general lack of interest in collection which I described in Chapter 1. It also exacerbated the problems which I had in documenting enforcement. Virtually nothing has been written on the subject.

distress fund; mans an information and advice department; co-ordinates locum services; assists in the registration of trade marks; tests drugs and so on.

It is clear that the occupation of collector is a loose category; collectors are a heterogeneous group, and membership of the occupation is by no means stable. Moreover, the various agencies are not at all closely connected with one another. The scarce commodity which most collectors market is their records of defaulters and they are reluctant to let competitors have access to their files. Similarly, they seldom communicate about their methods. The better established trade protection societies *are* organized into an association which enables co-operation and the exchange of information, but they cannot control the activities of their more disreputable colleagues. Although the association periodically condemns the enforcement techniques of marginal firms, its condemnation serves to underscore its own rectitude rather than hamper the unprincipled collectors. In 1934, for example, the *Daily Herald* reported (23 February 1934):

> Bogus debt-collectors have been reaping a big harvest recently, but their good time is now coming to an end. Tradesmen creditors have found they have lost more money through these collectors than if they themselves had gone on trying to collect their bad debts. So the various trade protection associations have got together, exchanged experiences, and drawn up a 'black list' of doubtful debt-collecting agencies . . . the identity of most of these black sheep is known, and the combined trade protection associations think they will be able to stop the bogus 'collecting' in future.

Two years later, the *Daily Herald* stated (7 May 1936):

> Bogus debt-collecting agencies were denounced as 'vampires' and 'swindling parasites' and many of their methods exposed at the annual conference of the National Association of Trade Protection Societies in London yesterday. Delegates from all parts of the country told stories of the growing activities of men who make large sums of money from debt-collecting and cost traders thousands of pounds a year. Conference made a strong demand for their suppression.

Whilst the larger collectors are organized, the small firms are entirely independent of one another. I gathered the impression that there is some enmity between the various agencies and, in particular, hostility exists between the giant central agencies and the smaller suburban firms. The former regard their rivals with suspicion, believing that they are unprofessional upstarts who might resort to force or dishonesty (cf. Greig, 1941, p. 162). The latter group define their colleagues as inefficient, unwieldy and complacent. As a result, liaisons are likely to be set up only between firms that are able to offer each other desired services. Thus, the large concerns often engage local agents to collect debts when their letters fail to have an impact. Something of the occupation's lack of cohesion and distrust is conveyed by Collector 13's observations:

> American Collectors' Association, I had them in here a little while ago, and apparently all the debt-collecting associations in America have got an association. And he came over here: he'd no idea of how the work was over here, he couldn't understand why we were all individuals and not joined together. And I had to explain to him, I said 'an Englishman is a very different type to an American. He is prepared to work on his own. He doesn't want a whole bank of people round him to make him any good. He's prepared to work on his own'. But they couldn't see it at all. Now, there's that one, it's a New Cross number, you see, 'no success, no charges',—— Company Ltd., S.E.4. . . . There's another one, 'debts collected, no charge'; ——, Oxford Street. So it goes on. And here's another, here's one in '64 that came about. But what happened to them, I've never heard any more. They were actually in this street . . . but they didn't seem to live very long. ——, that's the Balham one, that's another chap. You see, they spring up but we never hear anything of them. They seem to die away. . . . You see there's no capital required to set up a debt-collecting agency, there's only experience and people's trust in you.

So open an occupation naturally recruits its members from an incredible diversity of backgrounds. Whilst the larger firms hire, train and promote their staff in the manner followed by any other sizeable commercial concern, the smaller companies may be founded or joined by ex-policemen, ex-bailiffs, private detectives, erstwhile employees of other agencies, or by people with no relevant experience at all.

Debt-collectors man a stage in the career which is a further, sometimes final, probe of the serial testing system; a somewhat hurried interlude between private and public enforcement; or an amalgam of both. In its second and third guises, the stage bridges two significant periods of collection but is not itself a protracted or intensive episode. The use of dummy firms of collectors by some creditors underlines how insubstantial this phase can become. It is insubstantial because most of a collector's effectiveness lies in the ideas suggested by his name and function, ideas which can be as well conveyed by a bogus firm as by a genuine one. Most collectors do little more than add to a debtor's anxiety. Their engagement in enforcement is meant to signify that there has been a profound change in the pace and importance of the career:

> Normally, the member's sent in an account and, if he comes to us, he's asking us to write a formal letter from someone outside to show that he's seriously wanting to collect the money. (Debt-collector 8, a large trade protection society.)

The debt-collector's role is normally the manipulation of frightening images and it seldom entails the active pursuit of a debt. This role readily lends itself to a cheap extension of the empty threatening procedure of a creditor. The collector can be employed to launch a last attack on debtors whom the creditor does not propose to take to court:

> We get very small accounts. I think they [creditors] find it's worth their while to hand them to us just to *try* before they write them off because they'd never sue for these fiddling little accounts. But it is just an effort, if they've got a quantity and they've got to give them all to us, well, on average, we've got to get some of them. (Debt-collector 11, a small debt-collector.)

There are many reasons why debt-collection is usually based on letters alone. The first reason is that letters are cheap, expedient and pose few organizational problems. Collectors tend to charge a standard rate of a few pence for each letter sent and exact a commission on the debts they manage to recover. The commission may be a flat ten per cent or it may be calculated on a sliding scale but, in the main, the less a collector does the smaller are his fees. 'Inactive' agencies therefore satisfy a creditor's demand for economy. They may be less efficient than their colleagues who call on defaulters but a creditor who sought efficiency would probably not employ a collector at all. None of the debtors I interviewed in Brixton Prison, for example, recalled encountering a collector. Creditors who want to acquire power over defaulters and exploit career possibilities to the full typically proceed to court without an intervening debt-collection stage. They may simply regard an agency as an obstacle to recovery. Indeed, some collectors are quite disparaging about their own usefulness and argue that the county courts are more efficient institutions:

> There's very little point in coming to us rather than going to a county court. . . . The effect could be less because [creditors] have been trying to get the money out of these people and [the debtors] have been trying to put it off. Then they come to us and the person concerned re-opens all the back-log again, starts

> trying to go through the same procedure. Whereas, if you get a court order, you've got a greater opportunity of getting someone nailed down to a particular date.[4]

Despite their inability to impose physical sanctions, collectors variously claim to recover between fifty and ninety per cent of the accounts they are asked to handle. Whilst active agencies appear to be generally more successful than their inactive colleagues, they are also more expensive. It could be as costly for a creditor to use one of these collectors as it would be for him to use a county court. The court is often regarded as a more effective institution because it is able to inflict the stigma of a judgment which punishes the debtor and warns future credit sanctioners. It can also offer a variety of types of unpleasantness; bankruptcy, execution, imprisonment, and so on, which are more potent than those manipulated by a collector. As a result, a debt-collector is usually called upon to play a fairly minor role in enforcement. He may be asked to pursue either the smaller debts or debts which are about to be abandoned. The relationship between the time consumed in enforcement and the size of the sum enforced is an inverse one. Minor sums will be chased over a relatively long period of time and with relatively little action. Debt-collecting agencies are therefore best able to deal with cases involving a subordination of efficiency to economy. They can do so by sending letters rather than engaging in personal calls. The inactive agents are cheap substitutes for the court or a prelude to it; the active ones are its rivals.

The second major influence which predisposes collectors to send letters is the difficulty of doing anything else. One collector graphically described the complexities of active enforcement:

> Normally, they say 'right, pass your debt to us. We will collect, and of the money we collect we will take a percentage of blank.' Now, when they have these accounts, they are necessarily limited to a very small area if they're going to operate successfully. . . . Particularly you may go, say, for a debt of twenty pounds. When you get there and the people are out, and if you've got to go ten miles before you get to the next one, that's sheer waste. If you get there, the position may well be that the person'll say 'Well look, I'm absolutely flat broke. I admit I owe this money but I can't give you anything at the moment. Come back tomorrow.' Well, if you have sufficient business, you can't go back tomorrow! You've got to go back perhaps three or four or six days later and then perhaps you only get ten bob, you see. (Debt-collector 12.)

[4] Debt-collector 10, a large debt-collector and status reporter who usually acts against commercial organizations rather than private consumers.

Compared with the simple transmission of letters, active collection is often awkward to co-ordinate, expensive to run, and is not always more successful. Letter sending is not only simple, it also fits in well with a collector's other function of status reporter. Collection merely becomes another type of paper work which involves no esoteric skills or special personnel. It can be offered as a service by small institutions or by agencies with other roles. Above all, this kind of enforcement suits the collector who is concerned about his potential involvement in dirty work. He can dismiss active enforcement as 'strong-arm methods'. Such attempts to dissociate the good collector from bad collection are fairly common.

I argued in Chapter 1 that many Londoners fear debt-collectors and associate them with violent social control. This definition is sustained by what seems to be a deliberate ossification of ideas concerning collection; poor communication between enforcers and public; and the absence of a need to be publicly accountable. The employers of collectors subject them to some control, but employers are also the victims of the deviance that is being assaulted. Fear is highly useful to the collector and there seems to be no institutional means of dispelling it. The press usually harps on the exotic in enforcement, stressing the unpleasantness of agencies which are really unconnected with normal collection systems. Although the vast bulk of collection is carried on by a few firms who do nothing but send letters,[5] newspaper articles commonly foster apprehension and alarm about enforcement. One article (*Observer*, 21 November 1965), for instance, reported that 'throughout the week the men who make up the unscrupulous end of the debt collecting business will be warning bad payers that any violence will not be "the liability of the company" or that they will not accept responsibility for "damage caused by dogs"'. The scrupulous end of collection is not described because it is too dull or because it does not serve as a target for criticism. The behaviour of minor collectors thus colours the labels attached to major ones.

All the collectors I interviewed disassociated themselves from the 'unscrupulous end' of their occupation, but they also made obvious use of the advantages created by its reputation. Some exploited the symbols generated by their identification with violent collection.[6] Thus, the manager of one firm told me that he could easily label his company the 'Horrible Debt-Collecting Service' but 'we don't call

[5] In 1964, for example, one firm (which collects by letter alone) dealt with 42,823 debts in London and recovered £1,000,104 (122nd *Annual Report* of the International Association for Promotion and Protection of Trade Ltd).

[6] These symbols include a frightening name for the company, the use of ambiguous threats and an emphasis on the fact that the collector *is* a collector.

ourselves debt-collectors. We influence payment.' (Debt-collector 12.) Despite his disavowal of dirty work, his letter sequence is clearly characterized by the dirty work of others:

> *Letter 1:* **PRIVATE AND CONFIDENTIAL** We are advised that the applications by the above for the adjustment of your outstanding account have not resulted in payment being made by you.
>
> Please forward payment to the above *immediately* . . . and thus avoid unpleasantness.
>
> *Letter 2:* We have been advised by the above that despite applications by them you have defaulted in payment of your account.
>
> Therefore **TAKE NOTICE** that failure by you to make a payment *direct* to this Creditor within the next **SEVEN DAYS** may result in your name being registered as a **DEFAULTER** both *locally* and *nationally*. This registration will stop your obtaining any further credit in future.
>
> *Letter 3:* Having failed to pay the above sum the **CREDITOR** has no alternative but to take **LEGAL PROCEEDINGS** against you for recovery of same. . . . The return of this notice with payment . . . within eight days will stop such proceedings.

This stream of letters resembles its predecessors in the enforcement career. At first it suggests that it is the basis of a stage which will be final and really punitive, but it lamely ends with the threat of yet another stage. The first letter contained a typically vague threat of 'unpleasantness'; the second was unusual in that it prophesied a specific sanction; but the third was again orthodox. Registration as a defaulter is, of course, the one device that most collectors would use in any case. Their ancillary role as status reporters necessarily leads to the recording of information secured through enforcement. Indeed, many collectors automatically record the names and addresses of all the debtors they have dealings with. Although recording is a cheap, alarming and viable sanction, it is unlikely to be as effective as Debt-collector 12 predicted.[7]

The meaning of the unpleasantness threatened in the first letter, however, can be shaped only by a defaulter's beliefs about debt-collectors. Imagined unpleasantness acquires its awfulness from the notoriety of the occupation, a notoriety which is perpetuated by the press and by the occupation itself. The collectors I saw disowned their disreputable colleagues but they patently flirted with their stigma. This ambivalence is clearly demonstrated in the two statements made to me by a debt-collector who was also a private detective:

[7] For the reasons given in Chapter 2.

> I found that debt-collection required a certain type of mind. To be able to instruct a person to go up and collect debts was not the easiest subject to instruct them [employees] on where you have other work. Now, for instance, the attitude of mind of our operatives is this, that they will do debt-collection, but they don't like it because the very term 'debt-collector' incites smutty remarks and smutty smears. It's not, you know. . . . If somebody asked me what I did for a living, I wouldn't probably say I was a debt-collector.
>
> Now, we limit it [collection] to people via whom we know we will receive no criticism because of our other activities. If we were purely debt-collectors and nothing else, then publicity-wise, it wouldn't matter how much criticised we were. This would be good for debt. (Debt-collector 6.)

The ambivalence with which many collectors regard their stigma is of interest. It keeps alive the problem of resolving an occupational identity because it does not allow a collector to be completely 'good' or 'bad'. Whilst agencies seem to deplore the shameful aspects of their occupation, they often emphasize precisely these aspects in their attempts to recover debts. They disavow their connection with stigma by redefining their enforcement as not 'real' debt-collection. For example, collectors frequently abjure physical intimidation and protest that they reject work which is repugnant to them:

> There are strong-arm methods. One of our members . . . Well, I've just refused to work for them now because—I mean, he was always so full of bluff. 'Why don't you go and knock their so-and-so heads off?' and all the rest. Well, these are not my methods, I mean, and he was so abusive! I just wouldn't deal with it. (Debt-collector 11.)

> We always say, that we've raised the trade of debt-collecting to that of a profession. . . . That's the way we've built it up. . . . And that's the method on which we've done . . . I mean, some people write to us and say 'Look, I want to write a rude letter to this person.' I say, 'I'm sorry. We never write rude letters. We'll carry on in our usual way, but we don't write rude letters.' (Debt-collector 13.)

Attempts to resist contamination may induce collectors to discard the very name of 'debt-collector'. They may label themselves an 'agency', a 'trade protection society' or a 'default register'. They may define their place in enforcement in a way which is more compatible with their moral and social distance from the unscrupulous. They do not, therefore, collect debts but 'influence payments', make 'arrears calls', and act as 'impartial negotiators' or 'settlers of disputes':

> On the collection side, our job is to try and ensure that money which is properly owing is paid but, if there is a proper dispute and the debtor insists that he doesn't pay, then a proper account is taken of what he says. And, if the money is in fact not owing, he's not made to pay. (Debt-collector 3, a large trade protection society.)

However, there are pressures which make the assumption of such a neutral and scrupulous identity difficult. All collectors are to some extent forced into involvement with stigma. Firstly, there is an apparent lack of discrimination between the scrupulous and unscrupulous on the part of those who witness and report debt-collectors' actions. Press commentary seldom stresses the respectability of some collectors when it castigates others. Neutrality or the use of impeccable methods is also difficult when the collector is the paid agent of the victim. Large numbers of collectors receive commissions on the debts they manage to retrieve but nothing for those they cannot recover. They are impelled to make their limited methods as effective as possible. Effectiveness may well be seen as the maximization of the threatening capacity of letters. It will take this form especially when letters are the only method employed. Bluster can become a substitute for action.

Neutrality may be additionally offset by the manner in which collectors categorize defaulters. Throughout the career, from the first letter to imprisonment, debtors are reassessed when they are transferred to a new stage manned by new personnel. Creditors may assume that their letters have weeded out all unfortunate debtors, but debt-collectors and their successors do not share this assumption. All enforcers work in the same world of a few social types because they have a common need to explain why some debtors never pay, why some pay immediately coercion is applied, and others pay after protracted enforcement. The people who respond to a collector's letters are necessarily labelled unfortunate despite earlier classifications. As a result, the three-fold typology is systematically used throughout the whole enforcement. Each group of enforcers takes up its predecessor's feckless and professional debtors and redefines them. There is a constant process within and between stages, an oscillation between dichotomous and trichotomous classifications. A collector's typology thus closely resembles a creditor's typology:

> You have the debtor who unfortunately runs into bad circumstances, who is not what you regard as a bad debtor,

> he's just unfortunate, got into debt possibly through no fault of his own. . . . This is possibly the most common debtor, shall we say. Due to circumstances beyond their control. . . . You have the debtor who unfortunately runs into a bad account because he feels he can, under present existing circumstances, he can manage. They slightly differ, or he goes too far, and he finds that he runs into debt. . . . I think the third debtor can be classed as the out and out man who lives by debt alone, who just makes debts and leaves one address for another. He never finds any fear in anybody threatening legal proceedings. He has hundreds of county court judgments registered from one address to another and, in fact, doesn't care two hoots about it. (Debt-collector 5.)

Any classification is a guide to action. A collector who is confident that professional debtors exist is also confident that they should be punished if the creditor consents. His hostility to the deviant, although balanced by sympathy for the unfortunate, impairs his mask of impartiality. It is also partly responsible for his stigma. A collector's categorization of defaulters conflicts with views held by people outside the collection system. In Chapter 1, I argued that debtors are popularly defined as morally weak but non-deviant persons. Authoritative definitions tend to portray the debtor as a casualty of primary poverty or as an inadequate person.[8] This kind of explanation is most commonly given for the presence of debtors in prison, and it is in this context that the difference between esoteric and exoteric analyses of default is clearest. Women prisoners are, by the logic of the system's occasional rationality, the most deviant debtors. They have reached the zenith of the career, failed all its tests, resisted all punishment and have even escaped the special checks instituted to prevent females being incarcerated. Outsiders, however, label such debtors as inadequates. Xenia Field (1963, p. 20), for example, states:

> The high figure of debtors in the Civil Prisoners table is extremely worrying. It is made up mainly of housewives, many of them inadequate, bad housekeepers and managers, with large families and too little money. Unable to pay their way they get into deeper and deeper debt and are finally overwhelmed by it.

An obvious implication of such a portrait is that the machine which processes these feckless debtors is at best undiscriminating and at worst brutal.[9] The justification of a debt-collector and his colleagues

[8] Cf. Chapter 11.
[9] Moya Woodside (1962, pp. 29–30) gives a similar description.

for coercion depends on the credibility of the professional and of the devices that exist to identify him. Many outsiders do not believe in the professional and, if they do, distrust the filtering mechanisms of enforcement. This gulf inevitably stigmatizes anything a collector does in response to people he imagines to be professionals. Collectors often deplore this lack of understanding. A letter to the *Observer* (20 October 1968), for instance, reflected:

> Your last Sunday's report . . . on the wrong way to collect old debts, has a ring of truth in certain respects, but as usual for public consumption the article is slanted in favour of the debtor. The point is once again made that the public are ignorant of their rights. As far as we are concerned the opposite is often the case, and it would seem there is a certain class of bad debtors who know more about the law than the law itself. Nobody in their right minds should countenance the use of strong-arm tactics; certainly our company dissociates itself from any such action. However, it would be interesting to know just what would be the overall effect on prices if bad debts could be cut out completely. . . . A further point often forgotten is how often bad debts cause bankruptcy and regularly jeopardise legitimate positions and jobs. (From M. Brook, director of Herts and Essex Trade Protection Office Ltd.)

Actions motivated by professional and feckless debtors tend to taint the reputation of debt-collectors. The actions are responses to beliefs about the debtors' deviance which, at this stage, has automatically grown. The collector is aware of the significance of his place in the career structure and must conclude that his defaulters are necessarily more deviant than those successfully disposed of by a creditor. His classification of defaulters cannot exactly replicate its predecessors. His professional is rather more professional; his feckless more feckless; and his unfortunate less unfortunate. Collection must be organized around the assumption that his defaulters are not just 'ordinary' people or inadequates but people with special properties. One collector told me that he intervened 'very largely when everyone else has given up hope'. (Debt-collector 7.) The collectors are pushed into taking a coercive role because of their relations with the rest of the enforcement machine. They perform the dirty work of creditors and confront their failures.

This push is reinforced by the manner in which the collector is depicted by the machine itself. He is the threat offered in the previous stage and would disrupt the impression of increasing tempo and severity if he adopted a 'soft' stance. Most careers, and debt collection in particular, continually progress towards a discernible goal. The idea of progress is carefully nurtured in enforcement. A collector's wish to be mild or neutral is subversive to the structure and purpose of the career. The collector is the culmination of all that has occurred before him and he is defined by those other stages. As a creature of the machine, he has little influence over the kinds of action he can take and the interpretations which are made of that action. If he attempted to negotiate, his approaches might be read as devious manoeuvring. If he was direct and unthreatening, his behaviour could be identified as hectoring. He is a manufactured villain of a dramatic presentation laid on for defaulters and his efforts to make a more heroic role are inevitably frustrated.[10]

The chief constraint on collection style is imposed by a collector's links with his creditors. Large collectors are letter-sending agencies who are forced to fit neatly into the overall structure of mass enforcement. Their organization is geared to satisfy the needs of bureaucratic creditors whose demands for economy, speed and standardization stamp themselves on all the enforcement they control. As one collector observed:

> Mail order companies, as a matter of policy, with their mass-production techniques of advertising, mailing goods, the procedures of debt recovery, the follow-up letters, the handling of disputes (if any); the larger organization will not treat each account on its merits. . . . It would go through the normal channels. (Debt-collector 1.)

Collectors, as one of the normal channels, must try to mesh themselves closely with adjoining career stages, sometimes to become mere appendages of the creditor:

> We are really extensions of their [creditors'] own offices, we are clerks working for them. (Debt-collector 12.)

Restriction of autonomy leads to a smooth and uninterrupted career pattern. When the creditor's letter stream ends, a connected stream starts to flow from the collector's offices. Restriction produces efficiency but it also moulds collection techniques. It means that a collector cannot be idiosyncratic in his decisions about the content of letters, about the spacing of letters or the length of his own contribution to enforcement. He must convey the impression that recovery is relentless, more determined and accelerating.

There is another influence on the work of large collectors and

[10] Occupational factors are not, of course, the only determinants of the mode of collection. People who decide to take up collection must have prior attitudes towards enforcement and their place in it. The repute of the job might act as a bar to those who are seriously concerned about stigma. Nevertheless, it has been my impression that collectors are anxious to ward off attacks on their identities.

this is the functional importance which enforcement has in an organization. Many collectors perform more than one task; they may also be status-reporters, private detectives, enquiry agents or trade protection societies. The significance of collection and its relations with other areas of work will affect the way in which it is handled. When collection is relatively unimportant, the strains and pressures brought about by the structure of enforcement may be resisted. Trade protection societies, for instance, primarily exist to safeguard the interests of a particular occupation. They provide information, negotiate with such bodies as government departments, and publicize the commendable features of the occupation. Collection may be a minor function. One society's manager told me:

> We provide the debt-collection section of the service purely as a service. It's not done as a money making thing. In fact, it costs us far more for every case we deal with than the very minor charge we make for it. More than the debt in many cases! . . . It's just purely a series of letters, in effect, and advice to the member. (Debt-collector 8.)

Debt-collector 6 felt that his enforcement role should not be allowed to endanger his work as a private detective. He curtailed collection in order to promote more rewarding business. Not only did he avoid collection which might excite criticism, he also believed that collection corrupted:

> With debt you've got two very dangerous points from a private detective's point of view. You have this: if you put a man on to debt who's experienced in many other fields, he's going to feel that he isn't using his ability to the full. And therefore he's going to go about it with apathy unless he really enjoys the whole job and this is only part of it which he doesn't like but he's going to make the best of it. Secondly, you might turn a man who is otherwise absolutely honest and trustworthy into a thief because if he's calling on Mrs Bloggs and she pays a five pound note and his wife's seen a dress in the sale that she wants, and he's going to repay it next week; or is going to bet the dogs and is down a few bob, and wants to make his money up, you're giving him the opportunity of handling cash which otherwise he wouldn't be able to, and you could turn a very good operative into a thief.

Collector 6 thus turned some enforcement work away. Together with Collector 8, he was able to resist some of the demands placed on him by the enforcement process because his lack of commitment to debt-collection freed him of a number of its restraints. Such protection is, however, rare. Most agencies are so heavily dependent on collection that they must conform to the pattern set by it.

The final determinant of collection style is the way in which an agency regards its general population of defaulters. Deviance tends to be ascribed to people who already have some stigmatizing characteristics. Simmons (1965, p. 231), for example, has argued that 'amongst those who are known to have committed a deviant act, those who seem to possess additional qualities concurring with the stereotypic image of that kind of deviance are far more likely to be labelled and processed a deviate'. In the main, middle-class debtors receive different treatment from that meted out to the working class. When a collector believes that the bulk of his cases are middle class, he may deliberately alter his overall enforcement policy. Not only is a middle-class defaulter defined as less of an unambiguous deviant, the tactics employed against him will be based on different ideas of effectiveness. An agency may try to manipulate feelings of shame rather than of fear. It may also be true that a collector whose debtors are largely middle class will apply slightly altered labels; his feckless may well be less feckless: his professional less professional, and so on. A collector can infer the characteristics of his debtors from their occupations, addresses and from the types of account that go into default. If his employers are banks, credit card organizations or West End shops, he might legitimately conclude that he will encounter the middle class. Similarly, a debtor's skin colour can affect enforcement:

> A coloured debtor is so much more difficult to find and extract money from; this is because we know coloured boys who, every time they move their address (and they move fairly frequently), they change their name just by a matter of practice. Smith, Brown, Jones . . . (Debt-collector 6.)

There are variations in enforcement policy but they can find expression only within relatively narrow limits. Despite the attempts of some of the larger agencies to establish reputable images for themselves, it is apparent that the meaning and mode of collection are formed by influences over which they have very little control. The collectors' position in the career structure forces them to assume a threatening, partial and unambiguous relationship with their defaulters. Nevertheless, some variation is possible and the relationship can be interpreted in a number of ways. It may be marked by fairly mild letters:

> We are instructed by our Members M. . . of . . . to apply to you for immediate payment of £. . .
>
> You are aware our Members have given you every opportunity

> to settle this account without recourse to unpleasant measures, and this department is intended wherever possible to obviate the unnecessary trouble and expense of legal proceedings.
>
> We must request you, therefore, to remit to this office the above amount on or before . . . next, . . . or we shall have no alternative but to hand the matter to the Solicitors acting for our Member to issue summons. (Debt-collector 14, a medium-sized debt-collector.)

The relationship may be based on more overt intimidation:

> **NOTWITHSTANDING** your agreement with our clients and in spite of repeated requests from us to remit regular instalments we note that no recent payments have been received.
>
> You will appreciate that our clients are not prepared to wait indefinitely for settlement and unless you *immediately recommence* payments *to us* and continue without further lapse we cannot but assume that your intentions are to deliberately avoid payment for goods obtained and shall at once arrange for proceedings, the cost of which may have to be borne by you.
>
> We accept no responsibility for any report published in the local Press or publicity which may arise from this action, nor any listing in the **NATIONAL REGISTER OF DEFAULTERS** published by the Hire Purchase Trade Association. (Professional and Trade Services Ltd.)

There are letters which try to excite an even greater fear:

> You have made no payment to the Agency.
> We intend to collect if it takes us a Life Time.
> None of the steps to be taken are very pleasant.
> Our collectors will call by Day and Night.
> You will be on the next **BLACK LIST** to go out to **SHOPS, H.P.** Companies, etc.,
> If we find, once the Black List is out, that you owe to two or more creditors a total sum of £50 we will make you **BANKRUPT.**
> **BANKRUPT** Receiving Order/Public Examination/Name in Gazette/The Petition Etc.
> **REALISATION OF DEBTORS PROPERTY**
> The only goods we cannot take are your Tools of Trade, wearing apparel and bedding to the value of £20.
> Really the amount involved is not worth all the trouble it can cause you.
> **SO LET US HAVE A PAYMENT BY RETURN OF POST**
> (Premier Debt Recovery Agency.)

I think it is clear that all these letters share common features despite formal differences. Similarities between collectors outnumber dissimilarities because collection is inextricably tied to the enforcement system by links which permit little freedom. Most agencies carry the pursuit of a debtor through a tripartite stage consisting of a prologue, a threat and then a final phase which joins the stage to its successor. Each of the letters quoted above threatened defaulters with some kind of unpleasantness. In each case, the debtor was told that he might be registered as a defaulter, taken to court, or subjected to an unspecified punishment. The chief difference between the agencies' approaches was the extent to which the content of the letters was embroidered.[11] The third collector elaborated the consequences of legal action so that it appeared in its most disquieting light. However, he did not offer a more substantial sanction than his colleagues had offered. Although the first collector appears to be the only scrupulous member of the three, beneath their stylistic masks all three were substantively alike because they suffered the same constraints. It is, of course, true that style can be all-important in this type of impression-management. Form and substance cannot be conveniently disentangled. Nevertheless, inactive collectors tend to follow the same pattern of splitting their stage into three parts, flourishing identical warnings and ending with the same conclusion.

Letters from inactive collectors succeed one another rather quickly. Whilst a creditor usually contacts a defaulter at monthly intervals, a collector writes once every week or fortnight. The duration of the debt-collection stage is also comparatively brief. Creditors may pursue a debtor for five or six months before passing him on to an agency who will harass him for only a month.[12] At this stage, therefore, the career has become both truncated and accelerated.

Enforcement is organized around a serial testing system. Debtors who resist all a creditor's advances have failed his tests and are inevitably defined as 'tough', recalcitrant and deviant. The range of possibilities which any simplified career can contend with is limited. For these two reasons, debt-collectors are employed to subject the

11 A minor check on the content of dunning letters is the possibility of a successful libel action against the collector. I discovered two reports of libel actions in the press. Both actions were initiated against the same firm by women who were not, in fact, defaulters. The collector appeared to have adopted a somewhat eccentric approach. One of its letters stated, 'the Second Vice is Lying, the first is running into debt. It is a great comfort to be free from Guilt. A small regular payment would place your integrity above suspicion.' In the one case (reported in *The Times*, Law Report, 22 December 1937) the plaintiff was awarded damages of £50 plus costs. In the other (reported in the *Daily Mail*, 7 April 1938), the plaintiff was awarded damages of $\frac{3}{4}$d.

12 Debt-collector 7, for example, wanted the acceleration and truncation to start further back in the career structure because 'they ask us really too late'.

defaulter to a new type of experience which contains an even more stringent test. The creditor's definition of a collector's use is quite explicit:

> You've got to be tough in a lot of cases because you'll generally find (people are fantastic about falling into types) but you'll find, if there's anything genuine about a person, they don't fall into arrears, not badly into arrears. It's only the trouble-boys that really do get into trouble. And if you do get into trouble with people like that, you really must adopt a tough line with them. It's all they understand. (Creditor 25.)

A debt-collector serves to dramatize the seriousness of a debtor's position. His role is to create the impression that a 'tough line' has at last been taken:

> When we're asked to collect a debt, we assume that an account has been rendered on many occasions which have been ignored. Our members will have written several letters before passing it to us because, after all, it's going to cost them something when they pass it to us. If they're going to get it without employing us, they're going to do so. But when it's pretty obvious they're not going to get their money, well, they're going to pass it over to us. And it's surprising how, when a third party has got interested, the money comes in. The person or the firm can threaten several times and the customer gets the idea 'Oh, I've heard that before' and throw it in the basket. But when they get a letter from a firm such as ourselves, they say 'he means business. We'd better do something about it.' (Debt-collector 11.)

A collector's understanding of his function is unambiguous. He is there to cope with those defaulters who are unaffected by the lengthy and exhaustive probes of the creditor's enforcement stage. These defaulters are in some way deviant but not so deviant that the intervention of a stigmatized collector will have no impact. He must foster the idea that 'he means business' in order to coerce a debtor into payment. The impression of action and 'business' managed by an inactive collector is extremely frail. It must eventually become apparent to even the most obtuse defaulter that he does not mean business at all. The illusion of action is what a collector is paid to achieve and it must be sustained by whatever means are available to him. In part, that illusion may be created by an increase in the gravity of his letters' content and by shortening the gaps that elapse between them. Three aggressive letters in three weeks may suggest that a tough line *is* being taken.

The brevity and telescoping of the collector's stage are necessary products of the career's logic. A tough line and an increase in tempo can only be signified by an accelerated career. Brevity does not only support the collector's weakness, it also reinforces a general definition of the situation furnished by the creditor. 'Something' is at last being done, the defaulter can no longer safely withhold the money he owes. This movement from a leisurely to a rapid pace underscores the specific threats that are offered and the overall mood of this phase of the career. Thus spacing, pacing and content are all manipulated to create the most coercive impression and inspire the greatest anxiety.

In addition, it is supposed that the cynicism of an uncowed professional debtor will be encouraged by a phase that once again does nothing to him. If he resists a collector's threats, there is little point in prolonging the debt-collection stage. He must either be abandoned by his creditor or rushed on to the county court stage where he can be confronted by real sanctions. Collectors are aware that they are effective because they have some of the qualities of confidence tricksters. Under the heading 'Debt Collectors survive because of public ignorance', Egan (1968, p. 4) writes that 'the debt collector who sends a dunning letter or calls at your door has no status and no particular power. His position is no stronger than that of his employer, the creditor'. The collector's strength derives from his ability to frighten; if his representations to a debtor are discredited, his usefulness has become exhausted.

Furthermore, collectors and creditors often state that 'the biggest problem in this country is the constant movement of people that acquire goods on credit' (Debt-collector 1). There is not only a normal population movement brought about by rehousing and so on, there is also alleged to be some shifting of the professional debtor from one area to another in his attempts to evade enforcement. Mobility of this sort can pose acute problems: the inactive collector may have to become active in order to trace 'skips'; the costs of collection automatically rise; and creditors and collectors claim that many institutions and employers are unco-operative about providing information relating to debtors' new addresses.[13] Enforcement may cease when a debtor disappears:

> It means you've got to keep paying out to the enquiry agents to trace his present whereabouts. In some circumstances, they can't trace a chap as easy as that and you've also got to pay out more than is necessary. It does depend on whether he's got the vehicle still. In some cases, where he's got a vehicle worth five hundred pound then, of course, you can't just drop

[13] Thus, the Housing Department of Manchester Corporation refuses to disclose the new addresses of council tenants who move (*People*, 13 February 1966), and Birmingham Council does the same (*Daily Mail*, 11 February 1968).

> the case just like that. It's a case of paying out until you eventually either get your property back or get him in court under your thumb. . . . So, of course, where it is a case of where he keeps moving, we do consider every time whether it will be more reasonable to drop the case and leave it at that or continue. (Creditor 14.)

Many creditors who deal with small accounts are forced to ignore the debtors they cannot economically pursue. Enforcement may stop as soon as it threatens to become unduly expensive. Since tracing can be one of a creditor's major expenses, enforcement cannot afford to be dilatory at the debt-collection stage. Creditors and collectors believe that the professional debtor recognizes this stage as a warning which presages court action. If so, it might act as a cue for him to move and thereby elude the courts. As a result, the collection stage is foreshortened in order to reduce the professional's chances of escape and its attendant cost.

Finally, the serial testing system becomes less and less tentative as the career progresses. Hypotheses about the debtor's situation can be confirmed or falsified by increasingly sparse evidence. Collectors define the honest debtor as someone who will respond to their letters immediately. Any hesitation or delay indicates recalcitrance. The pressure applied to a defaulter does not gradually mount up during this stage because any encounter with a collector is regarded as very taxing for the normal consumer. There is no need, therefore, to build various surmises about the defaulter into the collector's letter stream. The debtor can either demonstrate his probity by payment or by negotiation or he risks being labelled recalcitrant. An economy of hypotheses also arises from the inactive collector's inability to muster a large range of responses. He can abruptly end his letter stream; continue it for a longer period of time; allow it to run its normal course; advise the creditor to sue or not to sue; or accept any offer of instalments. Delay is not attractive because he cannot put information derived from extensive probes to much use.

A collector who receives no response from a debtor assumes that he has moved (thereby falling under the suspicion that he is thoroughly deviant) or that he has not and is recalcitrant. He may then advise a creditor that checks should be made to see whether the defaulter has, in fact, moved and whether court action would be fruitful. In all cases, an absence of feedback from the debtor indicates that a choice has to be made between carrying the career on to another stage and abandoning it. This choice is partly shaped by the way in which a collector understands the significance of a debtor's lack of response. It may be taken to mean that court action is justified:

> The only way to get money out of them is to take them to court. They've no intention of paying. It's fairly obvious if they don't reply. (Debt-collector 8.)

A justification of this sort is based on two important ideas: that the test posed by the collector is not a critical one, and that court action is likely to be effective. The collection stage may well end the career if these ideas are not accepted. The evaluation of the test's reliability rests in part on the collector's reading of his own role in enforcement. Collector 8 was a representative of the trade protection society which engaged in enforcement merely to aid its subscribing members. He believed that he did little more than embellish the impressions created by others. Collector 7, however, had more faith in his own efficiency and placed greater stress on his ability to test debtors. He thought that his probes were so discerning and effective that a creditor would be mistaken to want action against a defaulter who made no response. A passive debtor must be too deviant to justify further enforcement:

> Very largely, when it gets to the stage of issuing a summons and you don't hear, against the individual debtor it's a write-off. It's just a waste of time going ahead. (Debt-collector 7.)

Collector 7 was typical of many collectors in his belief that his techniques filtered off all but the most recalcitrant defaulters. He also belittled the impact of the court:

> [Courts] give the benefit of the doubt nearly all the way, right the way through to the debtor. In fact, in some cases, quite ludicrously . . . [Debtors'] nominal repayments under the hire purchase agreements may have been, say, five pounds a month. You take them to court and the registrar of the county court says 'alright, you have obtained judgment against this person *but*, because of his circumstances, we give you an order for five *shillings* a month'. Which means, of course, that it's going to take years to collect that particular debt.

Collector 4 was similarly critical of the courts:

> Enforcement? There's no such thing. There's no such thing as enforcement! It's just a mockery really, honestly! English law, to me, I'm ashamed of being an Englishman! You see, the Hire Purchase Act of 1934; three year contract, debtor refuses to pay or render up the goods. She goes up in front of the judge and offers a ridiculous figure per week which the judge or registrar accepts. Now, which is correct? The Hire Purchase Act or the judge? You see, now we have a Parliament which makes and sets the hire purchase laws on the one hand, and a

registrar or judge on the other hand who breaks every law in the books! You see? The Hire Purchase Act, you can throw it out of the window!

Three factors are then responsible for forming the collector's assessment of a debtor's inactivity: the way in which he regards the tests he sets; the way in which he regards the county court as an agent of control; and the way in which he regards his own place in the debt collection system.

When there *is* a response, a collector's handling of a case is largely affected by a realization of his own impotence. An inactive agency must usually accept any offer of reduced payments because it cannot punish a debtor for not making a better offer; it cannot bargain; and it can only be grateful that the debtor has at last replied:

If he offers, you'd be a damn fool not to accept, even if it's a shilling a week, because a shilling a week's better than nothing. (Debt-collector 7.)

Self-deprecating collectors (such as Collector 8) tend to assume that any offer is worth accepting because of their low opinion of their ability to affect the debtor. Other collectors (such as Collector 7) argue that payments which are negotiated without court intervention are preferable to the expense and the risk presented by an excessively lenient judiciary. In both cases, the debtor has been defined by his place in the career as an unco-operative person, and some co-operation at this stage is recognized as an achievement.

A defaulter may respond, however, without suggesting any payment by instalments. Most collectors treat the reasons given for protracted default with some suspicion. They believe that they would not have had to deal with the debtor at all if he had not been somewhat dishonest. The feckless or the unfortunate debtor, for instance, is either unusually plagued by poor luck or is merely stalling:

Anyone can, you know, there but for the grace of God, anybody can fall on hard times. But it is curious that the people who fall on hard times tend to keep on falling on hard times. However good the times are at the moment, they're always dead unlucky. (Debt-collector 3.)

Within the span of its three or four letters, an agency can apply some hypotheses about the validity of the debtor's excuses:

We get a lot of people, I mean, they're always going to remit next week. They're expecting some money, it hasn't come, but it's bound to arrive by the week after next. There are, of course,

> in this trade we get a lot of very tragic things, but there again this is a thing you can feel. You accept it on the first or, say, the second letter, but after that you begin to tell whether it's just a feeble excuse or whether it's genuine. (Debt-collector 11.)

The opening up of an interaction with the debtor suggests that a further use of the testing system is worth while. A defaulter who is in communication with an agency is unlikely to be a professional. A professional would not reply and, if he *did* reply, would at least be amenable to court sanctions. A corresponding debtor tends to be an accessible debtor. Furthermore, since an agency cannot do very much to the defaulter, it may find it profitable to wait and see whether his promises are kept. The letter will become evidence of his truthfulness or deviousness, evidence which can direct policy if a summons is issued.

Sometimes this evidence will not be forthcoming in the near future. Alternatively, a collector may have to refer every decision to his employer with appropriate advice. In either case, the letter has to be assessed almost as soon as it is received. When this happens, the criteria employed are similar to those used by creditors in an earlier stage. There seems to be no institutional or generalized body of standards against which letters are matched. Familiarity with the process of judging letters eventually leads to an insight which cannot be described or communicated:

> Letters vary in texture very considerably. I mean it's very difficult. The circumstances differ as to which member we're collecting for. I think it's a matter of experience. I can't put it any other way. I've been in this business a long time. Something tells me, I don't know what it is. Something just doesn't ring true and somehow you feel you need a further explanation. It's something you can't pass on. This is one of the difficulties of a trade protection society. You can't pass the experience on to anybody. (Debt-collector 5.)

Probabilistic expectations of the outcomes of decisions, coupled with a sensitivity to subconsciously perceived clues, lead a collector to recommend acceptance or rejection of an application. Unwittingly, the collector may hold loosely formulated stereotypes of various kinds of debtor and may seek material which assigns the letter writer to one of these stereotypes.[14] He may discern flaws in the

14 Scheff's theme of simplicity is probably applicable to evaluations of the defaulting poor. It is likely that academic writers and lay people hold implicit assumptions about the social meaning of poverty and social types associated with it. Liebow (1967, esp. pp. 29–31), for instance, hints at these ideas in his discussion of the interaction between the potential employer and employed. The distinction between the morally deserving

presentation of an argument; logical inconsistencies or implausible accounts, which trigger off suspicion. Nevertheless, he is predisposed to trust a debtor if trust does not lead to excessive risk. Any reply is welcomed.

Active collectors

Creditors, debt-collectors and agency solicitors are embedded in a complex network of institutions which carry out esoteric functions in connection with enforcement. The establishment and maintenance of links with these institutions is a necessary part of their expertise. Their services can command a price on the market because, in addition to their own particular competence, they know whom to approach when certain tasks have to be performed. The enforcement system is not only made up of the major organizations which I have discussed so far, it also contains 'snatch-back men' who repossess goods on hire purchase, certificated bailiffs, enquiry agents, and so on.

Creditors may want their collector to trace a debtor or advise about the wisdom of taking him to court. An inactive collector will not welcome these demands. He is not equipped to carry out these tasks and they would disrupt his routine work. Tracing and advice require the same sort of organization as face-to-face enforcement and status reporting, and they are avoided for the same reasons. Moreover, enquiry work is manageable and profitable only when it is done in conjunction with other face-to-face work. It is therefore passed on to active agencies:

> The large organization . . . have a man in one town, but they are unable to give him sufficient business in the week to bring him a reasonable return. So, generally speaking what you find is that agencies as such do have representatives in towns, or chaps who represent *them*. Now, these blokes sitting down in a particular town are given enquiries from the various large enquiry agencies. This makes it a somewhat economic proposition then. They then have a bunch of things which they can sort out. (Debt-collector 12.)

Major institutions thus act as funnels, allocating tasks to the smaller agencies through the network. Delegation is brought into being because of the inactive collector's dislike of personal enforcement;

and the undeserving poor may still affect some decision-making. People who offer 'reasonable' excuses, suggesting that they are victims of primary poverty, would be identified as unfortunate debtors. Presumably, their tone would be deferential and their explanation would refer to illness, unavoidable unemployment and so on. The undeserving sufferers of secondary poverty would be recognized by their aggressive or disrespectful manner of writing, their feckless excuses, and so on.

the inability of any one organization to provide a national coverage; and the need to exploit economies of scale caused by inadequate supplies of local work.

In turn, the smaller agencies rely on a web of contacts and associates:

> We go round and see these people. Caretakers . . . A milkman is the debt-collector's friend. He knows everything. And then, of course, in the provinces and in the villages, we have agents all over England. (Debt-collector 13.)

Through filtering and delegation, the system of gathering information extends into most areas of Britain. The network allows an agency to gather some material on a defaulter anywhere in the country. The larger collector can offer creditors a service because of his links with others in the system. These other, second-tier collectors, are usually the active agencies. An inactive firm may commission them to undertake personal recovery in places it cannot afford to go to and using knowledge it has no access to. They are tied to their own localities and may deal with creditors in their vicinity. The large bureaucratic creditors, however, are rarely able to approach them directly. Active collectors may be too small to come to their attention; the collectors' reputation and choice of methods may be uncertain; and the funnelling role of the major agencies is attractive in its simplicity and in its capacity to cope with all debts rather than with small batches of them.

The small firms' use of face-to-face enforcement does not often seem to be based on overt intimidation of the defaulter. Egan (1968, p. 4), for instance, observed:

> All the firms I approached said that they opposed the use of physical force, guard dogs, debt-collection vans designed to announce the nature of the driver's business, and other similar methods popularly associated with this kind of business. . . .

Personal confrontation typically rests on other forms of control. Small collectors regularly patrol their local areas, calling on debtors at fixed times. They may have the goal of doing nothing more than recouping debts; they may seek information; or they may try to do both. When collection is the main object, they will visit a debtor until calls no longer seem to be a fruitful method of enforcement. Their contacts with the defaulter will become regulated and the collection of small sums will become routine. Debt-collector 4 attributed his success to 'insistence and regularity. If you know that Mr Bloggs is going to call every Friday night, regular, you're not going to object'. (Debt-collector 4.) The collector hopes to insert himself into the debtor's life, becoming a predictable occurrence which creates anxiety only when payment cannot be made.

A collector can establish this relationship once he has acquired a hold over the defaulter. The hold is frequently secured through the creation of a particular sort of impression. Collectors make defaulters compliant by asserting that they are both members of a moral community founded on shared conceptions of honour, trust and reciprocity. This idea of a moral community is intimately connected with the reluctance of the enforcement machine to confer stigma on debtors. The machine tries to avoid awarding deviant identities to the people it processes. Similarly, a collector will affirm the bonds that exist between himself and the defaulter, or he will try to bring the debtor back into a restraining relationship. He will reassure the debtor that the relationship will not have stigmatizing consequences. This 'cooling-out' (Goffman, 1952) phase marks the beginning of the collector's overtures. He will attempt to undo some of the feelings evoked by his own and others' threatening letters and present himself as a fairly sympathetic person. Cooling-out may be difficult:

> [People] obviously don't like collectors. . . . They've obviously been contacted several times over with all kinds of threats and suggestions from the people to whom the money is owned. (Debt-collector 6.)

There are numerous techniques of building up rewarding ties between collector and debtor. One collector stated:

> You get one person who calls on the door and you get nothing at all and no chance of ever collecting any money. You'll get another person calling at the door and the person will pay up immediately. It's paying to a personality.

He described the most effective personality as

> An elderly man or woman, probably in about the fifty-five to sixty range, who calls along and tells a story 'well, I've got to do this job because of my circumstances. If I get good results, you know, I'll be able to feed the kids next week. And, you know, with your help, I'll be able to get good results.' This type of approach has a far better chance of success than the 'pay up or else!' It's creating a sympathy. (Debt-collector 6.)

This kind of appeal to the defaulter can result in an ongoing relationship which will end when the debt is paid. In his search for the appropriate emotional hold, a collector will develop a skill at interpreting debtors' reactions and tailoring his own:

> I always tell my men 'speak to a person as you wish to be spoken unto yourself'. I mean, there are people who only know

> language by swearing all the time, and if you don't speak to them in the same language you're out! I mean, we have been to court where the woman has called us all the bathbuns under the sun. The children even tell their mother she's an old ——. And you've got to talk the same language in the house. And this particular woman used to pay us. We even used to say 'where's your purse dolly?', take her purse, take two pounds out of it, and say 'there you are doll'. And she'd call you all the effing so-and-so's under the sun, but she would love you just as much. (Debt-collector 4.)

Thus debt-collectors believe that they may be able to establish a curious *rapport* with many of their defaulters. The *rapport* is founded on their ability to understand and manipulate people. It leads to a routinization of contacts between the enforcer and his quarry:

> You see, these debtors—we get the same debtor time and time and time again. The same person. And they get to know us. There's more than one order of debtor. Ladies—there's one, a lady of title, that I refer to very often. I write to her and she writes back, 'Dear Mr ——, so nice to hear from you again'. (Debt-collector 13.)

Collectors try to change relations which are essentially secondary into relations which are primary in nature. A collector–debtor link normally suggests patterns of coercion and evasion; a collector hopes to transform this link into a connection which has some of the trappings of amiability and obligation. If the situation can be defined in this manner, a collector may be able to exploit a debtor's feelings of shame, guilt or even friendship. A woman defaulter was reported to have said, for example (Clements, 1969):

> . . . you get to the point where you have so many debts that it doesn't really bother you. I don't mind stinging letters when they are just threatening, but I don't like it when they go to court. . . . You get quite friendly with the collectors. You find a man standing outside your front door with a summons, and you start chatting with him. The actual fellow who collects the Co-op money is very decent, because he knows I'm hard up, and I do try to pay off £1 a week, because they're a good firm.

It is evident that the 'Co-op' collector was able to wield an influence which 'stinging letters' alone could not achieve. His capacity to do so was somewhat strengthened by the neutralizing techniques which debtors often employ. I shall discuss these techniques at length in my description of the way in which imprisoned debtors fight off attacks on their identity. I believe that many people are prepared to default on contracts made with large bureaucratic creditors because the contracts are not 'personalized'. That is, debtors sometimes deny the moral force of arrangements which are not made on a face-to-face level or enforced on this level. The system of social control used by most creditors is impersonal, conducted by letters only, and involves no threat to this neutralizing technique.

Gans (1962, p. 90) describes the culture of working-class Boston Italians as a 'person-oriented' morality. He argues that the over-riding aspiration of 'person-oriented individualism' is 'the desire to be a person within a group; to be liked and noticed by members of a group whom one likes and notices in turn'. This aspiration permeates the social life of Gans's Italians, and it is applied to situations which middle-class people would treat as impersonal:

> The West Ender's unilateral adherence to a religious morality... provides guides mainly for person-oriented behavior and for relationships between individuals. Norms such as equality, justice, independence, charity, reciprocity, and personal honesty are conceived as they apply to peer group relationships. The West Ender also applies these norms to the outside world, without, however, making adjustments necessary for secondary-group relationships. Businessman–client or government–citizen encounters are expected to follow peer group norms (Gans, 1962, p. 96).

My interviews with Brixton debtors indicate that some members of the London working class also subscribe to person-oriented norms. Many debt-collectors are convinced that these norms are influential and their methods are geared to exploiting the feelings which characterize peer group transactions.

There is another facet of a person-oriented morality which collectors try to combat. Debtors seem to award more legitimacy to property rights which are vested in possessions owned by identifiable people. Property held by corporations and socially distant groups is based on less legitimacy. Mannheim (quoted by Clayton, 1967, p. 158) makes much the same observation about general attitudes to property:

> It has become clear beyond reasonable doubt that there is in the minds of many people all the difference between public and private property: and, within the latter category, between the property of the small man and that of the rich, especially of the large company. It is, in fact, for many a facet of natural law that only the small man's property deserves to be respected, whereas the other categories of property are the legitimate objects of occasional or persistent predatory attacks.

The active collector personifies the creditor and introduces an affective tone into the creditor–debtor relationship. The pressures which he can exert undermine some of the props which support the defaulter's inaction. Because he can symbolically become the creditor in the enforcement situation, a collector restores some authority to the creditor's demands. Other bureaucratic victims are denied legitimacy and they also resort to such a personalization of the bureaucracy-deviant relationship. Thus Smigel and Ross (1970, p. 7) remark:

> . . . crimes against large organizations are more acceptable to the public than are other categories of crime [because] our system of ethics lacks rules which specifically apply to relationships between individuals and large organizations. All major historical religions originated in small communities, in which obligations concerned relatives, friends, and neighbors. From these static and personal communities a set of personal ethical norms developed; responsibility to great impersonal structures did not exist. Today, when large-scale organizations dominate our lives, men may be ethically unprepared to cope with the problem of the relationship between the individual and the corporation.
>
> The size, wealth and impersonality of big business . . . are attributes which make it seem excusable, according to many people, to steal from these victims. . . . Congruent with this thesis is the tactic frequently used by bureaucracies: the attempt to 'personalize' the loss. Witness this sign in a Midwestern motel: 'If any towels are missing when you leave, the maid cleaning the room will be responsible for them.' The notice attempts to deter theft by invoking sympathy for an individual rather than the bureaucracy. Some bureaucratic organizations, moreover, attempt to personalize the impersonal and to make the large corporation appear to be a family business.

This transformed and binding relationship is ideal from the collector's point of view, but it cannot always be sustained. Certain debtors, for instance, are taken to be obviously ineligible for membership of the normal moral community. 'The only people who are prepared to pay are people who aren't professional debtors.' (Debt-collector 6.) When a debtor can be identified as professional, appeals based on the person-oriented culture are useless. The collector feels that it is futile to claim bonds of sympathy or likemindedness with the defaulter. Instead, he resorts to intimidation and threats of court action. He must conspicuously demonstrate that he is so knowledgeable and alert that the debtor cannot possible escape him:

> On the average, they're fair, but when you come across one that's literally taken a firm for a ride, believe you me, they're as hard as nails. They know all the answers. We normally tell 'em how far we're prepared to go, what we know. For instance, if you say to a person 'now look, Mrs Brown alias Jones, something else, something else, something else', they'll say 'well how did you know that?' And this is the whole point! (Debt-collector 4.)

Whilst collectors may not hesitate to threaten an obvious professional, they are more circumspect in other cases. They will probably wait until their overtures are rejected. Active collectors meet defaulters in face-to-face situations, but they are often unable or unwilling to weigh them up on the basis of these encounters alone. Personal calls are usually made on a fairly massive scale and they are typically brief. In consequence, the collectors' classification methods resemble those employed by their inactive colleagues. Debtors are subjected to a serial testing system which simplifies and organizes the process of categorization. If, for example, a debtor makes no satisfactory response after three calls, he will be defined as too recalcitrant for the debt-collection stage. Again, if he pays after the first call, he is likely to be labelled an unfortunate. Collector 6 clearly describes how the pressures imposed by economy and speed do not allow for careful attention to each debtor:

> Even though people in our line of business are supposed to have an immediate assessment value of the people we're dealing with, this is only true within the sphere . . . within a limited sphere. If I approached a person, a Mr X, to make a statement, and he made a statement to me and it was inaccurate, I would put such questions to him that would show me very quickly whether it was inaccurate and I'd tear it up and throw it in his face. Now, this doesn't always apply as far as a debtor is concerned because this analysis of people—you're only involved in this analysis of people when you've got the time to actually do it. In divorce enquiries, one has the time because one has the financial backing to do it. But in the case of debt, you know what margin you're working on. You've got to work at speed. So therefore there isn't this time for assessment. One man may make twenty or thirty calls a day and therefore he hasn't got time. The whole question doesn't warrant it and the situation doesn't allow for it, and therefore you can only go by promises kept and promises broken.

The chief sanction available to an agency is the threat of county court proceedings. That threat is, however, equally accessible to anyone engaged in the collection of debts. What distinguishes the intimidation of the active agency from that of his passive colleague is the concreteness of the pressure which he exerts:

> Whereas before [debtors] have only been approached with letters they can tear up and throw in the fire, they can't tear one of our blokes up and throw him in the fire because they know they'll be called back on if they don't keep their promise. (Collector 6.)

Debt-collection is therefore a brief, accelerated phase of enforcement which is dominated by the large inactive firm. Most enforcement during this stage is a series of feints and threats. The effectiveness of most debt-collectors rests on the structural intimidation which they necessarily exert. No matter how a collector defines his work and the situations it engenders, he is always coloured by the ideas popularly associated with his calling. Moreover, although physical violence appears to play no part in routine enforcement, the participants in the enforcement transaction are so aligned that their relations are inevitably tinged with some fear. Coercion is built into the very structure of a collection system.

5 The solicitor

Criminal court proceedings are often formally organized around the task of discovering an acceptable version of what happened in a disputed case. The civil courts are also influenced by this contest model: a debtor might deny that he owes the sum for which a summons was issued; he might argue that the plaintiff did not adhere to his contractual obligations; and he might meet the plaintiffs' claim with a counterclaim. Complicated civil actions frequently involve skilled disputants who present conflicting versions of reality. Despite these elements of contest, solicitors are almost always the agents of a creditor when they appear in debt collection actions. The typical county court case is an undefended action. When a debtor defends himself, he usually does so alone and without legal aid or advice (cf. Abel-Smith and Stevens, 1967, and Marsden-Smedley, 1969). A survey of judgment summons hearings in a number of London county courts revealed, for instance, that the 169 cases were made up of 139 instances of a creditor being represented by a solicitor and only one instance of a debtor being represented. The solitary debtor had engaged a barrister to appear for him (Zander and Glasser, 1967, p. 815).

The solicitor's place in the enforcement structure is thus clear-cut. In the main, he is responsible for shepherding defaulters out of private areas of debt collection into public areas. His role is rather more complicated than those played by his predecessors. Whereas relations in the first one or two stages were dyadic (creditor–debtor), and triadic in the next stage (creditor–debt-collector–debtor), the solicitor's role entails transactions with many others: creditor, debtor, registrar, judge, bailiff, colleagues, and so on. His function is to provide a dominant perspective on what happened and what is happening for various others who can influence enforcement. He must depict the debtor–creditor situation to the court, and the solicitor–registrar–judge–bailiff situation to the debtor in ways which are most conducive to a favourable outcome for the creditor. Once again, enforcement is heavily committed to impression-management.

In this chapter, I shall discuss only those features of a solicitor's occupation which are concerned with his handling of defaulters before court proceedings are started. Some of the interactions between solicitors and other personnel during the county court stage will be described in the following two chapters. My aim here is to describe the split that exists between agency and 'ordinary' solicitors; to examine the opening phases of the relations between defaulters and solicitors; and to provide some preliminary guidance for understanding the working of debt collection in the county courts.

A solicitor can enter the career system at various points and can make various contributions to it. In some cases, a creditor defines him as a functional equivalent to a debt-collector. Active collectors are constrained by the size of the areas which they can patrol, and England could be presented as a mosaic made up of the territories controlled by different agencies. As a result, a creditor who maintains direct links with 'reliable' collectors may not know of an agency in a place where defaults occur. He may then hand cases over to a solicitor for enforcement in a local county court. This geographical determination of the career structure means that the first stage delegated by a creditor to an outside firm can sometimes involve a collector and sometimes a solicitor. The pattern becomes more complex when the creditor regularly submits some of his collector's failures to legal coercion. In other cases, a solicitor may be employed in conjunction with an agency; or he may be asked to pursue larger defaults whilst the smaller sums are pursued by agencies.

A solicitor's entrance is structured by other qualities of the career. Not only do different firms of creditors build different numbers, types and combinations of stages into their career systems; they also regulate the career in different ways. Spacing, pacing and quality may all be altered to achieve a creditor's goals. One firm may choose to send two peremptory letters to a debtor and then call upon its solicitor to intervene. Another may send a dozen letters, arrange for calls by representatives, demand lengthy intimidation of their defaulters by collectors, and only then pass the debt on. This latter model of action is usually followed by the large bureaucratic creditors who are owed numerous small debts. The former model is followed by smaller firms who have comparatively little experience of enforcement and have no need to routinize their collection practices. I shall discuss the differences between agency and non-specialist solicitors below. The agency solicitor is a person who frequently acts in his local county courts, enforcing cases devolved to him by colleagues whose primary interests are conveyancing or other work unconnected with enforcement. There are thus four possible patterns.

FIRMS	SOLICITORS	
	Agency	*Non-specialist*
Large	1	2
Small	3	4

Patterns 1 and 4 are the most common, 2 and 3 least common. The connection between the large firm and the non-specialist solicitor in pattern 2 resembles the earlier link between the creditor and the inactive collector. The solicitor merely passes the debt on to a practice that is able to tackle it. Pattern 3 is established when a specialist firm is given local business. One such solicitor told me rather plaintively 'occasionally we do have our *own* clients'. (Solicitor 7, an agency solicitor.) In cases 1 and 2, solicitors tend to believe that excessive delay is built into the career. A bureaucratic creditor's cautious preoccupation with economy impairs their own effectiveness.

> [Clients] usually wait an enormous length of time before getting in tough by sending a bill and several accounts rendered, perhaps over several months, and being fobbed off with useless telephone calls before they realize that the balloon is up. (Solicitor 8, an erstwhile agency solicitor but now in ordinary practice.)

There is not always a consensus about the significance of lengths of enforcement time. Solicitors and creditors do not invariably agree on common benchmarks. In part, this disagreement is based on the different positions which the two groups occupy. Whilst creditors rest their actions on threats and very weak sanctions, solicitors can mobilize weapons provided by the court. As a result, lawyers are rather more inclined to cut their stage short by proceeding rapidly to judgment. Similarly, solicitors tend to rely on the court's testing system which includes judgment, execution and judgment summons. Rather than establish their own means of assessing the debtor, they send one or two letters and then resort to official processes. Earlier stages were also characterized by a greater uncertainty about the defaulter's 'nature'. Events could not be rushed because, after all, the debtor might be honest or unfortunate. It is only at the solicitor's stage that some certainty is reached. Furthermore, solicitors are often anxious about the problem posed by the skipping defaulter. There is necessarily a disjunction between the views of the employer and employed in patterns 1 and 2.

The antithesis is frequently apparent in the other patterns. I have already referred to the absence of routinization and experience which marks the small creditor's enforcement policy. In consequence, solicitors may believe that the creditor has been too precipitate in demanding a summons. Their belief is supported by the knowledge that relations between a minor lender and his defaulter can become exceptionally strained. The hostility that may arise between landlord and tenant, doctor and patient, or small shopkeeper and customer is very different from the impersonal bonds that hire purchase companies and mail order firms contract:

> Very often, especially the dentists you know, because it seems to be such an intensely personal relationship, such a very personal service, they've bent over this man and attended to his wants, and then they feel as if they've been kicked in the stomach. (Solicitor 5, an ordinary solicitor.)

Thus solicitors may feel that collection in patterns 3 and 4 has been too brief and hurried. No meaningful benchmark has been passed by the defaulter. Instead, they believe that there may be other reasons for default than recalcitrance. The outraged client has been driven by distaste for the debtor into precipitate action. The debtor could well be an unfortunate or a feckless person.

Two distinct kinds of objection are thus made by solicitors: the first is that the career is too protracted; the second is that it has not been explored at all. A solicitor's ability to affect the shape of his client's enforcement system is dependent on his functional importance and, to a small extent, his personal influence. Agency solicitors can enjoy effective monopolies over the collection carried out in 'their' county courts. Their indispensability allows them to instruct their clients on collection tactics. Non-specialist firms, on the other hand, may have to take up cases without much opportunity to criticize their client's behaviour. In any case, it might be unwise to attempt to pacify an agitated client too abruptly. Their involvement in enforcement is so meagre that they feel it would be foolish to jeopardize their relations with people who offer them other desirable business. Solicitor 5, however, did try to regulate careers:

> If he's my client, I will ensure that he writes two or three letters himself. In other words, if he comes to me, the first thing I'll say to him is 'what have you done?' And quite often he says 'very little', and so one makes sure he writes. I will cheerfully draft the letter for him, but I will make sure he writes. . . .

Such a question and answer sequence would never occur when the client is a large bureaucratic creditor. Indeed, the fear would then be that the client has done too much already rather than too little. The solicitor's greatest anxiety would be that 'the trail has got cold'. (Solicitor 1.)

Once a solicitor has been engaged to act, he may be expected to perform one of two broad roles for the creditor. Each of the roles has three minor variants. The definition of an appropriate role is shaped by the type of creditor, the debtor and the sum of money in arrears. The first role is likely to be called for when a creditor has systematized his collection procedure. Creditor 6, a small mail order company, routinely fed all debts over £3 into court. Similarly, the gas board described in the previous chapter poured every unpaid debt it encountered into the legal system. Such creditors do not select out debts for legal coercion. All defaulters are forced to travel up through the career with no escape but payment. For example, the registrars' court at D[1] had a cause list of sixty-two actions in one week of May 1966. Forty-six of these (74 per cent) were issued in a batch by one large group of mail order companies. A second variant of this indiscriminate conveyor-belt model is found when a solicitor acts as a serial tester. Court sanctions will be threatened but they will not always be implemented. This is an unorthodox use of a solicitor's coercive powers. Even the solicitors who resort to it feel that it is rather unethical to send a letter conveying threats which are without substance. Nevertheless, this variant of the first role is fairly common:

> [Our letters] usually end with the phrase 'if it doesn't come, we expect instructions to take proceedings'. Whether or not we will advise a client to take proceedings will depend on the circumstances of the case. Very often a letter is only a try on. We write because we think 'well, it doesn't cost very much and it's worth it just to see in any case'. Sometimes it doesn't help in the least. (Solicitor 3, an ordinary solicitor.)

The threats may be extended into the opening phases of court enforcement itself:

> If a debt was fifty pounds, I think we would say, if there was any chance of recovering it, we would advise a client to have a shot. But if a summons in the county court produced nothing except a judgment . . . and the debtor doesn't keep to . . . payments, the matter is quite often dropped. (Solicitor 3.)

A solicitor can make a further adaptation of the testing system. He may sue for the defaults which he considers to be strategically or economically worth attacking. He will not immediately discard the rest but threaten court action although he is in no doubt about his

[1] I have adopted the convention of referring to the twelve major London county courts by letters rather than by their actual names.

intention to do nothing at all. This is the last attempt of the empty threatening process which distinguished the greater part of previous enforcement. In this role, therefore, a solicitor is expected to carry out rational and economic enforcement. He might be responsible for massive and indiscriminate litigation, he might serve as yet another test, or he might combine both tasks by subjecting small defaults to threats and large defaults to serious enforcement. In each case, he tends to act for a creditor whose chief interest is the minimization of loss and the maximization of efficiency.

The other major role focuses on the court as a means of punishing deviant debtors, deterring potential defaulters or upholding justice. Punishment, meted out by such firms as Creditor 7, is advocated because a debtor 'should not be allowed to get away with it'. Deterrence can override short-term economic loss in order to maximize long-term gains:

> If, for example, you have a firm which has a considerable number of debtors, and there's one of them that owes a pound (that's all) which, in normal circumstances, I'd advise him to write off, he says 'well look, if I let him get away with this, he's only going to tell all his pals, and they're going to do the same. If we endeavour to get this pound from him, within reason I don't care if it costs me five pound, I don't care. At least it will show the others that we're not prepared to forego the small debts.' (Solicitor 1.)

Finally, a client may instruct his solicitor to defend a set of abstract principles concerning the proper relations between lender and borrower. The defaulter has flouted a convention which must be sustained. Yet 'if you can't trace the debtor or you happen to know that there are thirty five other judgment creditors just round the corner, then even their principles will bend'. (Solicitor 8.) The desires to punish and enforce morality are often aspects of the same ascription of deviance to defaulters. Many solicitors, especially agency firms, are bemused by this ascription. Their bewilderment seems to be founded on a number of points: it is not their money which is owed; they may not even know the clients well enough to sympathize with them; they have more of an occupational acquaintance with 'real' deviance such as crime; and they feel that such righteous motives typically lead to an unfortunate outcome in court:

> It's very difficult for a lot of people to appreciate that debt isn't crime, and this applies to people with an enormous amount of experience and an enormous amount of knowledge of the subject. I mean lay people, I don't mean solicitors, I mean creditors. I think a very high proportion of creditors see

> no difference between a debt and fraud, and of course, there are circumstances where the distinction is absolutely non-existent. . . . Where the distinction between debt and fraud lies is a matter for jurisprudence, but from the creditor's point of view there's no difference at all about it, I think in that type of case that creditors are really quite vindictive, quite pressing. (Solicitor 7.)

In some cases, the 'vindictive' client will insist on court proceedings despite warnings from his solicitor. The solicitor will then feel constrained to act against his will. He may even exploit the situation to demonstrate his client's folly:

> With one or two I've adopted a very brutal method of showing them the light which is, after trying to persuade them not to proceed, letting them. And when they find out how much their time out of their surgery is worth and what they're getting for it, they see things more my way in future. (Solicitor 5.)

Some solicitors, of course, become quite as incensed as their clients. When they are consistently exposed to the frustrating task of recovering money from a reluctant and evasive defaulter, they may apply notions derived from feelings of moral shock:

> I have been doing debt collection for the last thirty years, shall we say? Ever since I've been in the law, let's say 1932, I mean particularly before the war, I've had a lot of experience of debt collecting. And my experience is that, I won't say that every debtor is the same, but a large proportion of debtors, if they can avoid paying, they will. They just don't want to pay! It's morally destroying that sort of thing! There's no sanctity of contract, nothing! (Solicitor 1.)

Solicitor 1, however, was alone in his condemnation of the debtor as an ethically reprehensible person. In the main, ordinary solicitors regard collection as a chore which involves little emotional commitment; and agency solicitors define it as a routine and massive operation which is impersonal and mechanical.

The two roles available to a solicitor are not entirely discrete; they may be fused, they may overlap or they may succeed one another during the enforcement of a single debt. Fusion occurs, for example, when a lawyer is expected to wield punitive sanctions against a person who 'deserves' to be 'made an example of', and whose debt is sizeable. Similarly, a county court may be used punitively against cases which have passed through the serial testing system. The two roles are the bases of a variety of approaches to collection. They tend to cluster around different kinds of creditor;

deterrence and principle, for instance, usually guide the smaller firms. On the whole, the solicitor's unwillingness or inability to feel heated about the iniquity of default leads him to find the second role relatively uncongenial. The demands placed on him by a vengeful and incensed creditor are much more taxing than those of a large, dispassionate firm.

I have not yet discussed the major functional division which separates agency and ordinary solicitors. There is a wide gulf between the two; a gulf that does not allow for gradations but sets up a radical disjunction between the work of the two types of firm. Debt collection is conducted on such a gigantic scale in London that it imposes taxing demands on those who are significantly connected with it. Efficient and rapid processing of defaults requires organization and attention which are incompatible with the normal operation of a non-specialist firm. Solicitor 1, an agency firm, stated:

> I find that it is remunerative, but you've got to have a really efficient organization. Now, I deal with more than a hundred different county courts up and down the country you see. Now, in order to keep on top of it, because I've got thousands of debtors . . . I've got to be on top of it.

Solicitor 5, on the other hand, realized that collection would impose organizational strains on his practice:

> I wouldn't be very keen on seeking that kind of work. I certainly wouldn't seek it if it were necessary for myself or one of my partners to devote our time to it, and I wouldn't like looking for the staff.

Enforcement demands specialization because it is remunerative only when it is performed in bulk. A perennial source of discontent amongst solicitors is the level of county court costs.[2] A letter to the *Guardian* argued, for example, that 'solicitors' fees are kept deliberately low, and in the county court can only be described as absurd'.[3] An ordinary solicitor's experience of the county court would normally entail appearances in single actions. In each case,

[2] A report in *The Times* (9 February 1968) referred to negotiations between the Law Society and the Prices and Incomes Board about solicitors' fees: 'the society feels that much county court business is being conducted at a loss.'

[3] Letter signed by the Chairman, Public Relations Subcommittee, British Legal Association (24 June 1966). Similarly, another letter from the Honorary Secretary of the British Legal Association stated, 'unless solicitors receive some relief in the form of a swift upward revision of the scales of County and High Court costs . . . many solicitors will be obliged to be selective about the work which they accept.' (*Guardian*, 12 May 1966.)

he would not only have to travel to and from the court but might also have to wait an hour or so before his case was heard. Work in the county courts is time-consuming and, according to the lawyer, inappropriately rewarded. An agency solicitor, however, typically spends each morning in court dealing with some twenty or thirty cases. The court presents him with an opportunity to exploit the economies of scale. Without much greater effort, he can earn at least ten times as much from a session in the court as can his non-specialist colleague.

Specialization also leads to an increased effectiveness. An agency solicitor will be familiar with the peculiarities of his local courts and will know how to manipulate these peculiarities to advantage. Much of this manipulation will be dealt with in the following chapter. It is apparent that the debt-collecting solicitor has access to knowledge which is denied the ordinary firm. The ignorance of the ordinary firm leads to bewilderment about the arbitrariness and uncertainty of judicial decisions. Thus, Solicitor 4 simply said, 'I can give no answer on the way the various courts deal with their debtors.' Similarly, Solicitor 6 remarked:

> We ourselves don't practice in any particular county court and we'd always get debt collection proceedings covered by agents. So our actual experience of particular judges or particular courts is practically zero. . . . Our experience is mainly of Bromley, Croydon and D, those are the main ones. I don't think the practice differs substantially between these courts but that's really all I can speak for. One does hear stories of peculiar judges or good judges in other courts, and I think the only person who can make a particular forecast of what might happen or what would be the appropriate course would be the solicitor who actually appears in court.

On the other hand, agency firms have a considerable expertise and sophistication about suitable strategies. Solicitor 7 said:

> You know, for instance, that in [D county court] the chances that anybody will actually be there to give evidence are minimal. So what one does is simply wait to see whether the defendant will turn up. If the defendant turns up, one cross-examines as to means. Normally the judge does most of the work. He kicks off and finds out all the things he wants to find out. . . . But you see, in some courts, for instance I have been in when a debtor has said that he has hire purchase commitments of, you know, a pound a week, he can be grilled for quite a few minutes as to the date he entered this new hire purchase commitment as opposed to the judgment debt he

> has. But in D, normally, the judge is very sensible. Once a bloke has got commitments of any other kind, they are always taken into consideration even though legally, perhaps, they should be deferred until the one that's being considered. . . .

Solicitor 7 was so knowledgeable about D county court that he had become a marginal member of the court's covert culture and had learned some of its folklore:

> The common saying at D is that while Judge A was sitting on the bench (and he was an extremely tough judge), that all the debtors moved out of D; and when Judge B came on the bench, all the debtors moved back into D. You often hear this remark at D: 'God, if only Judge A were sitting, he'd have rapped that bloke!'

A division of labour between solicitors is mirrored by what appears to be a parallel division of prestige. Ordinary firms seem to define the agency solicitor as something of a hack who performs the dull, undemanding and unrewarding work of his more sophisticated colleagues. Collection is conventionally regarded as boring and mechanical:

> [It] is terribly uninteresting as a whole because the excuses put out for nonpayments of debts are always the same. And one always finds the same people getting into this situation. (Solicitor 8.)

Every county court will have one or more agency solicitors attached to it. They become a part of the institutional structure of the court, appearing in the bulk of the routine debt collection actions. Their performances will only occasionally be punctuated by an ordinary lawyer who pursues a solitary action. Their situation is remarkably similar to that of the Public Defender's in the American criminal court. Both develop more intimate associations with the court than with their clients, and both tend to be more involved than their non-specialist colleagues with the court world (Sudnow, in Chambliss, 1969, p. 249):

> While the courtroom encounters of private attorneys are brief, businesslike and circumscribed, interactionally and temporally, by the particular cases that bring them there, the [Public Defender] attends the courtroom as his regular work place and conveys in his demeanor his place as a member of its core personnel.

The consequence of such an involvement will become more apparent when I discuss the routine bargaining that is pursued in the county courts, particularly at the judgment summons hearing.

The agency solicitor is usually asked to act for an abundance and variety of creditors from all over Britain. He receives his work from the creditors directly or it is channelled to him from debt-collectors or ordinary practices. Agency solicitors may be delegated work from other agency firms which have no links with a particular court. Legal practice thus resembles previous processes in enforcement: an extensive network exists to feed defaults into the most appropriate institutions for active handling.

Collection problems are aggravated for the non-specialist. He must develop a hybrid practice to accommodate them; he is not as expert as the agency firm; and the very nature of his relations with clients is more perilous. Whilst the agency solicitor typically manages debts owed to large concerns who have a comparatively realistic expectation of success, the ordinary firm has clients who are not so experienced and are dominated by a desire to recover money quickly. Collection can endanger an ordinary firm's other business:

> I think all solicitors dislike debt collection intensely. It's unremunerative, it's often unsuccessful and it's not usually a very good branch of public relations—solicitor–client relations. (Solicitor 6.)

An ordinary solicitor thus tends to turn away as much collection work as he can: it poses problems of economic reward; he dislikes acting as an agent of vengeance; he dislikes his position in the career structure; and so on. As a result, he will tend to act only for clients who can offer him other lucrative business:

> It is a service which we supply to our clients. Debt collecting, unless it is on a vast scale, or alternatively for large amounts, doesn't pay very well. (Solicitor 4.)
>
> These small county court debts are completely undesirable and, of course, we run them at a loss. . . . If one refuses to do a [client's] debt collection, the chances are that they'll go to someone else, and they'll probably take their other work with them. So it's a sort of blackmail if you like. (Solicitor 10, an ordinary firm.)
>
> [Collection] is as small as we can make it simply because it's the poorest paying of any kind of work you do. I sometimes feel like saying to clients when they instruct me to collect a small debt: 'look, let me give you a fiver and go away and leave me in peace!' I know I've got to lose money when I collect small debts . . . but I want to keep the client, you see, so I'm afraid to put this to him. (Solicitor 5.)

Antipathy to enforcement widens the gulf between the specialist and the non-specialist even further. It leads to a wholesale delegation of collection actions to the agency firm. This necessarily increases the cost of enforcement charged by the ordinary solicitor because he must exact his own fee on top of that charged by his colleague. An ordinary firm may have to charge more in any case since it is not equipped to handle collection as cheaply as an expert.

It seems that the ordinary solicitor often attempts to persuade his clients that it is not worth suing for sums which any agency firm would gladly try to recover. Such advice is deliberately offered in order to minimize the volume of collection undertaken by the non-specialist. Whilst Solicitors 1 and 7 were prepared to proceed against defaults of two pounds (the lowest figure for which costs are awarded), Solicitor 3 would inform his clients that they should not sue for 'anything up to twenty pounds because, generally speaking, people who don't pay twenty pounds haven't got them. These people aren't worth pursuing. They won't even be able to pay the county court costs.' When the creditor is not a valued client, the resistance to collection will be even stronger. The fees will be more substantial; the picture of likely success painted much blacker; and the minimum debt 'worth' enforcing will be raised. The ordinary firm will do its utmost to dissuade a stranger contemplating litigation. It may even refuse its help outright. Thus there is a complete contrast between the conveyancing firm which shuns enforcement and the agency practice which welcomes it.

Just as the debt-collector expanded the creditor's dichotomous typology before he refined it again, so do solicitors inherit feckless and professional debtors and extend the classification to include the unfortunate. After all, even at this stage some debtors *do* pay after very little coercion and must be labelled unfortunates. Nevertheless, the unfortunate category is a marginal one and solicitors attach almost no importance to the letter which they use to threaten court action. It is often described as the 'usual seven-day job' and is dismissed as a 'preliminary ritual'. (Solicitor 2.) The majority of debts are conveyed to solicitors by large creditors whose career systems are thought too stringent in their testing. Lawyers believe that defaulters have already been effectively typed long before they reach them. Their one letter will filter off the small residue of unfortunates who have been inefficiently passed on to them. The remainder are necessarily stupid or devious:

> You see, you've got to divide debtors, to my mind, into welfare problems and non-welfare problems. Now, it seems to me, that most debtors that get into debt because of financial difficulty—too many commitments—should not really be dealt with in a county court at all. There should be a comprehensive family court, one of whose aspects should be to see how the family

> income should best be applied in all sorts of ways. . . . But how you would sort these out from the ones where the defendant is not in financial difficulties really, except difficulties of his own making. . . . There are a number of cases, principally car hire purchase cases, where one feels that a man has not committed himself for necessity but for pleasure. (Solicitor 7.)

> Now, by the time he's got to court, his demeanour will count for very little because if he has, well shall we say, been irresponsible enough not to approach you personally about solving his problem before he got to court, then he's either very stupid or he's on the way to being a hardened debtor. (Solicitor 2.)

The 'seven-day letter' is nothing more than a symbolic opening of hostilities in most cases. 'My initial letter really is just to crystallize the position rather than to endeavour to get the money back. One doesn't, you know, expect to get it back on a letter before action. You've got to do that, you've got to open the gate before you can charge through.' (Solicitor 8.) A debtor is not expected to prove himself an unfortunate in the brief phase which elapses before a summons is issued. Whilst a solicitor is in sole charge of his stage, he makes little organized effort to discover the unfortunates because he believes that there are so few of them. His belief is confirmed when a judgment is made in his favour. It is a belief that inevitably engenders frustration when the county court officers again search for unfortunates amongst his cases.

When a letter does evoke a response other than full payment, the solicitor's typical reaction is suspicion. 'Occasionally, you'll get somebody coming in and you'll get people 'phoning up. It's a lot of old flannel, trying to get round you.' (Solicitor 9, a small agency solicitor.) Replies are slotted into stereotyped categories which the solicitor feels are too predictable to be trustworthy. Solicitor 5, for instance, who dealt with defaults incurred by dentists' patients, stated:

> The favourite reply seems to be 'he hurt me, I've got a counterclaim', or 'I didn't want all that done. I didn't know it was going to cost that much. I've been tricked', that sort of thing. That's a good favourite reply. In other words, a lot of these replies tend to raise spurious counterclaims. You suspect that these people are playing for time.

In the main, the ordinary solicitor will be more predisposed to accept an offer of instalments than his agency colleague would. Instalments can be monitored and they entail none of the difficulties associated with county court enforcement. 'If they are genuine offers, we would much prefer instalment offers which are being kept than to proceed.' (Solicitor 3.) An agency solicitor, on the other hand, is as adept at supervising payments made into court as he is at supervising ones made into his office. He would probably compare the offer with the order he anticipates his local registrar would make. His ability to gauge the size of a court order is necessarily superior to that of the ordinary solicitors. It can be a critical difference. Solicitors are replete with cautionary tales about lilliputian orders. In one case, for example, the judge of Middlesbrough County Court instructed a debtor to discharge his debt of £42 at the rate of 6d a week (*Daily Mirror*, 21 July 1965). Rather than risk such a calamity, an uncertain solicitor might cling to any offer he receives. When no offer is received, or a solicitor feels that negotiations are fruitless, the default will be transferred on to yet another stage.

6 The county court

Introduction[1]

Legal enforcement is almost invariably waged by the county courts. The courts make up a system which is the 'basic administrative unit of civil litigation' (Glasser, undated), a system which was designed by the County Courts Act, 1846, to provide a cheap and efficient means of collecting small debts.[2] The definition of a small debt has become progressively more liberal and, in 1969, the four hundred courts have jurisdiction over almost all civil actions for sums of up to £500. Table 6.1 clearly demonstrates the pre-eminence of the county court in debt collection actions.

TABLE 6.1 *County court actions started in 1964*

		%
County Court: plaints entered	1,510,324	92·5
Queen's Bench and District Registries: writs issued	123,220	7·5

1 It will be recalled that, in my discussion of processes that have been affected by the Administration of Justice Act, 1970, I have adopted the convention of using the present tense. The following chapters should be taken to refer to events as they stood in 1969. Any other practice would have led to a tortuous mixture of tenses which would have engendered more confusion than this simple expedient.

2 The long title of the Act is 'An Act for the more easy Recovery of Small Debts and Demands in England'. The Act established the county court as the 'grassroots court' and successive legislation has confirmed its character as the inexpensive local civil court. In 1961, for instance, the Lord Chancellor stated (*County Court Officer*, 16 June 1961, vol. 37, no. 4, p. 46) 'it would be fatal if the County Court were to lose its basic qualities of a poor man's court.'

Although the court is a major agent of social control, it is poorly integrated with other institutions concerned with coercion. Its links with the police, magistrates' courts and prisons are tenuous and they generate ambiguities and tensions. The problems posed by incomplete integration affect the performance of a number of the court's tasks and I shall discuss them at length. Formal links are maintained only with the county court's sister organization, the High Court. Actions are transferred between these courts and a High Court judgment might, for instance, be enforced by a judgment summons in the county court. County courts normally have bankruptcy jurisdiction but this has become, in London, the province of the High Court. Additionally, both courts may be in competition with one another for the goods and bodies of the same debtors. Possible sources of conflict are regulated and somewhat neutralized by the rules of the competing courts.

The court itself has a bureaucratic structure mapped out by Acts of Parliament and the County Court Rules. The court's blueprint specifies the function and power of each of the roles contained in its structure. In particular, the court centres around three crucial positions, those of judge, registrar and bailiff, whose occupants have all worked in other control agencies. Judges are drawn from the ranks of barristers, registrars were once solicitors, and bailiffs are largely recruited from retired members of the police force. These three actors are collectively responsible for carrying the enforcement process on to the threshold of prison. Although each one has a clearly defined task, there is some unofficial merging of functions. The bailiffs, for example, have conspicuously stepped outside their mandate and have acquired considerable judicial power, as I shall show shortly.

Judges are the most senior officials of a court and their role is supposed to be purely judicial. 'A judge sees only the sitting in court. Most of his time with County Courts is spent listening to the trial of actions. The worst side he sees consists of judgment summonses, a tiresome chore for him' ('Gaius', 1965, p. 140). In fact, judges also wield a great influence over a court's policy towards its debtors and they are able to shape their bailiff's enforcement behaviour. The most significant feature of their role is that judges are alone entrusted with the authority to commit people to prison. Imprisonment is so grave a sanction that sentencing cannot be delegated.[3] Formal sentencing normally takes place at judgment summons hearings which are routine and relatively simple procedures. In addition to

[3] In practice, there is considerable delegation to the bailiffs as I shall show in Chapter 8. The registrar of E court, in one of his memoranda to the Payne Committee, stated, 'it is not the judiciary but the bailiff who has the final say'.

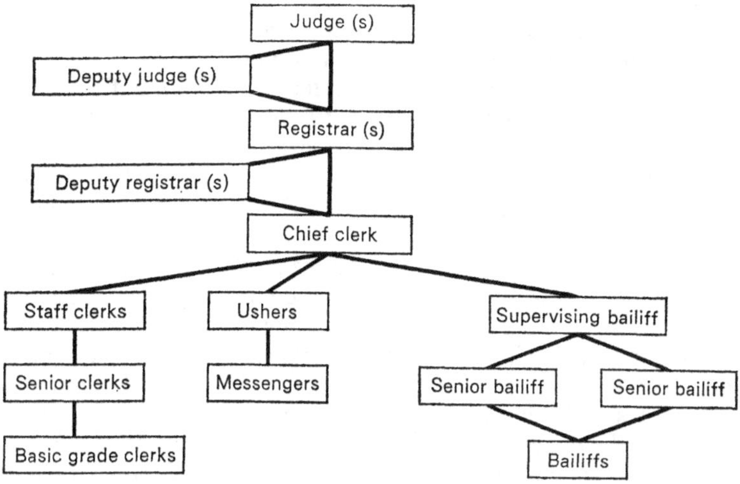

Figure 1. Organizational structure of a large county court.

making sentencing decisions, judges hear the more complicated actions involving sums of less than £30 and the bulk of those which are brought for larger sums.

Registrars are required to play three roles. They are minor judicial officers, hearing most of the actions concerned with debts of less than £30 and some of those which are more sizeable. In 1964, for instance, 9·7 per cent of the plaints heard by the registrars of the London courts were for amounts exceeding £30. The scope of the registrar's judicial function is constrained by his relations with the judge of his court. These relations are not rigorously defined by official rules and seem to be quite negotiable. For example, a registrar may give judgment in any uncontested action, but only by leave of his judge. Additionally, a judge may alter or reverse any decision given by a registrar if he believes that errors of procedure or legal interpretation have been committed.

Registrars also have two administrative functions. They control the court's staff and, as High Bailiffs (County Courts Act, 1959, Section 207), supervise its enforcement arm. 'In practice, however . . . many administrative duties are delegated by the registrar to the clerks and bailiffs.' (Gregory, 1962, p. 4.)

Bailiffs are responsible for translating the coercive power of a county court into action. They are the agents through whom social control is realized. One registrar (of E court) has defined enforcement as 'legal brutality wearing kid gloves' and it is the bailiff in his warrant officer role who is brutal when brutality has to be displayed. The bailiff's other role of Process Server is centred on the distribution of summonses and the collection of money.

Both activities are pursued in an esoteric context. Bailiffs cannot be recognized by outsiders because they do not wear uniforms or drive distinctive vehicles. Theirs is a largely invisible exercise of social control. Only the immediate members of the bailiff's world can recognize the signs which symbolize that enforcement is taking place.

Bailiffs occupy a strategic position in the work of the county court. They have acquired the means to man the most important posts in the enforcement process. They have command over the flow of information, the business of decision-making, and the implementation of decisions. In part, that position derives from a fairly common feature of social control agencies. The everyday work of bailiffs, like that of the police, is not of a kind which permits effective control from above. In the case of the American police, Gibbons (1968, p. 67) has remarked:

> Another general observation about police bureaucracies has to do with ecological peculiarities in these organizations. Many formal organizations are located in a single place, such as a college, a prison or a factory. Control of individuals is made easier by virtue of the visual surveillance which can be maintained over them. But the police organization is scattered about the community in headquarters and precinct stations. It is further scattered due to the fact that the largest single group of police employees are the patrolmen, most of whom are in patrol cars and not in the station house at all. These conditions make it difficult for police officials to conduct systematic evaluations of job performance of the workers, save through such devices as recording the number of arrests made by officers. The ecological structure of police work also creates difficulties in the way of control over deviant workers. Many of the deviant acts in which policemen sometimes engage, such as drinking on the job, are extremely difficult for administrators to observe. The spatial peculiarities of police systems probably go some way toward explaining the persistence of corrupt practices in the face of reform efforts occurring on the occasion of police scandals.

Although there are cultural traditions which account for differences between American and British control practices,[4] much of Gibbons' argument is appropriate to the bailiffs of a county court. Bailiffs are erstwhile policemen and they are familiar with formal and informal police processes. Indeed, their association with the police was probably of greater duration and significance than their connection with the court. They therefore apply many police work norms to debt collection and the link between the police model portrayed by Gibbons and a bailiff's situation is a close one.

The day-to-day work of bailiffs resembles the patrol behaviour of American policemen, but it is even less closely supervised. After all, the police are identifiable and are subject to the restraints imposed by countless witnesses. In this sense, bailiffs could be described as invisible and the public can rarely report their actions. Bailiffs are largely unmonitored and enjoy enormous autonomy despite their nominal subordination to a registrar. They are able to establish themselves as a substantially independent unit; setting their own goals, conceptions of suitable strategies and choice of targets for enforcement. The registrars of E and H courts told me that bailiffs are drawn from the police because they have to possess qualities which guarantee their integrity in situations which cannot be watched. The long-term consequences of a bailiff's performance can be assessed, but his job removes him from minute control. Bailiffs do, however, depart from Gibbons' model in a number of important respects. A county court has peculiar features which make its enforcement staff even more independent than their counterparts in the police.

The first feature is that bailiffs are unofficially required to feed incorrect information back to the court. Legal sanctions primarily operate as threats and bailiffs are expected to manipulate these threats in order to prise money out of defaulters. A sanction nevertheless tends to take the form of a warrant which instructs the bailiff to act against the debtor as soon as he is seen. Immediate implementation of a warrant to execute on goods or commit to prison would radically diminish a court's ability to control its debtors. Bailiffs

[4] The differences may not be as great as they sometimes appear. American police systems are rather more amenable to professional and public scrutiny than our own. It is quite possible that a number of features conventionally thought to be peculiar to America obtain in Britain as well. Maureen Cain, for example, in a discussion at the Symposium on Deviancy at the University of York on 2 November 1968, echoed Gibbons' argument in her analysis of the concealment practices of British policemen on the beat. Grigg comments on the manner in which Challenor's deviation was systematically supported. (Grigg, 1965, especially pp. 188–190.) Skolnick (1966, p. 70) also has doubts about the degree of divergence between American and British practices: 'those who too clearly contrast American and British police in favour of British are probably generally wrong.'

thus find and cajole debtors but tell their superiors that they were 'unable to see' them:

> The returns read, 'Not met', and we know they mean 'Bailiff avoiding Debtor'. . . . Bailiffs frankly admit that they meet and talk to commitment debtors without executing their orders to convey them to prison. Debtors come into court saying that they spoke to the Bailiff 'last night' who advised them to come into the court office. (Registrar of E Court.)

The institution thus lends highly recondite meanings to such words as 'see' and 'meet'. A debtor who has been seen is a debtor whom the bailiff has despaired of. This is often a successful process, but it manufactures a structured ignorance about the progress of any action. The registrar and senior bailiffs frequently do not know what their subordinates are doing or whether their inability to locate debtors is caused by laziness, ineptitude or skill in enforcement.

Bailiffs are tacitly given the role of censors. The information which they censor is, in any case, more detailed and vivid than that available to other court officials. They have daily interactions with debtors and see them in their 'natural surroundings'. 'Gaius' (1965, p. 140) observes:

> A bailiff sees practically only debtors, and that in the homes. They see the direct effect of County Courts on society and on the community. . . . As to the impact on the community, as to the type of person or family who is at the receiving end of County Courts, as to what process is effective, as to whether the County Court tribunal assesses the means of debtors correctly, the best evidence comes from bailiffs. They do not speak from hearsay.

Bailiffs can gauge more accurately than any judge the style of life of a debtor. Furthermore, the performances which debtors present in court are different from those witnessed by bailiffs. The court room is a strange situation for many debtors and it engenders strained behaviour. Bailiffs can approach defaulters in a more informally structured setting. Judges and registrars sometimes ask bailiffs to report on the debtors they encounter, but this is far from normal. As is the case in other bureaucracies, the lower ranks of the county court have face-to-face transactions with the people dealt with by the organization and they have a more intimate knowledge than their superiors.

Not only is there an ignorance about individual actions, there also appears to be uncertainty about the overall success achieved by the courts. Officials do not compile statistics of success-rates equivalent to the clear-up figures prepared by police forces. The

County Courts Branch of the Lord Chancellor's Office and court officials were unable to tell me what proportions of debts were eventually recovered by the courts. A number of judgment debts are, moreover, paid directly to creditors and solicitors and become wrongly identified as 'unsatisfied'. In consequence, officials have a rough idea only of which judgments are being paid, which are not being paid, and which warrants are outstanding. It does not necessarily follow that the courts are incompetent. Taylor (1966) has observed, 'we have a highly efficient system of justice running along . . . this is the justice of the county courts.' Similarly, a Working Party Report (1956, p. 6) commented 'the system functions reasonably well so far as the smaller debts are concerned.' The county court may not be inefficient, but bailiffs' enforcement practices cannot be made to respond to changes in rates of collection. Another source of control available to senior police officers is denied county court personnel.

The formal definition of legal enforcement as a process which threatens rather than sanctions also means that bailiffs have acquired much more power than they are entitled to. A bailiff must enforce warrants which will have unpleasant consequences for defaulters. He is not expected to implement them immediately. Instead, he is given wide discretion over the timing of enforcement. He may even aver that a debtor could not be seen at all. Bailiffs have thus taken over a judicial function in deciding whether to impose sanctions and when this imposition should take place. Some warrants may be too difficult to dispose of whilst others may be defined as an unmerited punishment for a debtor. There are pressures from creditors and the court which demand that a certain proportion of warrants must be cleared up. A bailiff believes that there are four situations in which warrants may be used: when pressures from his superiors are regarded as irresistible; when debtors are defined as professionals who 'deserve' punishment; when enforcement is likely to be uncomplicated; and when a bailiff has to maintain or regain control over his territory. 'To survive, the bailiff must be master of his patch. The debtor who has gone to prison will be respectful in his next dealing with the bailiff.' (Registrar of E court.) A latent function of the Warrant Officer role is the bailiff's use of a warrant as a device to engineer personal authority. Warrants are not primarily employed here to collect debts or express the court's displeasure with a debtor. In the two former cases, a bailiff is allowed to usurp a judicial role which is nominally located at the highest levels of the bureaucracy. Bailiffs have therefore become vastly more powerful than the formal plan of the court's organization suggests.

The autonomy of the bailiff force within the court has important ramifications for the style in which enforcement is pursued. Autonomy is coupled with two other characteristics of the bailiff's occupation: his feeling of impotence, and his belief that other agencies of control do not render him proper support. These three factors lead to a search for illegal solutions to recurring problems of control. I shall examine them later at some length.

Another consequence of this autonomy is the failure of bailiffs to play the parts which others would have them perform. The bailiffs' power to exercise discretion can frustrate other actors in the enforcement process. In particular, many solicitors feel that it is impermissible that bailiffs apply a three-fold typology to debtors. Solicitors believe that they have taken feckless and professional debtors to court, and they bitterly resent the tendency of bailiffs to dilute sanctions by classifying some people as unfortunates:

> . . . and the sheriff's officers and bailiffs and so on; some are very good but some we reckon are in league with the debtors. There's no doubt some are too lenient. They regard themselves as doing a *social service* and they are the arbiters of whether the debtors should receive some measure of time and so on at their hands. Which, of course, is very wrong. (Solicitor 2.)

The London county courts

My analysis of county court enforcement will dwell only on the London courts. These courts are not typical because they do not have jurisdiction in bankruptcy; they tend to be busier than the average court; and they deal with cases involving larger sums, as Table 6.2 shows.

TABLE 6.2 *The twelve Inner London county courts' share of all county court business in England and Wales (1964)*

	London courts	*Percentage of all courts' cases*
Total process	181,122	12·0
Amounts not exceeding £100	166,449	11·8
Amounts above £100 but not exceeding £200	6,147	16·0
Amounts above £200 but not exceeding £300	1,320	18·5
Amounts above £300 but not exceeding £400*	1,401	20·1
Amounts above £400*	64	34·4

* In 1964, with certain exceptions, the maximum sum for which a plaint could be entered in a county court was £400.

There is considerable variation between the London courts themselves. The heterogeneous nature of London reflects itself in the courts which control its areas. This variation has quantitative, qualitative and 'experiential' dimensions. E county court, for example, dealt with 21,000 cases in 1964 whilst A court dealt with only 6,327 plaints. As a result, the registrar of E tended to place stress on the organizational as well as the judicial aspects of his function. He was the only registrar I met who consistently referred to the need to implement business efficiency methods in enforcement. The complements of the courts again vary. K court had fifteen judges and a force of twelve bailiffs attached to it in 1964; A court had four judges and six bailiffs; whereas L court only had two bailiffs.[5]

Qualitative differences first appear in the type of business which a court handles. The majority of defendants in L court are commercial firms and, as a result, the court heard more than half (54·7 per cent in 1964) of the actions issuing for more than £400 in London. The court did not therefore tackle enforcement in the same manner as a normal court would. In 1964, for example, its bailiffs served only 0·3 per cent of the judgment summonses issued in London.

The ecological and social qualities of a district will stamp themselves on a court and differentiate it from its fellows. This may be illustrated by a comparison between C and D courts. C administers a middle-class and business district which has pockets of working-class inhabitants. D controls a predominantly working-class area. Compared with C, the registrar's court at D proportionately heard seven times as many plaints issued by mail order firms, but one thirtieth only of the cases brought by advertising companies, moneylenders and travel agents.

Let me describe some of the differences in experience by focusing on the bailiff staffs of the London courts. Quantitative and qualitative differences create, and interact with, cultural differences between the courts. One of the L court bailiffs, for instance, is mainly concerned with walking from one City office to another serving summonses on defendants' solicitors. He acts as an intermediary between sets of professional people whom he regards as awesome. His court sent one debtor to prison during the whole of 1964 and 1965. The L bailiff's work world is structured by a group of significant events and personalities which is foreign to the world of his colleagues at, say, the C or D courts.

The C bailiff encounters an extraordinary mixture of exotic defaulters (Jones, 1964, p. 179):

[5] These complements of judges represent various combinations of full judges, deputy judges, part-time judges and full-time judges. At K court, for instance, fifteen judges would never sit simultaneously.

> Let us see the type of person our Court deals with—particularly the Bailiffs. . . . Of titled people their names would fill several pages of Debrett, followed by financiers, gamblers, leading lights of the theatrical and cinema professions (and there are some!); doctors, solicitors, club proprietors, pimps and prostitutes, homosexuals, criminals, down to the working men of all nationalities and colour—these and many other types too numerous to describe here—in other words—the lot!

In such a world, bailiffs must be prepared to face a great variety of enforcement situations. They must be able to deal with a range of debtors who require entirely different approaches. A C bailiff's repertory of role-styles includes obsequiousness, forcefulness, intimacy, coldness, and so on. In contrast, the world of the D bailiff is considerably simpler. His role-set contains debtors (most of whom he defines as feckless or professional), fourteen other bailiffs, policemen, prison officers, and court officials. In 1964 alone, D court's bailiffs conveyed 155 defaulters to Brixton Prison. To the D bailiff, a county court is one of two warring camps. It symbolizes a legal order which is under constant attack from debtors attempting to evade social control. A county court simply does not mean the same thing to the various forces of bailiffs in London. Although the forces act within the same formal framework, there is enormous substantive differentiation between their work situations.

A county court is a social world with distinct boundaries. It has little contact with other enforcement agencies and none with the public which does not default or litigate. The courts also seem to be relatively insulated from one another. They are self-contained units of administration and enforcement which are more like Fielding's Bow Street court than modern control agencies. Unlike the police, for example, the bailiffs of one court rarely know their colleagues at another. The very structuring of bailiffs' time contributes towards the establishment of these separate worlds. Bailiffs must work when debtors can be found at home and they thus live on a time-scale which is out of phase with the behaviour patterns of the normal population. This not only divorces enforcement staff from outsiders, it also promotes a higher level of interaction between insiders. This is evinced by the common language which is spoken *within* but not *between* courts. Whilst the judge, registrar, chief clerk and bailiffs of one court may all call a deviant debtor a 'rogue'; in another court they will all label him a 'hard-core case'; and in a third a 'professional'.

Interaction between a court's members often assumes the form of a discussion about common professional problems. The judges and registrars of most courts regularly dine and consult together.

Bailiffs debate and formulate common ways of viewing their world. It is thus inevitable that a number of orthodoxies arise in any court which help its staff to interpret its role and its internal and external relations.

These orthodoxies are buttressed by three other factors. Important figures in a court are in a position to provide support for their subordinates' interpretations. In critical cases, this support is vital to the continued existence of a particular interpretation. Importance is largely derived from access to power. Formal control is vested in the judge, in the registrar, and, to a lesser extent, in the chief clerk of a county court. A judge's influence can be wielded through direct rulings; through indirect rulings communicated to his registrar; or by laying down a foundation for the rest of a court's actions. Thus, if a judge is reluctant to have debtors imprisoned, his chariness in issuing committal orders will emasculate the potential militancy of his registrar and bailiffs. He may also sanction the actions of his staff. One such sanctioning opportunity occurs when bailiffs bring debtors before him on an assault charge and submit them to his summary jurisdiction. In this situation, a judge's ideas of what constitutes correct behaviour can strengthen or weaken a bailiff's status and enforcement tactics. Two analogous cases with different outcomes demonstrate how definitions of model enforcement can vary.

> The judge of B court observed in an assault case that the debtor then lost his temper and he, without reason, threw water over this bailiff and the bailiff got cross and probably did say more than he should have done, namely, 'little bastard'. Bailiffs are only human beings and, if water is thrown over them, they could not be expected to act with complete equanimity. (Report of registrar of B court.)

A magistrate at P[6] court, however, refused to support an F bailiff. A local newspaper (*Kilburn Times*, 3 May 1957) reported:

> The magistrate, dismissing the charge, said that court bailiffs had a difficult task and often encountered troublesome people. At the same time, he said one expected a higher standard of conduct from them than from anybody else, and a performance of their tasks with tact, discretion and forbearance. . . . [The defendant] insisted on going into her room and shutting the door and that provoked the first violent incident in that the court bailiff called her a 'bitch'. [The bailiff] said it was merely an expression of surprise, but he [the magistrate] could

[6] Letters from M onwards refer to courts other than the twelve Inner London county courts.

> not accept that as a fair description. 'It is an expression', he said, 'which I venture to think that the bailiff, Mr ——, is the first to admit is not in accordance with the terms of his duty to address anybody in that way'. [sic]

Whether a bailiff is regarded by his superiors as 'only a human being' or a person from whom 'one expected a higher standard of conduct than from anybody else' is a question which has an immediate impact on his collection policy. It is a question which can also be decided by a registrar. The registrar of a court monitors both staff and bailiffs and can dismiss them if they do not conform to his expectations of reasonable behaviour. Ideas vary. In L court, the model of an ideal bailiff appeared to entail politeness and a 'respectable' front. The L bailiff was the only officer I accompanied who insisted that I should not smoke whilst enforcement was taking place. In D court, however, 'toughness' seemed to be required of bailiffs and, when I was appointed a bailiff there, I was asked to sign a disclaimer of responsibility in the event of my being assaulted. What is classed as *diplomacy* in one court might be construed as *softness* in another. A registrar can thereby prescribe his court's attitude towards its defaulters. This is especially apparent in the determination of when the execution of a warrant should be abandoned. Many enforcements can proceed only when illegal or unorthodox measures are used to aid a bailiff. Some registrars may refuse to countenance illegitimate techniques; others may demand that a higher success rate be achieved despite unconventional means.

The third important figure is the chief clerk who is responsible for the routine running of a court. He may choose to act as a buffer between the bailiffs and his registrar, tailoring the information which his superiors receive. In some courts, there is a measure of collusion between chief clerks and bailiffs. In D court, for instance, the chief clerk told me that only unimpeachable cases of assaults on bailiffs would be taken before the judge. He repeatedly stressed that D's area was populated by tough debtors and that, if bailiffs used violence, a blind eye might have to be turned on what took place. He also felt that he had to rely on his bailiffs because debtors frequently manufactured mischievous accusations against them. The more serious accusations would be investigated but the others would be ignored unless the police intervened. I was fortuitously shown a report of an assault case in which a bailiff had lost his temper and trampled a debtor's fur coat in the excrement that had been thrown at him. When I later saw a copy of the report in the files of the Lord Chancellor's Department, there was no reference at all to retaliation or to the coat. The account had been defensively altered by the chief clerk. Protective liaisons of this sort may be established to permit the continued use of illegitimate means of recovery. Common definitions of debtors as professionals on the one hand, and of the judiciary as structurally removed from opportunities to 'really' know the problems of enforcement staff on the other, lead to systematic evasions of the consequences of improper conduct.

The second buttress is provided by the tendency for bailiffs to be self-recruiting. Registrars and chief clerks may question established bailiffs about the reputations acquired by applicants whilst they were in the police force. This reinforces the existing orthodoxies because 'tough' bailiffs will support the acceptance of 'tough' recruits.

Third, each court has, or claims to have, its own unique problems and characteristics. In B court, for example, the diplomatic 'immunity' of some defaulters complicates enforcement. I was told about the belligerence of the dockworkers who live in the area controlled by N court and about the firearms owned by the debtors of D court. These problems can become of symbolic importance to the staff: they help to distinguish the courts and make a drab job colourful and exciting. Significant events in a court's history will become parts of its culture. Thus the judge, registrar and chief clerk of I court all severally told me the same anecdote about a recalcitrant barrister who was a persistent defendant.

These differences serve to justify distinctive policies and programmes of action. They can explain how the various courts approach their roles as enforcement agencies and how they are themselves approached by outsiders. The former is nicely illustrated by a written discussion which took place between the registrar of a court and officials of the County Courts Branch. A debtor had assaulted a solicitor whilst a case was being heard by the registrar in chambers. The solicitor issued a summons for common assault and the registrar asked:

> From the department's point of view, do you wish me to take any further steps, bearing in mind the district in which the court is situated, and that these things have a habit of being 'broadcast'? (Letter dated 5 June 1958.)

The debtor was fined by a magistrate and the registrar reported:

> Having regard to all the circumstances, my judge and I feel that the magistrate has taken a sufficiently serious view of the matter to justify leaving it, and I expect that you will feel the same. Our anxiety was that this being a 'tough' district, we have to act accordingly. (Letter dated 30 June 1958.)

The formation of discrete county court cultures engenders systematic predispositions towards certain courses of action.[7] The variation is often recognized by solicitors and others who have frequent dealings with the London courts and may, in turn, affect their behaviour:

> If the debt is a borderline one, let us say £190, I might possibly issue a county court summons. But when I see the X county court is the local court, I would advise my client to issue a High Court writ. This may be a little unfair but I think that the policy of the court, there *is* a policy of the court, . . . is determined by the judge or the registrar or both, and will depend on the district where the court is. . . . As a joke, I suppose, some courts have been labelled 'Debtors' Courts' and others 'Creditors' Courts'. It's not so much of a joke, really. There's some truth in it. (Solicitor 10.)

Judgment

There are two types of county court summons, a default summons and an ordinary summons, but my analysis will be concerned only with the former. Default summonses are issued for the bulk of the debts whose enforcement has been discussed so far, and the actual procedural differences between the two sorts of action are slight.[8] 'In substance, there is only one difference. . . . If the defendant does nothing at all, in the default action judgment is entered in default, whereas, in the ordinary action, there must be a hearing. In all other respects, default and ordinary actions proceed on parallel courses.' (Registrar of E court.)[9] In order to simplify my discussion, I shall deal with default actions alone.

7 Of course there are only a few courts which encompass a completely integrated cultural system with no possibilities of change or ambiguity. Important officers may leave and become replaced by others who subscribe to foreign beliefs. Again, bailiffs typically work alone and need pay only an overt allegiance to their colleagues' views.

8 The aim of the ordinary action is to afford the debtor greater protection. Default summonses cannot be issued '(a) against a person under disability; or (b) to recover money lent by a moneylender within the meaning of the Moneylenders Acts, 1900 to 1927, or interest on money so lent . . .; or (c) by an assignee of a debt or any other thing in action; or (d) to recover money secured by a mortgage or charge; or (e) under a hire-purchase agreement to recover more than the amount of any instalment or instalments of the hire-purchase price which is due or unpaid'; or (f) to recover interest accruing after the commencement of the action; or (g) an unliquidated demand. (*County Court Rules*, 1936, Order 6, Rule (2), and amendments.)

9 Indeed, the Payne Committee stated, 'We think that (with certain exceptions) no useful purpose is served by distinguishing between ordinary and default actions in claims for recovery of debts.' (Payne Committee, 1969, para. 144, p. 36.)

A county court judgment is the first stage in the often arduous process of legal enforcement. It serves three functions: first, it penalizes a defaulter by officially branding him as a poor credit risk; it also offers the creditor a chance to manipulate court sanctions if default is made on the judgment order; and it places the debtor under duress:

> What I tend to do is this: if I make contact with the debtor, what I want to do to protect my client is to get a judgment, either hostilely or with his consent, because then I'm in a position to start talking. Then, if I do any kind of settlement, it's on the basis that payment is made by instalments but, very important, should any one instalment become in arrears, the whole lot of the outstanding debt is payable instantly. (Solicitor 8.)

Judgment cannot be entered unless a default summons is first served. Unlike other court summonses and warrants, the default summons is not difficult to serve. The summons does not have to be personally received by a defendant and may, indeed, be served by post or through a notice in a newspaper. Service can also be delegated to people who are not employed by the court and solicitors sometimes find it expedient to deliver it themselves.

The distribution of default summonses is the largest single task performed by bailiffs. In 1964, the average bailiff of a London court was required to serve 1,959 of these summonses and he was successful with ninety per cent of them. Initial failure to serve a summons may prompt a bailiff to attempt further service, but he is unlikely to search for a debtor who has 'skipped'. Bailiffs tend to be stirred into taking vigorous action only when they feel that they are threatened in some way. The threat may be presented by seniors who define them as inefficient, or it may be presented by a debtor who undermines their personal authority. It is unusual for a bailiff to perceive the need to master a defaulter at so early a stage in enforcement. He probably does not know the debtor at all and feels no animus against him. If a bailiff recognizes the debtor from past unhappy meetings, it is possible that he may try to trace him. In most other cases, the onus reverts back to the debtor's creditor. When small debts are concerned, nonservice typically results in the abandonment of the action because creditors are reluctant to subsidize possibly fruitless enquiries. The summons will be officially struck out if it cannot be served within a year of its issue.

The default summons belittles the significance of judgment itself. The summons tells the debtor that 'judgment may be obtained against you and enforced without further notice unless within eight days of the service of this summons . . .' (County court form 22).

Judgment, in other words, is consequent upon the apathy or admission of the debtor. Most other procedures set up institutional checks to offset the possibility that enforcement will progress without negotiation from a debtor. The default summons, however, appears to be designed to minimize the chance of negotiation (Committee on County Court Procedure, 1949, p. 10):

> There was evidence that many creditors prefer the default procedure, because it often provides a speedier remedy than the ordinary procedure and there is always the possibility that judgment may be obtained in default of admission or defence without the necessity for any attendance by the creditor at court to give proof of the debt.

An assumption is written into the process that judgment is a natural successor to service of a default summons. Default actions are rarely contested; in 1964, for instance, only 3·4 per cent of cases heard in the London county courts were fought. This figure would have been even smaller if default actions alone had been represented. Again, only one per cent of the legal aid results reported for 1964–5 concerned the county courts. Table 6.3 shows how slight the problem of securing a judgment in the county court is.

TABLE 6.3 *Judgments in county court actions in 1966 and 1967*

	1966	*1967*
Actions disposed of in England and Wales	1,212,818	1,278,837
Actions by consent or on admission, or in default of appearance or defence	973,400	1,024,025

The defended actions which I witnessed seemed to have been fought on grounds derived from 'natural justice'. Caplovitz (1963, p. 157), writing on the American poor, remarks:

> Failure to maintain payments does not always stem from the consumer's inability to pay. Ironically, he may stop paying because the merchant has failed to live up to *his* obligations. When dissatisfied with the shoddy merchandise they receive, some families retaliate for the merchant's bad faith by withholding payments. But this logic . . . does not apply to the low-income marketing system. As most of the families soon learned, the contracts they signed precluded this form of redress.

It is not only when goods are shoddy that natural justice is invoked. It is enough that a debtor thinks of himself as shoddily treated. Equipment acquired on hire purchase may become defective or goods may be repossessed. In another context, the registrar of E court observed, 'we do overlook that debtors do not have the County Court Practice as their bedtime reading'. A debtor's conception of moral justification does not necessarily coincide with a valid legal defence to a default summons. Most solicitors are contemptuous of the defences that are put up against them. They rarely bother to prepare impeccable cases because judgment is so easily entered. They regard debtors' defences as feeble obstructions:

> Most of the collection defences . . . wilt away as soon as you go on. They usually, in excess of ninety per cent, are not truly being defended. (Solicitor 5.)

A registrar *may* attempt to work extra-legal compromises when a case is contested for such reasons. Certain firms seem to have acquired notorious reputations in the courts and registrars might wish to alter the flow of legal process by making it difficult for them to litigate routinely. The registrar may also wish to induce willingness to co-operate in a genuinely aggrieved defendant. Again, he may wish to regain some control over a mechanical and seemingly independent process. Thus, in G court, the registrar reduced a judgment debt by the ten pounds which he thought would pay for the repair of some prematurely aged furniture. This was an uncommon case because moral reasons for withholding payments are usually dismissed as irrelevant to a default action. For example, successive actions were fought in C court by defendants who owed money to advertising companies. It seemed that oral promises had been made to the debtors which had been negated by the contracts they had signed. All the court staff, including the registrar, told me that they thought the defendants had been deliberately misled. Nevertheless, their belief could not affect the entering of judgment and the debtors lost their cases.

On the other hand, a debtor may pay the debt when he receives a default summons. He might fear the stigma of judgment, knowing that it could jeopardize his ability to obtain credit in future.[10] He might also have been at last matched with a threat sufficient to create intolerable anxiety. 16·6 per cent of a sample of default actions taken from the files of E court were paid before judgment. Thus only

[10] It is significant that the defendants who would lose most from a poor credit record, commercial firms, were heavily represented in this group. 29·5 per cent of these debtors who paid before judgment were firms, although firms represented only 12 per cent of the sample of 450 actions initiated in E court in 1963.

75 per cent of actions progress through to the judgment stage itself.

A plaintiff can sign judgment in default and choose his own order if the defaulter does not appear or make an offer. He can ask for payment of the debt 'forthwith', by a specific time or in monthly instalments. His choice of the first two types of order could be prompted by a desire to punish the debtor with a more onerous order. He might also choose these orders because he has some knowledge of the defaulter's means; if the debtor defaults again, the plaintiff can immediately take full execution on his goods or initiate bankruptcy proceedings. Payment in one sum is most appropriate to a wealthy debtor.

Such an order could, however, stem from an ignorance about county court enforcement. Warrants of execution and judgment summonses cannot issue for less than the amount of the order. As a result, plaintiffs who resort to payment 'forthwith' or by a certain date have drastically reduced the flexibility of their coercive power (Working Party Report, 1956, p. 15):

> Unless [the plaintiff] has an instalment order he cannot use the method of issuing successive executions for part of the debt, and without such an order a judgment summons will not lead to an order of commitment, unless he can prove that a debtor has had the means to pay the full debt, whilst he can obtain an order of commitment if he proves that the debtor could have paid one or more instalments.

In addition to this diminution of their ability to manipulate the debtor, plaintiffs may attract the disfavour of registrars and judges. The effect of a warrant of execution or commitment can always be nullified by the debtor's successful application for its suspension. On the whole, debtors are treated more sympathetically if their creditors can be officially identified as malicious or unsophisticated. The usefulness of warrants issuing for the whole debt is also undermined by the bailiff's added difficulties in executing them. An attempt to recover fifty pounds is much more likely to be unrewarding than an attempt to collect five. Such orders are therefore liable to lead to one of two outcomes: rapid and effective enforcement or the abandonment of an action. Table 6.4 shows that they do not lead to protracted enforcement:[11]

[11] Cf. 'When judgment is given for the recovery of a debt it is very common, particularly in hire purchase cases, for the Judge [*sic*] to specify instalments by which the debt is to be paid. This is not of course done where there is a likelihood of the judgment being enforced by execution on the debtor's goods or by bankruptcy proceedings. From the point of view of the creditor the instalment order is desirable as laying the foundation for future proceedings by judgment summons if the instalments are not maintained.' (*Credit*, vol. 1, no. 4, p. 4.)

TABLE 6.4 *Fates of judgments entered in 1963 in E county court*

	Paid in 1963 (N=150)	*Paid in 1964 or 1965* (N=50)	*Dormant (Abandoned)* (N = 150)	*Live (Continuing in 1966)* (N = 100)
	%	%	%	%
Forthwith or by a specified time	36·0	6·0	44·2	11·0
Instalment order	64·0	94·0	55·8	89·0
Total	100·0	100·0	100·0	100·0

In the main, solicitors know so little about the debtors they pursue that they ask for standard small instalment orders which should be within the means of most defendants.[12] Agency solicitors mechanically process the masses of defaults they are requested to collect. The creditors who employ them are frequently unable to give any information about the defaulters and it would be expensive and time-consuming to search for it. Thus solicitors sometimes have no more to act on than a name, an address and a brief history of the debt:

> Often it's almost laughable. You get 'Please take proceedings against Mr Smith of such-and-such an address', and you then have no alternative but to sue someone just as 'Smith (male)'. And, of course, there can be more than one at the address and if they've gone, they've gone. (Solicitor 6.)

> One is very often working in the dark as regards the debtor, but one gets some background from the trade and the nature of the debt. (Solicitor 4.)

Agency solicitors are in no position to demand large judgment orders. They evolve uniform policies of requesting an order of a pound or two pounds a month for every debt and from every debtor. Their policy reduces the complexities of enforcement to a minimum: they do not have to pay attention to individual cases; they do not

12 Thus the Payne Committee comment (1969, para. 444, p. 120): 'one of the most unsatisfactory features of debt cases is the omission of creditors at any stage to obtain reliable information about the income, assets or property of the debtor. Frequently they supply the goods in the first place without any enquiries and without any knowledge of the financial position of the customer. In the event of default they institute proceedings without any further knowledge about the debtor and in the hope that some facts about his means and assets will come to light in the course of the proceedings.'

have to take account of the idiosyncrasies of particular courts; and they have little to fear from a registrar's or a defendant's opposition to their requests. Such opposition could force them to waste time on negotiations about the order, negotiations which they are ill-equipped to undertake. Moreover they believe that the demand for a substantial order considerably dwarfs their chances of success:

> It's much better to have an offer of ten shillings a month which he can pay than two pounds a month which he can never keep up. (Solicitor 6.)

> There should be judicial intervention to ensure that too high an order isn't made. Feckless debtors often make an offer of four pounds a month which they can't afford. (Solicitor 8.)

On occasion, however, it is the debtor who suggests an appropriate judgment order. A defendant who admits a debt is required to state the manner in which he proposes to pay it. If the creditor accepts the defendant's offer, judgment is entered and the proposed instalment order is judicially confirmed. Most bureaucratic creditors, through the solicitors who act for them, accept such an order because they have no evidence about the debtor which indicates any other course. The clients of the agency solicitors can again be identified by the court staff as co-operative and professional in their approach. Like the defendant in a criminal case who pleads guilty, the professional creditor allows mass legal collection to proceed smoothly. It seems to be an informal rule in some county courts that the professional creditor should be rewarded when his debtors apply for suspensions of warrants or when he asks for a committal order at a judgment summons hearing. This, again, has parallels in the administration of the criminal court; an American federal judge, for instance, remarked (*United States v. Wiley*, 184F. Supp. 679 (N.D. Ill., 1960):

> If in one year, 248 judges are to deal with 35,517 defendants, the district courts must encourage pleas of guilty. One way to encourage pleas of guilty is to establish or announce a policy that, in the ordinary case, leniency will not be granted to a defendant who stands trial.

Creditors who are not prepared to accept their debtors' offers must appear before the registrar to defend their objections. The court becomes arbiter and negotiations take place before the registrar in chambers. When the debt admitted is greater than £40, the debtor may be personally examined at this 'disposal' of an action. In such a case, if one of the disputants does not appear, a registrar will tend to approve the order of the person who does attend.

If the creditor is absent at a disposal, registrars are often unprepared to examine the objections to the defendant's offer and the debtor merely wins his case by default. When it is the debtor who is absent, the registrar's reasons for accepting the plaintiff's proposal are rather more complex. Instalment orders are always subject to alteration because either party can apply to vary the size of the payments. When a plaintiff's order is too onerous, his debtor can make an immediate application for its reduction. If the creditor chooses to dispute this application, the examination of the debtor and negotiations about methods of payment may now take place.

Registrars generally urge the wisdom of making small orders. They believe that these orders are less prone to default and, if default *does* ensue, subsequent enforcement is both easier and more just. They argue that a small order which a debtor can afford is superior to a large one which he cannot. Their contentions bring them into conflict with those creditors or solicitors who want retribution; who seek immediate payments or who define most defaulters as deviant. Solicitor 1, for instance, labelled the bulk of his defendants as professionals and felt their offers were invariably too low:

> . . . He comes before the court and we ask him how much he earns. . . . You say to the chap 'Well, I think that even on the information which you've given, you ought to pay the contractual instalments of a pound a week.' He says, 'Well, I can't.' 'Well, are you any worse off now than when you entered into the agreement six months ago?' 'No,' he says, 'I'm not any worse off, but things have gone up in price—cost of living.' And the registrar says to me, 'Well, Mr ——, are you going to accept this offer?' I say, 'Well, I don't think I ought to accept this offer. Well, the government (and this is the argument I always put forward) has said that goods of this description, the hire purchase agreement mustn't run for more than two years. Look, if you're going to reduce his payments from one pound a week to five shillings a week, you're going to make it run for eight years. Well, that's cutting right across parliamentary *legislation*!!' He says, 'I'm not interested. I'm the registrar of this court and I'm going to say what it's going to be.'

A registrar who confronts such opposition may wish to demonstrate his arguments by acceding to the plaintiff's request. Thus, in a case at K court, the registrar thought that a reasonable order would be £3 a month. After some debate with the plaintiff, he nevertheless agreed to a request for an order of £4 a week. He told me that he had confirmed the order because he hoped to educate the creditor. His prediction was that the debtor would become hostile to the creditor and default again. Because the judgment order had been excessive, the defendant would have no difficulty in getting it reduced on application. The outcome of the creditor's folly would be that payments were delayed; the debtor's good-will lost; and the registrar's more modest order would be inevitably confirmed.

Although this policy of approving orders in an automatic fashion was upheld on the occasions when I observed disposals,[13] it does not appear to be widespread. For instance, the Working Party (1956, p. 16) remarks that when a debtor does not attend a disposal:

> Some Registrars take the view that the onus is then on the creditor to prove that the debtor can pay more than he has offered, and, in default of evidence by the creditor, will make an order in terms of the offer. Other Registrars use their own knowledge of local wages and conditions and fix a figure which they believe would be fair.

I found that the Working Party's comments are more applicable to the situation in which creditor and debtor *do* confront one another. The three actors involved in the process bring different conceptions to bear on the bargaining, examination and adjudication which characterize disposals. Solicitors, for example, are generally hostile towards the defaulter. They have inherited debts against which creditors and others have already waged unsuccessful enforcement. The very signing of judgment means that they have themselves been defeated in their first encounters with the debtor. They are convinced that judgment debtors are either stupid or dishonest. In consequence, all solicitors (and those who appear at disposals in particular) entertain feelings of distrust about defaulters.

Their distrust may well resolve itself into outright condemnation. Some solicitors become quite heated in their hostility towards the deviance and deviants encountered in collection work. Solicitor 1, for example, maintained that many debtors attacked the 'sanctity of contract' in a way that was 'morally destroying'. Other solicitors, however, develop emotional and intellectual distance from enforcement:

> Generally, debt collection is quite an impersonal sort of thing, very dull and dreary from a solicitor's point of view. (Solicitor 11.)

Whatever their personal investment in collection may be, solicitors believe that they know the 'true' debtor and that the registrar in chambers cannot possibly do so. This volte-face of the defendant can be most infuriating:

> If he [the debtor] comes, he tells them a lot of untruths about his means and liabilities, and the court never calls, or very

13 I attended disposals once at C court, twice at G, twice at I, and three times at K.

rarely calls upon him to produce his pay slip or any evidence as to his liabilities. I think this is one of the unfair parts about it. (Solicitor 3.)

Complaints of this sort are made throughout county court enforcement.[14] The solicitor knows that a defaulter is 'really' feckless or professional, yet the court is so arranged that the registrar attempts to apply a threefold classification system. The wicked or the stupid constantly escape their proper deserts by gulling the judiciary into labelling them unfortunates.

Solicitors at disposals naturally distrust the debtor's statements about his means. They may act for a private creditor who has access to unusually full information about a defaulter but, generally, they work from assumptions about defaulters' propensities to evasiveness and dishonesty and not from sure knowledge. It is often very difficult to substantiate their opposition to a debtor whom they think to be lying. They may employ an enquiry agent to provide them with some evidence but, in many cases, this is not economically feasible. The same problem applies to the judgment summons hearing of which Solicitor 5 observed:

This is loaded entirely against the creditor. He can't win. He's got to prove the means of the debtor . . . and, unless he makes exhaustive and expensive enquiries, there's no guarantee that he'll be able to find out what he wants to know. If the debt's under fifty pounds, it's not worthwhile making these enquiries because they're so expensive. The solicitor therefore gambles on the outcome.

A solicitor's misgivings about a defaulter's honesty can be so great that the instalment offer is frequently dismissed as a ruse. The solicitor may believe that default is inevitable and intended and that any offer is sheer manoeuvring:

The great majority of them, if they're experienced in this matter, they know that this is a way of putting off the evil day. Because, once you've accepted this offer, then the first payment doesn't become due until a month after you pay it; and you can't take any action to recover the balance until the whole period's elapsed, and they jolly well know it. (Solicitor 11.)

[14] Interestingly enough, the Payne Committee (1969, p. 83) appeared to sympathize with such complaints: 'The more unscrupulous the debtor the more obstacles he raises against his creditors, and it is argued with great force that, since he has got himself into debt, he should be compelled to make a full disclosure to the court of his means, assets and circumstances so that the court can assess suitable instalments or order appropriate modes of enforcement.'

A registrar, however, treats defaulters with little suspicion at this stage. He will apply labels to them only when the court career has developed enough to provide useful feedback. At that stage, he will follow his predecessors and make use of a tripartite classification system. Thus the registrar of G court categorized debtors as 'rogues', 'unfortunates' and 'feckless'; and the registrar of I court referred to them as 'professionals' 'unfortunates' and 'feckless'. Feedback can be generated by a review of any action's history or by reports of unusual events submitted by subordinates. At a disposal, clues for social placement are still limited: a debtor may be identified as a member of the 'stage army' of defendants that frequent a court; he may seem too familiar with court etiquette to be an innocent; he may be currently involved in other process; or he may be typed by what the registrars of E and H courts called the unmistakable 'hang-dog' demeanour of the genuine unfortunate. A debtor's statements can also be matched against the expectations which a registrar has built up from his knowledge of local conditions. This is a difficult procedure, however, if the court's area is heterogeneous. Wages and rents may vary too widely to establish viable expectations. In uncertainty, a registrar can ask bailiffs to report; he can threaten to seek corroboration of evidence from an employer; or he can demand tangible evidence. Means might also be induced from the occupation, appearance and address of the defendant. They can, for instance, be assumed to be substantial if the debtor is represented by a solicitor himself. These clues are of limited utility and a registrar prefers to set up his own testing system:

> In our opinion, to give power . . . to make an order for payment by instalments . . . is one of the most convenient, fair and effective means of enforcement tending to hasten the process whereby the dishonest or recalcitrant debtor becomes liable to imprisonment under the Debtors Act upon failure to pay instalments when, in fact, he has or had the means to do so. (Joint Working Party, 1963, p. 27.)

Thus an instalment order is a test of a debtor's deviance and it follows that the smaller the order, the more positive are the test's results. The registrar's propensity to make small orders is reinforced by his belief that finer discrimination is built into a moderate demand. Registrars do not often class debtors at a disposal. Instead they activate a mechanism which will automatically detect 'the dishonest or recalcitrant debtor'. They cannot hope to judge the defendant's veracity so they postpone final decisions.

A registrar is better able to assess the plaintiff's case. There is a common universe of discourse between registrar and solicitor which excludes the defendant. They are both members of the same occupational and social groups. Registrars were once solicitors themselves and may indeed have played the role which is now enacted before them. Moreover, a close working relationship between the two can make them finely attuned to one another. The agency solicitor may spend a considerable portion of his working life in interaction with the registrar of one court. This cannot but lead to trust and reciprocity on the one hand, or breakdown and the development of hostility on the other. An agency solicitor will not survive as the possessor of a viable practice if he is unable to gain the trust of his registrar. He will be anxious to demonstrate his reliability to the judicial officers of the court he depends on. Reliability may involve open criticism of the quality of the cases his clients have handed him; or it may involve a display of neutrality in other actions. A registrar's conception of the solicitor's reliability will affect any decisions made about orders at disposals. This universe of discourse means that registrars will appreciate how expensive and difficult the collection of adequate evidence of means can be. It will also mean that the registrar is well placed to detect attempts at camouflaging inadequacies in the presentation of a case. In most instances, the burden of proof rests with the plaintiff. Registrars tend to accept the defendant's offer if objections to it cannot be sustained.

The transaction itself is informally conducted. At this stage, the court has not yet identified the defendant as a professional or feckless person who merits coercion. Disposals seem to be governed by an aspect of the doctrine of societal dualism; that is, they are concerned with arranging affairs between private individuals, not with assigning guilt or engineering degradation ceremonies. Although later stages closely resemble more conventional types of social control, disposals and applications follow a neutral policy.

The disposal places little stress on the formal proprieties of the situation. Proprieties become explicit only in the breach. Thus, in I court, a debtor brought out a lighter and cigarettes and was told by the registrar 'this is a court of law and you may not smoke cigarettes'. In addition to this assumption that the court was controlled by unwritten but 'obvious' rules of behaviour, there is a definite but undeclared structure imposed on the process. This was again exemplified in I court when a defendant asked whether he could put a question. He was told that he would be allowed to speak 'at the proper time'. That is, his spontaneous attempt to initiate an exchange was killed by his ignorance of rules which had never been stated to him. There were few props to support this structure or these rules; the court was defined as a place where the contesting parties are not guilty and accuser, but simply two negotiators. Bargaining over instalment orders is perhaps the last stage in which the conception of societal dualism is reflected in the county court.

Table 6.5 describes the outcomes of these negotiations in the case of E court. With the exception of orders made for payment in one sum, orders are, in fact, fairly uniform for all four groups. They are preponderantly modest instalment orders designed to discharge modest debts. In each type of debt, the largest group of orders is for payments of up to £2 a month. Another predictable finding is that, 'dormant' actions apart, the size of a judgment debt is related to the time taken to recover it. The larger the sum, the more prolonged is the enforcement. This relationship is not, however, a simple one: most of the dormant and live judgments should have been satisfied

TABLE 6.5 *Judgments and orders* made at E court in 1963*

Order	*Dead in 1963* (N = 150)		*Dead in 1964–5* (N = 50)		*Dormant in 1966* (N = 150)		*Live in 1966* (N = 100)	
Payment ordered in one sum:	%		%		%		%	
Forthwith	26·7		6·0		36·7		8·0	
		34·0		6·0		45·5		11·0
By a specific time	7·3		—		8·0		3·0	
Payment ordered in monthly instalments of:								
£ *s*								
10	5·9		14·0		8·0		9·0	
1	9·8	27·2	22·0	76·0	9·3	40·7	26·0	60·0
1 10	3·3		14·0		4·7		3·0	
2	6·7		26·0		18·7		22·0	
2 10	0·7		—		—		1·0	
3	2·7	6·0	4·0	10·0	3·3	7·3	5·0	16·0
3 10	1·3		—		—		—	
4	1·3		6·0		4·0		10·0	
10	4·7		6·0		6·7		12·0	
		6·0		8·0		6·7		13·0
10+	1·3		2·0		—		1·0	
	£ *s*		£ *s*		£ *s*		£ *s*	
Average instalment order	2 8		1 18		2 6		2 6	
Average judgment debt	11 4		26 4		23 14		42 2	
Average court costs	2 18		5 14		5 0		8 18	
Average amount recoverable	14 2		31 18		28 14		51 0	

* All orders are expressed as percentages.

in 1964 or 1965, but they were not. Two additional factors appear to be significant; the period of repayment is affected by the amount of coercion that is applied to the debtor, and it is also affected by the success of the coercive measures which are adopted.

This can be seen in Table 6.6 which shows that defaulters who paid their debts in 1964–5 received more coercion than those whose

TABLE 6.6 *Enforcement in E court of actions started in 1963*

	Dead in 1963 (N = 150)	*Dead in 1964–5* (N = 50)	*Dormant in 1966* (N = 150)	*Live in 1966* (N = 150)
	%	%	%	%
No execution and no judgment summons	46·6	14·0	30·0	6·0
Execution only	48·6	60·0	42·0	32·0
Judgment summons only	2·0	10·0	12·6	19·0
Execution and judgment summons	2·7	16·0	15·3	43·0
Totals	99·9	100·0	99·9	100·0

actions had fallen dormant. Whilst 14 per cent of the former group were not exposed to sanctions, 30 per cent of the dormant debtors encountered no control measures at all. The table also shows that, with the exception of the dormant actions, enforcement increases with the age of a debt. That is, unless a debt is recovered immediately, payments can be maintained only under repeated threats of punishment. Instalments are not effortlessly collected by a plaintiff. Indeed, most judgment debts in each group were subjected to some enforcement. Two-thirds of the plaints entered in E court (65·9 per cent) entailed the infliction of legal brutality. Those who are summoned before a county court for default will default again. The pessimistic argument I attributed to solicitors is sustained.*

* E court is a large county court situated in a working-class district but, for its size, it does not inflict an extraordinary number of sanctions. When size (as defined by the number of plaints entered in a year) is held constant, three of the twelve London courts issued execution warrants more frequently than E court in 1964. Similarly, three courts issued more judgment summonses in proportion than E court in the same year. Whilst E court made use of many warrants, it was by no means exceptionally punitive towards its debtors.

7 Execution

The history of a typical judgment debt is a long alternating sequence of defaults and threats. Legal control rests on a court's ability to frighten an erring defendant into obedience. The simple signing of judgment is no guarantee that a debt will be paid. 'The law works because its will prevails. . . . Judgment is a declaration of war. The arsenal of enforcements provides the means to wage that war successfully.' (Registrar of E court.) Similarly, the Final Report of the Evershed Committee (para. 399) observed that any system of enforcement must have a 'method which is extremely unpleasant to the judgment debtor'. In their conduct of the war, solicitors in the London courts avail themselves of remarkably few types of enforcement. Although they are offered charging orders on property, garnishee orders, bankruptcy, executions and judgment summonses, they overwhelmingly resort to executions and judgment summonses alone.

In part, their choice of weapons is constrained by their ignorance of the debtor and their unwillingness to devote time, thought or money to enforcement:

> It depends on the depth of consideration you're going to give to debt collection. We're back again to the question of costs. . . . (Solicitor 8.)

An order to garnishee permits a solicitor to seize a debtor's bank account or other assets and it is obviously misguided if the defaulter has nothing worth seizing. Garnishing has no place in routine enforcement because solicitors know very little about their debtors and are not prepared to learn more:

> With most debtors, one isn't sufficiently sure whether there's anything to garnishee. (Solicitor 7.)

The solicitor's distrust of any judgment debtor is another disincentive to attempt garnishee methods. The professional will not let his assets remain in any place long enough to be found by a plaintiff:

> Garnishee proceedings are very good if you can get the necessary information. The people who give you cheques which aren't honoured have a habit of going from bank to bank and branch to branch. You think you're lucky, you've got a cheque on X branch, and you go up and try garnishees and you discover there never was an account or it was transferred several months back. (Solicitor 8.)

Solicitors identify the stereotypical judgment debtor as a manual worker without a bank account or capital. Rather than misdirect their enforcement effort, most solicitors prefer to ignore garnishee techniques altogether. None of the 450 judgment debts that appeared in the E court sample entailed a charging or a garnishee order. Bankruptcy is similarly uncommon. A bankruptcy notice can issue only against a debt which is greater than £50 and, as Table 6.5 shows, it is thus seldom useful in the county court. Bankruptcy is thought to harbour no fears for the wage-earner and it is unlikely to lead to a satisfaction of the debt:

> I suppose one only goes for bankruptcy where bankruptcy will hurt. If the person's a rootless Nigerian who works for London Transport, it won't hurt him to go bankrupt. It won't have any effect at all. But if he's a company director, and can't be a company director if he's made bankrupt, it *does* hurt him and he'd rally round his family. (Solicitor 2.)

Abortive executions involve a solicitor in little work or cost; but injudicious bankruptcy proceedings can commit him to unusually tedious labour:

> It's an awful lot more trouble and more costly if they're not successful. (Solicitor 3.)

Moreover, bankruptcy might bring about the economic destruction of a debtor. Successive executions can wheedle small sums out of a defaulter until his debt is discharged, but bankruptcy can cause 'the whole building to cave in on the debtor'. (Solicitor 6.) Above all, poverty of information about a debtor does not allow solicitors to resort to bankruptcy as a routine measure. When a notice *is* sent, a solicitor normally intends to do nothing more than scare a debtor. The notice is inexpensive and it is 'the cheapest way of getting the debtor frightened'. (Solicitor 1.) As a result, a mere 1·1 per cent of the actions in the E court sample were taken to the High Court for bankruptcy proceedings. I shall therefore discuss executions and judgment summonses only.

A committal order is dependent on a judicial decision, but an execution warrant is not. The creditor is alone responsible for deciding whether the execution machinery should be set in motion. The warrant can be issued only when the defendant has defaulted on the judgment order, and it cannot issue for an amount less than the terms of the order itself. Agency solicitors are so sure that judgment debtors will default that they automatically apply for execution warrants when they sign judgment.

Creditors who secured orders for payment in one sum are constrained to issue warrants for 'full' execution, whilst those who had instalment orders made can enforce by 'full' or by 'part' warrants. A full warrant issues for the whole outstanding debt, but a part warrant is designed to recover the one or more instalments which have fallen into arrears. The smaller the initial order, the greater is the choice afforded a creditor, although it is a choice that narrows as the judgment debt nears satisfaction.

The full warrant is likely to lead to a more rapid recovery of the debt. It is, in any case, a cheap gambit which *might* have a happy outcome for the plaintiff:

> With a small debt I think you don't want to get bogged down in continuing judgment summonses and it's worth risking a few shillings or a pound or two to see if an execution which would finally dispose of the matter is likely to be successful. You do get people, of course, who pay out on the threat of an execution when the bailiff actually comes round. For what you might call medium-sized debts, one would have to think about it more carefully. For a very large debt, of course, where the outlay comes proportionately less in ratio to the debt, well it's often worth trying because you never know what might turn up! (Solicitor 6.)

If the warrant fails, the creditor will have gained a clearer idea of the resources of his quarry. The bailiff's report that a debtor has insufficient goods to meet the warrant can orient future enforcement. Indeed, warrants may be used as devices to obtain information about defaulters:[1]

[1] The Payne Committee (1969, para. 296, pp. 82–3) made much of the fact that the warrant is often used by ignorant creditors to obtain feedback: 'One would have thought it self-evident that there was every possible objection to proceeding with the enforcement of a money judgment against a debtor without first ascertaining what property, assets, earnings and means he has at his disposal. . . . And yet steps in enforcement are frequently taken before this information has been obtained and often as a means of obtaining the information itself. . . . Frequently applications for execution or for

> Most times, you don't know whether a man really owns his house or what. So the first thing you do is bring the bailiff in and try to get his goods and chattels. They do that pretty quickly if he's been a difficult person. You find that they all belong to his wife or are all on hire-purchase, you know, and then you have to think again. (Solicitor 5.)

The execution warrant can be an inexpensive substitute for an enquiry agent. It can also be a ritualized first feint in enforcement. If it is abortive, the plaintiff may abandon pursuit entirely or immediately proceed to the investigation of means and the coercion which a judgment summons hearing entails. When the bailiff's return states that the warrant *can* be satisfied, the creditor has two equally propitious choices: if the debtor does nothing, his goods are auctioned and the debt is discharged; if he applies for a suspension of the warrant on terms, the plaintiff can control him by threatening execution. A successful full warrant can be both punitive and efficacious. Creditors who surmise that debtors can afford to pay in a single amount also surmise that they have the means to meet one execution warrant.

The reasoning which is applied to the full warrant also holds good for the part warrant. A debtor who can only pay in instalments can only satisfy small warrants (Working Party Report, 1956, p. 17):

> If the debtor is a person without substantial assets which can be seized and is unlikely to be able to pay the full amount of the debt from one or two weekly wage packets (i.e., a typical county court debtor) the sensible creditor does not wish to issue execution for the full amount. He knows that he will not get paid out and will either get a return from the bailiff that the goods are not worth the cost of sale or a sale will take place which will bring in little to the creditor but cause a severe loss to and antagonize the debtor.

The part warrant is therefore less vulnerable to a *nulla bona* return and is more likely to bring about negotiations or sale. Successive part warrants can recoup sums which one full warrant could never recover. It is a cheap way of confronting a debtor with the legal brutality of social control (providing he has no time to take avoiding action):

> Executions are always a bit of a problem and I usually try to find out first whether the chap's in a house or in furnished

committal to prison under a judgment summons are made for the very purpose of ascertaining what property or assets are in the possession of the debtor or what is his salary, wage or other income. This is a singularly speculative method of enforcement and has serious objections.'

> premises. If possible, if that can be done, by me popping along there one evening . . . If it *is* a house, it's worth trying, although, again, it's not always very successful. But sometimes it is. You get this chap suddenly landing on your doorstep with a warrant and if it's the sort of debtor who hasn't been in this business before where he knows all he's got to say to a bailiff is 'well, all these things are on hire purchase' or alternatively 'all these things belong to my wife'. If he can be caught napping, it's the most successful way there is because it's all over in a flash and the money's into court and you're there. (Solicitor 3.)

If a debtor cannot meet even a small warrant for, say, two pounds, a creditor will know that enforcement will prove difficult if not impossible. In addition, it is thought by some[2] to be a more equitable mode of enforcement because it applies only a gentle pressure on a defaulter. Finally, it is extremely useful to agency solicitors because it is an unselective procedure. They can issue streams of part warrants without differentiating between their targets or knowing much about them:

> The creditors themselves are at fault inasmuch they know precious little about their debtors. They can't tell you whether a warrant's going to be any good or not unless they happen to be one of the firms that's decent. Creditors don't know what their debtors' circumstances are. (Solicitor 7.)

Table 7.1 shows that, although they are a minority group (having entered only 46·7 per cent of E court plaints in 1963), bureaucratic creditors not only exploit execution methods more fully, but also dominate the part warrants system.

It would follow that the bureaucratic creditors were under-represented in the groups of judgments which were paid quickly or abandoned. These groups involved more sizeable initial orders and executions which issued for larger amounts. Many of the debtors who owed money to the larger creditors might have been able to satisfy their judgments earlier, but they were subjected to indiscriminate techniques which were not sensitive enough to treat them as a special group. Table 7.2 describes these differences clearly. The bureaucratic creditors controlled the judgments which took a relatively long time to be paid, but they were outnumbered by smaller creditors in the groups of debts which were rapidly satisfied or foregone.

It should also follow that the smaller warrants have a higher

[2] The arguments for and against the system are put by the Working Party in para. 45, p. 17.

TABLE 7.1 *Bureaucratic* and other creditors' use of executions in E county court in 1963 (sample B)†*

	Full execution (N = 250)	*Part execution* (N = 250)
Bureaucratic creditors	49	133
Other creditors	44	24

* Bureaucratic creditors are the large companies, labelled 'professionals' by court staff, which include mail order firms, hire purchase firms, gas and electricity boards, and so on.

† Two samples are used in this analysis of executions. Sample A consists of 450 judgment debts entered in 1963 in E county court. Sample B is a special sample of 250 executions (including eleven deliveries) issued in the same court in the same year.

TABLE 7.2 *Repayments of creditors and sizes of execution warrants in E court in 1963 (sample A)*

	Proportions of creditors			
	1963	*1964–5*	*Dormant*	*Live*
		(N = 450)		
Bureaucratic creditors	44·3	64·0	40·0	64·0
Other creditors	55·7	36·0	60·0	36·0
Total	100·0	100·0	100·0	100·0
Mean sums on execution	£10 12*s.*	£6 0*s.*	£15 7*s.*	£7 2*s.*

TABLE 7.3 *Full and part warrants issued in 1963 in E court (sample B)*

	Full warrant	*Part warrant*
Proportions of total warrants*	35·6%	60·0%
Mean sums on execution	£21 0*s.*	£3 2*s.*
Proportions satisfied	60·0%	67·4%

* 4·4 per cent of the sample were warrants for the delivery of goods.

chance of being satisfied. In fact, the successfully executed warrants in sample B issued for an average sum of £5 12*s.*, those which were unsuccessful were for an average of £12 3*s.* Table 7.3 adds further support for this argument by showing that part warrants were more frequently used in E court and that, when they were used, they met with a greater degree of success.

Execution is the first and major mode of legal enforcement. Most judgment debtors are confronted with a succession of small warrants until an abortive return is made or the debt is paid. If execution fails, an action will be abandoned or taken on to the judgment summons stage. In the B sample, warrants employed against old judgment debts were conspicuously more successful than those used against recent ones. Table 7.4 demonstrates that, with the exception of

TABLE 7.4 *Age of judgments and success-rates of executions issued in 1963 (sample B)*

Date of issue of default summons	*Proportion of warrants paid*
%	%
1959 (1·2)	83·3
1960 (3·2)	50·0
1961 (15·9)	69·1
1962 (56·5)	59·9
1963 (23·2)	59·3
(N = 250)	

judgments entered in 1960, there is a pronounced tendency for executions against older debts to be paid in greater numbers. Warrants against recent judgments are directed at debtors who are unknown and untried.

Table 7.5 clarifies even more the patterns which enforcement by execution assumes in a county court. The bulk of the first executions in Table 7.5(a) were satisfied, but only a minority progressed on to second execution. Second executions were also satisfied. The fifty-five successful but solitary executions were presumably levied against debtors who were shocked into conformity. I assume that the shock engineered by bailiffs accounts for the few execution warrants that were issued. A second execution, like the first, can issue only after default and not many execution debtors in Table 7.5(a) seem to have defaulted again. The effect of execution threats in Table 7.5(b), however, does not appear to be shock. Instead, a stream of execution warrants becomes the main method of collection. Dormant judgments are patently invulnerable to the execution procedure. Execution cannot succeed when defaulters are elusive or too impoverished to offer substantial assets. These judgments either proceed to judgment

TABLE 7.5(a) *The relationship between the first and second execution for judgments obtained in 1963 and satisfied in that year (sample A)*

Second execution	*First execution*					
	a	b	c	d	e	f
a: No further execution	0	55	2	0	0	2
b: Satisfied	0	11	0	0	1	2
c: 'No goods'	0	1	1	0	0	0
d: 'Left—gone away'	0	1	0	0	0	0
e: Partially satisfied	0	0	0	0	0	0
f: Suspended	0	0	0	0	0	0

(Mean number of executions per execution debtor = 1·33)

TABLE 7.5(b) *The relationship between the first and second execution for judgments obtained in 1963 and satisfied in 1964–5 (sample A)*

Second execution	*First execution*					
	a	b	c	d	e	f
a: No further execution	0	5	11	1	0	2
b: Satisfied	0	29	0	3	0	0
c: 'No goods'	0	4	0	1	0	0
d: 'Left—gone away'	0	2	0	1	0	0
e: 'Stayed for a period'	0	1	0	0	0	0
f: Suspended	0	0	0	0	0	0

(Mean number of executions per execution debtor = 3·84)

TABLE 7.5(c) *The relationship between the first and second execution for judgments obtained in 1963 and which were not being enforced in 1966*

Second execution	*First execution*						
	a	b	c	d	e	f	g
a: No further execution	0	2	24	15	1	2	3
b: Satisfied	0	5	0	0	0	0	0
c: 'No goods'	0	4	3	2	0	1	0
d: 'Left—gone away'	0	2	0	2	0	3	0
e: 'Debtor not known'	0	0	0	0	0	0	0
f: Suspended	0	0	0	0	0	0	0
g: Debtor bankrupt	0	0	0	0	0	0	0

(Mean number of executions per execution debtor = 1·4)

summons or else they fall dormant immediately. The last Table, 7.5(d), is divided more or less equally between executions which were abortive and those which were not. The successful execution is successfully repeated. The other judgment debts are carried on to judgment summons hearings. Table 6.6 shows that live actions are enforced not so much by executions alone as by judgment summons.

TABLE 7.5(d) *The relationship between the first and second execution for judgments obtained in 1963 and still being enforced in 1966*

Second execution	*First execution*					
	a	b	c	d	e	f
a: No further execution	0	1	2	0	19	0
b: Satisfied	0	16	0	0	1	0
c: Abortive	0	0	0	0	0	0
d: 'Insufficient goods'	0	1	0	0	0	0
e: 'No goods'	0	4	0	0	1	0
f: Suspended	0	1	0	0	0	0

(Mean number of executions per execution debtor = 3·19)

The enforcement of warrants of execution

Committals seem to be regarded as sanctions of greater importance than executions. The committal order can be made only by a judge who has satisfied himself that a debtor wilfully refused to pay the judgment order. There is an elaborate system of checks and appeals which attempts to filter off all but the most recalcitrant 'commitment' debtors. Execution warrants, however, can automatically issue when a debtor defaults on a court order. They are supposed to serve the same threatening function as a committal order, yet they are not so carefully surrounded by mechanisms of negotiation. This disparity between the two sanctions might be explained by the facts that county courts are relatively sensitive to public criticism of imprisonment for debt;[3] that committal is the last stage of the

[3] A number of newspaper editorials, for example, have strongly condemned the place of imprisonment in debt collection, but I have not yet seen one which attacks execution. The London *Evening Standard* (24 May 1966) argues, 'there is no question that imprisonment for contempt is a fiction. Imprisonment for civil debt is still very much part of the British scene, even though it is often thought that with the passing of the Debtors' Act, 1869, the harsh days so graphically depicted by Dickens were gone forever. . . . Whatever ensues, the abolition of debtors' prisons is the essential step. When this happens the law on debts should at last be brought in line with modern

career and must be used judiciously; and that imprisonment is viewed as a more unpleasant sanction.

Nevertheless, in many cases it is possible that imprisonment is less onerous than execution.[4] Sentences are usually short; debtors seem able to neutralize adverse definitions of self, and the punishment generally ends with release. Execution, however, can denude a family of its possessions and create long-term problems:

> It will . . . be a mistake to suppose that enforcements against property cannot inflict greater hardship when successfully applied. . . . The home that has been carefully furnished over a period of years, presents a sad sight when stripped and sold for a song, leaving the debtor with the need to incur fresh debt to gather a few essential items about him. . . . As against this, successful commitment leaves the debtor untouched, albeit, a little poorer, but he cannot complain of that. . . . (Registrar of E court.)

Despite the misfortunes that can be caused by execution, effective communication between the court and debtor is not as carefully fostered as it is when imprisonment is imminent.

humanitarian thinking.' Similarly, the *Daily Mirror* (17 June 1966) states, 'what is the point of putting debtors in prison? Does prison deter them or help them or reform them? Is it meant to be punishment or rehabilitation? . . . Any liberal and reforming Home Secretary is up against archaic laws, narrow prejudice and illiberal entrenched attitudes. But Home Secretary Jenkins sounds as if he means business. His thinking is constructive. Like himself it belongs to the Twentieth Century, and not—like our grimmest prisons—to an age that has gone.' These editorials reflect trends in recent official thinking about the functions of imprisonment. In 1966, for instance, Lord Stonham observed that 'a prison sentence, however short, involves greater penalties than loss of liberty. . . . When we ask ourselves, if these extra inescapable punishments, when inflicted for minor crimes, bring a sufficiently worthwhile benefit to society at large, the answer must be no. For this reason, though offenders must be punished, we intend in specific fields, to substitute for prison, a system of treatment in freedom.' Lord Stonham then described alternative solutions which might be applied to the problems posed by drunks, epileptics, drug addicts, fine and debt defaulters, remanded prisoners, and first offenders. He continued, 'these changes, essential and beneficial in themselves, will, other things being equal, confer the added boon of a reduction of up to 15 per cent in prison population and a much bigger reduction in prison receptions . . .' (Address at the opening of the British Congress on Crime, 5 September 1966.) The Payne Committee (1969, para. 955, p. 246) were clearly aware of this when they wrote, 'social and economic changes which have occurred during the century which has elapsed since the passing of the Debtors Act 1869 make imprisonment for civil debt an outdated, often unjust and inappropriate method of enforcement.'

[4] Thus, the Payne Committee (1969, para. 630, p. 168) observe, execution 'is capable of occasioning greater hardship to the debtor and his family than most of the other methods since the goods seized and sold may comprise much of the home and contents'.

When an execution warrant is issued by a creditor, the registrar can warn the debtor by sending him a form similar to the Ex. 52 used in committal proceedings. His decision is structured by the way in which he classifies the execution debtor. The form will not be sent if he labels the defaulter a professional (General regulations for registrars, 1956, para. 39 (3)):

> In the case of warrants, Forms Ex. 50, 51 and 52 should be issued in the first instance particularly where a long journey by a bailiff is involved, but they should not be used in the case of large amounts, say, over £20, or in cases where past experience or knowledge of the debtor concerned makes it obvious that the issue of the form would be useless.

A creditor can hold the registrar personally responsible for an abortive full execution if the debtor was forewarned, but he is not responsible for unsuccessful part warrants. Form 160A[5] is thus sent selectively to debtors faced with part-execution. The form tells the debtor:

> As you have made default in payment as ordered by the Court in the above Action, the Plaintiff has issued a WARRANT OF EXECUTION for . . . If you bring this sum to the Court Office on or before . . . it will not be necessary for the bailiffs to call on you. If, however, the money is not paid by noon of that date, the Warrant will be handed to the Bailiffs to call upon you and to execute the warrant for the amount stated, together with such further costs as may become due.

Although solicitors and the plaintiffs they act for are certain that all execution debtors are confirmed professionals or feckless people, the registrar still employs a tripartite typology at this stage. He is, moreover, unsure about his ability to label debtors. He establishes one testing system by relying on the results of instalment orders but, since so many judgment debtors default, it is an inexact method of discriminating between the unfortunate, the feckless and the professional. Registrars therefore rarely commit themselves when they send out Forms 160A. Only three of the 157 part-execution debtors of Sample B were unwarned. The remainder were subjected to the characteristic opening phases of a collection stage.

The bailiffs are brought into action if the defaulter does not pay the warrant or have it suspended within seven days of receiving 160A. In the overwhelming majority of cases, further enforcement was necessary. The bailiffs had to proceed against 151 debtors. Their initial enforcement is split into two phases: they must enter

[5] Form 160A was instituted in 1957 to replace Forms Ex. 50 and 51.

the debtors' homes, and they must discover whether they have enough goods to justify execution. Both these phases of the levying stage are complex. Although a bailiff does not have to encounter the execution debtor personally, he must gain an entrance into his house. Table 7.6 shows that over a third (37·4 per cent) of enforcements were complicated by difficulties at this point.

TABLE 7.6 *First returns on warrants of execution issued in 1963 (sample B)*

Bailiff's return	*Full warrants*	*Part warrants*	*Total*
No entry	7	9	16
No entry (first attempt)— no goods (second attempt)	6	3	9
Return in 14 days—no entry	5	0	5
Not at address given	0	4	4
Debtor left and new address	2	1	3
Defendant is denied at the address	0	3	3
Only visits occasionally	1	1	2
No entry—appointment—suspension	1	0	1
	22	21	43
Sent to foreign court*	36	99	135
Other types of return	25	47	72
			250

* Actions need not be entered at a debtor's local court in London, but they must be enforced in his 'home' court.

A bailiff is not legally entitled to break into a house at the levying stage. Although he is often overcome by the problem of gaining access to a debtor's goods, he does minimize it by resorting to a number of ingenious techniques. A D court bailiff, for example, told me that he was 'up to all their dodges'. He stressed that he could conduct himself so that he would not be accused of impropriety; he could outmanoeuvre debtors who were evading him; he could cope with dogs and so on.[6] He also claimed that he could recognize signs which indicated that people were in a house although they were anxious to convey the opposite impression. He could ascertain what parts of a building were occupied and by which types of people.

[6] Dogs are enticed to the back of a house with meat by one bailiff whilst his colleague levies in the front.

He could gauge the reliability of informants. All these skills are essential parts of the expertise which bailiffs must acquire during their apprenticeships in the police force and county court.[7] Recurring problems find places in the culture of the Bailiffs' Room and are matched with stock solutions. A bailiff who did not avail himself of this accumulated wisdom would make too many abortive returns.

If a bailiff suspects that an elusive debtor has secreted himself in a dwelling, he can attract his attention by patterns of knocks or whistles which are calculated to trigger off an interested response. He may imitate a postman by calling out 'Post!' or a friend by knocking in an informal way. Once he has managed to enter the execution debtor's home, the ensuing interaction is not difficult for him. The bailiff is merely required to draw up an inventory of goods which would be suitable for execution. He is not expected to remove the goods or intimidate the defendant. The paternalistic role which he characteristically adopts can cope with most contingencies.[8]

A bailiff can predict and counter many of the debtor's reactions to the levying situation. Shock, indignation or suspicion can all be dispelled by a cool, authoritative and, above all, continuous patter of talk. This interaction can be useful to the bailiff. If the debtor is unfamiliar to the court, further enforcement will be oriented by the impressions gained during levying. Very often, however, the bailiff will not meet the debtor at all until the goods are actually seized.

There are three distinct restraints on the goods which can be selected for removal. The first is legal: a bailiff cannot seize 'the wearing apparel and bedding of (the debtor) or his family, and the tools and implements of his trade, to the prescribed value [£50].' (County Courts Act, 1959, sec. 124.) The bailiffs may be faced by empirical problems of what a family is, or what tools and implements of trade are, but these legal restrictions are not of great importance. A more significant restraint is that the bailiff can only levy on goods which belong to the debtor. Objects owned by others, including hire purchase companies and other members of the defaulter's family, are exempt. The responsibility lies with the court or creditor to prove that these disowned goods are, in fact, the debtor's. As High Bailiff, the registrar has a duty to

> ascertain what goods belong to the debtor and seize such goods as he believes do so belong. If he fails to seize goods belonging to the debtor, he may be liable in damages to the creditor. On

I spoke to several police officers who maintained that these techniques were all commonplace in the police force. They argued that the methods were evolved by the police and owed nothing to the peculiar skill of bailiffs.

8 For a description of the way in which the relations between social control agents and others tend to become tinged by some amiability and mutual support, see Cumming, Cumming and Edell, 1965, esp. p. 277.

> the other hand if he seizes goods belonging to third parties he may be liable in damages to them. In practice he can escape from this dilemma by seizing goods whose ownership is doubtful and passing the onus of dealing with the claim to the execution creditor . . . but he should clearly make enquiries through his bailiff before doing so. (Working Party Report, 1956, p. 25.)

In 1964, however, there were only forty-six such cases of adjudication ('interpleader actions') in London. The astute debtor can completely upset the execution procedure by disclaiming any seizable possessions. The average creditor seems to dislike the complexities of interpleaders so much that he will not dispute the debtor's contentions.

Second, selection is based upon an assessment of the market situation. It is not only the debt that has to be recovered through execution: auctioneers normally receive 12½ per cent of the money raised in a sale; and court costs and solicitors' costs have also to be met. The goods detailed in a levy must be valuable enough to cover all these expenses. In addition, auctioneers may not be prepared to deal in certain goods[9] whilst other objects are in little demand. Execution goods which remain unsold after three successive auctions are returned to the debtor. The aims of execution can again be upset by levying on the wrong kinds of possession. Bailiffs must become familiar with the marketability of goods and apply that knowledge during levy. They regularly attend auctions in order to gain this information. When seizure actually takes place, it is customary in some courts for an auctioneer's representative to check the bailiff's appraisal. Nevertheless, his checks cannot radically affect the execution because a bailiff can remove only the items which he selected at the levy.

The final restraint is formed by the culture of the court. A debtor may own enough to merit execution, but the sanction would constitute an 'unjust' hardship to him. It might involve removing all he owns; or selling vital objects which are unlikely to fetch much at a sale (Law Commission, 1966, p. 10):

> On account of the disproportionately low second-hand value of goods today, a family could lose all its possessions in satisfying a minimal debt. Clearly, the second-hand value of such things as washing machines, radio and T.V. sets . . . bears no relation to their cost when new.

[9] It may, indeed, be difficult to engage an auctioneer at all: 'In some courts there is great difficulty in finding an auctioneer willing to conduct a sale. Court sales are not popular with auctioneers as the goods may have to be withdrawn at the last moment if the debtor pays, which halves their fee and disappoints their customers.' (Working Party Report, 1956, para. 78, p. 26.)

Registrars may thus limit the range of items which their bailiffs are permitted to seize. In winter, for example, it is unlikely that heating apparatus will be levied on. The bailiffs themselves may define what is suitable for execution. Although a creditor can put pressure on a court if he feels that bailiffs are being tardy in implementing the warrant, he cannot dictate the style or objects of execution. Bailiffs do not have to justify their returns and 'the decision whether to seize or not is entirely the court's'. ('Dobb's Dilemmas', 1965, p. 174.) Bailiffs' choices are shaped by their relations with debtors; their classification of execution debtors; by their notions of what is essential; by their expectations of the likely consequences of seizure; and by their ideas of the connection between the 'real' worth of an object and its auction value. They therefore apply, amongst other criteria, the concept of the 'just price'. The last cultural factor is also the most important: certain types of execution can be very damaging to a bailiff's conception of himself. The warrant officer role is based on fundamental ideas of dignity, authority and prestige. It is not enhanced when, as one bailiff told me, it entails 'removing every scrap of lino from a poor bloke's home'. The bailiff does not like to see himself as a brutal oppressor of the poor or as an agent of malicious creditors. He defends the value of the warrant officer role by selecting possessions and execution debtors that will not undermine his self-definition.[10] This distinction between warrant officer and process server is not at all dissimilar to the gulf that divides the law officer and the peace officer in the police force (Banton, 1964, p. 7):

> A division is becoming apparent between specialist departments within police forces . . . and the ordinary patrolmen. The former are 'law officers' whose contacts with the public tend to be of a punitive or inquisitory character, whereas the patrolmen . . . are principally 'peace officers' operating with the moral consensus of the community. Whereas the former have occasion to speak chiefly to offenders or to persons who can supply information about an offense, the patrolmen interact with all sorts of people and more of their contacts center upon assisting citizens than upon offenses.

Warrant officers execute warrants whilst process servers distribute court summonses and cajole debtors. Bailiffs who valued their service in the police force may want to perpetuate the 'law officer'–'peace officer' distinction. The law officer role endows its occupant with more authority and significance. It would be besmirched if it

10 A bailiff of L court, for example, told me that he would warn an execution debtor about the malice of his creditor if he felt that unjust motives impelled the issuing of the execution warrant.

were transformed into the debt-collector role, a stigmatized role which involves the subservient and routine collection of paltry sums.

Even if a bailiff discovers a debtor with goods, there may be further complexities. He is in competition with other enforcement officers who may pre-empt him. Rate bailiffs, rent bailiffs, Inland Revenue bailiffs and sheriff's officers may all be seeking to levy on the same goods. It is inevitable that many execution warrants are abandoned at the levying stage. Table 7.7 shows that 44·3 per cent of the first returns made by a bailiff indicated that a warrant could not be satisfied.

TABLE 7.7 *First returns on warrants of execution issued in E court in 1963 (sample B)*

Bailiff's return	*Full warrant*	*Part warrant*	*Total*
No goods	10	26	36
Goods claimed by High Court Sheriff	1	0	1
No entry (first attempt)— No goods (second attempt)	6	3	9
No goods—prior warrants	1	0	1
Defendant bankrupt	2	0	2
Defendant has ceased trading and has no goods	1	0	1
Defendant claims that goods are on hire purchase	0	1	1
	21	30	51
Sent to foreign court	36	99	135
Other types of return	26	38	64
Total	83	167	250
	(N = 250)		

A bailiff may meet with greater success if the creditor applies for the warrant to be re-issued, but too few goods seem to be a decisive criterion. Only 16 of the 250 warrants in the B sample were re-issued.

When a bailiff has completed a successful levy, he leaves a notice at the debtor's home. The notice contains detailed statements about the costs and so on which are involved in an execution, but it does not mention the way in which the warrant can be suspended. The execution stage is inexplicably anomalous because it makes almost no attempt to guide a debtor back into obedience to his creditor.

Enforcement entails a sophisticated manipulation of threats and county court sanctions also 'primarily operate as threats'. (Working Party Report, 1956, p. 6.) A normal stage, moreover, is heralded by repeated warnings and the debtor is given abundant opportunities to escape punishment by resuming payments or negotiating. A solitary warning received by a special group (part execution debtors) is extremely unusual:

> When we are dealing with commitments, we are at pains, at every stage, even after imprisonment, to tell the debtor of his right to apply for stay. However, one will search in vain for any indication of the debtor's right to apply for stay, in any document handed to him in connection with a warrant of execution. . . . We are bad at communication. (Registrar of E court.)

Levied goods are tantamount to seized goods and it is an offence to move them or obstruct their removal by the court. The court might attempt to safeguard them by resorting to a device called 'walking possession'.[11] In this case, a bailiff will try to persuade the execution debtor to sign a form granting him walking possession. The debtor's consent nominally frees him from the 'possession man' who would become in 'close possession' of the goods. In fact, 'possession man' is not a role adopted by the London bailiffs. The consent may lead to an acknowledgment that the debtor has agreed to ultimate seizure, but he does not have to agree before execution can take place and it does not afford the bailiff much of an advantage in law.

At least five days must elapse between levy and sale but, in practice, the interval has lengthened:

> I could instruct bailiffs, 'With every warrant, you will levy at once. . . . If you are not paid in full, hand your warrant to the supervising bailiff, and he will arrange to move after 5 days.' I should be right. I should also immediately lose all my bailiffs. The one thing you must never do with a warrant of execution is to treat it as a warrant of execution, unless the circumstances are exceptional. (Registrar of E court.)

County court warrants are not defined as instructions to commit a debtor or sell his goods. Their aim is to place a defaulter under a compulsion to pay the money he owes. The most uncommon result

[11] 'A signed agreement to the effect that, in consideration of the bailiff not remaining in close possession of the goods seized, he should be allowed to re-enter at any time with force if necessary amounts in law to a seizure of the goods.' Notes on Section 124 of the County Courts Act, 1959, in *The County Court Practice*, 1963, p. 170.

of an execution warrant is the sale of goods, as Table 7.8 shows. Sale is so infrequent that it is virtually insignificant.

Even the vigorous enforcement staff of D court allowed 98·8 per cent of warrants to progress without an auction. The warrant of execution gives rise to an elaborate process of negotiation, control and interaction. It is no more a sanction which must be used than any of its predecessors.[12]

Bailiffs are responsible for carrying on these transactions between court and debtor. Their responsibility stems, in part, from the interval that occurs between levy and removal. During that time, they are required to cajole, threaten and inform the execution debtor. The part they play has been given no official sanction and is surrounded by ambiguity. It has been condemned by a number of court officials:

> It removes judicial control and, indeed, transfers judicial discretion from the judiciary to the bailiff, who is not equipped, by education and training, to exercise it. (Registrar of E court.)

TABLE 7.8 *Executions and sales in the London courts in 1964*

Court	*Number of execution warrants issued*	*Execution warrants issued as a percentage of plaints entered*	*Sales made*	*Sales made as a percentage of warrants issued*
A	6,435	86·7	32	0·5
B	7,153	40·0	11	0·3
C	8,375	51·2	27	0·2
D	14,733	77·4	178	1·2
E	19,678	79·2	79	0·4
F	19,372	118·9	19	0·9
G	12,024	53·6	16	0·1
H	11,006	60·2	4	0·04
I	5,544	33·0	18	0·3
J	11,784	62·9	74	0·6
K	15,199	73·1	8	0·06
L	8,379	63·2	5	0·06
Total	139,682	66·6	471	0·34

12 The Payne Committee (1969, para. 635, p. 169) observed, for instance, 'there can be no doubt that the effectiveness of execution as a mode of enforcement rests in the threat to sell, which exerts a powerful inducement on the debtor to avoid a sale by raising the sum required . . . and so avoiding the hardship which would otherwise follow.'

The Austin-Jones Committee were surprised at its occurrence (Committee on County Court Procedure, 1949, p. 26):

> It was suggested that a bailiff sometimes allows the debtor time to pay. No bailiff should be permitted to do this without express authority of the judge or registrar. . . . It would not in our opinion be right in any circumstances for the bailiff to refrain from levying under a warrant of execution.

A later committee, however, qualified this sentiment by stating (Working Party Report, 1956, p. 24):

> If this was . . . only intended to mean that a bailiff should always levy on the first occasion he obtains entry we fully agree with it, but clearly a bailiff must exercise some discretion . . . in deciding how much further time should elapse before the goods are removed for sale, and the Registrar cannot be consulted in every case.

A bailiff has thus been unwillingly given some licence to control the timing and style of execution. The absence of formal warnings gives rise to an unofficial delegation of the court's threatening function. Timing, in particular, is subject to the bailiff's decision. The court's culture provides him with a guide to assessing a 'reasonable' interval between levy and removal. A supervising bailiff of D court, for example, told me that the minimum period of five days was all the time that should be extended to an execution debtor. His colleagues, however, did not subscribe to his view and he felt constrained to give debtors slightly more time.

Interactions between the bailiff and debtor at this stage seem to pass through discernible stages. Initially, bailiffs are expected to use persuasion before they apply force. 'We like to be humane here. In fact, we're *encouraged* to be humane.' (Interview with a bailiff of Marylebone County Court in 'Is he looking for you?', *Nova*, January 1967, p. 18.) Bailiffs and debtors may have known one another for years and relationships which were originally secondary in nature can become marked by a certain amount of informality and reciprocity. Indeed, bailiffs and debtors may have known each other before in the roles of policeman and offender. The Senior Bailiff of G court, for instance, told me with some pride that he had been invited by a number of debtors to their sons' *barmitzvahs*. He felt that he could accept without compromising his position because the debtors were either unfortunates who would not meet him in his warrant officer role, or else they were roguish professionals who identified enforcement as a 'game' whose rules entitled him to be punitive at a later stage. Amiability does not only grow because close, regular contacts cannot remain formal for very long;[13] it is also fostered because bailiffs find it useful in enforcement, and because debtors hope that it will benefit them too. The moral consensus exploited by debt-collectors is thus resurrected by court staff.

Friendly relations are only one of the courses that bailiff–debtor interaction can take. It is possible that the bailiff will find himself unable to feel any warmth towards the defendant. Similarly, the debtor may dislike the bailiff and take evasive action when a meeting is likely. Transactions can develop into hostilities, secondary deviation can emerge, and executions will not be postponed at all. Certain debtors may arouse a court's especial dislike after a long period of time. One of D court's most unpopular debtors was forced by a stratagem to serve consecutive sentences although almost all county court terms of imprisonment are served *concurrently*. The debtor was released from Holloway Prison at the expiration of one sentence, she was met at the gate by bailiffs and immediately returned to prison on another warrant. Unfamiliar debtors who become defined as deviant are unlikely to be the objects of such elaborate planning.

In most cases, however, debtors are not labelled professionals. The bonds between the two place some obligation on the bailiff to delay removal of the goods. These bonds are rarely ones of genuine or deep liking. Cordiality may be feigned by both but it may be useful to both. A joking relationship certainly removes much of the tension latent in such a situation. The bailiff's delay can alleviate his anxiety at the debtor's inevitable distress. He can draw upon the rhetorical capital which it provides. He may argue that execution is not a result of the court's brutality, but of the debtor's reluctance to pay or suspend the warrant. Delay, moreover, is a constant feature of all enforcement processes.

Several factors curtail the period of grace offered to an execution debtor. First, a bailiff invariably applies his own serial testing system. Debtors defined by a bailiff as co-operative are usually granted an extension of the five-day period. They can demonstrate their 'reasonableness' by satisfying the warrant or having it suspended on terms. If they do neither, their co-operation will become less and less apparent as time passes. Rational excuses for inertia become progressively exhausted. The bailiff's notions of sensible behaviour and its connection with time impose an automatic limit on the probationary period given to debtors. Once that limit has been reached, no 'reasonable' person can be left vulnerable to execution proceedings. Any further postponement of action is useless because only

[13] An excellent fictional account of such friendly relations between bailiff and debtor is given in Story, 1966, pp. 112–16.

feckless and professional debtors have remained inactive. The bailiff's timetable thus mechanically categorizes defaulters.

Not only does the bailiff's definition of the debtor change over time, his definition of self also changes. A bailiff regards the regular harassment of debtors for petty sums of money as a tedious, time-consuming and degrading task. He feels that these tasks can dwarf his warrant officer role into the inferior role of debt-collector. When this threat is present, execution will be enforced and the dignity of his warrant officer role will be re-asserted. A bailiff's need to affirm his status thus sets a further limit on delay.

Furthermore, a bailiff depends on his superiors for continuing employment and promotion. He must therefore demonstrate his efficiency. As an execution warrant ages, he becomes exposed to mounting pressures which demand action on his part. Senior bailiffs, chief clerks, registrars and, indirectly, creditors may all become impatient with the slow progress of an action. The bailiff must respond to these pressures because he is a subordinate; he is dependent; and he ranks low in what Becker (1967) calls a 'hierarchy of credibility'. He may have his own understanding of the proper way to execute warrants, but he is constrained to act in accord with his superiors' conceptions of enforcement behaviour. Pressures can also emanate from a bailiff's equals. Each court prescribes a desirable work load for its bailiffs, and officers who fall short of these quotas will be suspected of incompetence or laziness. The fear that colleagues believe he is not doing his 'fair share' can be a powerful motive to act. Old warrants which are outstanding against tested and failed debtors are natural targets for this kind of enforcement.

The forces that define the timing of execution tend to act upon one another in concert. A levying stage must ultimately end in payment, stay or seizure of goods. Seizure has attendant enforcement problems which frequently worry bailiffs; it is one of a number of difficult work situations which demand special skills. The situations are difficult because they are fraught with uncertainty for a bailiff and might well have unpleasant outcomes for him. Bailiffs respond by evolving preventive strategies aimed at minimizing the risks which they face. The strategies rely on information-control, impression-management and complicated role-playing. Through them, a bailiff hopes to render a potentially dangerous debtor malleable by defining the situation for him in terms amenable to social control. I shall discuss the formation of these strategies at length in Chapters 9 and 10, and I do not want to repeat myself then. Some of them, however, are called into being by certain peculiarities of execution which ought to be described.

Execution has three distinguishing features: it is abrupt and sudden; it violates a debtor's 'material self'; and it is carried out by a bailiff who has had little time to establish his authority. There is abundant ritual to signify that the judgment summons hearing is an important stage of transition, but the execution warrant issues without ceremony. It occurs early in a debtor's career and its imminence is poorly heralded. The Assistant to the Head of the County Courts Branch attributed the number of assaults by execution debtors to the little warning which they had been given. Professional debtors will have been especially ignored by formal and informal processes of warning. A face-to-face confrontation with social control can be particularly shocking when the debtor is unprepared.

The removal of a debtor's possessions can also be most disturbing. Not only does it entail an invasion by outsiders of a person's 'private places' (cf. Stinchcombe, 1963, p. 18); it also means a denuding of the 'material me'. Doors and walls are conventional boundaries which mark off personal spaces from public places. Uninvited intrusions break down a debtor's sense of privacy and security. They destroy established understandings about the meaning of property. Intrusion has aggravated consequences when its aim is to strip a person of his possessions (James, 1963, p. 168):

> Although it is true that a part of our depression at the loss of possessions is due to our feeling that we must now go without certain goods that we expected the possessions to bring in their train, yet in every case there remains, over and above this, a sense of the shrinkage of our personality, a partial conversion of ourselves to nothingness, which is a psychological phenomenon by itself.

Debtors may also doubt the bailiff's right to act at all because the legitimacy of his authority has not always been accepted at this stage. The bailiff's power is symbolized only by the warrant which he holds and widespread public ignorance about his role cannot but complicate executions. In B court, for example, a trial was held of an execution debtor who had assaulted a bailiff. The registrar reported (Registrar's report, October 1960):

> Mr —— (the defendant). Did not realize Mr —— (the bailiff) was from the B County Court. Did not know he was a Bailiff and in any case did not know what a Bailiff was . . .
>
> Judge. 'It seems to me that the Defendant may not have understood that Mr —— was from the local County Court. . . . It seems to me that "I am from the local County Court" may be misinterpreted in many ways.'

An index of the difficulty encountered in an enforcement situation is the incidence of violence engendered by a particular mode of enforcement. Between 1960 and late 1966, several million enforcements were prosecuted by the London courts. Yet there were only sixty cases of assaults on London bailiffs reported to the County Courts Branch during that period. Although this figure is probably the peak of a small iceberg of violent incidents, it is clear that assaults are not very common. Recorded assaults are, in fact, so infrequent that they have almost no meaning when they are expressed as percentages of actions enforced by the courts. Represented in this way, it is apparent that executions are rather less dangerous procedures than evictions or committals. Table 7.9 shows that executions rank rather low in the hierarchy of risky enforcements.

TABLE 7.9 *Assaults on London bailiffs in 1964*

Warrants and summonses issued by the London county courts		*Number of assaults occurring during each type of enforcement*	*Assaults per 100,000 enforcements*
Service of default summonses	181,132	1	0·6
Executions	139,682	5	3·6
Deliveries*	9,482	3	31·6
Committals	5,319	2	37·6
Evictions	727	1	137·5

* Delivery and execution are similar in form and substance. Warrants of delivery for hire purchase goods issue for the return of goods which debtors have refused to pay for or hand over.

Despite the infrequency of reported violence, there are a great many encounters which *threaten* violence. In some courts, the idea of possible assault looms large in a bailiff's life. It affects his behaviour and is therefore important. In D court, for example, one of the bailiffs I accompanied often warned me that 'this next one will be a difficult case'. His counterpart in the American police force seems to respond to his work in the same way (Skolnick, 1966, pp. 45–6):

> The policeman, because his work requires him to be occupied continually with potential violence, develops a perceptual shorthand to identify certain kinds of people as symbolic assailants, that is, persons who use gesture, language, and attire that the policeman has come to recognize as a prelude

> to violence. This does not mean that violence by the symbolic assailant is necessarily predictable. On the contrary, the policeman responds to the vague indication of danger suggested by appearance. Like the animals of the experimental psychologist, the policeman finds the threat of random damage more compelling than a predetermined and inevitable punishment.

Execution debtors are symbolic assailants who threaten violence in one of the difficult situations confronted by bailiffs. Whilst executing, bailiffs employ the techniques which are characteristic of these situations: a preliminary tapping of the court's culture; social typing and adaptive role-playing (*Nova*, January 1967):

> See, in this job you don't go at things like a bull at a gate. Oh no. You always start out on a light foot. If you don't know the client, you make a little inquiry first, see what I mean? Always somebody knows. We talk here in the Bailiff's Room—I might say, 'I've got a Warrant of Execution here for a Mrs So-and-so, anyone know her?' and ten to one another bailiff says, 'Oh yes, you want to watch her, she's an awkward customer, that one.' So you know what kind of attitude to take, see what I mean?

Execution must pass through a number of defined stages. A bailiff may have found it difficult to enter a debtor's home when he was engaged in levying, and this obstruction can resurrect itself when he tries to remove the goods. The Working Party Report (1956, p. 26) comments:

> The law on the subject is complicated. . . . It was clear to us that bailiffs rarely broke in and the Department certainly does not encourage it.

The law allows a bailiff to break into a house in certain situations, but it denies him this right when he most needs it. He is given powers when he is inside the house but little authority when he is outside it. If he is expelled from the house or leaves under threat of violence, he can forcibly re-enter it. Nevertheless, a bailiff is fairly impotent in execution situations:

> There are far too many warrants brought to abortive conclusions by the return, 'Unable to enter' . . . We really must make up our minds whether warrants of execution against goods are a serious enforcement procedure which we intend to bring to conclusion, or whether they are mere opportunities for debtors to enjoy fun and games at the bailiff's expense. (Registrar of E court.)

This barrier to access is a prime example of the bailiff's weakness and the problems it presents. A bailiff may acknowledge his impotence and put in a final return of 'Unable to enter', or he may arrogate to himself privileges which he is not entitled to enjoy. This is a critical decision: bailiffs seem to be polarized into people who accept, albeit resentfully, their weaknesses; and those who overcome them by illicit means. When a bailiff of D court was told by an execution debtor that she would 'call the law in', he replied 'I am the law'. He meant not only that he was a properly accredited officer of the court, but also that he felt he was empowered to take any steps he considered appropriate. Tough courts must support the licence assumed by their bailiffs. Indeed, they may do so to such an extent that the illegal behaviour becomes overt. Thus, I observed two instances of illegal entry into a debtor's home in the course of one morning's executing.

As soon as a bailiff confronts the execution debtor, he is anxious to establish a personal mastery over the situation. He will parry potentially dangerous responses by adopting a cool, authoritative and paternalistic manner. He attempts to conceal any feelings of anxiety or animus he may hold. A bailiff hopes to avoid friction by forcing the debtor into a subordinate, child-like role; by removing the goods quickly and unostentatiously; and by acting so quickly and smoothly that the debtor is given no time to appreciate what is happening to him. He may achieve this by talking continuously and reassuringly: 'Good morning. Mrs ——? May I come in? I'm from the D county court. I've got a warrant here to seize your goods. May we look round? Bill [the auctioneer's representative], will you come in? What's down on the list? Where's the stove, love?' This patter was employed by a bailiff who labelled his ability 'conning'. He felt that it was an occupational skill which should be cultivated as much as possible, and he would rehearse it in unusual contexts. When, for example, he had decided to allow a debtor further time before execution, he would try to extract the costs of the warrant from him. No other bailiff I accompanied essayed such an act. The D bailiff would recite: 'There's a small matter of a guinea [or two guineas]. As you know, we've gone to a lot of trouble getting here. We've hired a van, and you know how expensive that is, thirty-five shillings an hour. The true charge should be three guineas, but I'm only going to ask for one . . .' He told me that his colleagues at the court were most amused that he asked for guineas, but he believed it sounded 'more professional'.

If a debtor is still 'difficult', a bailiff must rely on his capacity to impress him with his authority. He will fully exploit the fact that he is a warrant officer of a county court with a legal mandate to execute. If the debtor remains uncowed, a bailiff has powers under

Sections 30 and 127 of the County Courts Act, 1959, to arrest him and bring him before the judge for summary trial. His powers are only available when the judge is sitting and the bailiff may have to return with police officers to execute the warrant. Alternatively, he may rely on overt bullying or violence.

Goods taken in execution are normally lodged at the court for a while until they are removed to the salesrooms. A debtor may retrieve them at any stage before they are actually sold. In London, the auctioneers of execution goods tend to have links with a number of county courts. I attended, for example, a sale which was 'by order of the D, A, J, Q and R County Courts, Trustee Department of the —— Banks Ltd, Executors and others'. The auctioneer at that sale disposed of lots at the rate of a hundred an hour. The prices fetched by some lots illustrate the difficulties faced by bailiffs at the levying stage.[14] A lot containing 'a triple mirror dressing chest, chest of drawers, pedestal cabinet, and four foot six inches sprung interior overlay faulty' was sold for 15*s*. Similarly, a 'painted table, ironing board, folding tea trolley, pair of steps and Lloyd Loom chair' were purchased for 10*s*. The connection between court and auction was not underlined except when the auctioneer said, 'now, by order of our friend, the bailiff . . .'.

[14] It does, of course, also illustrate that executions can have very uneconomic results. The fact is that sales are mainly intended to lend credibility to threats. In 1964, for instance, a mere 0·34 per cent of execution warrants led to a sale. It is clear that they were not meant to be implemented. Poor returns at the stage of auction do not undermine the overall intention of the execution procedure.

8 The judgment summons hearing and committal orders

Debt collection before the judgment summons hearing revolves around unofficial definitions of the defaulter. Enforcers classify debtors into three groups and treat each group differently. Each stage inherits the professional and feckless debtors of its predecessor and expands the typology to include unfortunates. All previous stages are stamped by dualistic notions of social control; the professional may be a dishonest or obstinate person but he can be the concern only of a group of private citizens. Some of those citizens would like to reformulate this conception of the problem:

> The notorious debtor is dishonest, he is out to get something for nothing. There are a few who are obviously psychologically maladjusted, but one knows so little about the debtor that it's difficult to say that. But I would say that the great majority of them are dishonest, and that in other countries they would probably find themselves in prison long before, because they're obtaining goods by false pretences. They've no intention of paying for these goods at the time of ordering them. Very often they admit as much to you in private. (Solicitor 11.)

All the same, enforcement before the hearing is organized by the belief that collection should adjust relations between individuals. The debtor is of no interest to the 'state' or 'society'. When a default action is heard, for instance, a registrar is merely required to decide whether a creditor is legally entitled to claim a debt and, if he is, how he should be repaid. The judgment summons hearing introduces a qualitative change into the collection system. It entails an official pronouncement about whether the defaulter has been judged a deviant or not. Enforcement is completely lifted out of the private sphere and taken over by the representative of a wronged state.

The system is thus governed by both types of social control (Jenkins, 1953):

> It is no doubt true that from a judgment creditor's point of view the summons affords a means of enforcing payment of his debt; but in law the issue is not whether the court should take measures to enforce payment of the debt for the benefit of the judgment creditor; but whether (on proof of means and default) the judgment debtor merits punishment in the form of committal for his refusal or neglect to comply with the judgment or order. The function of the judgment creditor is to bring the facts to the notice of the court. Once that is done, the issue is between the court and the debtor.

The hearing, then, is aimed at discovering whether a debtor's default on a judgment order was wilful or not. Deliberate disobedience to the registrar is construed as an affront to the court, not the creditor. When this definition is rephrased, the significance of the hearing becomes more apparent. If a debtor has not obeyed a court judgment, the creditor must demonstrate to a judge that the debtor had, in fact, the means to pay the debt and that further enforcement is still justified. Greig (1964, p. 178), for example, argues:

> Where, owing to the defendant possessing no distrainable effects, there is no possibility of enforcing a judgment by way of an execution, the law throws upon the plaintiff the onus of proving, to the satisfaction of the judge, that the defendant has the means to pay.

Greig's statement can be further rephrased so that the most common understanding of the hearing emerges. This understanding stresses the value of the suspended committal order which may stem from the hearing. A person who has been categorized as a wilful or contumacious debtor may be forced to adhere to a court's orders under threat of imprisonment. A hearing is therefore usually defined as just another, and more punitive stage of enforcement:

> In the lifetime of nearly every judgment debt, being recovered by small warrants, there comes the time when the debtor digs in his toes and will not pay more. There are never any goods to seize. Rock bottom has been reached. To recover more, resort must be made to judgment summons. . . . The Debtors Act provides a means for overcoming his reluctance. (Registrar of E court.)

Although the hearing provides a creditor with a fresh power to coerce the debtor, plaintiffs and solicitors both seem to dislike it intensely. The Working Party (1956, para. 85) observed:

> Our recommendations with regard to judgment summonses are made on the basis of the onus (of proving means and wilful default) remaining on the creditor. It must, however, be realised that on that basis the judgment summons is bound to put the creditor to expense and give the debtor considerable opportunity for evasion and delay. Enforcement by this method will only be used if other methods fail.

The summons itself instructs the debtor to 'show cause why you should not be committed to prison for . . . default', but it is the creditor who must persuade the court.[1] Thus the Law Society observed:

> Judgment summonses have proved to be the source of the majority of complaints received from the profession abundantly confirming what was already known to the Council themselves. One main point on which complaint has been made is the present procedure under which the onus is on the creditor to prove that the debtor has or has had the means to pay the amount ordered but has failed to do so.

The creditor finds proof of means and contumacy difficult to obtain, and, when he does obtain it, it may not satisfy a judge. Courts differ in their policies towards the hearing and, since a judge is given wide discretionary powers, the outcome of a hearing may not be predictable:

> A number of complaints were made to us about the reluctance of some Judges to make effective orders and the differing practices of Judges in dealing with judgment summonses. Some Judges were said to be 'robust', whilst it was stated that others hardly ever made orders of commitment or, if they did, suspended them on payment of very small instalments (e.g., 4*s*. 0*d*. per month). Another point of difference is the length of the period of imprisonment normally imposed when a suspended order of commitment is made; here we found wide differences between the practice at different Courts we visited, which varied from 2–21 days, in comparable cases, according to the sex of the debtor. (Working Party, 1956, para. 97.)

[1] The Payne Committee (1969, para. 448, p. 121) recommended that the onus of proof should be partially transferred to the debtor: 'The judgment imposes a duty upon the debtor to discharge the debt and it should also carry the obligation to show why he cannot do so forthwith in whole or in part. We therefore recommend that there should be a legal obligation on the debtor to make a full disclosure of means and circumstances.'

The policy can even vary *within* courts:

> And, of course, the procedure varies from county court to county court. In some county courts, if you haven't got any evidence of means, the judge just throws you out; and in other courts he will make an order because the chap realises the practical difficulty here. I mean in ——, which is our local court, whilst Judge —— was there, no creditor could ever get a judgment summons without proof of means. Now he's been elevated to the High Court and it is easier again, because the deputy judges have been in the county court routine for years and know the practical difficulty. They don't stick to the book so much. (Solicitor 11.)

Table 8.1 illustrates the discrepancies in policy that can distinguish one London court from another. Whilst the judges of I court were prepared to make orders against a mere 7 per cent of the debtors who appeared before them, the judges at E court made orders against two-thirds.

TABLE 8.1 *Judgment summonses in the London courts in 1964*

Court	*Number of judgment summonses issued*	*Judgment summonses issued as a percentage of processes initiated*	*Number of judgment summonses heard*	*Number of committal orders made*	*Committal orders made as a percentage of judgment summonses heard*
		%			%
A	1,129	15·2	1,056	111	10·5
B	2,756	19·7	1,263	405	32·1
C*	595	3·4	388	69	17·8
D	4,579	24·1	2,897	555	19·2
E	4,952	23·4	2,706	1,837	67·9
F	2,209	13·6	1,623	642	39·6
G	4,450	24·8	3,350	1,800	53·7
H	3,155	17·3	2,993	456	15·2
I	1,392	8·3	1,237	82	6·6
J	4,236	22·6	2,841	813	28·6
K	3,749	18·0	1,642	238	14·5
L*	98	0·7	42	13	31·0
Total	33,480	15·9	22,038	7,021	31·8

* Courts C and L are the two courts in or near the City of London and they are not greatly involved in routine enforcement.

Although the judgment summons is employed by solicitors in all the London courts, it may be seen that there is very little uniformity in the courts' propensities to make committal orders. A solicitor is likely to be deterred from using the procedure if he has to act in a court which he defines as a 'debtor's court'. Yet, so unpopular is the judgment summons procedure that solicitors almost invariably depend on execution as their chief sanction. Although E court can obviously be identified as a 'creditor's court', the solicitors who work there rely heavily on executions and are loath to proceed to judgment summons hearings. Table 8.2 shows that a summons is generally regarded as a poor substitute for execution when executions prove abortive.

TABLE 8.2 *Relationship between the last execution on goods and the issuing of a judgment summons in E court*

	Dead 1963		*Dead 1964–5*		*Dormant*		*Live*	
Return on last execution	*Judgment summons*	*No judgment summons*	*Judgment summons*	*No judgment summons*	*Judgment summons*	*No judgment summons*	*Judgment summons*	*No judgment summons*
	%	%	%	%	%	%	%	%
Satisfied	6·7	41·9	11·0	39·6	1·7	21·5	2·3	43·9
Unsatisfied	53·3	7·1	56·0	37·5	55·2	42·3	66·0	29·3
Suspended	0·0	1·9	0·0	0·0	0·0	0·8	0·0	2·4
No execution	40·0	49·1	33·0	22·9	43·1	35·4	31·7	24·4
	100·0	100·0	100·0	100·0	100·0	100·0	100·0	100·0

A summons will seldom become a stage in a debtor's career if execution has been tried and found successful. Table 6.6 further suggests that a plaintiff will not issue a summons without first attempting execution. Only 7 per cent of judgments were enforced by judgment summons alone. The procedure thus appears to be generally unfavoured and many solicitors never resort to it. They define it as expensive, often unrewarding and excessively lengthy. 'Life's too short for most clients.' (Solicitor 2.) Some plaintiffs fear the publicity that may be created by the imprisonment of their debtors. Other people feel that imprisonment is an inappropriately severe sanction. The application of societal dualism to the judgment summons can be viewed in a number of ways: it can be adhered to in orthodox Durkheimian fashion; it can be regarded as a useful fiction; or it can be dismissed as an anachronistic and specious form of legal brutality:

> It's a question of morality. How important is it to society that people's debts should be recovered on the one hand, and

> bearing in mind the liberty of the civilian on the other hand for something which is a civil matter. It's a very difficult problem this, in this day and age. I never did agree with the sort of debtor's prison attitude, you know, 'you step out of line on money matters and inside you go!' Because crime, basically, is an offence against the state, not against the individual; and I don't really think you can really equate non-payment of a debt with crime. (Solicitor 8.)

The express purpose of the hearing is to grade defaulters into the contumacious and the feckless. Solicitors regard it as a last resort. In consequence, plaintiffs issue judgment summonses against debtors they have labelled as intransigent. The hearing is such a significant benchmark in a career that it automatically identifies a debtor who passes it as a stupid or dishonest person. Whatever the judge's decision may be, a judgment summons debtor is commonly thought to have become appreciably more deviant simply because he *is* a judgment summons debtor. A solicitor may endow the hearing with so much meaning that he abandons any defaulter who becomes eligible for it:

> If the man's the type of man who's willing to go to that depth, one probably advises the client to give up. (Solicitor 5.)

Service

A judgment summons must be personally served on the defendant at least ten days before the hearing. Personal service is more arduous than the simple service of a default summons which can, after all, be effected through the post. A bailiff finds this task complicated. Most judgment summons debtors are male[2] and are therefore unlikely to be found at home during normal working hours. The bailiff must either encounter them at work or at home, in the very early morning or evening. Many of the debtors of G court, for example, are lorry drivers who leave home at five o'clock in the morning. Bailiffs of G court must attempt service before this time. The bailiff's problems are aggravated by the fact that secondary deviation may have occurred at this stage of enforcement. Judgment summons debtors have usually been exposed to at least one sanction and they may try to elude the bailiff. The bailiff's work load is also rather heavy. In 1964, the bailiffs of the ten London courts outside

[2] The 450 judgment debts of the E court sample involved 317 male defendants; 96 of them were taken to judgment summons. None of the 54 companies experienced a summons; and only 24 of the 79 females were required to attend a hearing.

the City were required to serve an average of 267 judgment summonses each. The Working Party (1956, para. 90) stated:

> Personal service of a judgment summons is not easy and, next to committals, is the task most disliked by bailiffs. It frequently involves early morning or late night work, and many types of debtors . . . are extremely difficult to meet with, to say nothing of those debtors who know the bailiff from previous experience and deliberately evade service.

However, a bailiff who has 267 summonses to dispose of has to meet substantially fewer than 267 people. Thus, members of the four groups of judgment summons debtors in the E court sample (Dead 1963, Dead 1964–5, and so on) received an average of 1·3, 1·9, 1·4 and 2·2 summonses each in the enforcement of a single debt. Second, many defendants are known to the courts as 'multiple debtors'. They are caught up in more than one court action at a time and may have to attend an abundance of hearings. Their heavy indebtedness further reduces the number of *persons* involved in service. Multiple debtors are no strangers to the bailiffs who must serve them. Because they are recurrent targets for enforcement and are known to more than one bailiff, it is likely that their habits and acquaintances will be subjects of discussion in the Bailiffs' Room.

Bailiffs need to have a great familiarity with the multiple debtors who inhabit their areas. They map out their districts in terms of the defaulters who live there. It is not the physical structure of the area which lends it character, but its notorious debtors and significant events. Thus, when a bailiff wishes to direct a colleague to a place, he may refer to it by its street name. He may equally well use debtors' homes as reference points. An address might be No. X, Y Street; or it might be 'opposite old Mr —— 's place'. However, a bailiff's capacity to know an area is undermined by his superiors' insistence that he be moved every so often. In a large London court, for example, a bailiff will probably return to patrol the same district at four-yearly intervals. This rotation is imposed because court officials fear that too great a knowledge of a district will corrupt a bailiff, and it is resented by bailiffs ('The Stalwarts', 1966, p. 270):

> Bailiffs are disgruntled because the present system of interchange means: (i) Inefficiency—in that locally-acquired knowledge of defendants' habits and whereabouts is valueless when a Bailiff is required to work in a district some miles away . . . (iii) That Bailiffs (most of whom are Police or Service Pensioners—and not without pride) would rather furnish a

> Bond, indemnifying the Department against criminal loss, than spend the remainder of their working days somewhat blatantly regarded by their employers as potential thieves. Every few months we are uprooted from our districts, just when we are getting to know the 'artful dodgers', their haunts and habits. By the time we have completed the cycle of districts, many changes have taken place and once more we commence to grope and waste time.

Bailiffs impose another structure on this geography of defaulters. Information about an area's inhabitants is unevenly distributed amongst its population. Certain people have unusual knowledge because they occupy key roles in particular occupations; they include milkmen, postmen, policemen, porters in blocks of flats, door-keepers, café owners, and so on. Other people are centrally placed in immigrant, friendship and kinship groups. Bailiffs who gain access to them can, in turn, tap useful information about debtors' behaviour and movements. They attempt to construct a network of informants and contacts.[3] The network's functioning is sporadically upset by the interchange system but, if carefully nurtured, it can act as a source of abundant information.

A bailiff searching for a judgment summons debtor is guided by clues which are unavailable to a layman. Nevertheless, some debtors are not easy to find. If his initial attempts fail, he is presented with a choice. He may put in a return that the defaulter has 'Gone away' or was 'Not at address given', or he may continue his search. A negative return is often more attractive to the bailiff: it does not make him undertake further work; exploit the good-will of members of his network; or delay other process. Renewed search has to be prompted by exceptional motives.

A bailiff who hesitates to make a negative return must overcome a major obstacle before making a decision. The obstacle is caused by the way in which he defines his occupational role. Bailiffs are anxious to differentiate their role from the part played by enquiry agents and debt-collectors. They attach importance to the fact they are county court warrant officers and feel degraded by the routine collection of petty sums or the harassment of feckless and unfortunate debtors. They would like to present themselves as the impartial representatives of a court. Thus a bailiff of G court told me that he acted for his court, not for the plaintiff, and he hoped that debtors recognized this allegiance. Zeal in the creditor's interest would undermine a bailiff's display of impartiality. Such neutrality not

[3] If a bailiff once patrolled an area as a policeman, he is likely to have already established a network which can be converted to enforcement use. For the police resort to such a network, see Bittner, 1967, p. 702.

only enhances the dignity of his warrant officer status, it also contributes towards smoother relations with debtors. Neutrality is valued by the police and for much the same reasons (McNamara, 1967, p. 175):

> The last set of problems for officers in face-to-face interaction with citizens involved their failure to communicate an impersonal or decisive demeanor to the citizens. The failure to appear impersonally concerned with a citizen was especially problematic in cases involving some punitive action: the threat of using force, the use of force to gain compliance, an arrest, or the issuance of a summons (a ticket). The officer's failure to appear impersonally interested in such cases increased the probability of a citizen's feeling he was not treated impartially before the law.

Bailiffs therefore object to 'rate-busting'[4] because it manifests improper enthusiasm for a creditor's cause. Rate-busting also upsets established work quotas because it increases a bailiff's load. An example of this opposition to rate-busting was provided by the actions of a bailiff of K court. A bailiff of another London court had transferred a judgment summons for service in K court's district with a report that the defendant had moved, 'believed gone to —— in K'. The boundary of K court's territory is on one side of a road and the foreign bailiff's report had suggested an address on the other side of this road. It was just outside the jurisdiction of the court. The county court rules would have allowed the K bailiff to serve the summons, but he refused to do so. He argued that the action of the foreign bailiff was unnecessary and overly enthusiastic. He would not follow up the foreign bailiff's suggestion because his action might become 'the thin end of the wedge'. These beliefs proscribe the tracing of elusive or moved debtors.

Proscriptions about enforcement work are not categorical. A bailiff of C court, for example, told me that the onus of tracing debtors would normally revert back to the creditor. He was not interested in finding them. Nevertheless, he stressed that he made exceptions to this rule. Similarly, a bailiff of B court said that if an 'ordinary' defaulter moved he would allow the creditor to trace him, but if a 'hard-core' debtor moved he would pursue him himself. When a bailiff defines a debtor as a professional, impartiality and the ban on rate-busting need no longer be maintained. The relationship between bailiff and debtor has become a personal contest for control. An evasive professional threatens the bailiff's ability to

[4] Bailiffs do not themselves refer to this behaviour as 'rate-busting'; I have used the term because it is a convenient shorthand expression.

master his territory and sustain his authority. The selfsame bailiff of K court asserted that he would strenuously chase a 'wrong debtor' who had 'mucked him about' by breaking promises and not keeping appointments. By the judgment summons stage, bailiff and debtor have usually encountered one another several times and formed opinions of each other. The bailiff will have decided which debtors he must serve and which ones he can safely ignore.

Service itself is uncomplicated when a debtor *is* found. The bailiff is required to hand the debtor the summons, sometimes with a small sum as 'conduct money'.[5] Even this simple act may be affected by the bailiff's classification of the judgment summons debtor. When a feckless or unfortunate debtor is served, the bailiff may try to ensure that outsiders do not observe the action. If he is serving a shopkeeper, for instance, he may wait until there are no customers present to witness what takes place. When a professional is served, however, the transaction will be made as conspicuous and shaming as possible.

Despite these difficulties, some three-quarters of all judgment summonses are effectively served. I sampled one in ten of all the judgment summonses which were issued in D court between October 1965 and March 1966. Fifty-five of the 233 summonses in the sample (23 per cent) could not be served in time. A similar success rate was achieved by the courts of an earlier survey. The county court audit staff investigated the service of summonses which were to be heard in the last two months of 1955. The investigation was prompted by a Law Society complaint that the county courts of three cities were peculiarly inefficient (Working Party, 1956, para. 88):

> The results of that examination show that out of 2,082 summonses given to the bailiffs to serve 1,647 (79 per cent) were served in time, and that in over half the cases not served in time there was a good explanation (e.g., 'defendant left address given').

Hearing

A judgment for payment in one sum can be enforced only by a judgment summons issuing for the whole outstanding debt. When an order is made for payment by instalments, the summons

[5] A plaintiff provides 'conduct money' to ensure that a debtor manages to travel to the hearing. When a debtor lives and works outside the court's area, conduct money must be paid to him. A plaintiff may decide to pay the money to a defendant who *does* frequent the area. Two shillings and sixpence is the sum I normally saw handed over to a debtor. (*County Court Rules*, 1936, Rules 38 and 39(4).)

must issue for the instalments in arrears. The summons itself instructs the debtor 'to be examined on oath as to the means you have had . . . '. The hearing may be the first time in his career that the debtor has occasion to visit the court. It may indeed precipitate the only face-to-face encounter between the defaulter and the plaintiff or his representative:

> Correspondence with any debtor is unusual. It's not often that one gets into correspondence. I mean, you usually write a letter and get no reply. You issue a summons, it's served and you enter judgment. The only contact with a debtor comes if he happens to turn up in judgment summons proceedings. (Solicitor 6.)

Only a minority of defendants do, in fact, attend the hearing. A mere 17 per cent of the judgment summons debtors of the D court sample came in person. 'A debtor attending is an inconvenient spanner in the works of a delicately balanced time machine. If every debtor turned up and had his affairs fully probed, no Judge, in a busy court, would ever get through his list.' (Registrar of E court.)

Hearings are usually held at weekly intervals in the London courts. They are the one major ritual of debt collection. The judge is robed in lilac and black, he is wigged and sits above the court. He is surrounded by ceremonial furniture and his court is adorned by the Royal Coat of Arms. Solicitors and barristers are also robed and they may be wigged. Evidence is taken on oath before a public audience. Although it is an impressive procedure, the formal decision about a debtor's deviance has been transformed into a matter of routine. In 1964, for example, the average cause list of a London judgment summons court was made up of 65 actions of which 45 were heard. The size of the lists allowed judges somewhat less than four minutes to devote to each action heard. The judges not only have to contend with the debtors who appeared, they must also examine written evidence submitted by absent debtors and issue summonses compelling the attendance of other defendants.

The conduct of the hearing has necessarily been adapted to the demands imposed by such massive litigation. Thus a large part of the transactions between judge, debtor and agency solicitor have become non-verbal:

> [Debtors] are not pressed to produce their hire purchase agreements to show their other commitments simply because it's difficult enough to get through the list just asking standard questions as to means. If each one were turned into

> a minute Federal investigation, you'd finish perhaps three cases in an afternoon. Each court imposes its own system, its own rules. (Solicitor 7.)

Agency solicitors are masters of their court's idiosyncratic system and rules. When a judge hesitates or pauses, for instance, the solicitor will rapidly change his demand to an order which he believes will be more acceptable to the court. A number of understandings arise in any judgment summons court to replace formal argument. (Cf. Sudnow, 1965.) It is interesting that eloquence seems to be employed only by ordinary solicitors. The agency solicitor will be brief because he understands the cues that prompt judicial decisions. For example, a solicitor appearing in an action at E court said, 'as this case is four years old, since the debtor has paid nothing for a year, and the debt is a small one, I will ask for a committal order', and that was all. He had emphasized the critical arguments which were likely to lead to the making of an order of commitment.

An agency solicitor's mastery is based on three factors. First, judges are often explicit about the grounds of their decision-making. A judge of B court observed, for instance, 'I always make it a policy to order £4 a month where there is a weekly income of £20.' It is obviously advantageous for an agency solicitor to remember these judicial statements. His regular attendance at a court will give him privileged access to his judge's thinking about the judgment summons. He also has non-verbal clues to the reasoning which underlies judicial policy. Thus a judge who never commits on a summons issuing for a sum above £40 will not be asked for a committal order when the judgment summons debt exceeds that amount. An ordinary solicitor, however, cannot be aware of a judge's policy. Thus, a judge at E court told an ordinary solicitor, 'I'm not going to make a committal order here because the amount for which the judgment summons issued is too large. The Law Society should have learned that by now.' The agency solicitor, who had been securing orders of commitment, looked rather smug when he heard this.

Finally, a measure of reciprocity develops between judge and agency solicitor. An agency solicitor who acts for a great variety and number of creditors inevitably develops more detachment than his ordinary colleagues. He can afford to be judicious in his requests for committal orders, selecting only those debtors whom a judge would define as professional. He may happily agree with the judge that his clients have acted foolishly. One case I observed in G court, for example, was concerned with the considerable costs incurred in an undefended divorce action. The judge ordered the debt of £190 to be paid off in monthly instalments of £1. The Law Society's representative, an agency solicitor, told me that he thought the debt 'absurdly large' and he agreed with the wisdom of the judge's order. The outcome had been contrary to his client's interests, but it was apparent that the solicitor felt closer to the judge's position than the creditor's (cf. Blumberg, 1967).

Compared with an ordinary solicitor, an agency solicitor is heavily dependent on a judge's good will and is less inclined to dispute an order. He will further minimize friction by accurately anticipating judicial decisions. He thereby allows a judgment summons hearing to proceed quickly and smoothly. In exchange, a judge may trust his evidence of means rather more than he would the evidence of a strange solicitor, and he may be more predisposed to make committal orders when requested to do so.

The summons issues under the Debtors Act, 1869, whose long title is 'An Act for the Abolition of Imprisonment for Debt, for the punishment of fraudulent debtors, and for other purposes'. The hearing attempts to detect the professional debtor and punish him. A creditor who applies for the summons commits himself to proving that his defaulter had been deliberately dishonest.[6] He must show that a debtor has defaulted on a court order but that he could have paid the order if he had chosen to do so.

Judges must make three related decisions in each judgment summons case: was the debtor able to pay the judgment order; was his default on the order wilful; and should an order of commitment be made against him? These questions must be answered in sequence. A judge cannot, for instance, pronounce a suspended sentence of imprisonment if he is unsure about means and contumacy. The first and most important step is the examination of the plaintiff's evidence of means because this evidence is the basis of all that follows. J. McCardie said in an appeal case, 'the county court judge had several hearings before he made the instalment order, but when he made the committal order . . . he had no evidence upon which he could properly make it.' (Nesom *v.* Metcalfe (1912), K. B. 400 at p. 407.) Proof of means, moreover, must be recent. Hearings at which no recent evidence is offered will probably be adjourned.

A judge is forced to rely on the plaintiff's solicitor and the defendant for information about means. He hears so many summonses that he cannot even attempt a thorough investigation. A hearing therefore centres on the oral examination of the debtor. Solicitors claim that they find this process particularly frustrating. They

[6] The *praecipe* (Form 170) includes this statement: 'I am aware that, if I do not prove to the satisfaction of the court at the hearing that the defendant has, or has had, since the date of the judgment . . . the means to pay the sum in respect of which he has made default, and that he has refused or neglected, or refuses or neglects, to pay the said sum, I may have to pay the costs of this summons.'

argue that defendants do not bring documents with them and are often ignorant about their financial position:

> You get a judgment against a woman and her husband. You issue judgment summons. The bailiff can only serve the wife so the summons is effective. You come along to the court, and let's assume that you're fortunate enough that the woman turns up. Then you ask her whether she works and she says 'no'. She's got five children ranging from seven months to eleven years. 'How much does your husband earn?' 'I don't know.' 'What do you mean "I don't know"?' 'All I know is he gives me ten pounds a week housekeeping and I don't know', she says, 'how much he keeps for himself.' (Solicitor 1.)

Many solicitors are so convinced that judgment summons debtors are professionals they they disbelieve every word they say at the hearing:

> You go along there and perhaps in eighty per cent of the cases the debtor doesn't turn up on the first application. Then you issue what's called a Form 179 and he's got to come back. There's another adjournment. Maybe he comes this time, maybe he doesn't, this is fifty-fifty. If he comes, he tells them a lot of untruths about his means and liabilities; and the court never calls, or very rarely calls upon him to produce his pay-slip or any evidence as to his liabilities. (Solicitor 11.)

Others fear that judgment summons debtors will be turned into secondary deviants because the hearing publicly exhibits the success of evasive techniques:

> So many debtors have had periods of unemployment or have had periods of illness. Now, if during the time the arrears have been running, there's been a fairly substantial period of illness or of unemployment, you can take it for granted that in D no committal order will be made. And the snag is, of course, that the debtors come up to the court, sit in the court and listen to the other cases, realise they've only got to say they were out of work for two months during the summer, will not be pressed on this, and no committal order will be made. (Solicitor 7.)

Agency solicitors are armed with slender evidence by their clients; and they feel that the feckless debtor is too disorganized, and the professional too sophisticated to reveal much in court. Enquiry agents may make up this deficiency. They appear in many courts outside London but I saw them giving evidence at one London court only. They are treated with considerable suspicion by court officials. The registrar of E court, where I noticed enquiry agents, labelled them 'an unlovely parasitic growth'. Similarly, the registrar of N court told me that an enquiry agent had appeared at the court in the past, but he had been found guilty of perjury and the presence of such agents would no longer be tolerated by the court.[7]

In 1966, some London courts (including D, I and K) introduced another expedient to overcome the difficulty of obtaining information about means. Solicitors were made to send questionnaires to judgment summons debtors before the hearing. If the debtor attended the hearing the questionnaire would be used as a basis for oral examination. It would not only dispense with the need to ask many standard questions, but also act as a test of the debtor's consistency. If the debtor did not attend, the questionnaire would act as a substitute for the examination. A debtor who neither attended nor returned the questionnaire would be forced to appear under threat of imprisonment, a threat which would not be offered if the solicitor had neglected to send the form. The main aim of this system is to reduce the large proportion of judgment summons actions which are hampered by the debtor not turning up at the court or communicating with it. The evidence of an enquiry agent or a questionnaire cannot satisfactorily replace a formal questioning of the defendant.

Many judges feel uncertain about their ability to gauge a debtor's truthfulness. They can learn what a certain type of debtor is likely to earn and will then distrust any statements which suggest that he receives a sum substantially different from this norm. They can also guess what a debtor's expenditure is likely to be. A county court is a 'grass roots' court and its judges are constantly informed about living and employment conditions in its area. The accuracy of the judge's yardsticks depends upon the homogeneity of the area. In some districts, one industry will employ the bulk of a court's debtors and the oral examination will be uncomplicated. A defendant will also be easily placed if he works in a large industry which has clearly defined pay scales. For instance, a judge has little difficulty in ascertaining the income of a railway porter or a civil servant.

Judges have evolved standard techniques to prise as much information out of defendants as they can. They tend to work through a routine list of questions about the debtor's occupation, income, family, outgoings and court orders, which is designed to reveal his

[7] Another instance of perjury was described in the *County Court Officer* (23 July 1961, vol. 37, no. 5, p. 91): 'On the 6th of June, 1961, Captain John William Stearn was convicted of perjury at Chelmsford and sentenced to 18 months imprisonment. Stearn, who has given evidence of means at Judgment Summonses in many courts in Southern England, was said to have given evidence 50,000 times in 30 years.' Many agents, however, are considered reliable by the courts and the Law Society's Memorandum to the Payne Committee commends them.

economic condition. Thus, they will follow a question about earnings with a separate enquiry about overtime pay. They may let their interpretation of a debtor's manner guide their evaluation of his responses. They may tell him that they will seek corroborative evidence from his employer. If a solicitor is the sole source of information, they can simply refuse to make the order which he requests or adjourn the hearing.

These enquiries and decisions must all be completed in a few minutes. As a result, judges may come to regard certain pieces of information as critical tests of a debtor's means. Some solicitors maintain, for instance, that a number of judges are swayed by the knowledge that a judgment summons debtor is the owner of a car or a television set. These possessions will stamp the debtor as a relatively affluent person. An inquisition which lasts for so little time cannot but attribute enormous significance to such symbols of a debtor's life-style.

Table 8.3 shows that most hearings are transacted in a debtor's absence. The hearing could normally proceed when a debtor volunteered information by letter. In some cases, the debtor's

TABLE 8.3 *Judgment summonses in D court between September 1965 and March 1966*

Outcome	*Summons not served*	*Debtor did not appear*	*Debtor paid debt*	*Debtor sent letter*	*Debtor sent letter and medical certificate*	*Debtor appeared in person*	*Total*
Form 179	0	50	0	1	0	0	51
Application to revoke Form 179A	0	0	0	0	0	1	1
Form 179A 7 days	0	14	0	0	0	0	14
Form 179A 14 days	0	2	0	0	0	0	2
Adjourned	55	3	0	0	0	6	64
Struck out	0	1	0	0	0	3	4
Paid	0	3	18	0	0	1	22
New order	0	17	0	13	1	24	55
Committal order	0	5	0	1	1	3	10
Cases for costs only	0	7	2	0	0	1	10
Total	55	102	20	15	2	39	233

absence did not delay a decision. Half the committal orders and just under one-third of the new orders[8] were made although the debtor was not present. One-third of the cases when a debtor did not attend produced a result other than an adjournment or the summons being struck out.[9] The judge was not satisfied with the evidence of means in the other two-thirds and, typically, issued a summons to compel the debtor's attendance. A debtor who has not turned up at a hearing may be summoned under Section 144 of the County Courts Act, 1959, to attend an adjourned hearing under threat of imprisonment.[10] If the debtor fails to come to the hearing, the judge may pronounce a sentence of up to two weeks' imprisonment for contempt of court. [11] The sanction is designed to force the debtor's appearance and is usually lifted when the defendant apologizes and promises to attend court. It may be seen that the hearing is not so much taken up with investigating the means of judgment summons debtors as coping with the problems of non-attendance.

The second phase in the hearing is concerned with demonstrating a debtor's contumacy. Lord Bramwell (Stonor *v.* Fowle (1887), 13 App. Cas. 20, p. 28) stated:

> An adjudication of committal ought only to take place where there has been a wilful default; because in truth this power of committal is not an imprisonment for debt, it is an imprisonment for past dishonesty with the prospect of the plaintiff getting his money.

Although the debtor may have had the means to pay the debt or instalment order, his default was not necessarily prompted by dishonesty. The second phase is supposed to decide whether a judgment summons debtor should be treated as a feckless or professional defaulter, but 'the difficulty of distinguishing the feckless debtor from the dishonest one makes it inevitable that some of the latter should escape in the guise of the former'. (Working Party, 1956, para. 12.) Judges deal with this classification dilemma by adopting one of two polar solutions.[12] They can refuse to categorize a debtor as professional unless he is manifestly deviant.

8 A new order is simply a judgment summons order which is not backed by a suspended sentence of commitment.

9 When neither solicitor nor defendant appears at a hearing, the summons will be 'struck out'; that is, the action will be dismissed and cannot be started again unless the judgment summons is issued afresh.

10 The summons to an adjourned hearing is Form 179, known as a '179' in the courts.

11 The warrant to imprison is Form 179A.

12 It is interesting that the judgment summons makes no attempt to discover whether a debtor has been unfortunate. At this stage, a dichotomous typology is applied by the judge.

They may insist on such evidence as persistent default; reports from the bailiffs about the debtor's intransigence and lack of co-operation; and, possibly, surliness in court. These tests are relied upon to ensure that no incompetent can ever be mistaken for a professional.

The other solution has two components. It belittles the importance of classifying a debtor as professional by arguing that the classification itself is insignificant. What matters is the judgment summons debtor's subsequent behaviour. One component derives its justification from the self-fulfilling prophecy. Judges can argue that, if 75 per cent of suspended committal orders are disobeyed, then at least that proportion of orders was rightly made. The debtor's default is a fresh act of contumacy which proves his deviance. The other 25 per cent of orders may have been made against debtors who needed discipline. Judges may also believe that creditors should not be denied the right to threaten imprisonment. Other means of enforcement have failed and the debt may become irrecoverable if a committal order is not made. The order will be justified if the debtor *is* a professional. If he is not, he will pay anyway and be little affected by a very remote threat. Whilst the first solution excludes almost all judgment summons debtors from the professional category, the second labels most of them as deviants.

When a judge has assured himself that a debtor has been contumacious, he must further decide whether a committal order is warranted. Although he is entitled to make the order, the threat of imprisonment is not automatically offered after the act of classification. Judges may believe that imprisonment is appropriate only for cases of extreme recalcitrance. Even so, a judge of M court told me that he would not make an order unless the judgment summons issued for a small sum. He argued that the most deviant debtors would rather suffer prison than pay their debts. An order would not benefit the plaintiff, the defendant or the court.

An order will be made when three further criteria have been satisfied. The most important criterion is the size of the judgment summons debt. Judges employ a felicitous calculus when they award committal orders. They impute to debtors a rationality which compares the pains of imprisonment with the pains of obedience to the court. Obedience will be forthcoming only if it is less unpleasant than incarceration. The effectiveness of a committal order depends on the sum owed: it is greatest against a small debt and small instalments; and it does not exist when the debt or instalments are large.

The second consequence of the felicitous calculus is the size of the suspended instalment order. Judges usually approve an order which is half the sum offered by a defendant. I heard the following dialogue between judge and solicitor at E court:

Judge: 'I have received a letter saying that his circumstances are now improved. He offers £3 a month.'

Solicitor: 'This has been going on for three years. I'd ask for a committal order on £2 a month [which was the original order].'

Judge: 'Very well, I'll give a committal order on £2 a month.'

Table 8.4 shows that there is an unwritten system of compensation behind this philosophy; solicitors can achieve either a large new order or a committal order.

TABLE 8.4 *Average monthly orders made at judgment summons hearings in E court*

Type of order	*Dead 1963*	*Dead 1964–5*	*Dormant*	*Live*
	£ s.	£ s.	£ s.	£ s.
New order	2 10	2 7	2 0	3 9
Committal order	2 0	4 4	1 15	1 10
Judgment order	2 8	1 18	2 6	2 6

(Note. In all four groups, the committal orders were very low. The modal instalment orders were for less than £1 in each group.)

Table 8.4 also demonstrates that committal orders are usually smaller than the original judgment orders. This is not only a product of the felicitous calculus. Judges claim that they are guided by the two canons of enforceability and justice when they fix the size of an instalment order. Part of the reason for low judgment summons orders lies in the inadequacy of the evidence of means. Judges can argue that the instalment order will be payable whatever the debtor's resources may be. The unreliability of evidence is thus neutralized and there is only a slight chance that an order will prove harsh. A judgment summons order can also act as a test of a debtor's recalcitrance. A judge can make a new order when he is unsure whether a debtor is professional or feckless. A debtor who defaults on the new order will be classed as a professional and subjected to a suspended sentence of imprisonment.

The second criterion applied by a judge at this stage is his assessment of the plaintiff. Judges regard the hearing as an important stage in the debtor's career and are reluctant to make a committal order which will benefit a lax or malicious creditor. Judges may refuse to make an order when the judgment debt is old and the creditor has not been vigilant in enforcing it.

The final criterion is the deviance of the debtor. Judges will be unlikely to make committal orders against feckless debtors if they believe they can recognize them. Contumacious debtors will either receive a long sentence or an order for a trifling amount. A judge of G court told me that he had only once sentenced a debtor to six weeks' imprisonment, and that had been when the man was an 'obvious rogue'. If the debtor is female (particularly a married female), the judge may feel that any deviance is offset by her femininity. Indeed, he may argue that a married woman is not properly responsible for her financial affairs and cannot wilfully default.

Many judges, however, are unconfident about their ability to distinguish between feckless and professional debtors. They may be unwilling to make an order unless the debtor is transparently deviant. On the other hand, they may routinely pronounce sentences and rely on others to ensure that justice is done:

> All with County Court experience know that certain debtors will not pay until they are on the threshold of prison. The others are on judgment summons because they are feckless, disorganized, muddled, confused, forgetful—call it what you will—it is hopeless trying to distinguish, in court, between the 'will nots' and the 'do nots', . . . so we commit the lot. The orders are then nullified administratively. (Registrar of E court.)

Judges know that a small proportion only of committal warrants will actually lead to imprisonment. They entrust their bailiffs with the judicial task of selecting the genuine 'will nots' and incarcerating them. Officially, judges control the committal process. In fact, it is the bailiff who makes the critical decision (Proteus, 1965, p. 153):

> It is evidently . . . the duty of the Bailiff, before apprehending the debtor, to ascertain whether or not his failure to comply with the order is due to a wilful refusal to pay, or whether it is because of an inability to satisfactorily manage his financial affairs; questions which should, in a properly ordered society, have been resolved at the hearing, before the debtor was committed. The . . . instructions would seem to constitute the Bailiff with an unofficial form of appeal from the judge's order and, in consequence, to endow him with a degree of discretion on whether or not the debtor, already committed by the judge, should in fact be deprived of his liberty.

Committal orders are thus made fairly freely because, even if further default takes place, they are not expected to result in imprisonment. Table 8.5 shows that, although most committal orders are disobeyed and warrants are issued, very few warrants are executed. The warrant is regarded as a threat and not as an instruction to act.

TABLE 8.5(a) *Committal orders made in the London courts in 1964*

Court	*Number of committal warrants issued under Section 5 of the Debtors Act, 1869*	*(Column 1) Committal warrants issued as a percentage of orders made*	*Number of debtors conveyed to prison*	*(Column 2) Debtors conveyed to prison as a percentage of warrants issued*
		%		%
A	107	96·4	14	13·1
B	243	60·0	8	3·3
C	48	69·6	5	10·4
D	518	93·3	134	25·9
E	1,525	73·9	71	4·6
F	407	63·4	19	4·7
G	1,382	76·8	102	7·4
H	318	69·7	11	3·5
I	82	73·8	8	9·8
J	502	61·7	63	12·5
K	147	61·8	6	4·1
L	11	84·6	—	—
Total	5,290	75·3	441	8·3

TABLE 8.5(b) *Committal orders made in the London courts in 1964*

Court	*Number of Forms 179 issued under Section 144 of the County Courts Act, 1959*	*Forms 179 issued as a percentage of judgment summonses issued*	*Forms 179A issued*	*Forms 179A issued as a percentage of Forms 179 issued*	*Number of debtors conveyed to prison*
		%		%	
A	33	2·9	33	100·0	6
B	330	12·0	32	9·7	3
C	99	16·6	9	9·1	—
D	368	7·8	368	100·0	20
E	198	4·0	38	19·1	1
F	106	4·8	20	18·9	3
G	184	4·1	20	10·9	—
H	87	2·8	66	75·9	6
I	201	14·4	28	13·9	5
J	364	11·6	54	14·8	5
K	110	2·9	110	100·0	8
L	3	3·1	2	66·6	-
Total	2,083	7·3	780	37·4	57

It may also be seen that bailiffs execute a larger percentage of warrants in those courts whose debtors disobey committal orders most frequently. When columns 1 and 2 of Table 8.5(a) are ranked and then compared with one another, there is a modest correlation between the debtors' propensity to default and the bailiffs' propensity to imprison. (Spearman's 'r' = 0·35.) Bailiffs tend to be most punitive in the areas where debtors are the most contumacious. As I shall later show, bailiffs often regard the committal warrants as a means of asserting their authority over 'difficult' defendants. Their attitude towards committals makes the relationship between the debtors' contumacy and strenuous enforcement intelligible. It is clear that problems of authority are greatest in such courts as A and D, and the bailiffs respond by imprisoning more debtors.

Table 8.5 shows that three-quarters of the orders made in the London courts were disobeyed in 1964, but only 8 per cent of the warrants culminated in incarceration. From Table 8.6 it may be further seen that the history of a typical committal warrant is a long sequence of suspensions, re-issuings, and so on. The warrant is the last attempt of the enforcement machine to make a debtor pay; if it *is* implemented, debt collection has usually failed.

TABLE 8.6 *E court judgments resulting in committal orders*

*Fate of Order**	*Dead 1963*	*Dead 1964–5*	*Dormant*	*Live*
Debtor imprisoned	—	—	1	1
Warrant not issued	3	1	2	13
Warrant issued and paid	1	5	2	9
Suspended and re-issued	—	—	2	2
Issued and debtor 'Gone away'	—	—	1	1
Suspended	—	—	3	1
Suspended—re-issued—suspended	—	—	—	5
Suspended—re-issued—suspended—debtor 'Gone away'	—	—	—	6
Issued but not executed	—	—	—	1
Issued and debtor died	—	—	—	1
Total	4	6	11	40
Other judgments	146	44	139	60
Total	150	50	150	100

* The sample was taken in 1966 when the final outcome of the dormant and live actions had not been resolved.

Committal warrants issue automatically upon default, but between their issue and the imprisonment of a debtor there is a complex chain of interactions and deliberations. Creditors who feel that their debtors are extraordinarily deviant may want a warrant to end in imprisonment. With this exception, the last thing that a warrant should achieve is commitment. Some creditors believe that it is morally defensible to threaten prison but indefensible to realize the threat. Other plaintiffs fear publicity and give their solicitors explicit instructions to do everything they can to prevent a debtor being incarcerated:

> Banks are funny. At least —— is. They instruct us to press for committal orders which '*in no circumstances*' are to be enforced. (Solicitor 7.)

Courts set up an elaborate machinery to avert imprisonment.[13] Bailiffs are told that they should not regard a warrant as the automatic precursor of commitment. Debtors are fully warned that they are liable to be sanctioned. They are sent a notice which states:

> As you have made default in payment under the Order of Commitment . . . the Plaintiff has issued the ORDER for your COMMITMENT TO PRISON, unless you pay the sum of. . . . If you bring this sum to this Office before . . . there will be no need for the Bailiffs to call upon you. The Judge has power to suspend the Order if you satisfy him that you are unable to pay the amount stated above.

Moreover, most judges ask bailiffs to bring debtors before them immediately prior to the execution of the warrant in a last attempt to suspend it. The decision to issue a committal warrant is anything but the last to elapse before imprisonment.

[3] Pressures to limit the numbers of imprisoned debtors emanated from three sources at the time I investigated the courts (1966). The first pressure stemmed from the demands of the enforcement system itself; warrants are supposed to serve as threats rather than instructions to commit. The second pressure arose from official and 'public' opinion. Newspapers, ministers of state and criminologists (such as P. Morris and P. de Berker) combined to criticize imprisonment for civil debt. Finally, the Payne Committee acted as a powerful brake on vigorous enforcement. The Lord Chancellor urged registrars to curtail committals and there was a very apparent drop in the rate of imprisonment after the establishment of the Committee in 1965.

9 The bailiff's 'working personality'[1]

Before discussing the execution of committal warrants, I would like to expand my analysis of enforcement work. There are peculiarities about the bailiff's position which must be understood before legal control processes become intelligible. A bailiff's handling of his role has profound effects on the selection of debtors for imprisonment and the style in which they are committed. The working personality of a bailiff merits detailed examination.

Most county court work is routine and uneventful. Table 9.1

TABLE 9.1 *The work loads of London bailiffs in 1964*

	Average amount of process per bailiff					
Court	*Service of default and ordinary summonses*	*Service of judgment summonses*	*Enforcement of committal warrants*	*Service of warrants of execution*	*Removal of goods for sale*	*Enforcement of Form 179A*
A	1,237	188	2·3	1,073	5·3	1·0
B	1,398	276	0·8	715	1·1	0·3
C*	5,231	149	1·3	2,094	6·75	0·0
D	1,269	305	8·9	982	11·8	1·3
E	1,554	310	4·4	1,230	4·9	0·1
F	1,629	221	1·9	937	1·9	0·3
G	1,728	342	7·8	925	1·2	0·0
H	1,662	287	1·0	1,000	0·4	0·5
I	2,401	199	1·1	792	2·6	0·7
J	1,561	353	5·3	982	6·2	0·4
K	1,733	312	0·5	1,267	0·75	0·75

[1] I have borrowed this phrase from Skolnick (1966, pp. 42–70).

shows that bailiffs are predominantly concerned with the dull activity of distributing summonses and are only infrequently called upon to enforce sanctions.

Many debtors know the bailiff only as a process server and their encounters with him are fleeting. Table 7.2 demonstrates that most enforcement careers are brief and entail few prolonged exposures to the bailiff in his role of warrant officer. Even then, transactions between bailiff and execution debtor or commitment debtor are generally smooth.

TABLE 9.2 *Judgments obtained at E court in 1963*

Outcome	*Percentage*
Paid in 1963	57·5
Paid in 1964 or 1965	6·6
Inactive in 1966	26·4
Continuing in 1966	9·5
Total	100·0

Although the bulk of their work is unexciting, bailiffs are continually preoccupied with the dangers facing them as warrant officers. Active enforcement assumes considerable significance in their lives. They are aware that they may confront a violence which they feel singularly ill-prepared for. They retire from jobs in the police force which had a central theme of danger, and enter the county courts where the theme is again stressed. According to Skolnick (1966, p. 47), the theme is all-pervasive:

> Policemen themselves do not necessarily emphasize the peril associated with their work when questioned directly, and may even have well-developed strategies of denial. The element of danger is so integral to the policeman's work that explicit recognition might induce emotional barriers to work performance.

Bailiffs' anxiety does not only focus on physical attack, but also on social and psychological risks which may be almost as distressing. Social risk is created every time a bailiff tries to maintain a difficult role before hostile debtors. His ability to act efficiently and safely is threatened by the people he has to deal with. Lyman and Scott (1968, p. 14) have argued that everyday, peaceful relations are constantly threatened by certain risks. Their description of ordinary interaction conveys something of the much greater discomfort that attends enforcement work:

> Encounters are hazardous because of the ever present possibility that identity and status will be disconfirmed or damaged by behavior. Whenever an individual . . . has to stage an encounter before a particular audience in order to establish a distinctive identity and meaning, the management of the staging becomes crucial to the endeavor. The efforts can fail not simply because of the inadequacies or the conflict of the presented material, but also, and perhaps more importantly, because of the failure to maintain expressive identity and control. Thus individuals . . .—for a successful performance—must not only manage what they have planned, but also carry off the presentation smoothly in the face of interruptions, intrusions, and prop failures.

Hazards of this sort are multiplied when the audience is belligerent, evasive or merely unco-operative. All enforcement is thus potentially injurious to a bailiff's performance because it requires a role which is antipathetic to a debtor's interests. The bailiff's social problems are exacerbated by other factors. He dislikes being involved in public conflict because it is personally embarrassing, it increases the numbers of people he must adjust to, and because it may attract troublesome or hostile outsiders. Public brawls also tarnish his professional reputation and, in this respect, he experiences an anxiety which has been described in a study of Denver policemen (Bayley and Mendelsohn, 1969, p. 100):

> A policeman's guiding imperative is to quiet things down. If he must make an arrest, he wants to do so in the least disruptive way. Indeed, policemen get reputations among fellow officers for being unable to make an unobtrusive arrest. The officer who gets embroiled in an unruly public scene attracts a good deal of derisive humor from his colleagues. If a man shows himself chronically unable to intercede without raising emotions to a higher level, the fact is noted by his superiors. Officers may be cautioned or moved to other jobs if they do not have the gift of anonymous intervention.

The clumsy execution of warrants may then do irreparable damage to the bailiff's career and work relations. In order to avoid this, bailiffs try to foster a quasi-parental relationship with their debtors, warding off friction through the use of a joking manner. They expect their role-playing to cope with dangerous situations but realize that it is a fragile support. They may suggest to a debtor that his indignation and surprise are perfectly reasonable and that they sympathize with it. They argue, however, that their function is to act as the impartial agents of a court and the debtor should take up the matter with the court or creditor. They are 'only doing their job'.

A bailiff's authority is most easily established when the debtor's status is not very different from his own. The bailiff suffers some role-strain when there is a disparity in status not only because it is difficult to talk to the debtor 'in his own language', but also because the disparity may be used as a protective device by the debtor. A bailiff can respond to people of high status by depicting himself as a neutral but respectful inferior who must regretfully obey court orders. These elements of impression-management were all conveyed by the bailiffs who invaded Framley Parsonage. Trollope portrayed the bailiffs as well-rehearsed but troubled actors who rapidly exchanged supportive remarks in order to prop up a dominant definition of the situation (Trollope, 1947, pp. 480–1):

> 'And we is only a-doing our bounden dooties', said one of the bailiffs.
>
> 'As we is sworn to do, so please your lordship', said the other.
>
> 'And we is wery sorry to be unconvenient, my lord, to any gen'lman or lady as is a gen'lman or lady. But accidents will happen, and then what can the likes of us do?' said the first.
>
> 'Because we is sworn, my lord', said the second.

Some bailiffs seem to search for flaws in debtors of higher status so that they can alleviate their discomfort (cf. Gold, 1952). A bailiff of D court, for example, was delighted to find homosexual photographs in a debtor's flat. His discovery degraded the defaulter and overcame blocks which inhibited his performance. Such informal degradation processes suggest that there is a major difference between debt collection and other types of enforcement. Garfinkel argued that status degradation ceremonies strip deviants and reveal them as they 'really are'. Degradation and denunciation justify and guide subsequent social control practices. Similarly, Lemert (1951, p. 64) observes:

> Stereotyped stigmas tend to be attached to the deviant along with societal definitions of the deviant and his or her putative role. Often it is possible to distinguish a definite folklore and mythology built up around the deviant in the oral tradition and literature of the society which rejects him. An integral part of this is the body of rationalizations which are employed to justify the rejections and penalties inflicted upon the deviant as a result of the societal reactions.

Although the agents engaged in debt collection have a flourishing folklore which centres around stereotypes of the defaulter, the folklore is unofficial and is not supported by formal ceremony. The absence of degradation rituals poses two problems for bailiffs: selection problems are exacerbated by the fact that debtors are not neatly placed in discrete roles; and the motivations provided by myths are lacking. Whereas it might be easy for a policeman to justify his actions against a homosexual because there is a stereotype of the simpering, mincing queen who deserves no respect, the bailiff is denied such a public stereotype of the debtor. The attempts of certain bailiffs to compensate for the missing degradation ceremony might be interpreted as a quest for reassurance that brutality is really necessary.

Enforcement can also be distressing to bailiffs because it inflicts grief on debtors. Being ex-policemen, bailiffs have become used to withstanding such distress. Yet there is an ever-present psychological risk that they will become too involved in their work and too sensitive to its consequences. Involvement would make the job depressing and difficult to carry out. They therefore try to cut their 'work selves' off from their 'normal selves'. They may agree profusely with a debtor that he has been a victim of injustice, but they will later dismiss what he has said as 'flannel'. They may preserve role-distance by showing outsiders that their sympathy for a debtor is counterfeit. Thus, when I was present at an execution, a bailiff ostentatiously winked at me whilst he dried the execution debtor's tears.

Bailiffs may also wish to maintain social distance. A bailiff of L court told me that he avoided visiting shops owned by debtors and did not acknowledge debtors in the street. Bailiffs also display this divorce by emphasizing the moral and aesthetic qualities which separate them from certain debtors. A bailiff of D court, for example, referred to a debtor as 'that one, that one's a disgusting, dirty old heap. Quite a young girl she is too!' By denying the sympathetic qualities of a debtor, the bailiff can reduce the likelihood that he will suffer the discomfort of vicarious pain. The risk always remains, however, because pain is imposed only in the later stages of a bailiff–debtor relationship. The opening stages were marked by the bailiff's attempts to cultivate a debtor's friendship and feelings of reciprocity. His responses to a debtor during enforcement may be contaminated by these earlier bonds. Goffman (1968a, pp. 758–9) makes much the same point in his description of the staff of mental hospitals:

> However distant the staff tries to stay from human materials, they can become objects of fellow feeling and even affection. There is always the danger that an inmate will appear human; and if what are felt to be hardships must be inflicted on the inmate, then sympathetic staff will suffer.

Above all, a bailiff fears physical assault because his is a dangerous occupation:

> The county court bailiff occupies a unique position. Outside of the police force no other civilian is called on to combine such duties as arrest, levy on goods, and enforce possession of property without protection. . . . (Editorial, *County Court Officer*, vol. 38, no. 1, p. 3.)

There is a strong consensus in the courts that bailiffs have an unpleasant job which exposes them to seaminess and to violence.[2] There is also agreement that bailiffs are given very little organized support by other agencies of social control. Bailiffs feel they are not given the help they are entitled to receive from the police and magistrates.

Although the 1959 County Courts Act recites three versions of 'it shall be the duty of every constable within (the registrar's) jurisdiction to assist in the execution of every such warrant' (Sections 120(4), 158(2) and 161(4)), assistance seems unwillingly given. I spoke to a chief superintendent, an inspector and three sergeants of police. They all expressed no interest in civil matters or the problems of bailiffs, and they did not consider that aiding bailiffs was a proper part of their work. They felt that they should act as impartial arbiters when they are required to intervene in enforcement. They would be concerned to ensure not only that a breach of the peace or assaults did not occur, but also that bailiffs did not obstruct the pavement with goods seized in execution, take too much money from debtors, and so on. They did not therefore identify bailiffs as colleagues working in another area of social control.[3] Indeed, one policeman told me that he did not regard the prevention of conflict between bailiff and debtor as different in kind from interference in a fight between brawling drunks.

The attitudes of these policemen seem widespread in the force. Police support is not evenly rendered to courts throughout the country. Registrars and chief constables are expected jointly to define the working relations which should exist between the two agencies; in some courts this connection has been successfully established, in others it has not. The nature of the connection often seems to be shaped by odd contingencies. Relations between the police and bailiffs in G court, for example, were close because the

[2] The evidence supplied to the Royal Commission on the Police suggests that there is a probability that one policeman in every fourteen will be assaulted during the course of a year. The comparable figure for bailiffs is one in twenty-four.

[3] Bailiffs are frequently hurt by what they define as a betrayal by former colleagues.

senior bailiff's son was a member of the local force. Liaison may be poor; the superintending bailiff of one court wrote (letter to County Court Officers Association):

> Regarding assistance of P.C.s in general, they seem to think they are there only to prevent a breach of the peace, e.g., last week assistance was requested for arrest of a Defendant who had already tried to assault a Bailiff and finished with a broken nose. Police refused to take action . . .

Similarly, the chief clerk of another court observed 'concerning the passive attitude adopted by the police, this is usually found to be the case in this district also'. An integral feature of police–bailiff co-operation is uncertainty:

> What, if any, are the limits of . . . assistance? Constables do not appear to know. Has the Home Office made any Regulations on the subject? It ought to be laid down, somewhere, for all bailiffs and clerks to see, exactly what assistance they are entitled to receive. (Registrar of E court.)

This uncertainty prompted the County Court Officers Association to demand from the Lord Chancellor's Department an explicit definition of the relationship that should exist between police and bailiffs. The Department replied (*County Court Officer*, vol. 38, no. 3, p. 39):

> From a perusal of the previous correspondence which has passed between the Department and the Home Office concerning the interpretation of the duties of the police under . . . the County Courts Act, 1959, it is evident that the Home Office have been reluctant to give any general interpretation of these sections or of the respective sections of Acts preceding the 1959 Act. In fact, they have said that to define more closely the nature of the aid which the police are able to afford the bailiffs might result in loss of elasticity and indeed that new doubts might be created as to the duty of the police.

Thus, when bailiffs contemplate tackling a difficult enforcement situation, they have little assurance that the police will come to their aid. They feel that they are forced to act alone, relying entirely on their own resources. These resources, however, are no substitute for police co-operation. Bailiffs are not as powerful as police officers and are unlikely ever to become so. The Treasury Solicitor asserted (letter to the Head of the County Courts Branch):

> The question to be considered is whether it is necessary to give a bailiff any greater powers. . . . I have come to the conclusion

> that it is not necessary and I see no reason to equip a bailiff with all the powers of a police officer.

The powers vested in a bailiff are few, and his impotence can engender difficulties in such situations as executing on goods. A bailiff can arrest a debtor who has assaulted him and bring him before a county court judge for summary trial under Section 30 of the County Courts Act, 1959. However, he cannot arrest him if the judge is not sitting. In an appeal case, a bailiff had arrested a defaulter and charged him at a police station because his judge was not sitting. The subsequent trial underwent a *bouleversement*. The debtor was acquitted and the bailiff convicted of technical assault because he had no right to arrest him. His appeal against the conviction was dismissed because 'in the circumstances, the arrest was unlawful and there was a technical assault. . . . We think he thought he had the right to do what he did.' (Chairman of London Sessions Appeals Committee, 29 November 1961.)

When a judge is not sitting, therefore, a bailiff cannot arrest a violent defaulter. He is allowed to charge him with common assault as any citizen is entitled to do. Yet this is regarded as a very poor alternative by many court officials. There are ubiquitous complaints about the results of prosecutions in magistrates' courts. The registrar of M court told me, for instance, that on the last occasions when debtors had been taken before the magistrates of O court, the sentences had been so lenient that no debtor would again be taken before them.

A county court judge's powers to sentence are more limited than those of a magistrate. He is able to impose a fine not exceeding twenty pounds or a sentence of imprisonment of not more than a month. Magistrates can inflict severer penalties and some county courts adopt the policy of prosecuting the graver assault cases in magistrates' courts. Nevertheless, there is a widespread conviction amongst bailiffs that magistrates are not prepared to defend them or support them in a difficult job. A correspondence on this subject took place between the registrar of B court and an official of the County Courts Branch of the Lord Chancellor's Department.

The registrar asked the official whether a prosecution should be brought before the magistrates or his judge. He was told:

> It is usual . . . for such proceedings to be before the County Court Judge, and since the penalties were increased by the Administration of Justice Act, 1956, it has been found from experience that better results are obtained in so doing, than by bringing the defendant before the local magistrates.

The registrar replied:

> I do not know what is meant by the phrase 'better results' are obtained in a County Court than in a Police Court. By better results you surely cannot mean more frequent convictions or more severe fines—whether just or unjust.

The registrar put forward the argument that prosecution in a magistrates' court was a more just procedure than prosecution by a bailiff in the bailiff's court before the bailiff's judge. He was informed:

> Even before the Administration of Justice Act came into operation, at least 50% of assault on bailiff cases were dealt with by the County Court Judge. Since that Act came into operation, I should think 99% of the cases have been heard by a Judge, and it has at no time been reported to us that either the defendant or the bailiff felt aggrieved at such a course. As regards my reference to 'better results', I can only say that from experience it has been found that more sentences of imprisonment or the maximum, or near maximum, fines have been imposed by County Court Judges than by Magistrates, even though it is usually the more serious cases which go before the Magistrates. I appreciate, of course, that one cannot properly comment on any sentence which is imposed, but as we receive reports of assaults on bailiffs at the rate of an average of at least one a week, we cannot help forming our own ideas, based on the report of the circumstances and the result of the prosecution in each case.

Bailiffs thus feel unfairly deserted by the two agencies who should give them support. They are not given many powers themselves, but they *do* enjoy unusual autonomy. The consequence of this position is that bailiffs frequently resort to illegal solutions to problems posed by difficult enforcement situations. They are given generous opportunities to experiment with enforcement strategies. The position of the police is not dissimilar and their discontent with judicial policies can also express itself in anomic innovation (Reiss and Bordua, 1967, p. 33):

> Police dissatisfaction with the administration of justice by the courts results in their doing justice, a tendency to settle things outside the courts to be sure that 'justice is done'. Nowhere is this more apparent than when police are expected to continue law enforcement involving violators that the court sends back to the community. The police may then take the law into their own hands and dispense justice, even if it means using violence.

Bailiffs, however, are perhaps more prone to adopt illegitimate solutions than the police. They are as perturbed about the possibility of violence but feel less able to cope with it. Not only are they older and less fit, they are also not armed with the powers of the police and do not even have the authority of a uniform. Their evidence is less likely to be trusted by magistrates. They cannot rely on colleagues being near at hand, although a policeman may be rescued when he calls out, blows on his whistle or summons help by pocket radio. Moreover, bailiffs acquired an expertise in illegitimate techniques when they served as policemen. To this expertise they add other methods which are created by a dual frustration not shared by the police. They are less powerful than the police and this engenders its own dissatisfactions. Not only do they confront similar situations to those faced by the police, they also resent the stripping of power that occurred when they left the force. On the other hand bailiffs are able to innovate to a greater extent. They are less visible than the police; court officials and the public cannot monitor them as easily; and debtors (and bailiffs) are often far less aware of the limits of their authority. Abuses of police power have a better chance of being sanctioned because they are more widely discussed, recognized and deplored. Bailiffs can be more sure than the police that the people they arrest are ignorant of what is legal or illegal in procedure.[4] A bailiff of C court told me, for example, 'if the debtors knew their rights, I could never carry on my job'.

A bailiff's impotence places constraints on the manner in which he tackles difficult enforcement situations. He cannot rely on a display of force and authority so he tries to gain a debtor's co-operation instead. He is dependent on a debtor's acquiescence to proceedings. In many cases, a debtor will be amenable and a bailiff will be able to execute a warrant without difficulty. Nevertheless, there are cases where the bailiff knows that the debtor will not be compliant, and there are innumerable occasions when the bailiff simply does not know what will happen. Personal control and manipulation become a bailiff's chief preoccupation. He has to negate threats to his ability to master debtors. The debtors who threaten him will be the debtors who are sent to prison or whose goods are sold.

Threats can also be dealt with by role-playing. This is another form of social risk and the crucial importance of skill at interaction is a source of anxiety to bailiffs. Failure of a performance can lead to assault, embarrassment or inefficiency. Because it is so important, role-playing will be embellished by whatever inventions the ingenious and troubled bailiff can devise. He may withhold items of information and add incorrect details in order to sustain an authoritative

[4] It is interesting, for instance, that the debtor involved in the appeal case mentioned above was a barrister.

definition of the situation. A bailiff's impression-management is of a two-fold nature: he assumes rights and duties which he has no mandate to claim, and he disguises the 'true' nature of a situation. Some bailiffs enter into this impression-management so fully that they carry it over into situations where it is not really useful.

A bailiff's response to difficult enforcement situations is paralleled in other contexts. The situation's essential features are uncertainty; sophisticated role-playing; inadequate authority; and the possibility of an unpleasant outcome for the nominal master of the situation. In other words, it is a form of confidence game. 'Big-con games call for finished acting ability, versatility, keen insights into human behavior, judgment, and sense of timing, all skills which are not easily acquired' (Lemert, 1951, p. 301). It is extremely significant that a bailiff of D court labelled his behaviour 'conning'.

The difficult enforcement situation appears in other guises. It occurs whenever an unpredictable relationship can have an unpleasant or a pleasant result for the dominant participant. The pleasant result for a bailiff is the attainment of efficiency and the absence of violence or discomposure. In a totally different context, a cab driver may have a payoff in the form of a generous tip and his approach to work is remarkably similar to the methods adopted by bailiffs (Davis, 1959, pp. 162–3):

> There exists among drivers an extensive typology of cab users, the attributes imputed to each type having a certain predictive value, particularly as regards tipping . . . the cab culture's typology stems in a large part from the attempt to order experience, reduce uncertainty, and further calculability of the tip. . . . To protect and insure themselves against an unfavorable outcome of tipping, many drivers will, depending upon circumstances, employ diverse tactics and stratagems (some of them more premeditated than others) to increase the amount of tip or to compensate for its loss should it not be forthcoming.

The poolroom hustler is another illustration of the confidence game pursued in a difficult social situation (Polsky, 1967, p. 62):

> Hustling demands a continuous and complicated concern with how one is seen by others. Attention to this matter is an ineluctably pervasive requirement of the hustler's trade, and is beset by risks and contradictions. The hustler has not only the concerns that one ordinarily has about being esteemed for one's skills, but develops, in addition to and partly in conflict with such concerns, a complex set of special needs or desires about how others should evaluate him, reactions to their evaluations, and behaviors designed to manipulate such evaluating. The hustler is a certain kind of con man.

'Conning' seems to be generally practised by bailiffs in difficult enforcement situations. In another chapter, I shall discuss at length how bailiffs persuade debtors that prison extinguishes a debt; that appeals for release are readily granted; that prison is a sensible way of discharging a debt, and so on. So important is the bailiff's ability to 'con' that he will studiously cultivate it. In particular, he must become accustomed to dealing with a great variety of debtors in many different situations. A technique which is appropriate in one situation may be disastrously inappropriate in another. In consequence, bailiffs frequently stand back from themselves and view their performances as works of art which must be continually improved and revised. This kind of attitude characterizes the purest form of impression-management, the confidence trick. Maurer (1940, p. 186) remarks that confidence tricksters 'have cultivated the social side more than any other criminal group. They are able to fit in unobtrusively on any social level. . . . Although their culture is not deep, it is surprisingly wide and versatile.'

The extent to which a bailiff is prepared to con does not only depend on his ability and need, it is also determined by his court's culture. Collection techniques are systematically interpreted and altered by a court staff's conceptions of their roles and of the function which the court should serve. Although courts share structural features in common, these similarities are not sufficient to prevent the development of idiosyncratic cultures. Some courts are identified by outsiders as tough 'creditors' courts' because they maintain an aggressive policy towards defaulters. An exponent of this policy wrote (letter to *County Court Officer*, vol. 39, no. 6, p. 153):

> Is it not time we tried to regain some of those true values we lost some 25 years ago? Then, if a man could not afford something, he went without. Owing money was morally wrong and if it was wilful, you deserved and got punishment. The latest innovation of leading defendants by the hand and practically forcing them to apply for a suspension of an Order which itself tells them they have that right is in my view ludicrous. . . . County Courts were established to provide a speedy means of recovering small debts; surprising though it may seem, that is still their function today. Up to the obtaining of judgment, they fulfil their purpose, but from there on, if execution is unsuccessful, every conceivable obstacle is put in the way of the Creditor and the Legislature in their wisdom seem determined to make the course tougher still.

Other courts are called 'debtors' courts' because they are based on a culture sympathetic to defaulters (letter to *County Court Officer* vol. 39, no. 6, p. 153):

> The debtor is not someone who just keeps us in a job. He is a person who has become a great social problem. The needs of modern life, coupled with the shortage of money, have created the vast problem of hire purchase. The County Courts are filled to overflowing with debt cases. . . . We, as an Association, would do well to look out, beyond our own problems, into the world around us and see what miseries are suffered by people in debt. . . . I feel the moral aspect is the key to the situation. We must ask ourselves, individually, and as an Association: do we care?

Over time, most groups develop esoteric ways of viewing the world. Cultures grow when they are reinforced by closure against outsiders, intimacy between insiders, and common problems. I argued in Chapter 6 that county courts are fertile grounds for the breeding of cultures which direct their members towards the 'creditors' court' model or the 'debtors' court' model. A court's culture acts as a repository of solutions for recurring problems. It defines which problems are insuperable and how bailiffs can overcome the others. Certain courts refuse to entertain the use of illegal enforcement strategems. They will simply abandon the warrants which cannot be executed according to due process. The court's bailiffs may have difficulty in asserting their authority, but there will be few of the frustrations associated with harassing unco-operative debtors. Other courts unofficially urge illegal remedies for enforcement problems. They expect their bailiffs to clear up a high proportion of warrants resorting, if necessary, to officially proscribed methods.

A bailiff's choice of tactics is shaped by his court's culture. He served part of his apprenticeship in the court and learned its norms. Formal and informal pressures are likely to bring an errant officer back into conformity. A vigorous bailiff may be punished for brutality in one court but praised for efficiency in another. Moreover, many enforcement tasks are performed by teams of bailiffs. Group cohesion based on shared attitudes is essential for effective functioning. Bailiffs are also dependent on their superiors because their peccadilloes may need support in the form of censorship or a refusal to act on damaging information. Thus courts can contain systematic and enduring tendencies towards illegitimate modes of control. The police forces of the United States (and probably Britain) are very similar to the enforcement staff of a county court (President's Commission on Law Enforcement, 1967, p. 16):

> While neither articulated nor officially recognised, common responses obviously tend to develop in frequently recurring situations. A new police officer quickly learns these responses through his associations with more seasoned officers. The fact

that a response is routine does not mean that it is satisfactory. To the contrary, many routine responses are applied on the basis of indefensible and improper criteria. But once developed, the routine response is generally immune to critical re-evaluation unless a crisis situation should arise. Because of their informal character, such responses tend not to be influenced by developments in police training. And, because they consist of the accumulated experiences of frontline officers, they tend to take on a vitality which continues even without the active support of the higher echelon of police administration.

Execution of committal warrants

Elaborate checks exist to ensure that committal warrants will act as threats rather than sanctions. Yet bailiffs have to commit some debtors if only to keep the threats credible. Bailiffs must account for outstanding warrants and they can be dismissed for inefficiency. They can also be sanctioned for an enforcement manner defined as rash, impatient or unpolished. They must resolve some mean which will satisfy the two injunctions placed on committal warrants: 'do not commit too many debtors' and 'do not commit too few debtors'.

Committing is the most difficult part of a bailiff's job. It is a task which must be accomplished without any of the paraphernalia of handcuffs or special vehicles available to the police. Debtors must be taken to prison by public transport or in the bailiff's car. The task of shepherding a debtor through public places on his way to an unpleasant fate, or driving a car containing an unwilling passenger, exposes the bailiff to danger and calls for extreme skill. Some bailiffs prefer to work alone. Others may be on their own but will still arrest a commitment debtor whom they have seen but were not searching for. Committing is more complicated when a solitary bailiff has to concentrate on driving as well as on his prisoner. Even bailiffs who work in teams have little protection. They cannot rely on the police or arrest a debtor for assault when their judge is not sitting. They may be confronted by debtors brandishing spears,[5] guns,[6] iron bars,[7] or merely fists.[8] All the risks attendant on a difficult enforcement situation are present in commitment.

5 Assault on a bailiff of Oldham court reported in *County Court Officer*, 3 May 1963, vol. 38, no. 3, p. 47.

6 Assault on a bailiff of Liverpool court reported in *County Court Officer*, 9 September 1960, vol. 35, no. 14, p. 224; and assault on a Nottingham bailiff reported in *County Court Officer*, 8 February 1963, vol. 38, no. 1, p. 3.

7 Assault on a Chesterfield bailiff reported in *County Court Officer*, 14 December 1962, vol. 37, no. 16, p. 286.

8 Assault on a Nottingham bailiff reported in *County Court Officer*, 22 March 1963, vol. 38, no. 2, p. 26.

The further a bailiff has to escort his prisoner to Brixton, the more unwilling is he to commit. Even when he has little distance to travel, the typical bailiff does not undertake commitment lightly. He not only dislikes the process, but also respects the importance attached to the warrant as a threat and may feel some reluctance to inflict pain.

A bailiff is thus predisposed to delay the enforcement of a committal warrant. He acts in much the same way at this stage as he did at the earlier stage of execution on goods. He will use the warrant as a bargaining counter in his transactions with the debtor. Cajolery and threats are employed to make the defaulter pay the sum he owes or apply for the suspension of the warrant. A bailiff may try to exploit the remains of the moral consensus he built up at the beginning of his relationship with the debtor. Such exploitation will reassure the bailiff that he is not really responsible for the defaulter's eventual imprisonment, after all 'he did his best'. It will also reassure him that the debtor was recalcitrant enough to deserve prison. Bailiffs thus apply their own tests, neutralize their disquiet and classify debtors.

Bailiffs learn something about the people they pursue when they engage in prolonged coercion. Not only will lengthy transactions inevitably convey information, a bailiff must also categorize debtors before making a decision about imprisonment. The act of social typing becomes of paramount importance. Typing has two functions: because bailiffs exercise considerable discretion in enforcement, they must carry out continuous and active selection; they also have to evaluate the partners of a delicate interaction. That is, they must decide which debtors they are going to commit and, having done so, must decide how they are going to commit them. The period which lapses between the issuing and the execution of a warrant is therefore put to a number of uses.

A major candidate for prison is the debtor who undermines a bailiff's authority. A bailiff's anxiety about his impotence is so great that he will do his utmost to punish debtors who increase that anxiety. 'Bailiffs are human. They do imprison debtors. The reason is that the debtor has upset the bailiff. I have never yet heard a bailiff express any regret at imprisoning a debtor' (Registrar of E court). Debtors who upset bailiffs may be labelled professionals by judges and registrars, but they may not. The criteria applied by bailiffs are often congruent with the intentions of the Debtors Act, 1869. Thus debtors who are pliable and respectful in their dealings with bailiffs could well be people who pay their debts or negotiate with the court. Nevertheless, secondary definitions employed by bailiffs are not necessarily relevant to the aims of enforcement. Feckless debtors can expose a bailiff's weakness as fully as any professional can. If the feckless defaulters live in a block of flats, for instance, a bailiff might fear them as contaminating agents. The debtors might demonstrate the bailiff's ineffectiveness to other potential or actual debtors. When he attempts to exorcise their influence, he punishes people who have not 'wilfully defaulted'. The subversive debtor will be an obvious choice for imprisonment and the bailiff is unlikely to devote much time to persuasion before he executes the warrant that commits him.

The fates of other defaulters are decided by less straightforward criteria. Bailiffs have work quotas which determine the volume of enforcement they must carry out. The quotas are in part set by superiors, in part by colleagues, and they will vary from court to court. A bailiff of K court who commits some four debtors a year would be regarded as intemperate by officials of K court but cautious by officials at D court. The differences between courts' cultures are nowhere clearer than in the perspectives offered on committal warrants. At one extreme, the warrant will be defined as an instruction to imprison and, at the other, as a means of collecting debts. A bailiff of D court, for instance, told me that he saw no reason why other bailiffs should 'twist the rules'. A warrant was 'there to be enforced' and procrastination was 'nonsense'. He argued that debtors had been given ample opportunities to satisfy their judgments and it was 'disgusting to see them jumping around at the last moment' to evade a warrant which he had to execute. He believed that warrants were issued because debtors had committed the serious offence of flouting the orders of a judge. They deserved punishment. The attitude which prevailed at D court explained why its bailiffs imprisoned the largest proportion of debtors against whom orders were made. Most bailiffs, however, use the warrant as a threat and are reluctant to enforce it. The size of a quota affects the bailiff's selection problems. If he has a small quota and sends enough subversive debtors to prison, he may well achieve his work target without becoming unduly concerned about further classification. If there are few 'obvious' targets for enforcement, categorization will become more important.

A bailiff's freedom to act is restricted by his quota and the way in which he fills it. He can use his freedom in his treatment of debtors he defines as feckless or unfortunate. When he places a defaulter in one of these categories, he will 'not see' him when he is found. If he is satisfying his quota, the bailiff can persist in not seeing the unthreatening debtor for some time. Similarly, if the debtor is difficult to meet or has moved, the bailiff can return the warrant with a report that he was 'unable to find' him. Such a report is not seen as a defeat because there is no threat to combat. A bailiff of G court, for example, called at the home of a commitment debtor. He told me that he would have executed the warrant if the debtor had been 'hard', but the debtor and his wife were both hard-working and frank in their relations with him. Although he had spoken to them in my presence, he entered a return of 'unable to meet'.

This kind of situation poses a dilemma for bailiffs. They wish to present themselves as vigilant employees but are continually forced to upset their presentation by false returns which disguise a very real vigilance. Registrars recognize this dilemma when they interpret returns. Yet they cannot but look askance at abundant reports which state that no progress is being made with enforcements. Bailiffs can afford the luxury of delaying sanctions aimed at the feckless or unfortunate only if they demonstrate their efficiency by imprisoning others.

The next most vulnerable group after the subversives are the lesser professionals. Bailiffs regard this group as troublesome and deserving of punishment. They will be impelled to commit its members when their quota is unsatisfied; and when plaintiffs and solicitors agree with their classification. When this agreement is reached, bailiffs are directed by internal and external drives to execute warrants. People able to put pressure on a bailiff will appreciate the value of delay in the case of the feckless. They will, however, become impatient to reach a crisis when professionals are involved. Many plaintiffs and solicitors believe that the recalcitrant debtor will pay only when he is on the threshold of prison. They can plague bailiffs and registrars with continual demands for action. I found such a demand from a solicitor attached to a warrant lodged at Brixton:

> We have your Notice of an Application being made by the Defendant for the suspension of an outstanding Committal Warrant, to be heard on the 25th inst.
>
> It is not our intention to incur additional costs in attending this hearing but we ask that this be dismissed. This man's offers to pay are quite valueless, as we have found since the summons was first issued in February 1960.
>
> Judgment was obtained at a defended hearing in the sum of —— . . . Our letter of instructions to our local Agents when the last Judgment Summons was due to be heard is attached. . . .
>
> This is self-explanatory and there is nothing we can add thereto. Not one penny has been paid by this evasive and reluctant Debtor since April 1964 when the third J.S. was heard.
>
> In our opinion it is time we had the support of the Court and pressure is brought to bear on this Debtor. The Warrant was issued on the 27th March last.

Although registrars and bailiffs do not have to respond to this type of letter, it must have some influence on enforcement decisions. At the least, staff have to have a plausible explanation for their inactivity.

Bailiffs apply a wide range of tests when they fix upon the third most eligible group of defaulters. They may consider a debtor's employment record; his deference to their status; the size of his debt; his history of payments into court; the ages of the judgment and the committal warrant; the number of times the warrant or its predecessors have been suspended; the amount of work which the debtor has imposed on bailiffs in the past; the debtor's family; and so on. Their decisions about this group are somewhat arbitrary. They may be determined by the sheer accessibility of the defaulter or the belief that enforcement will be uncomplicated.

In particular, decisions will be affected by proscriptions imposed by a court's culture. A bailiff's choice will inevitably be constrained by the culture's perspective on illegal remedies. If a bailiff is not unofficially allowed to match difficult situations with illegitimate methods, he will not venture into those situations. A court which stresses the binding nature of the due process model will deny a bailiff many targets for enforcement. He will be forced to make returns of 'unable to find' in these cases. Most of his efforts will be directed against debtors whom he can imprison in an approved manner.

Indeed, ease of enforcement can be a critical factor in the selection of third rank debtors. A bailiff may suspect that the arrest and imprisonment of some eligible defaulters will prove unduly troublesome. He has no animus against them and is unprepared to exert himself in executing their warrants. Bailiffs may rule out many of the difficult warrants issued against this group. They have innumerable clues to identify how complicated particular arrests are likely to be. They have probably assessed the defendants in earlier transactions and their colleagues may well know them. They also know that certain conditions will upset successful impression-management. The felicitous calculus can provide useful arguments about the wisdom of a debtor's consenting to imprisonment. When the debt is large, a defaulter may be persuaded that prison is a sensible way of extinguishing it. When it is small, however, the calculus generates contrary arguments. Impression-management can also be exploded when a debtor learns from others that the bailiff's statements are often false. The execution of a warrant can be further complicated when a debtor is young, male and physically strong.

Final returns on warrants cannot be indefinitely delayed. When a feckless or unfortunate debtor is elusive, the bailiff will report that he was 'unable to find' him. The debtor *may* be immediately imprisoned if he can be found, but he is far more likely to undergo a ritual confrontation with the judge. A bailiff usually takes unthreatening debtors to court in a last attempt to suspend the warrant. He will ensure that subversive defaulters are arrested when his judge is not sitting so that a final application cannot be made. He will argue that the subversives could not be encountered during court hours. He feels compelled, however, to present other debtors before the judge. Not only will the judge be reassured that his system of checks is functioning, the bailiff may himself be uneasy about incarcerating these defaulters. Judges appreciate that they see only those debtors who are defined by bailiffs as harmless. They can merely hope that the bailiffs' definitions coincide with their own. Suspensions seem to be freely granted because a warrant is supposed to coerce payments rather than punish. A refusal to suspend a warrant again indicates that a judge believes further enforcement would be fruitless. Decisions about suspensions are based on the criteria that the judge employed at the hearing, but they appear to be applied more leniently.

I have already discussed the formation of a bailiff's enforcement techniques and I shall continue the discussion in the next chapter. His techniques are divided into the two main areas of tracing evasive defaulters and manipulating them when they are found. The search for commitment debtors is often frustrating because males are rarely at home in the day time and may not even be there at night. Thus, I accompanied a bailiff of D court who managed to find only two debtors in the space of five hours. Bailiffs typically encounter the children and wives of debtors rather than the debtors themselves. Both encounters can be put to use. Bailiffs may question children about their parents' whereabouts and whether provision would exist for them if an arrest were made. The second set of questions were directly phrased: small children would be asked about their parents' relations with their neighbours and so on. Bailiffs often refrain from telling wives why their husbands are sought. A bailiff will pose as a friend of the debtor who wishes to meet him on 'urgent business' or to 'play cards' with him. Debtors on the verge of imprisonment have already been warned by Form Ex. 52 and bailiffs are unwilling to make them any more defensive.

Bailiffs resort to the whole gamut of stratagems they employ in difficult enforcement situations. They will knock on doors in a friendly manner but, if this fails, they will thump on the knocker in an ominous way. They will attempt some preliminary social typing of the debtor, adapting their role-playing to his expected responses. Their chief concern is to avoid violence and they place great reliance on their ability to persuade a debtor to come to prison with them. They may reconcile a debtor to his fate by disarming him with humour. A bailiff of D court, for instance, would routinely tell a female debtor that he would wait fifteen minutes before they left the house together. When asked why, he would reply, 'I'll give you ten minutes to wash your feet and five minutes to change your "unmentionables".' In many cases, the woman's amusement would make committal easier. Such gambits reduce the level of tension that inevitably build up between an enforcement officer and his prisoner. In the case of the policeman confronting a prostitute, for example (Skolnick, 1966, p. 106):

> The prostitute neutralizes the immorality of her illegal activity by emphasizing those aspects of her work that are tiresome, inconvenient, and dangerous, with the labor involved representing a moral justification for her fee. If the policeman challenges this conception by calling her a 'dirty nigger' or by emphasizing that she is a whore . . . he will have 'trouble on his hands'. By contrast, if the policeman treats the arrest as a competition or a game he has won rather than as a moral victory or a harsh joke, the woman will be more disposed to being arrested.

Similarly, bailiffs will show a real or feigned sympathy for the debtor. They will present the situation as one in which they are both victims of an impersonal system of control. The bailiff is no more a moral agent than the debtor. Bailiffs assure debtors that their wives and children will be cared for; that there will be no publicity attached to their imprisonment; that the sentence is short and will discharge the debt; and so on. Above all, they try not to let the debtor think too much about the impending prison itself. They talk continuously and, they hope, divertingly, about anything that will distract their prisoner. Once the debtor is inside the prison, he can be left alone with his shock. Up to then, bailiffs attempt to distract debtors and allow them no time to brood.

The bailiff's techniques are prompted by an awareness of what might happen when enforcement goes awry. The difficult enforcement situation is not only difficult because it calls for interactional skill, it is also capable of involving a bailiff in physical conflict. Something of what a bailiff fears is described in the following account of an incident that occurred at C—— (A.L.L., 1962, p. 286):

> C——, no doubt like most other Courts, takes a pride in the speed with which it deals with its process, so when a warrant of commitment issued in June, was still outstanding in the middle of August, drastic measures were called for. The defendant was a young man of 24, living with his father and working with him as demolition contractors. Both were well known to the bailiffs and some difficulty was anticipated. All the usual tricks of the trade—early morning visit, etc.—had proved abortive.

> Then it was learned that the defendant and his father were demolishing some old cottages about seven miles out in the country. Five bailiffs, in two cars, went at once to the site. They were not there but were expected back. The bailiffs parked nearby and waited. Some time later they arrived, in a lorry. . . . On seeing the reception committee waiting for them they increased speed and kept going with the bailiffs in pursuit. Soon they turned into a narrow lane and, when the leading car was close behind, the lorry suddenly stopped and reversed. Fortunately, the bailiffs managed to do the same, just in time to avoid a collision. The chase continued. The defendant's father then leaned out of the cab and threw an iron bar, about two feet long, at the nearest car, which was struck on the front wheel. More iron bars and pieces of wood followed during the course of the next mile or so. . . . After a while, the father jumped down from the lorry and stood in the middle of the lane holding above his head a large coping stone which he had taken from the wall at the roadside, and threatened to 'bash the head' of anyone who came any nearer.

The son escaped in the lorry and was pursued by one of the cars. The chase was unsuccessful, and enforcement was abandoned until the next day:

> Later the same evening one of the bailiffs concerned was outside his own house . . . when the defendant drove up in a private car and asked what the bailiff was going to do about it now that he was on his own. . . . He did not wait for any answer, but immediately drove off, to return in a few minutes with his father. Both got out and set upon the bailiff, the son with a paling from a fence and his father with a piece of wood like a truncheon, causing severe bruising and some lacerations.

The C—— incident was somewhat extraordinary, but bailiffs are influenced by what they read and hear about similar predicaments. They may have encountered extremely threatening situations themselves. The fear that violent debtors could create this type of enforcement problem explains the great caution with which some bailiffs approach committing. I spent some time observing the tactics of a bailiff of D court, and caution was evident in his behaviour. He refused, for example, to use the word 'prison' in his conversations with commitment debtors. One debtor was escorted to a telephone so that he could arrange a meeting at which the debt would be paid. The bailiff insisted throughout the journey to prison that he was taking the debtor to the meeting place.[9] In

[9] I have no idea how widespread this practice is. The bailiff's definition of the warrant as a punitive instrument rather than as an enforcement prop is, of

another case, he told a debtor that they were going to court in order to disentangle his difficulties. He was immensely affable with both debtors, agreeing with their statements, sympathizing with them, joking with them, and so on. He was very amused at the impression which he had conveyed, calling it 'a big con'.[10] It was only when the debtors were received at Brixton that they realized what had happened to them. Neither of them understood his changed status. They informed the prison officer that they would immediately leave the prison and return with the money they owed. They were obviously upset and took time to be calmed down by the reception officer. The officer, apparently familiar with the results of this expedient, told them, 'I don't care what happened on the outside, you're in nick now!' In a later examination of his tactics, the bailiff remarked to me, 'did you see their faces? Oh what a con!'

course, immensely significant. (Indeed, his views could be construed as a proper interpretation of the meaning of Section 5 of the Debtors Act, 1869.) The Payne Committee clearly did not know that this kind of practice existed (1969, para. 979, p. 250): 'A debtor who is experienced in the debtors' court knows that the county court judge is most reluctant to make any order which will result in a debtor going to prison. . . . Such a debtor will ignore the summons, the judgment, the judgment summons and notice of commitment, and will not normally make any payment until at the eleventh hour the bailiff arrives to arrest him. He will then pay what is outstanding on the warrant and the process may start all over again.' A bailiff in a tough court executing a warrant against a subversive debtor will try to ensure that the debtor cannot appeal to the judge. He may also insist on execution if the debtor cannot immediately satisfy the warrant. In other words, some bailiffs deliberately attempt to prevent an eleventh hour escape.

10 A 'big con' is one of the two types of confidence game; the short con and the big con. It depends on elaborate planning and should be highly profitable. It is interesting that the bailiff used criminal argot to describe his stratagem. It suggests that he was not only aware of the kind of impression-management he was achieving, but also that he felt some links with other confidence tricksters.

10 The prison

Introduction

A debtor destined for prison will attract increasing attention from the court staff. The enforcement directed against him will eventually become so intensive that he will be singled out for the exceptional fate of imprisonment. He will find that the judiciary have hardened against him when he applies for suspensions. Bailiffs will accelerate his once leisurely career so that it becomes harassing and relentless. In one respect, this tendency continues after his reception into prison. An imprisoned debtor has lost his freedom, he is subjected to uninterrupted punishment, and he is monitored all the time. Indeed, if executions proved abortive, prison might well be the first legal sanction experienced by him. Because it is the most severe stage in a debtor's career, prison 'naturally' fits into the pattern set by preceding phases.

However, the prison stage breaks with the pattern in other ways. A county court is an institution with its own peculiar culture, and the debtor was imprisoned because he was defined as a subversive or a professional by members of that culture. A prison is another institution whose perspectives on debtors and default have little in common with those of the court. There seems to be no agreement, for instance, on what the function of prison should be.

A prison might have at least five functions for an enforcement system. The aims of imprisonment could be retribution, deterrence, coercion, denunciation and stigmatization. Any stigmatization that occurs is an unintended consequence of imprisonment. When a judge makes committal orders at judgment summons hearings, he does not usually expect them to lead to incarceration. He may occasionally criticize the debtors who appear before him, but he is unlikely to want them punished unless they display further contumacy. At the hearing stage, therefore, he does not wish to inflict stigma. The way in which the committal warrant is actually used tends to be outside judicial control. Instead, the bailiff influences the manner in which debtors can interpret the significance of what is happening to them. Since he is generally anxious to avoid antagonizing debtors, the bailiff will try not to give the impression that they are undergoing some sort of public degradation ceremony. Although many bailiffs might be pleased that a subversive debtor has received stigma, they cannot afford to impose it themselves. Committals are made as undramatic as possible because bailiffs are unwilling to create extra enforcement problems. As a result, court officials do not ascribe a stigmatizing function to prison. The general tendency of the press to ignore county court proceedings is a further guarantee that debtors will not be intentionally stigmatized. It is, of course, possible that people will learn about a debtor's imprisonment, but there are no mechanisms established to inform them about his experience.

Prison serves the other four functions of retribution, deterrence, denunciation and coercion. The court staff sees prison as a useful threat and imprisonment as the failure of that threat. Debtors are incarcerated for two main reasons. The first, and more important reason, is that the debtor has imperilled the bailiff's efficiency. The General Secretary of the County Court Officers Association argued (Yeoman, 1965, p. 179):

> I believe the realisation that continued neglect may eventually lead to prison is the one thing above all others which leads debtors to respect bailiffs and gives them an authority without which they would find their job more difficult than it is at present.

Second, imprisonment represents the abortive conclusion of a final attempt to coerce the defaulter. The warrant is used to offer the debtor a critical choice between payment and prison (County Court Officers Association):

> Our experience is that the order of commitment operates primarily as a threat. . . . Many hardened debtors know every step in the procedure and will only pay when the final stage is reached and the bailiff has actually apprehended the debtor with the intention of conveying him to prison.

An order of commitment is valuable *before* imprisonment, not during it. The county court ascribes a *punitive function* to prison: 'The intention and effect of the existing law on imprisonment for debt is that a fraudulent debtor shall be punished. . . .' (*County Court Practice*, 1963, p. 1045.) Payment of a debt in order to secure release is a 'desirable' but secondary consequence of incarceration. Coercion is a very minor function of the prison because payment was expected during the previous stages. Prison thus acts as a threat; as a way of ritually denouncing contempt of court; and as a means of punishing debtors for their contumacy and lack of respect for bailiffs. The court does not seem to ascribe other functions because imprisonment is not an intended or significant product of the judgment summons procedure. County courts are more concerned with the 92 per cent of the debtors who do *not* enter prison despite the issue of a warrant. The minority of commitment debtors who become prisoners are unimportant failures.

Prison staff are unclear about their role in debt collection. Indeed, it was clear in the period of my research that they would soon have no role to play at all. Lord Stonham had stated, 'we shall employ means other than prison for dealing with many of the 20,000 fine and debt defaulters who are annually committed into custody at our expense' (an intention later realized in the 1970 Administration of Justice Act). Prison does not serve a punitive function (as the courts would like it to do) but a coercive one (Home Office, 1960, p. 39):

> The function of the prison in relation to the majority of these ['civil'] prisoners may be described as coercive, since it is intended to make them more disposed to pay their debts, or purge their contempt, as the case may be; and if they do so, they may be released. The treatment, therefore, falls somewhere between the custodial conditions of untried prisoners and the corrective treatment of convicted prisoners.

I have argued that imprisonment is viewed by the court as a sanction for contempt. It is a punishment devised to support correct relations between the debtor and the state's institutional representative. The sanction is threatened for enforcement purposes, but executed for other reasons. It thus plays a part in both aspects of the legal philosophy of societal dualism; prison simultaneously acts as a threat in enforcement, and as a punishment for disobedience to an agent of the state. Warrants are infrequently implemented because prison marks the unsuccessful end of debt collection. Prison will become a stage only when a judge and bailiff separately apply the label of contumacy to a debtor, and it is not part of a normal enforcement career.

I have put the court's argument because this conception of the prison's role enjoys an extremely limited circulation. It is curious that the court's application of the doctrine of societal dualism is not understood by outsiders. The Law Society (1965) have stated that they are

> aware of the disquiet that has recently been expressed over the fact that each year a number of debtors are committed to prison as a result of proceedings to enforce judgments for debt. Prior to the Debtors Act, 1869, debtors were regarded as quasi-criminals liable to imprisonment which was inflicted partly as a means of extracting payment and partly as an expression of public indignation against a wrong-doer. The Act abolished imprisonment for debt, and substituted imprisonment for contempt of court in the failure to obey an order of the court. . . . Though this is the legal position, there is a widespread impression on the part of the public that imprisonment is imposed for debt *per se*, rather than for disobedience to an order of the court.

The Prison Department believes that its establishments should play a pragmatic role rather than defending deep-seated and central social values. Some outsiders dismiss the court's philosophy as a legitimating myth which is cynically used to aid debt recovery. Two lawyers, for instance, have written (Foster and Blom-Cooper):

> Although in form committed for contempt of court, in reality [debtors] are imprisoned for non-fulfilment of their obligations to pay their debts. . . . We venture to think that people will look back with disapproval at our continuing use of prison as a means of debt-collecting, much as we look back at the barbarities of a hundred years ago.

The court thus expects prison to pursue the aims of retribution, deterrence and denunciation. Prison staff, on the other hand, see themselves in a coercive role. Not only are there misunderstandings about functional requirements;[1] the court and prison do not entertain common definitions of the debtor. Like any other complex and fragmented system, debt collection harbours multiple realities for those who are responsible for its operation. That is, creditors, debt-collectors, debtors, bailiffs and prison officers each inhabit their own world with its peculiar system of interpretation. 'Another consequence of institutional segmentation is the possibility of socially segregated sub-universes of meaning. These result from accentuations of role specialization to the point where role-specific knowledge becomes altogether esoteric as against the common stock of knowledge.' (Berger and Luckman, 1967, p. 102.) Defaulters are simply not the same people to bailiffs as they are to prison officers. They occupy different places in different role-clusters and

[1] The consequences in terms of the regimes imposed on debtors need not, of course, be great. Presumably coercion and punishment entail similar or even identical treatment. Nevertheless, it is important that the assumptions underlying the treatment are dissimilar.

thereby become different social figures. The courts tend to regard prisoners as fraudulent and deviant persons who *wilfully* display contempt. The judgment summons hearing and succeeding stages were expressly organized to detect and punish the wilful defaulter. Indeed, the word 'wilful' appears innumerable times in the praecipes, summonses and warrants connected with commitment proceedings. The court maintains that the prisoner was able to make choices and that his persistent default indicates moral *guilt*. 'The attitude always is "he asked for it and he got it".' (Registrar of E court.)

Again this definition is not widespread[2] and has no currency amongst the prison officers I talked to. When a debtor is imprisoned, he is evaluated by prison staff who compare him with other inmates. The debtor's sentence is brief and his offence is mild when it is contrasted with the crimes committed by burglars, murderers, assailants, rapists, and so on. Moreover, he is an unthreatening and marginal member of the prison community; he is not well versed in inmate behaviour and takes a respectful 'Square John' role.[3] Defaulters were the centre of interest when bailiffs pursued them, but they occupy a very insignificant place in prison. As a result, there is a very prevalent assumption that debtors suffer from *psychological* difficulty. Because they are unthreatening and comparatively unsophisticated, they are described in terms culled from a psychiatric vocabulary. They are not 'rogues' or 'professionals' but 'inadequates'. Thus the Governor of Brixton observed:

> It is apparent . . . that the debtor is an inadequate person and, in general, the reasons for his predicament stem from this inadequacy. . . . It appears clear . . . that inadequacy, or similar defects of personality, plays a large part in the predicament of debtors.

Similarly, the Principal Psychologist of Brixton wrote (de Berker, 1965, p. 313):

> It is safe to say that in all cases debt was a facet of a much more generalized picture of social difficulty such as marginal employment, general incompetence in social planning and the like.

2 One outside body, however, appeared to agree with the county court position (National Association of Discharged Prisoners' Aid Societies: *Indebtedness*, a paper submitted to the Payne Committee): 'it is in the interest of society that indebtedness should be recognised as a social evil. . . . In all future legislation the moral evil should be clearly stated and it would be a matter of social shame to incur indebtedness.'

3 Cf. Sykes and Messinger, 1960, p. 10: 'And if an inmate makes the mistake of allying himself with officialdom by taking on and expressing the values of conformity, he may be called a *square John* and ridiculed accordingly.'

The psychological label may be embellished by a further characteristic of the debtor, the size of the debt on committal. Pauline Morris (1965, p. 240) has stated, 'the civil prisoners were in debt for what were often paltry sums, a fact which underlines their poverty and ineptitude generally'. An exponent of the county court culture would point out that, according to the felicitous calculus, orders of commitment should be made only on small debts and that default on these orders is clear proof of contumacy. The official prison culture generates a different conclusion; debtors are inadequates who have been harassed for trifling amounts of money which they are too disorganized to pay. Prison officers cannot be expected to understand the felicitous calculus. They surmise that prison is an inappropriate place for debtors and it should not be their function to guard them.[4]

An even more upsetting description of the female debtor has been given by Moya Woodside. The evasiveness and dishonesty of the professional confirm her as a deviant in the eyes of county court staff. Woodside (1962, pp. 29–30), however, argues that these traits can also be attributed to inadequacy. They are not the signs of a subversive who has free will:

> The many sentences for debt give cause for concern. These women are not calculating impostors, running up bills for goods and services which they never intend to repay. They are, with a few exceptions, muddled housewives who have got in tangles with hire-purchase or other domestic commitments, often without their husband's knowledge. They may have resorted to fraud or to selling unpaid-for articles, in an attempt to stave off the eventual day of reckoning. Those with a large family of children, trying to manage on a marginal income, are particularly liable to find themselves in difficulties.

Associated with the debtor's appearance of inadequacy, confusion and poverty is a further factor which fixes him as a feckless person. Almost all English prisoners undergo status degradation ceremonies before they enter prison.[5] They are pushed into a stereotyped category which leaves the public (and prison officers) in no doubt about their danger, non-conformity and inferiority. However, there is no such ceremony laid on for debtors. In this respect, defaulters resemble Lemert's (1951, p. 55) 'innovating' deviant:

4 This view seems to have been behind the comments of the Commissioners of Prisons on the increase in civil prisoners (1959 Report): '. . . these prisoners come, we have reason to believe, largely as a result of failure to pay commercial debts of which the bulk have been incurred through hire purchase agreements. We view with misgivings the effect of this development on our limited accommodation.'

5 Reception at the prison itself can, of course, form another such ceremony.

> A sociopathic deviation which is entirely new and for which there is no historical antecedent often leaves a group or society at a loss for effective means of coping with it . . . Under conditions such as these the members of the group must rely or fall back upon informal expressions of their disapproval. These reactions may make the deviants uncomfortable and distressed but they do not necessarily impair their formal status. Recurrent deviations and the growth of a deviant population bring alterations in the culture and social organization of the community within which they occur. Mythologies, stigma, stereotypes, patterns of exploitation, accommodation, segregation, and methods of control spring up and crystallize in the interaction between the deviants and the rest of society. The informal societal reaction is extended and formalized in the routinized procedure of agents and agencies delegated with direct responsibility for penalizing and restraining or reforming the deviants. The status of the deviants is redefined, and special pariah roles may be assigned to them.

The parallel between debt collection and the informal reaction is a strikingly close one. Many of the people who know and deal with debtors *as* debtors do disapprove of them. Nevertheless, bailiffs conceal their disapproval of the professional and there is no formal assignation to a pariah role. Debtors may experience disquiet but their status is not redefined. Moreover, default is not surrounded by the mythologies, stigma and so on which accompany the reaction to Lemert's 'recurrent' deviation. Debtors thus enter prison as people who have not been degraded. Prison officers are not members of the informally reacting group and debtors are received as if they were a specially innocent class of inmate. In this sense, defaulters manifestly do not fit in with the rest of the prison population. They alone have not been denounced. Prison staff cannot but define them in terms of inadequacy or other non-deviant characteristics. The staff feel that there is very little they can do for debtors and that their relation with them has almost no meaning. The care of convicted (that is, degraded) prisoners is their 'proper' job. Thus, an officer in charge of civil prisoners at Eastchurch Prison frequently referred to his inmates as 'cons'. Immediately he used the wrong name, he would correct himself resentfully. (In his conversation with me, he preferred to dwell on his happier and more meaningful period of service in Pentonville, than on his present post.)

The most interesting feature of the debtor in prison is his total lack of importance. 'The civil prisoner is the forgotten man of the penal system.' (Morris, 1965, p. 228.) Prisoners committed by the

High Court, by the magistrates' courts for default, and by the county courts are all alike labelled 'civils' in prison. Although these groups are socially dissimilar, they are not differentiated by name. When I wished to interview county court debtors, a prison officer had to inspect the prisoners' files in order to distinguish them from other civils. The fact that a county court debtor is lost in a more general category of prisoners suggests that he is not important enough to merit special attention. The debtor's insignificance is also symbolized by the type of accommodation in which he is housed. All civils in Brixton Prison are placed in F Wing which is the shabbiest and least secure part of the institution. In addition, although the prison was being painted and renovated when I visited it, F Wing was going to be the last section decorated. If the official status of an inmate is reflected in the accommodation he is given, civil prisoners have a very low status indeed. When the prison is exceptionally crowded, civils may not even remain in F Wing:

> During recent months . . . owing to the marked increase in the number of remand prisoners committed into custody it has become necessary to accommodate civil prisoners under dormitory conditions in the classroom block. . . . In a review of accommodation available, it is evident that facilities are under pressure by the increase in remanded prisoners which in turn pushes out accommodation for civil prisoners at Brixton. (Governor of Brixton.)

The poor integration of court and prison is clearly illustrated by the breakdown in communication about procedural matters. The two institutions are jointly involved in three processes: the reception of the debtor; the discharging of his debt; and the purging of his contempt.[6] There are uncertainties about all these processes. In the case of reception, for instance, an official at the Prison Department told me (letter dated 23 January 1967):

> There is no time, official or otherwise, when a prison does not receive prisoners committed by the County Courts. There are no difficulties attached to the reception or discharge of debtors. The Sheriff's Officer [sic] is nearly always known to the prison gate staff.

On the other hand, the President of the County Court Officers Association stated (letter dated 8 February 1967):

6 Committal under Section 5 of the Debtors Act, 1869, is for a contempt of court which can be purged by an apology to the committing judge. Releases are, however, secured on these grounds in very exceptional circumstances only. It is far more common for debtors committed on a 179A warrant to discharge themselves by affidavit.

> In my own Court we have excellent co-operation from the police to the extent that in the event of our arresting anyone outside the *normal reception hours* at Brixton we are usually able to lodge a prisoner overnight at the Police Station. (My italics.)

The discharge procedure suffered from similar confusion. The chief clerk of Brixton complained that, for a long while, there was no standardized method by which county court debtors could discharge their contempt. A debtor was forced to compose an affidavit which could be returned to the prison for redrafting if the judge considered it unacceptable. Because of this delay, a debtor sentenced to a short term of imprisonment might have to serve his full sentence. Although he was in ignorance of what the judges required, the chief clerk had drawn up an affidavit which seemed to be approved by the courts.[7] He told me that the prison did not possess a copy of the *County Court Practice* and no court officials had advised him about how debtors could be helped. He claimed that his makeshift form was constructed in circumstances which exemplified the prison's relations with the courts.[8]

Court and prison are thus insulated worlds which have little contact with one another. Whilst prisoners are of little moment to the courts, debtors are regarded as insignificant by prison staff. When a debtor enters prison, all the labels that were applied to him in earlier stages are discarded. Instead, he is primarily identified as a nuisance. He may release himself at any time if he consents to pay the outstanding debt and, as a result, prison officers must always be near him. They cannot attempt to reform or rehabilitate him and 'there is little opportunity for staff appreciation of personal problems, or discussions. . . .' (Governor of Brixton.) Any officer who interprets his role in an approved manner cannot but find his relations with the debtor frustrating.[9] He resents having to deal with debtors at

7 The chief clerk's account was supported by a memorandum written by the Governor of Brixton. The Lord Chancellor's Department had asked him to comment upon some proposals about ways of simplifying the release of civil prisoners (31 August 1965): 'enclosed are three proposed forms for consideration. (A) For Contempt of Court. This is the form which has been brought into use here by agreement with the solicitor who usually attends in such cases where affidavits are required. . . .'

8 The chief clerk of D court made a similar complaint. He told me of an occasion when a female debtor was needlessly retained at Holloway Prison because of the gate staff's ignorance of correct release procedure. The staff had told the debtor's relative that the debt had to be paid to the court and that the prison was unable to receive money.

9 *Prisons and Borstals*, for example, urges, on p. 12: 'above all every member of staff who comes into contact with a prisoner should, by the influence of example and by advice in season, seek to show him the right way and to help him along it.'

all and his association with prisoners of low status reflects adversely on his own position. Moreover, the debtor's stay at prison may be short, but it requires all the complex processing involved in the reception and discharge of any other prisoner. A clerk who worked on part of this processing remarked, 'they're no damn good. They come here and then their wife rushes up five minutes later and pays cash and says "you can't keep my husband here a second longer".' There was thus an unconcealed satisfaction shown at Brixton when it was announced that the imprisonment of debtors would cease.

The passage of the debtor out of the jurisdiction of the court into that of the prison is not smooth. The two institutions are badly integrated, they ascribe different purposes to imprisonment and they do not share a common conception of the debtor. When they do have dealings with each other, their relations are sometimes complicated by misunderstandings. The debtor is assigned to a most marginal place in prison. There is some irony here because English prison history has been largely a history of debtors' prisons. Imprisonment for debt is an ancient means of enforcement[10] and, before the 1800s, prisons existed primarily to house debtors. Indeed, the connection between the debtor and prison was so close at one time that Ludgate gaol lent its name to debtors in general: 'Ludgatians'. The diminished status of the defaulter is a recent phenomenon.

Brixton

Brixton Prison was founded in 1820 as one of the metropolitan houses of correction for the county of Surrey. In 1824, it had the distinction of being the first English prison to make use of the tread-wheel. It was acquired by the government in 1862 and converted into an establishment for female convicts and then, later, into a remand and short-term prison serving the London courts. The prison is shaped in the form of a rough crescent with the administration block (which was once the Governor's house) as a separate building in its centre. Other structures have been added to this basic design and one of these, the civil prisoners' F Wing, stands apart as an isolated unit.

Brixton caters for three groups of prisoners: remanded prisoners awaiting trial in the London criminal courts (35·3 per cent of the daily average population in 1964); 'stars' serving sentences of less than six months (56·7 per cent); and civil prisoners from south-eastern England (8·0 per cent). The prison community is thus governed by a number of different regimes. There are murderers and

[10] Livy mentions it, for instance, in his *History of Rome*, Book 13(14). Execution against goods is also a venerable means of enforcement (cf. Matthew 18: 24–5).

others who are closely guarded; civil prisoners who are not regarded as security risks; short-term prisoners who are not strenuously protected; and remand prisoners who enjoy privileges and freedoms denied their fellow inmates. Brixton is simultaneously a maximum security prison; a local prison and something of a minimum security prison. The various types of prisoner are forcibly segregated although the barriers set up between them are often ineffectual. The prison's population is not only heterogeneous, it is also in a continual state of flux. In 1961, Brixton received some twelve thousand inmates but few of them stayed for a long period. The size of the population can fluctuate wildly and there is a constant turnover.

The flux is reflected in the prison's formal structure. The housing of prisoners can present problems, for example, because their numbers can unexpectedly change. Although Brixton may have ample accommodation one week, inmates may have to be transferred into classrooms and corridors the next. The deployment of staff is also affected:

> As the manning and supervision of Higher Courts is a responsibility of the prison, the provision of sufficient staff for duties in the prison reaches crisis proportions from time to time. The picture of staffing may appear in sharper context if demonstrated by an average staff requirement, i.e., from an authorised strength of 116 discipline officers (103 actually in post), some 70/100 are needed for external court duties in one category or another. (Governor of Brixton.)

Staff alternate between six months of escort duty and six months of work within the walls. Much of the work in prison is devoted to the routine tasks of receiving and discharging prisoners, and officers have few opportunities to develop stable relations with inmates.[11] Instead, the prisoners and staff seem to be split into a number of fragmentary groups. Because Brixton lacks cohesion, debtors can escape some of the penalties which are often inflicted on prisoners adopting the Square John role. They can espouse conventional attitudes without risk. As I shall show below, these attitudes are of considerable importance in the formation of a more general orientation towards imprisonment.

A maximum security prison with a strictly custodial regime might be viewed as an inappropriate institution for county court debtors. However, a prison's function is the coercion of payment and Brixton

[11] One inmate present when I visited Brixton was serving his sixth sentence there for contempt of the High Court. Although other reasons accounted for their attitude, the fact that the staff regarded him as something of an institutional mascot suggests that they regretted the poverty of their contacts with other inmates.

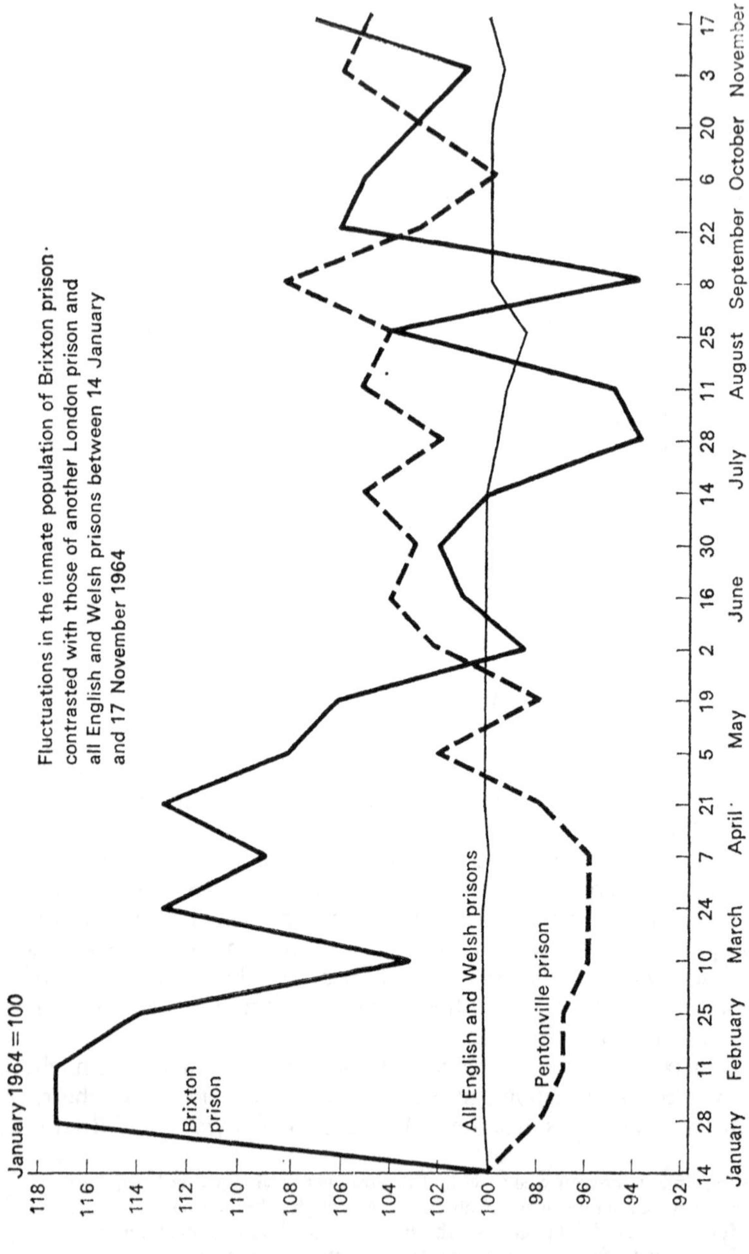
Fluctuations in the inmate population of Brixton prison contrasted with those of another London prison and all English and Welsh prisons between 14 January and 17 November 1964
January 1964 = 100
Brixton prison
All English and Welsh prisons
Pentonville prison
118
116
114
112
110
108
106
104
102
100
98
96
94
92
14 28 11 25 10 24 7 21 5 19 2 16 30 14 28 11 25 8 22 6 20 3 17
January February March April May June July August September October November

Figure 2.

is used because of its geographical position. A London prison serving the London county courts[12] must be located near sources of aid for its debtor inmates. In 1961, 90 per cent of the debts discharged during the prison stage were paid by people who visited Brixton to rescue debtors. There are two ironies involved in the fact that Brixton is the London debtors' prison. First, there is the unintended consequence that a prison of Brixton's nature is likely to satisfy a county court's demand for punishment.[13] Second, only recalcitrant debtors will be offered the more attractive alternative of transfer to an open prison.

Brixton does not normally send county court debtors to its affiliated open prison, Eastchurch. Transfers will be considered only when Brixton suffers a crisis of over-population and, even then, a debtor has to pass a number of tests. In 1966, prisoners were moved from the one prison to the other on Wednesdays. Since debtors receive short sentences, an inmate will not be moved unless he is admitted to Brixton on or near a Wednesday. A defaulter's sentence must also be unusually long and he must express a great reluctance to pay his debt.[14] Extraordinarily few debtors meet these conditions and they may not be transferred when they do. Yet it is evident that the people who are moved would be defined by the courts as hardened professionals. That is, the only prisoners who are allowed to escape the more punitive conditions of Brixton are debtors whom the courts would most like to have punished.[15]

[12] In 1961, two-fifths of the debtors in Brixton (39·7 per cent) were sent there by the inner London county courts.

[13] Some other regions commit county court debtors to open prisons as a matter of routine. Drake Hall in Staffordshire is an example.

[14] The other criteria are the absence of a criminal record; and good health (because demanding work is often required of a prisoner at Eastchurch, and hospital facilities are better at Brixton).

[15] When I visited Eastchurch in 1966, thirty-two of the thirty-three civil prisoners interned there were maintenance offenders.

11 The debtor as inmate

This chapter will take the form of an ideal-typical account of the debtor's career up to and during imprisonment. It will focus on three main themes: why debtors do not pay before they enter Brixton; why they do not pay whilst they are in Brixton; and how they manage to preserve an acceptable image of themselves despite Brixton. My discussion must repeat some of the arguments I made in earlier chapters because it dwells on the relations between bailiff and debtor.

A prison is supposed to coerce a debtor into paying the money which he owes. In Brixton, however, there is little publicity attached to the methods which can secure release. Thus, a typewritten information sheet drawn up for the inmates of F Wing showed how maintenance offenders could apply for the cancellation of their warrants. It did not mention the county court debtor at all. Similarly, the *General Information* notes handed to civil prisoners explain how inmates committed by magistrates courts, but not by county courts, can pay their debts. ('Notes for Civil Prisoners (Men)' no. 126M(1).) Indeed, the words 'county court' do not appear in either document although maintenance offenders are frequently referred to.[1] A county court debtor is not an important inmate. When he was asked if anyone had advised him about what he should expect in prison, Debtor 25[2] told me, 'no, and I still haven't been. There's supposed to

1 The first document has eight paragraphs and the second has thirty-four. One paragraph of the first, and eight of the second, are devoted to maintenance offenders.

2 I interviewed thirty-four debtors in Brixton over a period of six weeks. I initially intended to use a standard, pre-coded questionnaire but, later on, it became evident that an unstructured interview was the most fruitful approach. The debtors were fairly voluble and my standardized questions served only to interrupt what was often a valuable narration. After the first

be a Rule Book. I haven't seen it, I do as I'm told. Nobody knows what's going on.'[3] In a similar vein, Debtor 14 remarked, 'people should be given a book of rules. I don't know the ropes here.'[4]

Debtors are forced to rely on other sources of information, yet there are few knowledgeable people to whom they can safely turn. They have no wish to advertise their dilemma to outsiders who are unaware of its existence. They thus try to keep their enforcement careers private. 'It's not the sort of thing you like to talk about. You don't like people to know you're in debt.' (Debtor 23.)[5] They believe that their association with debt collection is a shameful fact that would harm them if it were known. Concealment can be achieved only by withholding information about their default from as many people as possible. As Goffman (1963, p. 77) observes:

> If there is something discreditable about the individual's past or present, it would seem that the precariousness of his position will vary directly with the number of persons who are in on the secret; the more who know about his shady side the more treacherous his situation.

Consequently, Debtor 2 told me that he had not mentioned his career at all to outsiders. 'Nothing like that! Last thing in the world I'd dream of doing! I've got to keep up the shopfront.'[6] The maintenance of a respectable front calls for a considerable reduction in the number of people who can provide guidance. 'I don't like people knowing my business, my downfalls.' (Debtor 24.)[7]

The prison officers of Brixton could be another agent of help for debtors but 'consistent staffing problems . . . obviously are reflected in the amount of personal contact or staff/inmate participation which is practicable beyond the normal requirements or supervision and control . . . This seldom allows for more than the essential chores of day to day administration.' (Governor of Brixton.) Whilst bailiffs consistently attempted to cajole the debtor, prison officers cannot do anything but act out a custodial role. Moreover, debtors are somewhat in awe of the officers and do not readily approach them. The social gulf that divides the two groups discourages any voluntary overtures by the debtors. Debtor 21 said,

couple of interviews, I decided to rely on encouraging the debtors' conversation and recording as much of it as I could. I used the questionnaire solely as an aid when the conversation started to flag.

3 Debtor 25 was a middle-aged builder who had been imprisoned by Croydon county court.

4 Debtor 14 was a middle-aged painter, committed by G court, on a 179A.

5 Debtor 23 was a young tent erector imprisoned by Kingston upon Thames court.

6 Debtor 2 was a middle-aged builder imprisoned by Epsom court on a 179A.

7 Debtor 24 was a labourer in his fifties committed by F court.

'I haven't had much to do with them, none of them's been nasty.'[8] Similarly, Debtor 19 remarked, 'I've nothing to say to them. I haven't seen them shout or anything yet. They're better than I've heard.'[9]

The defaulter has contact with many groups, but the county court is the only official body which devoted attention to him. In particular, bailiffs have had frequent and intense dealings with him.

I have outlined the influence of the difficult enforcement situation on the selection of debtors for Brixton. Bailiffs handle problematic enforcement by developing special techniques which include the control and distortion of information. It is inevitable that a debtor's orientation to prison will be affected by what he is told by the bailiff who takes him there. The influence of the difficult enforcement situation is not only confined to events which occur before imprisonment. In fact, the prisoner's actions may be best understood as a product of his transactions with the bailiff.

Imprisonment is the terminal stage of a long career, and bailiffs are unlikely to label the debtor as a subversive or a professional in the opening stages. They earn the debtor's trust in the beginning by adopting a paternalistic manner. Later on, this trust is maintained by skilful role-playing. Diplomacy will not be abandoned unless it proves ineffectual in a difficult enforcement situation. The bailiff's opinion of the debtor may have been revised, but the change remains covert because it could be dangerous for the court staff to reveal their informal feelings. These concealment practices are integral features of many arrests. When shoplifters are arrested, for instance, Edwards (1958, p. 134) believes:

> A gentle approach will usually disarm any shoplifter, amateur or professional, while a rough seizure or loud accusation may immediately put him on the defensive. At other times, it may result in a nervous or hysterical condition accompanied by an involuntary discharge which may be embarrassing to the arrestor and arrested.

Bailiffs employ persuasion rather than force in their relations with a commitment debtor. The ends of persuasion change over time; they are initially concerned with debt collection and then, subsequently, with the maintenance of personal control. As a result, a bailiff is usually able to create and sustain a fund of good-will which he can draw on later. Indeed, most of the debtors I interviewed seemed to like and respect their bailiffs. Debtor 13 said, 'the bailiff

[8] Debtor 21 was a young mechanic committed by Watford court.

[9] Debtor 19 was a young upholsterer committed by Ilford court.

was very generous. He even offered me money. I couldn't abuse him, he was too gentle. He looked as if he was more prepared to help than take me to prison.'[10] Debtor 5 observed, 'he's been a proper gentleman about it.'[11] In consequence, it is the bailiff who shapes the defaulters' definitions of the situation. Debtor 23 remarked that his bailiff was 'very informative like. He went out of his way to instruct you on the full consequences.'

If my analysis has been correct, several interesting arguments can be traced. Debtors seek clarification about prison conditions from the committing bailiff and he may well volunteer information. However, whereas the debtor is acquiring an orientation towards the next stage, the bailiff is achieving impression-management. That is, the bailiff's chief preoccupation is to control the debtor by persuading him into prison. The prison is used by a bailiff to prop up his authority. At this stage he is *not* interested in its debt-collecting powers. What a debtor is told, therefore, may not only be misleading, it may also be detrimental to the enforcement system.

A bailiff hopes to convey a fourfold impression to his prisoner. First, he would have him believe that his arrest and imprisonment are reluctantly carried out, and that he sympathizes with the debtor. Debtor 2, for example, stated, 'the bailiff resented bringing me. He thought it as unnecessary to bring me under Section 144.' Debtor 16 told me 'the two bailiffs who took me here . . . chatted to me. One bailiff said it's bloody ridiculous for a bloke like me to be here.'[12]

Second, the bailiff wants to communicate his lack of personal involvement in the situation; he is only 'doing his job'. 'They've got a job to do, same as anyone else, despite what they've got to do.' (Debtor 28.)[13] Any resentment or hostility which a defaulter may feel should not be directed against the bailiff. 'When the bailiff took me, I had nothing against the man. He was quite nice.' (Debtor 20.)[14] Debtor 24 echoed this when he said, 'he was just doing his job, that's all. I don't bear no grudge.' This kind of impression-management is aimed at by any agent of social control who is forced to pacify a deviant in a difficult enforcement situation. The debtors' reactions to bailiffs are remarkably similar to the feelings described by an American who was taken by two policeman to a mental hospital (Dahl, 1968, p. 86):

> [The police] seemed nice enough. In different circumstances I would have liked to know them better. They were just carrying out their orders and neither of them seemed to be taking any

10 Debtor 13 was a middle-aged seaman committed by N court.

11 Debtor 5 was a young steel erector imprisoned by Wandsworth court.

12 Debtor 16 was a young painter committed by Kingston upon Thames court.

13 Debtor 28 was a young machine operator committed by Ilford court.

14 Debtor 20 was a young bricklayer committed by G court.

joy in their duty. They were courteous and sympathetic. If they had been out of uniform, without the guns at their sides, I doubt if I'd have been afraid of them at all.

Bailiffs may even embroider this theme of their neutrality by expressing their dislike of the warrant officer role. Debtor 9 remarked 'this fellow was very reasonable, no bullying attitude or nothing like that. He said he didn't like this sort of thing, but that's his job.'[15] The first two items are thus used to emphasize one point: the bailiff as a bailiff has a function to perform; but the bailiff as a *person* detests this function. The function and the *person* must not be confused by the debtor. 'If a man is born to a job. . . . But if he's got to do it, then I don't hold it against him. The bailiff said he didn't like his job.' (Debtor 13.) The debtor is not allowed to question the legitimacy of the bailiff's authority. He must suffer imprisonment. Nevertheless, he cannot direct any anger at the bailiff himself. In its extreme form, the bailiff depicts the situation as one in which he and the debtor alike are victims of the same enforcement system.

The last two items contribute more to an understanding of how debtors react to prison. A bailiff may have established a smooth relationship with his prisoner, but he must still reconcile him to the goal which the relationship was set up to achieve. The defaulter is told that prison may be quite a pleasant institution. 'The bailiff said it wouldn't be too bad.' (Debtor 33.)[16] 'The bailiff said, "if you don't intend to pay, get it over with. You might get open prison".' (Debtor 6.)[17] If the debtor is committed for his failure to attend an adjourned judgment summons hearing, a bailiff can make an even stronger case. 'I'd forgotten about the summons. I saw the bailiff near my home and he told me that I'd be in serious trouble and that I'd have to go to prison. He said it would only be a formality, one night only. The bailiff is a very reasonable man indeed, he helps you in any way he can.' (Debtor 15.)[18]

The last of the bailiff's arguments is the most effective means of persuasion. It is also the most likely to emasculate the coercive power of the prison. Judges make committal orders on the basis of a felicitous calculus and, ironically, it is to this selfsame calculus that the bailiff appeals. He uses it in his attempt to convince the defaulter that imprisonment can be a sensible way of discharging a debt. Imprisonment does *not* extinguish the debt, but a bailiff seldom tells the debtor this. 'Imprisonment . . . does not operate as a satisfaction of the judgment debt . . . and although the defendant cannot

15 Debtor 9 was an old painter committed by E court.

16 Debtor 33 was a young mason committed by Southend court.

17 Debtor 6 was a young painter committed by St Albans court.

18 Debtor 15 was a middle-aged shopkeeper committed by Kingston upon Thames court.

be committed twice in respect of the same sum . . . execution may subsequently be levied on his goods in respect of a sum for which he has already been committed.' (Gregory, 1962, p. 60.) Furthermore, when a judgment summons has issued for instalments rather than the whole judgment debt, a creditor can ask for more than one committal in the enforcement of a single action. As the missing instalments mount up, so the sum grows and *changes.* Thus successive orders of imprisonment would be made against a different sum each time. In practice, however, imprisonment does end a career. Creditors tend to regard any enforcement after prison as futile. After all, a committal order can issue only for small sums and executions had probably proved abortive in the past. Moreover, commitment debtors are defined as the most professional of all defaulters. If one period of imprisonment has no effect, few creditors are prepared to spend time or money on further enforcement.

The bailiff's arguments often transform a debtor who might have paid into a debtor who will not pay. In large measure, therefore, the bailiff is responsible for undermining the effectiveness of imprisonment. He persuades defaulters that they can extinguish their debts by undergoing imprisonment. In so doing, he changes them into people whom creditors regard as thoroughly deviant. The bailiff's prediction thus acts as a self-fulfilling prophecy; prison *does* effectively act as a means of satisfying a judgment debt. The assumptions which debtors entertain about imprisonment are correct in fact, if not in law. 'It surprised me when the bailiff told me it wiped the £31 out. It surprised me. I thought I had to pay.' (Debtor 19.)

When prison is defined in this way, compliance with the bailiff becomes quite a 'rational' course for a debtor to adopt. Debtor 33 was asked if anyone would pay for his release. He replied, 'oh no, I hope not! I might as well work it off this way. I'll just say I've done ten days in Brixton and settled the debt up. . . . I didn't make an application because ten days for £41 was worth it. If it had been twenty-eight days, I would have paid. £41 is a good week's money i'n't it?' The bailiff's appeal to the calculus is often quite explicit. 'The bailiff told me how lucky I was to get in for both things. He told me if I went in for twenty-one days, that'd be the end of it.' (Debtor 6.) The bailiff's task will be complete when he convinces a debtor that prison will help him. The larger the debt on committal, the easier becomes the bailiff's job of persuasion. 'I didn't go to court when the committal order was out. I'd rather be brought for £15 10*s*. than £7 10*s*. I wouldn't bother [to ask anyone for assistance]. I'll sit here till Saturday. I've spoken to the bailiff, they can't get the debt again.' (Debtor 23.) 'The bailiff said it's worth ten quid a week.' (Debtor 3.)[19]

[19] Debtor 3 was a middle-aged groundsman committed by Ilford court.

It is interesting that two facets of county court enforcement help the bailiff. The very issue of a committal warrant increases the amount to be collected, thereby rendering prison more attractive. In the 1961 sample, the mean sum for which a committal order was made was £33 18*s*. but when it was issued this had become £34 18*s*. In addition, it is customary for a court to commit a debtor on all outstanding warrants concurrently.

TABLE 11.1 *Number of warrants per prisoner in 1961*

Warrants	*Number of prisoners*	*Proportion*
		%
	369	78·5
	72	15·3
	20	4·3
	5	1·1
	2	0·4
	1	0·2
	—	—
	1	0·2
Total	470	100·0

As Table 11.1 shows, the average number of warrants issued against each Brixton debtor in 1961 was 1·5. Although judges take other orders into account at a judgment summons hearing, this practice of imprisoning debtors on more than one warrant cannot but lend weight to the bailiff's argument. It appears that the difficult enforcement situation has a very immediate effect on the imprisonment stage. When a bailiff's conning is successful, the debtor willingly enters prison. However, the difficult enforcement situation would not *be* difficult if bailiffs were always successful in their impression-management. It is difficult because a bailiff is vulnerable. The impression which he hopes to convey can be exploded. If his technique does fail, his job will become more demanding and may become dangerous.

Before I examine the responses of the debtors who were disarmed, I would like to describe some of the weaknesses in the bailiff's presentation. The production of a 'correct' impression depends on a debtor's trust and this may not be forthcoming. Although a bailiff may manage to 'cool in' a debtor, he does not often have the opportunity to 'cool him out'. In Goffman's (1968b, p. 231) words, the defaulter is fed through a 'betrayal funnel' which can lead to a profound feeling of disillusionment. The debtor's career has much in common with the treatment of the mental patient:

> When the pre-patient arrives he is likely to learn quite quickly, quite differently. He then finds that the information given him about life in the hospital has had the effect of his having put up less resistance to entering than he now sees he would have put up had he known the facts. Whatever the intentions of those who participated in his transition from person to patient, he may sense they have in effect 'conned' him into his present predicament. . . . As the pre-patient may see it, the circuit of significant figures can function as a kind of *betrayal funnel.*

The bailiff's impression-management may be based on the communication of grossly inaccurate information, and the debtor who has been conned will also feel betrayed. Whilst a disarmed inmate may welcome imprisonment, the jaundiced debtor will have a radically different conception of what happened to him. Such a response will have little effect on the bailiff because he has got rid of the debtor. Nevertheless, a bailiff may have reason to fear that his relationship with a debtor will be contaminated by the latter's contacts with other 'marks'. Debtor 17,[20] for instance, observed, 'I don't know his name. "Bastard", that's what I call him. The wife said the bailiff came round and he's coming on Friday for thirteen quid. I said "fuck that". I know his reputation, he's a rough monkey. He nicked a mate of mine.'

Unskilful conning can force a bailiff to contend with a shocked debtor before they arrive at Brixton. Some cases of impression-management have inbuilt weaknesses which lead to premature insights about the betrayal funnel. A bailiff may present a portrait of the situation which will be contradicted by what actually takes place. 'I gave him[21] the guvnor's address and he said the next stop would be that one. But he didn't go. He's not straight, he lied. He told me he would take me to court to clear things up. . . . The other bailiffs are gentlemen compared with him. . . . Even when I was in the car, he told me he would take me to the guvnor. When we got to the Oval, he said "I've taken a wrong turning", but I said "you're taking me to Brixton", and he said "yes".' (Debtor 26.)[22]

[20] Debtor 17 was a young driver committed by D court. (It is interesting that the hostility of the bailiffs of D court is mirrored in the reactions of its debtors.)

[21] Debtor 26 was committed by the bailiff of D court whose tactics I described in the previous chapter. His experience is identical to the situation I recounted there.

[22] Debtor 26 was a young plasterer committed by D court.

An impression cannot be indefinitely sustained if it contains specific propositions which are falsifiable.

There are other complications which can upset smooth enforcement. The logic of the felicitous calculus, for example, will be convincing only when the debt is considered large. When the debt is small, the calculus would suggest that prison is not 'sensible'. If a bailiff is not taking a debtor to prison for the prisoner's 'own good', it must be for some other reason, and the debtor may find his predicament inexplicable.

> The bailiffs came to the door when I was having a cup of tea. 'I've got a warrant here for your arrest.' 'What's it for?' 'Eight pound ten or ten days.' 'Give me till tomorrow.' 'No, not then.' What's another day to them? Nothing! They had three of them come down. Blow me, it worried me! One was in the back door, two in the front door! Blimey! You'd think I was a criminal or something! Eight pound ten? It's not much! (Debtor 28.)

Furthermore, the bailiff's clumsiness can destroy a debtor's trust. Debtors selected for prison are people who have been defined as deviant. This definition usually remains hidden during the enforcement situation but an inept bailiff may not be able to conceal it. 'I didn't like it at all. I didn't mind the last bailiff; but he came up as if he was the law himself, as if you owed *him* the money. The way he messed me about on Thursday morning! His manner with the court order in his hand! That's worse than being here. I've got a nice lot of neighbours. They like to rabbit. The other just came to do his duty and that was it.' (Debtor 26.) The bailiff's inability to communicate his lack of involvement and neutrality can lead to friction and resentment.

Some bailiffs may feel so much animus against a debtor that they are unable to con. Others may identify certain debtors as too deviant to respond to persuasion. In either case, any attempt at impression-management might be abandoned. The bailiff relies on a display of force instead, allowing his opinion of the debtor to become overt. Debtor 1 complained, 'the bailiffs weren't interested in my troubles. They said they wanted me inside. They're sadists. They called me "boy". They gloated about it.'[23] The difficult enforcement situation has turned into a trial of strength between the two.

> I thought they were just doing a job, but when they come to a door . . . Fascists! Little Hitlers! Don't like the way they shove their way in through doors . . . explaining their rights over and above ordinary people . . . shoving you around. Their trump

[23] Debtor 1 was a young bricklayer committed by Hastings court.

card is 'if you don't come quietly, I'll bring three or four other bailiffs'. They use threats. They like to have a little trouble. They enjoy a good argument. I told him what I was going to do, if he thought he could do it alone, he should try it. (Debtor 8.)[24]

When an attempt at impression-management is abandoned or has failed, debtors cannot always convince themselves that imprisonment is a rational step. When it is sustained, however, debtors tend to treat prison as a kind of penance to which they have given their tacit consent. 'I made up my mind I was going to do it, and that was it. . . . Three weeks is not a long time, but I miss fags. It doesn't matter how bad it is, I'll just have to take it.' (Debtor 6.) The belief that imprisonment ends a debtor's involvement in enforcement is a strong one. Because of it, a debtor feels that he should stoically endure the final stage of his career. He may even feel that he is at last coping with his indebtedness. This is probably why two-thirds (64·3 per cent in 1961) of debtors serve their full sentence.

As Table 11.2 shows, the factor with which release is clearly connected is the size of the debt.

TABLE 11.2 *Size of debt and release from imprisonment in 1961*

Debt	*Debt paid and debtor released before the expiration of his full sentence*
	%
£15	38·0
£35	32·7
£100	19·2
£200	15·4

The sum on a committal warrant is directly tied to the felicitous calculus. Release cannot be simply explained by a debtor's ability to pay the debt because many debtors who could afford to free themselves refused to do so. Debtor 13 said, 'I asked the wife not to pay. The children are sure to ask where the wife's gone. I'd sooner stay to Saturday than pay on Thursday.' Indeed, it is likely that many debtors are unwillingly released. Table 11.3 shows that only 11 per cent of the debts settled in 1961 were paid by the prisoners themselves.

Prolonged incarceration may thus be explained by at least three variables. The assumptions manufactured by bailiffs are strikingly prevalent in prison and they shape the debtor's responses to his

[24] Debtor 8 was a young painter committed by Colchester and Clacton court.

TABLE 11.3 *Who paid for the release of debtors in 1961*

Prisoner's wife	48
Male of different name	24
Prisoner	11
Married female	10
Male of the same name as the prisoner	9
Female relative	2
Firm	1
Record not available	66
Total	171

debts. One debtor shared them to the extent that he could not understand why he had been imprisoned. 'I still feel it's rather silly. I don't see what satisfaction they get. Fourteen days squashes it. They could have got something, now they'll get nothing.' (Debtor 21.) Second, a number of debtors may not be able to afford to pay their debts. 'I never knew nothing about these places. If I could get the money, I'd be out straight away.' (Debtor 9.) Finally, many debtors want to conceal the shameful details of their career from as many others as possible. 'I don't want no-one to know.' (Debtor 30.)[25] Debtor 15 had not even told his wife about his fate. She believed that he was in hospital being treated for Addison's disease. This kind of reticence lessens the chance that an outsider will come to discharge the defaulter.

Because their definitions of the situation are structured by the felicitous calculus, debtors do not seem able to understand why they have been imprisoned.[26] They surmise that their imprisonment is a punishment which gives a mysterious pleasure to enforcers. None of the debtors I interviewed had been pursued by a debt-collector; on the whole, bailiffs are concerned to develop an amiable relationship with debtors; and the rest of the debtors' enforcement was conducted by a distant bureaucratic machine. Debtors are therefore unlikely to feel that they were the subjects of personal hatred. They reason that, if they were not the targets of hatred, their incarceration could give satisfaction to no one. Imprisonment thus becomes an inexplicable event. 'I couldn't tell you [why I have been imprisoned]. That's their procedure, what they do. No special reason.' (Debtor 9.) 'I can't understand it at all. I'm just passed down the line. There's

25 Debtor 30 was a middle-aged labourer committed by Wandsworth court.

26 It is interesting that a judge's idea of what constitutes an excess of pain over pleasure is not always shared by the debtor. An upper middle-class judge may sometimes miscalculate, especially when his assessment is challenged by a persuasive bailiff.

a channel for this, it's a routine. If they called and discriminated . . .' (Debtor 25.) They cannot understand that they have been defined as deviant from afar. Such definitions, they feel, must emerge from face-to-face interaction.[27] 'The gear was so rough that they don't want the stuff back. It's not personal because I haven't met anybody from there.' (Debtor 19.) 'Don't even know me, does he?' (Debtor 11.)[28] One debtor only (21) provided a reason which agreed with my own argument: 'only a personal opinion, but they want to scare you into paying at the last minute. If you haven't got it then that's it, they've pulled the last stroke.' Debtors therefore believe that they cannot be the victims of their creditors' dislike. They are subjected to a mechanical process which does not seem to stimulate feelings of guilt or degradation. Instead, imprisonment is an ambiguous stage which remains open to interpretation.

This belief is reinforced by a structural peculiarity of enforcement which allows debtors to regard themselves as 'normal' people. The debtor's evil is never dramatized because the whole process of identifying the deviant remains covert. The debtor's career is a highly articulate sequence of events yet, even at the ritualized stage of the judgment summons hearing, no clear bench mark is set up. A debtor is always treated as a redeemable person. The ever-present possibility of redemption is the curious aspect of debt collection which denies it a Rubicon. At any stage up to the gates of prison, a debtor can change himself. Unlike Goffman's mental patient, the debtor is able to switch back and forth between the status of person and the status of defaulter. McIntosh (1968, p. 184) argues:

> The disadvantage of this [labelling] practice as a technique of social control is that there may be a tendency for people to become fixed in their deviance once they have become labelled.

27 The debtors' understanding of bureaucratic processes was similar to the perspectives of Boston working-class West Enders described by Gans (1962, p. 95): 'The West Ender has considerable difficulty in understanding object-oriented behavior. He is unable to visualize people organized in cooperative group activity towards a common goal. Although he can see, observe, and describe this activity, he cannot see himself in such a role, and therefore cannot quite understand how others carry it out. Similarly, he has difficulty in comprehending the nature of administrative procedure, and the rules of bureaucratic government. He can explain these only by concepts based on individual motivation and morality, for example, by honesty, selfishness, and greed. Thus, he personalizes all of what are in part, at least, impersonal relationships.'

The debtors also tended to personalize the workings of bureaucracy. However, since the bureaucrats could gain no *personal* satisfaction from their imprisonment, the debtors were unable to explain the creditors' behaviour. If the debtors had viewed their creditors as impersonal organizations, they might well have stated that imprisonment served the goals of retribution, deterrence or denunciation.

28 Debtor 11 was a young labourer committed by St Albans court.

Enforcement does not suffer from this disadvantage of conventional control systems. There is no explicit labelling in debt collection. As a result, the debtor knows himself to be a marginal deviant who can still dispute his pariah status. Because he has not been placed in a fixed category, he feels that he can change his social position. Nevertheless, prison provoked enormous anxiety. Debtors fear stigma and, more especially, they fear that their own self-definition will become affected by their experience. I believe that it is this pre-occupation with self-evaluation that dominates the debtor's stay in Brixton.

I asked the debtors what they felt the worst features of their imprisonment were. Two-thirds of them referred chiefly to physiological deprivation: they objected to the lack of cigarettes, to the food and to boredom. Debtor 16 said 'the worst is night-times, locked up for a long time and no cigarettes. I'm used to smoking and drinking. The night seems long.' Debtor 13 complained, 'the worst thing is the boredom and the fact that I can't smoke.' Just under half the debtors (47·6 per cent) were distressed at their novel lack of autonomy. 'It's bad enough just the fact that you've lost your freedom and got to do as you're told.' (Debtor 21.) 'Not being able to walk out without someone else opening and shutting doors. The loss of freedom, it's amazing!' (Debtor 14.) Only one debtor (24) was explicitly concerned about the stigma inflicted by his imprisonment: '. . . me character, it don't stand very good for that. It's a shame on the family coming here.'

Inmates were thus most vociferous about the immediate physical effects of Brixton. They nevertheless revealed a considerable disquiet about the manner in which prison threatened their self-definition. Their whole career was thought to be potentially shaming. Debtor 6, for example, observed, 'people say "oh yes, the bailiff, he's alright", but my wife's a bit old-fashioned. She thinks it's a terrible thing for the bailiff to come.' Debtor 10 himself applied stigma to other debtors; he told me that he had known nothing about enforcement because 'I've never been in that company.'[29]

The debtors' anxiety was first triggered off by their meetings with enforcement staff. Their upset was allayed only by the bailiff's role-playing. Debtor 18 had felt 'worried and embarrassed. I'm still worried. [The bailiff] was decent and tried to explain what it was all about.'[30] Similarly, Debtor 19 said, 'I felt that big. He was a decent bailiff, one you could talk to.' Thus the debtors' initial experience of social control was marked by an apprehension that they had been critically labelled. Debtor 2 recalled that he had been 'embarrassed

[29] Debtor 10 was a young plumber committed by Kingston upon Thames court.

[30] Debtor 18 was a young labourer committed by D court.

and ashamed. I felt very furtive about it. I felt cornered.' Embarrassment can stem from an inability to handle an unfamiliar role. It can also be caused by discrepant demands being placed on a person. It seems clear that the debtors felt that they had been assigned to a foreign and unwelcome status. It was only when the bailiff translated this status into an acceptable form that the debtors believed themselves able to enter a relationship.

Another source of anxiety disturbed the debtors. They expected that their imprisonment would have damaging effects on their life after release. The extent of the possible damage depended on the relation which the defaulter had with significant people outside. One type of relation existed when these people were aware of the debtor's stay in Brixton and disapproved of it. Debtor 9 said, 'although you're only in for debt, once you've been in this sort of place, people are going to think different of you. Bosses will try to get rid of you.' Debtor 10 observed, 'it's troubling me now, these friends of mine. It's not nice to have gone to prison, very degrading. It doesn't go down well in club life.' A second possibility exists when a debtor is unsure about the people's response. Debtor 19 stated, 'I don't know. It's when you find who your friends are.' In the same way, Debtor 30 said, 'I don't know if they'll shun me or not.'

Third, a debtor may believe that his sentence will not stigmatize him although others know about it. Debtor 33 remarked, 'they treat it as a bit of a joke. Most of them are old cons, they're always in for assault and drunkenness.' 'They'll have a good laugh, they're used to it.' (Debtor 26.) The last, and most common, case is that of a group of significant people who know nothing of the imprisonment but who would apply sanctions to the inmate if they did know. 'They treat you as a criminal if they find out; but it doesn't get in the paper.' (Debtor 28.) 'If anybody asks, I'll tell 'em I've been working away. If they did know, I'd be proper choked.' (Debtor 6.)

This last category of debtors will take measures to protect itself and the bailiff may even assist its endeavours. A bailiff's task is manifestly easier if his prisoner is reassured about the improbability of disclosure. 'Fortunately, the bailiff is a gentleman. He said "go sick for a week and cover yourself that way".' (Debtor 13.) These debtors hope that their absence will be covered by an innocuous explanation. 'I come and go a reasonable amount. I quite often don't come home for a week.' (Debtor 2.) 'They think I've gone to see me mother.' (Debtor 3.) They refuse to advertise their association with Brixton. 'I don't want people to know I'm here, so I don't write from here. I'd rather have 'phoned, but the bailiff didn't let me.' (Debtor 30.)

I have argued so far that debtors are misled by their bailiffs into thinking that imprisonment extinguishes a debt. They are also persuaded that their sentence is quite a useful way of dealing with their indebtedness. As a result, most of them are prepared to serve their full sentence. Nevertheless, they tend to be anxious about their presence in Brixton because they are aware that it may stigmatize them. I would like to discuss the way in which they adapt to the prison community in the light of this argument. My main theme will be the reassurance debtors seek that they are not eligible for pariah status. They not only want to cope with their audience, they also wish to convince themselves. Such a desire is commonly felt by marginal groups who hope to demonstrate their 'normalcy'. The mental patient, for instance, suffers the same anxieties and seeks the same reassurance (Messinger, *et al.*, 1968, pp. 9–11):[31]

> There can be little doubt but that mental patients are in a situation productive of being 'on'. Bereft of membership in the group of reasonable men, they are forced to address the task of restoring their 'character', of becoming 'sane persons' again. It does not take mental patients long to discover that, as they lost their 'sanity' in the eyes of others through what they did and said, so may they regain it. . . . 'Normality' is an aspect of self the mental patient *himself* profoundly desires to take for granted again. . . . We are led to see . . . that the mental patient is not satisfied to *appear* 'normal', he strives to *be* 'normal'.

Relief cannot be obtained through release because debtors are unwilling to leave prison before they have completed their full sentence. 'I can't blame anyone. I made the offer but they didn't want to accept it. I'd rather pay than be here, but they wanted me to be here instead.' (Debtor 23.) Prison precludes payment and it is therefore something that must be suffered. 'I had to come, and that's all there is to it. It's no good crying about it. Nobody wants to come here.' (Debtor 11.) The debtors believed that prison was unpleasant but physically tolerable. Indeed, many of them had found it to be more pleasant than they had imagined it would be. 'I'm right choked, but it's better than I expected.' (Debtor 12.)[32]

[31] Dahl (pp. 91–2) describes his own feelings thus: 'Beside the doorway leading to the hall, there was a small mirror. I hesitated before it, glanced into it. It seemed to me that my eyes were opened wider than usual. . . . *If you're ever going to get out of here, you're going to have to narrow those eyes. People can see clear through you, they're so wide open. You look like a maniac all right. Narrow the eyes. There, that's better, and you're going to have to quit talking so much. Only a lunatic tells people everything he knows. . . .*'

[32] Debtor 12 was a young cutter committed by Kingston upon Thames court.

But it is not the physical impact of Brixton that disturbs the debtor most. He is more concerned about the meaning of his committal there and, whilst he is a prisoner, about his proper place within the walls.

Debtors equate a prison with punishment but rarely feel that they committed a wrong. 'I'd rather be out than in. I've never done nothing wrong.' (Debtor 20.)[33] A prison is a suitable place for the housing of criminals, but debtors feel that they have nothing in common with criminals. They are often extremely conscious of the identity which they have been given by the institution. 'From the moment you come in, you're treated as if you're a criminal. All your belongings are taken away. Shoved in a shower irrespective of whether you're clean or dirty. That's when it hits you, you know you're in.' (Debtor 25.) This new identity can be frightening and alien to the defaulter. 'I feel profoundly ashamed. I try to hide away. It's very bad.' (Debtor 15.) It may be strenuously resisted by protestations of how inapposite it is. 'I've been at work. I've got references. I've been in people's houses and never took anything. I couldn't sleep last night. I'm not a gambler. I've got a clean record.' (Debtor 9.)

Debtors are thus prepared to brave prison, but they also feel a need to ward off the attacks it directs against their selves. This protection can be afforded by the creation of a special status, a status which will sharply differentiate them from the threatening criminals. It is founded on a triple basis. The first part consists of a declaration of loyalty to 'orthodox' values.

The Prison Regulations (Section 13, Subsection 3) state that 'civil prisoners who elect to wear their own clothing should not be permitted to associate with any other class of prisoners.' However, 'adequate segregation of civil prisoners, from those convicted, is almost impossible in the prevailing circumstances.' (Governor of Brixton.) Despite the efforts of prison officers, a Brixton debtor is likely to encounter a criminal. Like any other inmate, the defaulter finds the prison community an uncongenial environment (Sykes and Messinger, 1960, p. 15):

> The remaining significant features of the inmate's social environment is the presence of other imprisoned criminals. Murderers, rapists, thieves, confidence men, and sexual deviants are the inmate's constant companions, and this enforced intimacy may prove to be disquieting even for the hardened recidivist.

The debtor's normal reaction is thus simple avoidance. 'I've nothing

[33] Debtor 20 was a young bricklayer committed by G court.

to do with them. I stay clear of them. I just don't want to get involved. Seven days is more than enough.' (Debtor 5.)[34] Social distance is increased by the criminals' manifest lack of interest in the county court inmate. 'They look down on you a bit. Debtors are rather a scurvy lot.' (Debtor 2.)[35] Criminals are avoided for two reasons. Debtors attach conventional labels to them and are therefore distressed at their threatening proximity. 'Some of them deserve to be here, by the look of them. Some of them are frightening.' (Debtor 25.)[36] Criminals are also immoral; Debtor 23[37] told me that he knew nothing about the convicted prisoners: '. . . no, I don't know. I'm doing my own time. They've been dishonest.'

Second, association carries with it the risk of contamination. Not only might people class the debtor and criminal together, the debtor may accept this classification himself. 'I don't mix with the criminal type. They talk to you if you talk to them. I wouldn't mix with 'em. I'm not that sort. If you mix you become a criminal yourself. It's bad enough coming to one of these places without being damned as a criminal yourself.' (Debtor 28.)[38]

Debtors define the criminal in a curiously conventional manner. They conspicuously display their distance from the wickedness of crime and thereby emphasize their own rectitude. Their sharing of a common fate with criminals leads them to disavow any similarity that may exist between them. Debtor 8 observed of criminals that they are 'damn fools to get into trouble. Crime doesn't pay!' Similarly, Debtor 10 remarked, 'I can't understand why they do the crimes they do. Bloody robbing people!' Again, Debtor 23 argued, 'if I was in their position, I wouldn't touch crime myself. Trying to get something for nothing!' The rejection of comparisons with stigmatized others occurs in other contexts. A more extreme example is provided by the Puerto Rican schizophrenic who dissociates himself from the status of a 'loco' or lunatic (Rogler and Hollingshead, 1965, p. 218):

> Schizophrenic persons are particularly vulnerable to being assigned the role of the loco. Consequently, we explored the possibility that the schizophrenic's portrayal of this role would be drawn in less harsh and more benign terms than that drawn by well people. This idea was erroneous! There is no tendency on the part of the schizophrenics to soften the portrait of the loco; sick and well persons describe him as violent, immoral, criminal, filthy, idiosyncratic and worthless.

[34] Debtor 5 had no civil or criminal record.
[35] Debtor 2 had a criminal record.
[36] Debtor 25 had no civil or criminal record.
[37] Debtor 23 had a civil record only.
[38] Debtor 28 had a civil record only.

The felicitous calculus acts as another strong support for the debtor's status differential. According to the calculus, civil prisoners are superior to the criminal because they tend to receive shorter sentences for larger sums of money. Debtor 26 believed, 'they probably resent me. I'm only in for a week. They'd like me more if I was in for six months. They boast about the lengths of their sentences to boost their morale. They say my sentence is a piece of cake.'[39] The debtors regard criminals as a negative reference group from whom they are estranged by a reciprocated dislike. As Debtor 9 put it, 'they don't make no comments.'[40] In some cases the felicitous calculus can only be imputed to the criminals' evaluation of defaulters. 'I suppose they think I'm lucky whereas they're unlucky. Some have three months for twenty pounds.' (Debtor 12.)[41]

Debtors are clearly reluctant to enter into relationships with other prisoners. Their sentences are short, prison awes them and they are unwilling to involve themselves in the prison community. Debtor 24, for instance, stated, 'I don't talk much to other prisoners, I don't talk much to anybody.'[42] Similarly, Debtor 30 remarked, 'I don't have much to do with them. I don't ask a lot of questions.'[43]

However, debtors *are* forced to have dealings with maintenance offenders because both groups share F Wing or the classroom dormitories. 'They say "seven days? You're a bed and breakfast chap!" We're stuck in the same classroom so you've got to have conversation.' (Debtor 5.) Whereas all the debtors feared convicted prisoners, they did not agree about maintenance offenders. Forty per cent of the defaulters approved their actions. Debtor 6 reflected, 'their wives seem to have told them a pack of lies. They've had a raw deal.' Nevertheless, another 40 per cent censored them in a way which seemed to entail an incongruous condemnation of default. 'They're only slags. If they can't pay their wives, they deserve to be here.' (Debtor 17.) This kind of incongruity often colours a deviant's perspectives on his own and others' behaviour: Sykes and Matza (1967, p. 134), for example, have suggested that delinquency can be neutralized by a denial of the victim:

> The existence of the victim can be denied for the delinquent . . . by the circumstances of the delinquent act. Insofar as the victim is physically absent, unknown or a vague abstraction . . . the awareness of the victim's existence is weakened.

In much the same way, county court debtors are able to deny

39 Debtor 26 had no criminal or civil record.

40 Debtor 9 had no criminal or civil record.

41 Debtor 12, who had no civil or criminal record, had been sentenced to one week's imprisonment on a £32 debt.

42 Debtor 24 had a civil record.

43 Debtor 30 had a civil record.

bureaucratic creditors their role as victim, but they cannot neutralize the force of personal commitments. Pauline Morris (1965, p. 238) observed, 'those who were in prison for debt, as opposed to non-payment of maintenance, claimed to get on very well with their wives. . . .' This discrimination between victims (which is also exemplified by the debtors' description of criminals) may illuminate the causes of the defaulters' contumacy and their puzzlement at imprisonment. Debtor 23, for instance, clearly ascribed moral weight to arrangements made and enforced in face-to-face meetings. He said of maintenance offenders, 'they're silly. They was married once. If I left my wife, I'd expect to pay.' He also said, 'the clothing club people called at the door so I'm still paying. Anybody who called got paid'. The impersonal enforcement machinery of large creditors prevented them from becoming meaningful victims.

Debtors do not appear to seek each other out. I assumed that my presence in Brixton would form the subject of conversation but none of the debtors had heard of me. Their avoidance of prisoners in general may contribute to their isolation from their fellows. It does not allow them to recognize other county court inmates. Debtor 9 said, 'I don't know who's who.' Moreover, debtors entered Brixton in such few numbers and stayed there for such short periods that it was unlikely that an appreciable group would be formed at any one time. County court debtors influenced one another in two situations only. First, their admissions might be bunched together. Debtor 14 said, 'there's a little section here who're all debtors. We're all in the classroom. We talk because we've had similar experiences. They're not too bad.' Second, debtors who applied to purge their contempt sought guidance and reassurance from each other. In all other cases, debtors are forced to work out individual solutions to their problems.

This, then, is the manner in which debtors adapt to Brixton. They are marginal to the social structure of the prison because they serve their sentences in a forced and sought isolation. Whereas 'both the staff and other prisoners regarded them as the dregs of the prison population' (Morris, 1965, p. 234), they define themselves as superior to, and different from, the rest of the inmate community. Their desire to detach themselves from the penal experience makes them reduce their contacts with others to the very minimum. 'We don't want to mix with cons.' (Debtor 1.)[44] They avoid possible sources of friction: 'there's only one way to act in prison—"keep your mouth shut." I'm not supposed to work but I'm not going to question it.' (Debtor 5.) Predictably, this feeling is also reflected in their attitude towards prison officers. Debtor 17 said simply, 'I keep out of their way.'

[44] Debtor 1 had a civil record.

Debtors' relations with other figures in Brixton act as a basis for their rejection of the deviant label. Only four debtors did not share the belief that they were innocent. Debtor 13, for example, argued that he had been imprisoned because of 'wrong-doing what I've done' and Debtor 26 said, 'I've been messing them about.' Debtor 2, who was one of the few identifiable professional debtors I interviewed, was more explicit. 'I didn't want to expose my circumstances to all and sundry. I'm trying to do a few manoeuvres financially. I was in such a position, dodging about, that I couldn't do anything. I knew it was a question of time before I sorted things out. . . . My attitude was to wait and see how much rope you could get. I rather miscalculated. It blew up in my face.' Debtor 2 also remarked, 'there's a bit of the criminal in every debtor.'

These four debtors were unusual; their fellows all felt that they had been improperly treated. Other people have commented on the debtors' rejection of the deviant label. The Governor of Brixton, for instance, has described the typical debtor 'bewailing his "innocence".' Similarly, Morris (1965, p. 238) said, 'one of the most striking differences between the criminals and the civils was in their views of themselves as people. The civils saw themselves as being, on the whole, pretty reasonable and decent fellows. . . .' Paul de Berker (1965, p. 313) has made much the same point.

Although I am unable to furnish a psychological analysis of this rejection, I am not prepared to accept that it is solely a reflection of the debtors' 'inadequacy', 'fecklessness' or ingenuousness.[45] I would argue instead that it is directly related to the structure of the enforcement system. The system denies a debtor subcultural support and, even in prison, he is a solitary person. In this respect, defaulters have much in common with certain shoplifters and their reactions are identical (Cameron, 1968, pp. 333–6):

> Pilferers differ in one outstanding respect, at least, from other thieves. They generally do not think of themselves as thieves. In fact, even when arrested, they resist strongly being pushed to admit their behavior is theft. . . . Pilferers feel that if their family or friends learn about their arrest they will be thoroughly disgraced. The fear, shame and remorse expressed by arrested pilferers could not be other than genuine or a reflection of their appraisal of the attitudes they believe others will take toward them. . . . Because the adult pilferer does not think of himself, prior to his arrest, as a thief and can conceive of no in-group support for himself in that role, his arrest forces him to reject the role.

The suddenness of the shock faced by conned debtors resembles

[45] I shall examine the concept of 'inadequacy' in the next chapter.

the abrupt hurt of arrested pilferers. They both fear and disown stigma. These similarities demand a sociological explanation, not an explanation couched in the language of psychopathology. My explanation will be based on the answers which I received to questions that I asked the debtors about why they had originally defaulted and why they had persisted in their default.

The answers seemed to fall into four areas. The first is a novel version of what Sykes and Matza (1967, pp. 134–5) call the condemnation of the condemners:

> The delinquent shifts the focus of attention from his own deviant acts to the motives and behavior of those who disapprove of his violations. His condemners, he may claim, are hypocrites, deviants in disguise, or impelled by personal spite.

Whilst delinquents are forced to deal with outright verbal degradation, debtors are gently persuaded to take an ignominious role. I have argued that debtors rarely encounter overt manifestations of disapproval. As a result, debtors merely fail to comprehend the motives and behaviour of their condemners. These, they argue, are not related to enforcement goals, since 'the majority believed that their debt would be cancelled because they had come to prison.' (de Berker, 1965, p. 312.) They could not attribute their imprisonment to 'personal spite'. It was due to 'no personal reason. It's too big a firm to get personal.' (Debtor 20.) Debt collection relies on a manipulation of techniques. Debtors face techniques, not motives, and it is the techniques which they condemn.

Debtors seem to respond most frequently to pressure which is applied in a face-to-face situation. Indeed, the registrar of E court told me that he believed very few debts would remain unpaid if bailiffs undertook to make regular calls. The more complicated enforcement methods are employed only because they are cheaper. Defaulters can thus neutralize their deviance by asserting that their default is due to the enforcers' irresponsibility. 'The Co-op man failed to call. I asked him why not but he didn't give a reason. I told the court that if somebody called, I'd paid.' (Debtor 13.) I asked Debtor 16 why he had defaulted. He replied, 'no particular reason. I just didn't have it. If they'd come to the door, I'd have paid them, but they didn't and it seemed easy not to.' The debtor refuses to legitimate the impersonal sanctions of the creditor and court. He believes that the only compelling mode of collection is a direct confrontation. The responsibility for action thus reverts back to the enforcer. A debtor can claim that it was the enforcer's inertia which produced default, not his own.

The second reason for inaction is sometimes fused with the first.

Whilst the condemnation of the condemners is a somewhat negative justification based on the formula 'I would have paid, if only . . .', the second reason argues 'I did not pay because . . .' A sympathetic excuse made default an innocent act. The cause was either innocent itself (and therefore not blameworthy), or else it lay outside the debtor's control. The innocent cause *and* condemnation were both present in Debtor 1's statement. He said, 'it was partly my fault. I forgot to appear and pay. When they come round, I pay. With four or five orders, I forget to pay. So I pay when they come round, I don't send it. The bailiffs have got to know me, they know I forget. I pay it when they come.' Debtor 1 not only blamed the bailiffs, he also attributed his default to the natural human failing of forgetfulness.

Forgetfulness is one of a number of human conditions which, although they give rise to unfortunate consequences, are commonly accepted as legitimate excuses for those consequences. If a man is rude, he may later dismiss his rudeness as insignificant because he was 'not himself'. In other words, he was so out of role that his behaviour did not convey anything of his 'real' self. Human relations are so prone to breakdown that it seems necessary to create conventions which automatically restore order (cf. Goffman, 1969, pp. 14–18). The most common convention is the simple apology. If an apology has to be expanded, there is a further class of apologetic formulae which have become incorporated in the vocabulary of social relations. The formulae are relatively few in number and their sole intention is to signify that relations should be resumed. They are not supposed to be closely examined or even queried. Indeed, questioning would imply that the apologetic gesture has been rejected. Thus, one of the 'correct' responses to 'I was upset' is 'that's alright', it cannot be 'why were you upset?'

These gestures cannot be used in certain situations simply because they are conventions. It would seem that they are acceptable only when they deal with relatively minor breaches. If an individual does not answer a statement, he can safely say that he 'was lost in thought', but he cannot defend a major discourtesy by saying this. A man can only 'lose himself' politely when he is in reasonable control of himself. When a major breach of etiquette occurs, the use of the conventional gesture might be regarded as an added rudeness.

Debtors resort to this kind of explanation, but extend its credibility. Serious delictions cannot be normally covered by this class of response. Defaulters might satisfactorily account for their not having posted a letter by saying that they had 'just forgotten' to do so; but they use this formula to excuse protracted default. 'I've just been working away and, one thing and another, I just forgot.' (Debtor 24.) 'When I got reminders, I tried to pay. But then I stopped paying, it just slipped my mind. I forgot when payments were due.' (Debtor 12.) 'I put it on one side and said "I must pay that", but I just more or less forgot about it. Went to the back of my mind.' (Debtor 14.)

Debtors believe that this is a useful recipe for warding off threatening labels. They are not 'different' or 'wicked' for, after all, 'anyone can forget'. Although enforcers subscribe to these common conventions, their credibility has been strained. This partially accounts for the gulf which separates the debtors' and the enforcers' definitions of the situation.

The other alternative has two variants. One of them uses the concept of alienation. Debtors are preponderantly working class and various sociologists have argued that a belief in fate is a component of working-class culture. Miller (1958, p. 11), for example, states, 'many lower class individuals feel that their lives are subject to a set of forces over which they have relatively little control.' Miller's stress is placed on the importance of the ideas of good and bad luck. The Brixton debtors, however, echoed a slightly different form of the belief in fate. Many of their statements suggested that they felt powerless before outside forces. They had become the objects rather than the subjects of their lives, abdicating responsibility for their actions. 'They tended to see the cause of their troubles as external to themselves, usually in the form of "bad luck".' (Morris, 1965, p. 241.) 'Somebody came from the shop to tell me to pay ten bob a week. I did pay for a couple of weeks, then things got on top of me again.' (Debtor 6.) 'I just got into a rut and that was it.' (Debtor 11.) 'Things got on top of me and I didn't know whether I was coming or going.' (Debtor 12.)

The second version locates the reason for inertia in a more specifically caused impotence. Actions are related back to a significant precipitating event which dominates the debtor's default. The debtor can transfer blame from himself to an outside phenomenon which justifies all subsequent inaction. A debtor may have been ill or unemployed several years before his imprisonment but such a cause would inhibit all further activity on his part. A feature of this version is that (in the interview replies at least) events have become telescoped. The connections which debtors trace between cause and effect are rendered implausible by the long period of time which lapses between them. Temporal association becomes less important than symbolic association. There is a timeless quality about this mode of explanation which requires a willing suspension of disbelief. A debtor's account of his past would have one think that the cause of default occurred immediately before his imprisonment.

Illness or unemployment not only serves as a reasonable excuse for default, it also provides the basis for an acceptable model of the self. If the debtor believes that he was incapable of paying because he was prevented by outside forces, he cannot define himself as unprincipled or deviant. Cressey's (1953, pp. 98–9) embezzlers reacted to the threat of stigma in much the same way:

> In a 'non-shareable problem-position-of-trust' situation trusted persons 'objectify' their own actions to the extent that they place themselves in the place of another person or group of persons with the status of 'trustee' and hypothesize their reactions. The hypothesized reactions to 'borrowing' in order to solve a non-shareable problem, for example, are much different from hypothesized reactions to 'stealing', and the trusted person behaves accordingly. Similarly, the hypothesized reactions to a conception of self as an 'ill' person or as a 'pressed' person have different implications for behavior than hypothesized reactions to a conception of self as 'criminal'.

The debtor's movement from the status of honest customer to that of defaulter is not nearly so abrupt as the change brought about by the embezzler's betrayal of trust. Furthermore, the stigma imposed by criminal sanctions is more upsetting than that imposed by county court enforcement. In consequence, the embezzler's need to provide a favourable interpretation of his behaviour is rather more urgent than the defaulter's. Moreover, an articulate, white-collar criminal is better equipped to stand outside himself than a working-class defaulter. As Gans (1962, pp. 98–9) points out, someone who is person-oriented has difficulty in objectifying his own actions:

> . . . the society of voluntary organizations and purposive community participation . . . often requires the kind of behavior I have . . . described as object-oriented. In order to participate in this type of group life, the individual must develop some detachment and self-consciousness about his activities and about himself, which leads to the creation of a *self-image*. . . . The person-oriented West Ender, however, does not live in this society. His social life takes place in peer groups that are not given to cooperative activity or purposive goal-seeking. Indeed, much of his behavior is based on impulsive, but time-tested, reactions to the people he has known since childhood—a type of social life that does not encourage or require the detachment demanded in voluntary organizations. Thus the West Ender develops a different 'me', with a different type of 'generalized other', and operates without a self-image.

To the extent that the Brixton debtors were person-oriented, their protestations would have been less detached and sophisticated than the embezzler's. Nevertheless, I believe that they attempted to construct a viable self which could deal with attacks by citing illness or calamity as excuses.

The third type of answer appeals to what might be termed a higher morality. Debtors recognize that payment is a desirable act, but they argue that it is only one of a number of competing goods. They may have to forgo payment if they are to respond to the most pressing claims that are made on them. The most competitive claim is the defence of principle and it is tied up with the debtors' conception of honour. 'It's not as if I was skint at the time, it was on principle. The car was on six months guarantee, the company went bankrupt.' (Debtor 25.) An interesting feature of the debtors' neutralizing arguments is that many reasons may be invoked simultaneously. Debtor 25, for instance, also cited the single precipitating event. 'My wife and I didn't see eye to eye. I came home and found a letter from the council threatening eviction. It was the first time I'd heard of arrears. I gave money to the wife but she hasn't been paying. I lost heart, things go along and then everything goes bust on you at once.' Similarly, Debtor 34 invoked principle: 'one H.P. debt I had no intention of paying. It was a second-hand car that didn't go. A matter of principle . . .' But he also resorted to the conventional explanation: 'I didn't have time. They just picked me up. I had forgot all about it.'

The higher morality may be employed in the context of a hierarchy of economic ends. The lower ends may have to be sacrificed in favour of the higher. 'I always kept the important things square, the rent and household things. You can always do without a motorcar.' (Debtor 5.) The hierarchy may be constructed around a successful presentation of self. Debtor 2, for example, was preoccupied with the way in which others evaluated his front. He told me that he wanted to appear confident and affluent. In consequence, he was most concerned about some money which he owed to a newsagent because he feared that his default would be broadcast around his village.

The final class of justification has been extensively described in this thesis. It is based on the exceptional ease with which debtors can move out of the deviant role. Defaulters are seldom told that they are irrevocably deviant and the simple payment of a debt will automatically restore them to the normal population. A debtor can argue that his intention to repay is proof of his true normality. The argument takes the form: 'I meant to pay all the time and, if only . . . had not happened, I *would* have discharged my debt. It is merely bad luck that I am in prison because I am really no defaulter.' The intention acts as an anchor for the debtor's conviction that he is essentially honest. It therefore becomes a focus of much of his explanation (de Berker, 1965, p. 313):

> After long discussion with such people their basic negative attitude to repayment of the debt often comes through to the interviewer although they maintain to the end their intention to pay.

Thus Debtor 16 said, 'I knew I'd have to pay but I didn't know I'd come here', and Debtor 23 stated, 'yes, I was willing to do so [pay] in two weeks.' Debtor 2 remarked that he was aware he had to settle his debts because 'I'm not in Noddyland, I'm not psychopathic.' Because imprisonment is viewed as a symbolic substitute for monetary payment, debtors in Brixton felt that they had discharged their obligations in an honourable way. They could maintain that they had always intended to pay and that, because they have made expiation, their integrity has not been undermined.

There are two other minor influences which seem to perpetuate default. A few debtors made statements which suggested that they were acquainted with a default subculture. Debtor 23, for instance, said of bailiffs, 'they bring court orders. Everyone round our road thinks its an everyday occurrence. They don't think it's too bad.' Again, Debtor 1 told me that it was 'common knowledge' that bailiffs force their committed women debtors to sleep with them. Differential association was further suggested by a meagre subcultural vocabulary. Some debtors talked of being 'county courted'. For instance, Debtor 11 said, 'I knew you'd get county courted. That's obvious, everybody knows that.' Another debtor called bailiffs 'bums', a perfectly correct term. Most defaulters, however, kept their careers private and did not seem to be members of a subculture.

In contrast, one or two defaulters seemed to be quite ignorant about county court procedure. Debtor 21 had written to his creditor: 'I explained I couldn't afford it and offered it back. The snatch man got me to ride the machine back to the yard. He said, "by letting me have it back, you'll hear no more about it, no black-listing on H.P." All smooth talk!' Conning at the repossession stage can complicate legal collection later. The same debtor argued, 'if it was repossessed, I thought that was it. As far as I'm concerned, I don't owe this. I told them about the snatch-back . . .' There were other misconceptions about the courts but they were relatively insignificant. The courts rely heavily on their negotiating mechanisms. Unlike most social control agencies, they are anxious to inform the deviant about the ways in which sanctions can be averted. Despite some curious omissions (execution, for example) warrants tend to be implemented only when protracted overtures to the debtor have failed. The formal lines of communication between the court and debtor are reinforced by the informal links which are set up by bailiffs. Although the debtors seemed surprised that they had been imprisoned, they appeared knowledgeable about the other phases of enforcement.

Enforcement has no official degradation ceremonies which would prevent debtors from protesting their innocence. They are allowed to retain innumerable props for their self-evaluation and are never rewarded for playing a deviant role. Up to the gates of Brixton, the bailiff's actions continually affirm that they are normal (if unfortunate) people. Other control systems sometimes rely on an encouragement of deviance, but debt collection does not. Furthermore, as I shall show in the next chapter, there is no general condemnation of default. There is no widespread concern about debt or the measures that are taken to combat it. As a result, few debtors are subjected to pressures which induce crippling feelings of guilt or anxiety about their identity. Instead, there are subsidiary but pressing problems about what people might think about their involvement with bailiffs or with imprisonment. I have argued that bailiffs are usually able to solve these problems by proferring explanations of why a stay in Brixton is a desirable and sensible experience.

12 Typifications of debtors

Debt collection organizes and is organized by visions of social reality which direct and account for all central activity. It is the interpretations which collectors bring to bear on their work that make it a systematic and coherent enterprise. In particular, those interpretations are structured by typifications of the defaulter. The feckless, professional and unfortunate debtors dominate most critical decision-making. Until now, I have not examined the origins and nature of these master typifications in any detail. It is clear that such an examination is necessary and, in this chapter, I shall offer a rudimentary explanation of how important perspectives on defaulters arise. I shall separately discuss the typifications maintained by legislators, by the public, by collectors and by authoritative outsiders.

Legislators

Because enforcement is waged as unobtrusively as possible, it does not occupy a salient position in the life of many people. It is rarely a matter of public debate or concern. Uninvolved outsiders consequently exercise little control over the structuring of collection processes. There is relatively little public negotiation of the place and meaning of a collection system. Rather, its shape is unilaterally determined by a few powerful groups. Chief amongst them is the legal profession. Many of the major features of enforcement are regulated by legal definitions.

The essential elements of deviancy are frequently construed as a combination of action and intention. Deviant intention without concomitant activity is almost never sanctioned in the West; deviant action without intention is often neutralized. Default is only marginally deviant because it consists of inaction with a problematic intention. It is a conditional deviancy whose full significance is to be retrospectively understood at some point in future time. Certainty about the meaning of a default must always be suspended. The marginality of default is enhanced by the fact that the stage when a definitive judgment is made cannot but be arbitrary.

Default itself is not taken to be deviant; what is significant is the defaulter's motives. Beccaria (1963, pp. 76–7) expressed this view most forcefully:

> I think it important to distinguish between the fraudulent and the innocent bankrupt: the first should be assigned the same punishment that counterfeiters of money receive, for to counterfeit a piece of coined metal, which is a pledge of the obligations of citizens, is not a greater crime than to counterfeit the obligations themselves. But the innocent bankrupt, who, after a rigorous examination, has demonstrated before his judge that either the malice or the misfortune of others, or events which human prudence cannot avoid, have stripped him of his possession—upon what barbarous pretence is he thrown into prison, deprived of the sole sad good that yet remains to him, that of mere liberty, to experience the agonies of the guilty, and perhaps, with the desperation of violated honesty, to repent of the very innocence that permitted him to live peacefully under the tutelage of those laws which it was not in his power to offend?—laws dictated by the powerful out of greed and suffered by the weak for the sake of that hope glittering now and then in the human heart, which makes us believe that unlucky accidents are reserved for others and only advantageous ones for us?

Until 1971, the county courts system was still dominated by this perspective. The 1869 Debtors Act, and the debate that preceded it, make it clear that legislators believe in the existence of two discrete groups of debtors, the honest and the dishonest.[1] A Member of Parliament, who spoke at the debate, urged Beccaria's principles when he said 'he believed that imprisonment in cases of fraudulent indebtedness was right, but that the man who was merely unfortunate should not be regarded or treated as a criminal.' (Candlish, Hansard, vol. 195, p. 176.) The Act abolished imprisonment for *debt*, but it retained a penal sanction for the fraudulent debtor. In consequence, the judgment summons procedure under Section 5 of the Act was expressly designed to discriminate between the honest and the dishonest defaulter. The legal emphasis on *intention* and *motive* rather than on action colours the bulk of enforcement.

[1] For a recent echo of this argument, see the Hansard report of Parliamentary questions about the Payne Committee Report (Hansard, 1969, pp. 461, 462).

The county courts are thus based on a system of checks which are supposed to ensure that the fraudulent debtor will be punished but the feckless and the unfortunate will escape relatively unscathed. The Payne Committee's (1969, p. 252) recommendation that imprisonment for debt should be totally abolished reflected this concern about efficient discrimination:

> The evidence which has been put before us leads inevitably to the conclusion that the vast majority of debtors who are actually received in prison under orders of the county courts are inadequate, unfortunate, feckless or irresponsible persons; they are, for the most part, not dishonest and do not therefore require punishment; many of them do not really qualify for imprisonment under the Debtors Act 1869 and we do not think that they would have been committed to prison by the courts if the system had been properly adapted to enable the persistent or dishonest debtors to be distinguished from the inadequate persons and if adequate evidence of the character, mentality, background and general circumstances of the latter at the time of their arrest had been put before the court in addition to the sometimes meagre evidence of their means and assets.

Coupled with uncertainties about problematic intention is what is construed to be the equivocal role of the creditor or collector. Default has not been conventionally treated as a product of individual delinquency. It has, instead, been regarded as the outcome of a delinquent social system. Such doubts about creditors, money-lenders and middlemen have long characterized the more paternalistic legislator (cf. Thompson, 1971). The legal perspective does not clearly indicate whether the creditor or the debtor is primarily to blame for default. The sympathies of law-givers have constantly oscillated between the two. Thus, the preamble to an Act of 1760 (1 Geo. III, c. 17, ss. 46–49, preamble to s. 46) complained 'many people who are prisoners for debt too often choose to continue in prison, and spend their substance there, than discover and deliver up to their creditors their estates or effects towards satisfying their just debts.' The Act compelled debtors to surrender certain kinds of property, but it remained in force for a mere two years because 'great inconveniences have arisen from such powers being given to creditors' (2 Geo. III, c. 2). Similarly, a Member of Parliament argued in the debate on the 1869 Act (M'Mahon, Hansard, vol. 195, p. 175) that creditors and the credit system should be held responsible for default:

> At present the County Courts were converted into agencies for the collection of small debts, many of which were incurred by the wives of poor men in consequence of the importunities of

> traders. These debts were frequently left outstanding till the harvest season, when the creditors insisted upon payment or sent the debtors to prison, and the men so imprisoned were committed again and again unless they satisfied the harpies to whom they were indebted. . . . All political economists, from Adam Smith to Mill, laid down that it was not for the interest of a State to encourage credit, and he believed that if they were tomorrow to abolish imprisonment for debt trade would be all the more flourishing. . . .

A hundred years later, the Payne Committee (1969, p. 321) observed of brutal harassment:

> It may be urged that defaulting debtors have only themselves to blame and they have no call for protection against those who are seeking to collect their lawful debts. In our view, it cannot be tolerated that just claims be pursued by unjust methods. It may not be forgotten that the debtor class includes many who by misfortune or mischance have drifted into debt and they are peculiarly exposed and vulnerable to the methods which we condemn.

Such reticence about assigning culpability to the creditor or debtor alone is not confined to lawyers and legislators. Hire purchase companies and door-to-door salesmen have been more frequently lambasted than defaulters in the press. Many collectors themselves are aware of their part in the deliberate fostering of default. Greig (1964, p. 16) states, for instance:

> Readers may be reminded also that it is not always a sign of efficiency when the business can show an entirely clean sheet and say with pride: 'Not a single bad debt'. Before regarding such a state of affairs with satisfaction, it is well for a management to be sure that the credit manager has not been frightened into playing for safety to such an extent that the volume of trade has been unnecessarily restricted. . . . The point to be remembered is that there will always exist a small percentage of bad debts in any really live, progressive business. . . .

Anxiety about default may thus become diffused. Debt is unusual in that it is just as commonly attributed to social institutions and policies as to faults in the rule-breakers themselves. A *Times* editorial (26 June 1963) argued, for example:

> The national hire-purchase debt is now about £900m. Yet the law as it stands is pregnant with social evil and legal injustice. . . . Larger pay packets have made almost every housewife the potential victim of high pressure salesmanship

on hire-purchase terms. . . . Parliament should intervene to protect the poor or less well educated.

Similarly, the 1965 Hire Purchase Act was described as providing some 'safeguards for people who are browbeaten by doorstep salesmen and persuaded to buy goods they do not want'. (*Focus*, 3 April 1966, p. 18.) Such pronouncements about creditors tend to prevent persistent defaulters from becoming a distinct pariah group.

Laws have thus been framed by people who believe that creditors are not always innocents, and debtors not always villains. Uncertainty has produced an enforcement system which denies either party a clear advantage in law. Restraints have been imposed on a creditor's ability to recover debts, and collectors are not allowed to take precipitate action. Instead, they are constrained to wait until systematic checks have graded defaulters because lawyers maintain that default itself is not deviant.

Lawyers and philosophers have typically regarded civil law as a body of rules which adjust relations between individuals. Society, the 'State' or the community are not harmed by the actions of debtors. There is no need, therefore, to pay special attention to the processing of defaulters or present it in a dignified and ritualistic manner (Mead, 1918, p. 586):

> A very large part, perhaps the largest part, of civil law proceedings are undertaken and carried out with the intent of defining and readjusting social situations without the hostile attitudes which characterize the criminal procedure. . . . No stigma attaches to the one who loses. Our emotional attitude toward this body of law is that of interest, of condemnation and approval as it fails or succeeds in its social function. It is not an institution that must be respected even in its disastrous failures. On the contrary it must be changed. It is hedged about in our feelings by no majesty. It is efficient or inefficient and as such awakens satisfaction or dissatisfaction. . . .

The county court does not degrade defaulters or redefine them. Instead, it withholds stereotypes and avoids dramatizing its work. A further consequence of the doctrine of social dualism, then, is the deliberately engineered incapacity of the enforcement system to furnish legislators with unambiguously stigmatized typifications of defaulters. Uncertainty and the application of the doctrine conspired to make debtors ineligible for punitive laws. In turn, the absence of punitive laws promotes further uncertainty.

The public

Popular understandings of default and its control provide a vital context for enforcement. They shape the extent to which the enforcement system will undergo external interference. They provide a reservoir of beliefs which may enter the system and become influential. Most important, they constitute the basic materials for the response of naïve debtors who pass through the collection career.

There is almost no information available about these understandings, and my account must rest chiefly on surmise. However, it is apparent that the public face of a collection system is profoundly influenced by the organized groups which have some control over its presentation. Because enforcement is socially invisible, authoritative interpretations of its meaning become unusually important. As I have argued, those interpretations are marked by an absence of concrete directives for imputing deviancy. Legal thinking, and its reflection in the structures of collection, offer no guidance for the formation of distinct typifications of the defaulter. Courtroom ritual and routine enforcement work are not taken up with denunciation or public pronouncements.

In my first chapter, I argued that the public seems to be largely unaware of the private skirmishing that is waged between collectors and defaulters. Official or unofficial enforcers do not draw attention to their activities. They cannot be recognized by outsiders. Debtors themselves are indistinguishable from anyone else. It is impossible to recognize a debtor unless he is present in some special context, such as a court or prison, that proclaims his identity. Many deviants *are* highly visible; they may be known by 'such things as the grimaces the stutterer makes in trying to speak, the bizarre posturings of crippled or blind persons, the mannerisms which the professional criminal elects to symbolize his difference from other members of society or . . . the flamboyant dress of the traditional prostitute'. (Lemert, 1951, p. 52.) Distinctive styles of behaviour or appearance are often adopted by groups who have to contend with the problems posed by segregation or ridicule. They can serve as expressive means of advertising one's status and common links with fellow pariahs. They can also express one's rejection of what is conceived to be the conventional world. Deviants may also be singled out by their resort to certain notorious places. Defaulters provide none of these cues. There are no symbols or meanings peculiarly associated with default.

Invisibility itself is no check on typifying processes. Instead, these processes may flourish when there is a poverty of information. They are, however, checked when the candidate for social typing is not separated from the typer by any great social distance. Rubington and Weinberg (1960, p. 10) contend, 'one rule on typing, inferred from many observations, may be summarized as the greater the social distance between the typer and the person singled out for typing, the broader the type and the quicker it may be applied.' Default is so widespread that there is no wide gulf dividing the debtor from his fellow members of society. Whilst debtors who are advanced in their movement through the career may keep their involvement covert, there is enough overt participation to prevent debtors becoming an estranged group. Indebtedness is a familiar state and exposure to enforcement is taken to be commonplace and unremarkable.[2]

Enforcement has probably been the type of formal social control most commonly experienced by the population of England and Wales. It loomed large in the lives of the population during the last few hundred years and novels describing those lives necessarily paid attention to it. Works such as Smollett's *Roderick Random*, Fielding's *Amelia* and Dickens' *Little Dorrit* are replete with references to collection. It has, indeed, been estimated that 0·4 per cent of the adult male population of 1832 were imprisoned debtors (Heynen, 1970).

Credit is becoming an ever more significant part of the British economy. The Board of Trade has estimated, for example, that the total amount of outstanding consumer debt was £934,000,000 in 1961. This sum had grown to £1,371,000,000 by December 1965. Concomitant with this growth has been a swelling in the numbers of defaulters. About a million people are sued for default each year (Payne Committee, 1969, p. 16) and, of these, several hundred thousand must receive judgments for the first time. That million is no more than the apex of a vast pyramid of default. Many more people travel far enough through the career but leave it before the judgment stage. In Chapter 3, I suggested that some 2½ per cent of all defaulters actually face county court proceedings, and the Payne Committee (1969, p. 15) also believed 'a tiny proportion only of the total value of contractual debts are sued for'. It is thus possible that almost every adult in the country has defaulted at some time. So pervasive is default that it is qualitatively different from any other kind of formal rule-breaking. It is, of course, probable that most defaulters do not attach importance to their incumbency of the defaulter role. That incumbency does not necessarily lead to a transformation of their stance towards the generalized debtor. Yet default cannot be simply typified as the behaviour of an alienated minority.

Wilkins (1964, p. 85) has argued that the emergence of deviant

[2] My argument is based on the assumption that the deviant is not already stigmatized by a familiar and unflattering stereotype. When an unpleasant typification *is* available, the definer might well minimize any similarity between himself and the deviant.

typifications depends on the communication properties of particular social systems. When a group is structurally isolated from the central institutions of a society, communication lacunae tend to transform the nature of the information which those institutions receive about it. There is a reduction in the volume of information and a distortion of its content. Misleading feedback generates a process of deviancy amplification: poor information directs control work; the typified group is constrained to respond to the misdirected control efforts of the centre; its responses are, in turn, defined as symptomatic of further deviancy; and the cycle is then repeated.

Defaulters do not constitute an isolated group and communication lacunae are unlikely to develop. Default is not a matter of great opprobrium and much of it is not concealed. Thus, although the survey described in my first chapter indicated that public knowledge about default was sparse, it also showed that debtors were not regarded as transparently deviant. Indebtedness is too familiar to permit gross caricature.

Institutions which process default render it unspectacular, but it is also a poor subject for dramatization in its own right. Offences revolving around the regular exchange of petty sums of money offer few opportunities for exciting moral outrage. Money can impersonalize transactions between people. Very rarely does a defaulter's breach of contract give rise to heated encounters between victim and deviant. On the contrary, a debtor is a passive deviant. Moreover, default is typically the routine concern of large organizations: it involves few personal victims and it cannot be construed as an eventful break in the everyday life of a community. Debt collection and debtors attract little attention.

The collectors

Public indifference and legal concern about intention provide a context for the work of enforcement agencies. Those agencies mechanically employ a threefold scheme of classification: defaulters are feckless or professional or unfortunate. The scheme is essentially a bureaucratic product: it is generated by the conventional workings of institutions which manage millions of people.

A bureaucracy is based on a division of labour which cannot be viable unless it offers its members a coherent paradigm for interpreting the tasks which they perform. The world must be made orderly and intelligible before it can be acted upon. Concerted action requires a common vocabulary so that men may co-operate in their dealings with important objects. Any bureaucratic vocabulary will represent a store of stock solutions to stock problems. It will reduce the recalcitrant and the complex to a series of repetitive operations. The greater the scale of the bureaucratic enterprise, the greater will be the dependence upon a simplifying paradigm. In the case of debt collection, economy and speed of response combine with scale to raise the paradigm to a position of paramount importance.

One crucial facet of such vocabularies is the transformation of an uncertain world into a set of predictable occurrences. It is the business of bureaucratic rules to stabilize work material and outline characteristic ways of managing it. No system of rules can ever be exhaustive. The structure and vocabulary of an organization will necessarily impose a selective grid upon the cases which it handles. Only a few features of those cases will be recognized by that grid; and those features will be systematically organized so that they become capable of processing. The typical bureaucratic operation is conducted on material which has been made serviceable by the pre-structuring work of the grid. When an organization has considerable control over its material, ambiguous or anomalous events are likely to be forced into a familiar cast. Such recasting is made more likely when the organization has little information about its material and when it is structurally ill-equipped to prepare more than a few standard responses to it. In the case of debt collection, again, the richly textured world of default is stripped down to a skeletal set of paradigmatic cases.

Rubington and Weinberg (1968, pp. 110–11) describe how paradigmatic cases are routinely employed by social control agencies:

> The office developed to solve a problem in social management. A number of strangers typed as deviants have either gotten caught or have given themselves up for public regulation. The theory of the office supplies the answer to the question of what is to be done with them. . . . The office goes on to specify who shall be designated as the defining agent, how he shall go into official action against some of these persons, and under what conditions he will be permitted to type them as deviants. Once official typing has gotten underway, the deviant career has been launched, frequently in what the office would consider a rite de passage. This deviant career must now be managed in accordance with the theory that the office dictates, administered according to certain routine conceptions. Unless this administration proceeds according to the plan, the deviant career is likely to become inoperative or uncontrollable. However, when administration goes according to plan, the office is handling what it takes to be its usual run of business, its 'normal cases' . . . the system by which it will type and categorize its deviant clientele is of crucial importance. These categories

> become the basis for issuing official reports and for indicating the rates at which the office is actually both producing and processing deviants. More important, the system establishes the official perspective by means of which agents of social control will define and deal with the deviants they type. For so long and only so long as these agents type the deviants they encounter in their work, to that extent can the agency manage social deviance.

The genesis of normal cases is a complicated matter. It may be explained partly as a result of the social organization of knowledge which takes its form from the structure of a bureaucracy. It is partly a response to the world which is manipulated by the bureaucracy. Yet the control agency's structure is an embodiment of what was conceived to be an appropriate reaction to that world; and the manipulated world is moulded by the agency's reaction. There is no world which can be considered until it receives definition from the organization.

One strategy of explanation would hold that the bureaucratic paradigm is a pragmatic construction. Normal cases emerge out of the practical tasks of management which are performed by the bureaucracy. They reflect what must be done to a phenomenon, how that phenomenon might respond and, more generally, the nature of the routine contacts which make that phenomenon knowable. Classification schemes which evolve in occupational settings mirror their practical concerns (Strauss, 1959, p. 21):

> Any group of people that has any permanence develops a 'special language', a lingo or jargon, which represents its way of identifying those objects important for group action. Waitresses classify types of customers and other workers in the restaurant, give shorthand names to foods, and have special signs and gestures standing for important activities. So do criminals; and even ministers are not immune from the necessity of classifying their clientele and colleagues, otherwise how could they organize activity in an orderly and sensible manner?

Enforcement can be visualized as a series of actions and reactions; it is a progressive interaction which mechanically builds up a composite portrait of the defaulter. It is only through this interaction that the defaulter emerges as a knowable figure. What is identified by the bureaucracy as a debtor is no more than what the enforcement process itself can create. Typifications of debtors are constructed out of the knowledge which is generated by collection tasks.

Enforcement work can be described as a system of coercive probes which elicit information-bearing responses. The organization of those probes determines the resultant image of the defaulter. By examining those probes, I shall be able to explain how the collector's master typifications are constituted.

Most collection is mediated entirely by letters. Personal confrontation between creditor and debtor is an uncommon event. Interaction which is conducted across a wide area of social space is grounded in a form of knowledge which is qualitatively different from that available to people in face-to-face contexts. There is a wealth of detail which is simply unavailable to the participants. Responses cannot be made to facial expression, body gestures and the positioning of the self in significant environments. Language and symbolic communication take on highly conventional forms. There is certainly little scope for complex elaborations of meaning in the letter exchanges that take place in collection. On the contrary, interaction is reduced to a few standard formulae which are incapable of conveying much information. Ideas of the other person in such mediated transactions tend to become correspondingly featureless. The other becomes relatively anonymous and unchanging. He is seen as predictable and as saturated by a few definitive characteristics. He may be readily classed as a member of a relatively homogeneous category of people.

The mediated relations of collection are commonly no more than sequences of action without reaction from the defaulter. The information conveyed by the process then becomes merely that the debtor is inert. Enforcement must proceed with no sure knowledge of the deviant. Its stages follow upon one another in hierarchical fashion; each evoking no response. When interaction translates inactivity as meaningful, scope is created for an organizational solipsism which defines the defaulter solely in terms of organizationally-derived understandings. The structural influence of the career is then paramount. The defaulter is simply a phantasm of the collection machine, responsive to any procedural changes introduced in the machine, slavishly reflecting the assumptions that are automatically fed into the machine.

Collection conducted by large financial bureaucracies allows little opportunity for debtors to negotiate identities for themselves. Typically, the paucity of the debtors' responses prepares the ground for the exercise of a total mastery over the definition of defaulters. When there is little legitimate power behind debtors' reactions, the possibility of negotiation is further reduced.

Debt collection in England is a massive enterprise which is regulated by minute calculations of cost. It is an enterprise which is forced to respond immediately and effectively to default. None of its constituent probes can be designed to convey a fully-rounded portrait of the defaulter. The expense and time devoted to such work would militate against the smooth operation of a cheap control system. Rather, the informational poverty that distinguishes the system imposes its mark upon the typifications which are employed. Judgments must be rapid, simple and decisive. The debtor is forced through one of the career routes that have been mapped out for the limited number of cases which the system can manage.

The pre-eminent goal of collection is the restoration of money, but that goal rests on the companion task of organizing an adequate understanding of default. Enforcement is unusual because it does not simply represent an attempt to control the consequences of an accomplished act. The deviancy of defaulters remains persistently problematic. It is only in the gradual unfolding of a defaulter's reactions that clear meanings emerge about the significance of his default. The interpretative procedures of enforcement are thus necessarily organized around the development of default over time. The emergent qualities of default are reinforced by the nature of enforcement work. Debt-collectors are unwilling and unable to employ sanctions which will bring the course of a default to an abrupt conclusion. They rely instead on threat and the symbolic work performed by the changing sequence of the collection career. Their operations are also extended in time. The typifications of defaulters which flow from debt collection necessarily reflect its temporal organization.

It is plausible that these influences conjointly bring about the tripartite classification of debtors. The paucity of information leads to a simplistic typing of defaulters as static and discrete entities. The economy and scale of collection generates a limited number of typifications. A preoccupation with intention fills out the content of the typifications with qualities relating to motivation. The temporal structure of default explains both the threefold classification and the procedures which are used to place debtors.

Extending his judgment along a temporal continuum, a collector will know whether default was made at the beginning of an agreement (a professional), in the middle (feckless) or at the end (an unfortunate). He will find that some debtors always reply to his overtures and are always accessible to his representatives (unfortunates); others reply erratically and are not always accessible (the feckless); whilst others never respond and are extremely difficult to meet (the professionals). The debtor might pay as soon as any pressure is applied (the unfortunate); he might repay after some time (the feckless), or he might never repay (the professional). One group of debtors will require almost no enforcement effort (the unfortunates), another will require more sustained effort (the feckless) and another considerable effort (the professional).

Fecklessness, misfortune and professional deceit are the inevitable concomitants of a process which is engineered to discover a defaulter's plans about future action. They are qualities which are related to the timing of activity, and they are qualities which are unearthed by the timing of activity. The probes put out by collection are staggered over a length of time, and the typifications they produce reflect that staggering.

These typifications are highly functional to enforcement. A collection strategy must recognize that some debtors default for innocent reasons and that they would be alienated by tactics that impute dishonesty to them. Other debtors are considered too insensitive to appreciate the significance of what is done to them. A third group is defined as evasive and dishonest. It is not disturbed by a creditor's attribution of deviant motives. A parsimonious typology must provide for at least these three contingencies. Failure to do so would generate possibilities of unwanted secondary deviation, allegations of improper coercion, and excessive leniency, in different cases.

Because the threefold classification has solipsist features, and because it stems from routine collection work, the scheme is applied throughout the career. At every stage of enforcement, three types of debtor are regulated. At every stage, the unfortunates are eliminated and professional and feckless debtors are passed on to the personnel who man the next phase. The unfortunate defaulter is resurrected afresh with each movement. His re-appearance might be attributed to a number of causes. Successive collectors might be increasingly sensitive and discriminating in their filtering work, or they could designate as unfortunate people who are progressively less unfortunate. Thus, the solicitor's unfortunate debtor would be unlucky only in the context of those other defaulters who are passed on to the pre-court stage. Yet it is more plausible that the collectors' actions are always calculated to have three responses. Each enforcement stage has a beginning, a middle and an end; and debtors who respond are classified according to the timing of their reaction.

Of course, once such a system of classification becomes institutionalized, its parts do not require constant rediscovery every time a collector undertakes enforcement. Although the validity of a system requires reinforcement through feedback, the system itself will acquire a quality of objectivity and common sense which can make it highly resistant to change. The professional, unfortunate and feckless debtors will become parts of the natural world, independent of the collector's will. Schutz (1962, vol. 1, p. 12) observes:

> It is obvious that both idealizations, that of the interchangeability of the standpoints and that of the congruency of relevances—together constituting the *general thesis of reciprocal perspectives*—are typifying constructs of objects of thought which supersede the thought objects of my and my fellow-man's private experience. By the operation of these constructs of common-sense thinking it is assumed that the sector of the world taken for granted by me is also taken for granted by you, my individual fellow-man, even more, that it is taken for granted by 'Us'. But this 'We' does not merely include you and me but 'everyone who is one of us', i.e. everyone whose system of relevance is substantially (sufficiently) in conformity with yours and mine. Thus, the general thesis of reciprocal perspectives leads to the apprehension of objects and their aspects actually known by me and potentially known to you as everyone's knowledge. Such knowledge is conceived to be objective and anonymous, i.e. detached from and independent of my and my fellow-man's definition of the situation, our unique biographical circumstances and the actual and potential purposes at hand involved therein.

Every action in enforcement can have three broad outcomes. There can, for instance, be an adequate response, an inadequate response, and no response at all. Every action is thus tied to a discrete set of reactions. Collectors believe that the sets overlap to such an extent that they can be melded together. The man who defaults as soon as he receives credit, for example, will not reply to letters or pay anything unless he is under extreme duress. The professional, the feckless and the unfortunate are composite portraits based on information which emerges out of enforcement behaviour. The professional is an elusive, predatory person who has no wish to retain any links with the creditor; the feckless debtor is too disorganized and irresponsible to make moral decisions; and the unfortunate is a co-operative, guilt-ridden individual who will pay whatever he can afford. It is clear that a creditor cannot really know why a debtor defaulted. The portraits are based on surmises about the meanings of certain responses. As Cicourel and Kitsuse (1968, p. 126) observe:

> The motivational processes which presumably lead to deviant behaviour are conceptually independent of the social processes by which the members of the social organization *impute* motives and perceive regularities in their construction of the deviant, the grounds for such decisions, and the subsequent treatment of persons so defined.

Enforcement proceeds as if debtors' characteristics were invariably clustered together in clumps. Labelling can therefore take place without very much being known about a debtor's intentions or attitudes. A person who does not reply to letters will be mechanically identified as a professional, although it is obvious that other inferences *could* be made about him. An excellent example of misinterpretation has been furnished by a member of the John Hilton Bureau:[3]

> We did hear from a man who got a demand stating that he had bought a bicycle for £28, that he had paid £3 several years ago and nothing more. Well, our reader didn't worry about this because he knew it was a mistake. He'd never bought a bicycle from the firm so he did nothing more about it.
>
> Well, if you get a court summons and you don't do anything about it, the automatic result of that is that a court order is made in default of defence. You must officially defend a summons or you will land in trouble. This man didn't, so after a while he received a court order. Well, he felt very annoyed about this but again he stressed his annoyance in a rather unorthodox way.
>
> Instead of going round to the County Court office, he wrote on the back of the court order 'Get stuffed' and posted it back to the County Court office and, as he told us, the next thing he knew of was a bailiff banging on the door with a summons, worrying his wife silly about it.

The man's indignation about faulty accounting procedures prompted him to ignore enforcement. He was propelled quite far through the career, becoming increasingly deviant as he passed critical benchmarks. Towards the end, he was obviously identified as a subversive debtor by the court bailiffs. Although his was probably an exceptional case, it does illustrate how autonomous the stereotyping process can be. A passive and innocent man was thrown into the role of professional debtor. A completely sinister interpretation of his behaviour was provided by the enforcement machine.

This kind of labelling machinery has profound effects on enforcement. The debtor who is least well known to collectors is the most likely candidate for the role of professional defaulter. The stereotype can be applied precisely because there has been no response from the debtor. A professional tends to be the person who does not reply to

[3] The John Hilton Bureau, *News of the World*, is an organization which attempts to answer readers' questions about such matters as debt. This quotation comes from the preliminary typescript of a projected BBC Radio Three programme on debt collection and the law.

letters, appear at court, meet bailiffs or other agents, or make any payments. Nothing may be known about him except his total passivity. Passivity can stem from many causes: the debtor might be indignant at some injustice; he might be illiterate,[4] ashamed, or so intimidated that he is unable to react. All the same, the inactive debtor will eventually be treated as a deviant if enforcement continues for any length of time.

When this label is applied, collection may become so intensive that collector and deviant will meet face-to-face. The collector will typically approach the debtor with assumptions manufactured by the labelling process. He will expect to meet an unscrupulous master of evasion. If he is heavily involved in the day-to-day work of collection, he may well find that his notions are reinforced by the debtor's behaviour. He will probably pay special attention to features which confirm the stereotype but ignore others which undermine it. This appears to be a fairly common response of people operating with an interpretative paradigm. Vernon (1962, p. 200), for instance, reported a study which investigated perceptions of Negroes:

> Observers were asked to rate photographs of Negroes and whites as to the degree they showed of certain Negro characteristics such as width of nose, fullness of lips etc. These characteristics are related to the stereotyped notion of Negro appearance. Those observers who were prejudiced against Negroes exaggerated the degree to which these characteristics appeared in the Negro photographs, by comparison with the less prejudiced observers.

In the same way, collectors may be so committed to a classification that they will also exaggerate the deviant characteristics displayed by the debtors they meet. This sensitivity may be accompanied by a superior insight into the debtor. The professional debtor is thought to be a thoroughly devious person. According to this stereotype, he would act in character if he tried to pass himself off as a feckless or unfortunate defaulter. Highly prejudiced collectors might therefore treat an honest appearance as no proof of a debtor's innocence. What *seems* to be a sign of ill-luck or fecklessness could, in fact, be a clever deceit. Some bailiffs for example, dismissed debtors' explanations as 'flannel'. They knew that they had the ability to probe beneath the debtors' cunning masks. Similarly, Creditor 16 endowed the professional with a quite extraordinary degree of deviousness:

[4] Two of the Brixton debtors I interviewed confessed that they were illiterate. It is more than possible that other defaulters were also unable to read or write.

> If you stick out long enough and if you're willing to put up with bad conditions in the home without furniture etc., or buying old rubbish which is not worth anything, you can get away with literally murder.

A person with this type of insight cannot easily be refuted. Any information can substantiate his definition of the situation. Facts which threaten his definition are shown to be nothing more than manifestations of a deeper level of reality, a level at which they are no longer threatening. Insightful people who cling to their classifications are not only confined to the prejudiced or the debt-collector. They include such people as psychiatrists.[5] Stanton and Schwartz (1954, pp. 200, 203) demonstrate how superior understanding enlightens members of this profession:

> The most common, most conspicuous, and most serious misunderstanding occurred when someone . . . ignored the explicit meaning of a statement or action and focused attention on an inferred meaning. . . . Restriction of attention to 'deep' interpretation was not . . . confined to dealings with patients; on the contrary, many psychiatrists seemed to pride themselves on ignoring the face value of what their colleagues said to them, focusing instead on what they believed to be 'really going on' . . . information was frequently lost . . . particularly when a junior staff member protested to a senior about certain aspects of the hospital; the protest was likely to be interpreted as a transference rebellion.

People immersed in enforcement are likely to believe that their environment is a complicated one which is never as straightforward as it seems. They may take a professional pleasure in recognizing the esoteric significance of phenomena associated with default. The idea that deviants lurk beneath seemingly innocent exteriors is an important prop to such active agents as bailiffs. It allows them to dispel their anxiety about the pain which they can inflict on people. They can be comforted by the knowledge that the debtors who suffered were really dishonest. Faith in the labelling process also reduces uncertainty and hesitation. If the career's benchmarks serve as valid measures of a person's deviance, problems of classification and suitable action do not often arise. Collectors must therefore rely heavily on their stereotypes of the defaulter. A with-

[5] According to Wootton (1963, p. 277), they also include social workers: 'in consequence of this conviction on the part of the caseworker that she can understand other people better than they understand themselves, a practice has grown up of refusing to accept at their face value the emergencies which cause people to seek the aid of a social work agency.'

drawal of respect for the predictive power of the typology would lead to confusion, disruption and inefficiency. If, as Rubington and Weinberg contend, the normal case is necessary to an ordinary agency, it is vital to the collector. Bailiffs and others must have an exceptional commitment to the belief that the professional exists and that he can be accurately identified by the testing system.

The social work culture

The response of authoritative outsiders is in complete contrast to this acceptance of the labelling process. Perhaps the clearest exposition of this view was put forward by the Payne Committee (1969, p. 251):

> We have received a considerable amount of evidence from those engaged in welfare and social services that many of the debtors who, in fact, go to prison are inadequate men who are incapable of managing their own affairs; they are men who have become overwhelmed by a burden of debt through illness, unemployment or other misfortune; they are irresponsible or feckless people who need control or temporary help. . . .

That is, the professional label is regarded as completely inappropriate to the debtors who enter prison. I do not pretend to know why debtors defaulted, but I feel that valid objections can be made to a stereotyping of the defaulter in terms of fecklessness. At the very least, the difference in definition seems to stem as much from differences in occupation ideology as from a clear disparity in competence or understanding. The bailiff is primarily concerned with problems of *control*. The professional is a person who undermines authority and requires discipline. He is the 'wise guy' whom the police also fear (Westley, 1967, pp. 174–5):

> [Police] were all aware of the fact that the public and, therefore, the researcher were critical of violence. Ordinarily they talked the formal line and maintained an aversion to its use. Yet there were times when they advocated it unabashedly. For example, there were many accounts of that unpleasant public character the 'wise guy', the fellow who talks back to the police or *speaks to them disrespectfully*. They maintained that it would be a good thing to teach a fellow like that a little respect, and some men told of occasions when they did.

The social control culture is based on certain central values. It emphasizes such notions as choice, responsibility, deterrence and punishment. That is, social control agents are wedded to the belief that deviants have free-will and can make rational decisions.[6] County court enforcement, in particular, stresses the 'wilful' nature of the 'fraudulent' debtor's acts and, when he is arrested, the bailiff's 'attitude always is "he asked for it and he got it".' (Registrar of E court.)

The culture of the welfare and social services, on the other hand, provides a radically different model of human behaviour. My description of the culture will obviously be something of a caricature, yet the social work perspective is clearly dominated by a number of pronounced themes. Firstly, the perspective is generally dependent on psychiatric definitions of human behaviour. As McCormick (1966, p. 635) observes, 'the readiness of social workers to follow the dictates of psychology and psychiatry is too well-known to warrant elaboration.' Occupational situations are described in the professional language of the psychiatrist: a social worker is a 'caseworker' who attempts to achieve a 'positive therapeutic relationship' with her 'client'. Treatment is directed at changing the client, rather than the social network in which he is embedded, because psychiatry and psychology emphasize the paramount importance of *personality*. 'To the extent that behaviour is governed by personality, contemporary situations are important only in that they remind us of previous events and thus elicit appropriate responses. This does not rule out the relevance of other situational factors; it merely relegates them to a secondary postion.' (Matza, 1964, p. 16.)

Social work is also governed by a determinism which suggests that most behaviour is outside a man's rational control.[7] Since

6 Except, of course, when the law admits psychiatric evidence of a person's lack of responsibility. In this case, however, it seems that legal conceptions of psychiatric states are often anachronistic. The application of the M'Naghten rule, for instance, appears to entail an outmoded distinction between the responsible and normal person and the abnormal and irresponsible person. 'Most psychiatrists today do not believe that knowledge of right and wrong is what distinguishes a "normal" person from a mentally disturbed person, but they are willing to perjure themselves on this question because they believe a mentally disturbed criminal should be treated rather than punished.' (Rose, 1968, p. 35.)

7 Dinitz, Dynes and Clarke (1969, p. 21) have neatly portrayed the contrasts between the two perspectives:

> The 'hard' determinists, which would generally include most of the social and behavioural scientists, suggest the 'cause' of the deviancy is more or less out of the hands of the deviant himself. Various explanations can be given—poor genes, glands, or body structure; inadequate family, housing, or status characteristics; or a variety of other 'causes'—and these may be offered singly or in combination. The causal factors are seen to be 'outside' the individual. The 'soft' determinists, among them many law enforcement

people are not responsible for their actions, they cannot be properly described as moral or immoral. Furthermore, punishment cannot be an effective solution to many social problems. This determinism is largely derived from psycho-analysis (Stephenson, 1961, p. 48):

> I referred . . . to the psycho-analytic theory which explicitly or implicitly underlies much casework teaching. Few of us realise, without pausing to consider, how much of such theory has become part of our thinking as social workers, without our ever having examined the basic hypotheses. Yet examination of such ideas by the student inevitably raises anxieties when, probably for the first time, he follows them through to their (apparently) logical conclusions. The age-old 'determinist' problem rears its ugly head; can anyone ever help what they do, and as a social worker, can I assume they could have stopped short at any point? . . . Closely related to this is another worrying thought for students. If people are not able to help their badness, can they help their goodness either?

Social work is thus organized around the belief that there can be no moral condemnation because people lack free-will. As Leighton (1965, p. 279) argues, 'the adopted father of social work, psycho-analysis, has probably done more to undermine people's faith in their ability to take moral decisions than any other influence in this century.'

Because personality is the dominant factor in the creation of problems, treatment is designed to alter people rather than social structures. Casework's 'aim is to help the client to manage in the community either simply with the aid of encouragement from the caseworker or also by changing some of the client's attitudes if they are proving harmful.' (Moffett, 1968, pp. 3–4.) People must adapt because they are not functioning properly and because it is more difficult to change a society than an individual. Adaptation can be assessed by the social worker as more or less adequate (Perlman, 1963, pp. 200–1):

> Within each phase of problem-solving work there is the exercise of the client's adaptation capacities, whether to an idea, a relationship, or a situation, and whether about some small or some large part of the problem. The caseworker acts so that adaptation is promoted and sustained by his stable relationship, his communication, and the tangible opportunities he may provide. . . . Within the boundaries of the client's wants,

officials . . . , often embrace the view that 'free will' and personal choice are central and decisive in human motivation. . . . The 'decision' to engage in deviant behaviour is seen as a result of conscious choice.

> his capacities, and the resources of skill and material means of the agency . . . the specific goal is to help him achieve his previous level of functioning and/or to promote the most effective functioning of which he is capable at this time.

In large part, the criteria that are used to evaluate effective functioning or harmful attitudes are adopted from a middle-class culture. Social work is a middle-class occupation which attracts middle-class recruits. It is inevitable that the occupation and the class will have repercussions on one another in the area of ideas and standards. The standards which caseworkers apply often seem to emphasize the desirability of planning, foresight, budgeting, stability, and the seizing of opportunities which will improve life-chances. These criteria are not always applied by the working class (McCormick, 1965, p. 134):

> The professions sometimes have as much difficulty helping the poor as the poor have in seeking and using their help. Professional people are committed to an orientation diametrically opposed to the apathy and lack of initiative that seem almost indigenous to poverty. Theirs is a world in which a person is expected to exercise control over his problems and initiative in solving them. He does this by the intelligent use of his own personal resources, augmented, when necessary, by those of the community.

When there is a discrepancy between middle-class and working-class attitudes and behaviour, there is always the possibility that the latter's adaptation will be defined as 'inadequate'. A social worker may largely ignore the effects of the working-class culture. After all, a client's personality is the primary object of intellectual and occupational interest. If the client is making a good adjustment, then, he may have to do so by adopting a middle-class set of perspectives in a working-class situation. Indeed, in some cases, those maintaining the social work paradigm consider that middle-class standards are the only significant or attractive ones. A not untypical example of such an orientation is Ausubel's (1958, p. 42) characterization of the inadequate:

> The inadequate personality fails to conceive of himself as an independent adult and fails to identify with such normal adult goals as financial independence, stable employment, and the establishment of his own home and family. He is passive, dependent, unreliable and unwilling to postpone immediate gratification of pleasurable impulses. He demonstrates no desire to persevere in the face of environmental difficulties, or to accept responsibilities which he finds distasteful.

Duster (1970, pp. 155–6) believes:

> This description treats 'immaturity' as a total quality of the personality rather than a selective one which emerges in some situations and not in others. Yet, using the criteria listed above, all of us are mature in some situations and immature in others. Where lies the compelling set of criteria which determine why certain situations are more important than others in indicating whether the *personality* is immature or inadequate? From the account above, the set of criteria used comes from a single social class's view of appropriate behavior: note the use of 'financial independence, stable employment. . . .' There is a remarkable bias here toward labeling of one social segment of the society as mature and adequate at the expense of another.

Middle-class professionals can also experience difficulty in interpreting the organization and beliefs of working-class groups. There may be simple misunderstanding or confusion about the meaning and structure of certain events. There may be an attempt by the interpreter to impose his own understanding on what he sees. Wallace (1968, pp. 139, 160) claims, for example, that there is a profound difference between the insider's and the outsider's analysis of Skid Row. Whilst the insider knows that Skid Row is based on a complex network of stable relations, the outsider assumes that it lacks community. Similarly, the middle-class person's incomprehension might lead him to describe an organized group as disorganized or a culture as meaningless (Gusfield, 1963, p. 70):

> Commentators on contemporary social welfare practices have pointed out the discrepancies between the values and norms of the social worker and the culture of residents in the slum community. Faced by the facts that crime, political corruption, limited motivation in school, high rates of desertion, and delinquency characterize an area, sociologists in past generations have pronounced the slum an 'area of disorganization'. Recently sociologists have shown that this designation hides the fact of very real differences in values between one level of society and another. Slum life often is highly organized, although the values around which the organization of behavior occurs may seem immoral, unjust, or incredible to observers.

Although my description of the social work philosophy has been simplistic, it is clear that the welfare and social services bring certain perspectives to bear on the defaulter.[8] Because of their

[8] In fact, there is some evidence that social workers have renewed their interest in sociological analysis. Accompanying this change, there has been

occupational and class culture, social workers are likely to have certain suppositions about the meaning of debt. Firstly, they are not predisposed to find or recognize professional debtors in prison because the very conception of purposeful, free-willed dishonesty is alien to them. Hard determinism does not permit the idea that defaulters are culpable. Instead, the prisoner's behaviour must be explained by personality factors which have prevented a successful adaptation. The conception of deviancy as a chosen course is replaced by that of immaturity as an inability to identify and judge between courses. In its most crass form, the treatment orientation assumes that adaptation is possible in almost every situation because the personality is the critical variable.

> We social caseworkers do not aim at radical personality changes but at changes in underlying attitudes which affect the individual's solving of his problem. This we attempt to do by mobilising the healthy parts of the personality to try to set in motion the natural healing forces present in everyone. (Lloyd Davies, 1963, p. 32.)

Nobody should become overwhelmed by debt because the adjusted person will tailor his expenditure in a sensible manner. A seemingly insoluble financial problem will thus become proof of the debtor's poor adjustment. If social work is professionally interested in the 'human being's capacity for self-maintenance' (American Association of Social Workers, 1929, p. 3), the caseworker will regard the debtor as a palpable failure. The middle class is commonly supposed to be concerned with promoting such activities as budgeting and saving, and it correspondingly disapproves of indebtedness. Default cannot be justified by arguing that debtors have large families, for instance, because an adequate person would have practised

a slight decline in their preoccupation with psychiatric models and the paramount influence of the personality. Meyer (1966, p. 280), for example, states, 'in the latter part of the nineteenth century, the concept of individualized services had the conservative flavor of the times. Notwithstanding the social action programs of the community organization society and the settlement house movement, this was the prevailing dictum: caring for the individual will improve society—society cannot be changed, and it is the individual who must learn to adjust to society. . . . The changing role, substance, and characteristics of individualized services in the modern world may be accounted for to a large extent by changes in social values. . . . For example, we no longer hold the individual totally responsible for his condition. Services are now viewed as the individual's right, not only because he makes a contribution to society but also because—unless he bands together with others—he is practically helpless to affect the social, political, and economic forces that govern his life.' I suspect that Meyer somewhat underestimates the contemporary strength of what she calls 'nineteenth century' concepts. It is my impression that the adaptational approach is still subscribed to by the bulk of social and welfare workers.

contraception. The inmate debtor has not coped in the crucial middle-class area of economy, and he is by definition an inadequate.[9]

'Fecklessness' is another label which seems to emanate from the social work culture. It carries with it implications of irrationality, irresponsibility, impulsiveness and unpredictability. A feckless person is somewhat less than human because he is not properly versed in the sophisticated laws which govern the adult world. He is a poorly equipped, childish occupant of a grown-up role. Fecklessness and inadequacy are types of incompetence whose causation is attributed to an underdeveloped or malfunctioning personality. I believe that they are unsatisfactory explanations of human behaviour for a number of reasons.

The hard determinist theory which accounts for the feckless personality has certain drawbacks. It seems to allocate the personality to a place of secondary importance in the causal system. The personality is more caused than causal. There is little interaction or action suggested by this model. Instead, the inadequate personality is a piece of psychological machinery which fails to work properly in certain situations. The language of social work is phrased in such terms as *adjustment* and *adaptation.* A man has to respond to his environment because he is unable to mould it himself.

The environment in which the man was raised and lives can be more or less well integrated. To the extent that it is poorly integrated, the inadequate person is self-determining. He has a greater scope for exercising his real or apparent freedom. Even if his choice is irrevocably determined by what he did and experienced in the past, his present actions are *relatively* uncompelled. In such a loosely-knit system, the idea of inadequacy becomes less useful. His passivity is transformed into behaviour which is more akin to activity. Furthermore, the inappropriateness of the incompetent man's reactions matters less because they can be more easily accommodated by a flexible and loose structure.

In a well-integrated system, however, a different pattern should prevail. It is true that a group has a moral and social force which is usually superior to that of any of its members. Nevertheless, because he is part of an inter-related whole, the inadequate must have an influence on his environment. By definition, such an influence would be disturbing because it stems from a feckless person who does not articulate well with his surroundings. The inadequate's response to

[9] Cf. Miles (1954, p. 128), who argues: 'In the days of the classical economists the individual was poverty stricken through personal fault. In the heyday of Freudianism he got that way because of his early childhood. At neither time did social workers have to become agitated about simple environmental factors, such as low wages, inadequate housing, and lack of protective labor legislation.'

the effects he produces would, in turn, be ill-judged. Hence he would be part of an increasingly destructive amplification system. The inadequate disturbs the structure rather than adapts to it. He brings about a loss of equilibrium which reacts back on his personality and makes it even more feckless. Increased fecklessness leads to a greater instability in the environment, and so on. This spiral could culminate in a collapse of the person's immediate environment. Social workers designate such a collapse 'social breakdown' and the crisis of imprisonment for debt is an instance of it. Despite the fact that the intervention of social work or social control agencies might restore the damage, the havoc caused by inadequates is presumably devastating. In contrast to this crisis model of social breakdown, the debtors at Brixton were rather innocuous: 88 per cent had had no previous record of imprisonment for debt, and 58 per cent had no criminal record. Either the bulk of debtors were not feckless, or one must conclude that the notion of inadequacy is based on poor theory. The sovereignty of the personality in social work philosophy seems to lead to intellectual difficulties. People do not simply fail or succeed in their attempts to adjust to a stable, relatively unchanging environment. Instead, they may well have an impact on the environment and thereby engage in a more complicated set of relationships than that posed by the crude psychiatric model. 'Those who oppose determinism to "free will" are apt to forget that human beings, as individuals and as groups are themselves dynamic participants within the causal order.' (Maciver, 1942, p. 236.)

If personality and environment act upon one another, the definition of inadequacy as unsuccessful adaptation needs some revision. By designating a person 'inadequate', a social worker has contributed little to the explanation of his behaviour. The label is nothing more than a 'technical' description, a prediction that things are likely to be handled ineptly by an 'inadequate'. However, it is an unfortunate label because it has the appearance of an explanation. It stops short of the point at which understanding might be reached. Indeed, the concept hinders *Verstehen* because it sheds no light on the logic and rules governing the inadequate's world. The inadequate is merely an incompetent person whose responses are dulled and inefficient. The label seems to deny the inmate debtor his full humanity.

Another major difficulty is the choice of criteria that are applied when adequacy is gauged. The concept tacitly rests on some 'objective' test which can assess to whom and for what the inmate is adequate. Definitions of mental health and illness, harmful and beneficial attitudes, adequacy and inadequacy all flow from an unwritten doctrine (Leighton, 1965, p. 280):

> Decisions have gone largely by default from the hands of the moralists into those of the technicians of mental and social health, 'good' and 'bad' behaviour is evaluated as 'mature' or 'immature', to live without conscience is to live in a very 'unreal' way and the only 'reality' is the ability to form stable and satisfying relationships.

'Adequacy' presupposes the existence of some universally valid yardstick. Such a presuppostion masks the very real diversity of standards that are routinely applied to Britain. As Donnison (1955, p. 349) remarks, 'there is no generally understood state of "social health" toward which all people strive; our disagreements on this question form the subject matter of politics the world over.' A boy in the D stream of a comprehensive school, for instance, might be adequate when judged by the fellow members of his class, inadequate when judged by his teacher, adequate when judged by the standards of the lower working class, inadequate when judged by the middle class, and so on. Similarly, the psychological and social problems faced by the nondelinquent in a highly delinquent area may be more acute than those faced by the conforming and adjusted delinquents. It is difficult to know whether the social work philosophy I have described would define such a boy as adequate or inadequate. To which norms is the nondelinquent supposed to adapt? Either choice could be regarded as evidence of inadequacy.

Inadequacy and fecklessness appear to be concepts of the same order as social disorganization. Whilst disorganization has undoubtedly characterized some social phenomena, the description is often applied to situations which have been misunderstood by outside observers. It is possible that an inadequate debtor is simply a person whose behaviour does not make obvious sense to one who describes it. Ascriptions of adequacy or inadequacy should be made only when the context of behaviour is fully explored. Many people are unintelligent, illiterate or foolish, but many others cope sensibly with unusual situations. Suttles (1968, p. 3), who produced an ethnography of a Chicago slum area, states:

> Measured by the usual yardsticks of success it is tempting to think that the local residents are simply inadequate and disadvantaged people suffering from cultural deprivation, unemployment, and a number of other 'urban ills'. If the residents insist upon the irrelevance of public standards and the primacy of their own, this can be dismissed as sour grapes or only an attempt to make necessity a virtue. Seen from the inside, however, the Addams area is intricately organized according to its own standards and the residents are fairly insistent on their demands. These demands require discipline and self-

restraint in the same way as do the moral dictates of the wider community. Conventional norms are not rejected but differentially emphasized or suspended for established reasons.

The treatment orientation focuses on personality defects. It argues that there is no need to understand the debtor's situation because his problems are the fruits of psychological disorder. As Wootton (1963, p. 286) argues, 'the contemporary emphasis upon the "casework process" or upon "relationship" is open to the further charge that it deflects attention away from the problems created by evil environments. Always plumbing the depths of her client's personality, the social worker all too easily ignores glaring evils on the surrounding surface. . . .' Thus, the social environment is assumed to be somehow normal and unproblematic. Like Suttles' and Wallace's outsider, the social and welfare services can dismiss the context of behaviour as unimportant or meaningless. The ideas that underlie the concept of inadequacy thus lead to a neglect of the situations which generate indebtedness (Davis, 1964, p. 23):

> Interpretation in terms of specific factors, such as mental abnormality, bad home conditions, or bad employment situations, generally assumes a stable institutional system (and the values that go with it) without which the factors could not operate. But this system is assumed only unconsciously and is hence left unanalyzed.

When attempts are made to analyse these situations, however, it becomes apparent that indebtedness is often a reasonable response to particular events. Economists such as Katona, Garvy and Fisher[10] have created theoretical models which suggest that *anyone* would 'dissave' if he were provided with certain information and had enjoyed a certain personal history. Debt can be construed as a normal consequence of normal causes. Furthermore, the causes are typically located in the social structure rather than the personalities of the people who contract debt. Katona (1949a), for instance, uses reference group theory to explain one kind of dissaving:

> If the income of a family declines in a year in which most families experience the same fate and national income therefore declines, optimistic income expectations may be infrequent and expenditure standards may be adjusted rather promptly. If, however, the income of a family declines in a prosperous year in contrast to the general trend . . . dissaving may be the result in a substantial number of cases.

Similarly, indebtedness may occur when a family experiences income

[10] See, for example, Fisher, 1950.

fluctuations (Garvy, 1948); when there is an illness or emergency (Garvy, 1948); when income declines but is expected to rise again in the immediate future (Garvy, 1948); when income rises and is expected to rise again (Katona, 1949); or when a family makes exceptional purchases (Katona, 1949). In many cases, therefore, debt can be lifted out of the area of psychopathology and restored to the category of normal behaviour. When the economists' models are applied, what seemed to be inadequacy often ceases to be so clearly inadequate. Fecklessness and inadequacy may thus be labels which are applied by people who are unaware of the events that affect the debtor's actions. Indeed, it is possible that this lack of awareness stems from a simple lack of interest in phenomena which are not pathological. In another context, Davis (1964, p. 23) observes, 'being in the habit of focussing attention upon things that require remedial work anyway, it is natural that [the welfare worker] should fall into a species of like-causes-like fallacy—in this case, the theory that evil causes evil.' Wootton (1963, pp. 291, 292) has admirably described the social work orientation towards problems associated with poverty:

> . . . conceptions of what is meant by social work seem to have taken a remarkable—and, in the view of the present writer, a most unfortunate—turn during the past thirty years or so. The root of the trouble seems once again to be traceable to the habit of confusing economic difficulties with personal failure or misconduct. . . . the modern caseworker, under obligation to maintain an attitude of 'neither tolerance nor intolerance', and conceiving her function as concerned with 'psychological maladjustment rather than material need', necessarily finds it hard to say clearly what she is driving at. The one explicit and consistent factor in her handling of every kind of social problem is her unwavering dependence upon psychiatric interpretation. Moral and economic problems alike are reduced to common psychiatric denominators and expressed in identical terms.

Although indebtedness cannot be automatically explained by faults in the debtor, it is possible that the Brixton inmates' behaviour *can* be explained by a form of inadequacy. Yet an important condition must be satisfied before debtors are classified in this way. The concept of inadequacy obviously needs considerable reformulation. It will continue to obscure analysis until it explicitly refers to the context in which the debtor's actions occur and the standards that are used to assess those actions. It must also describe or account for the events that led up to his incarceration. Without these additions, the observations of the social and welfare services are not particularly illuminating.

However, it is not difficult to understand why the imprisoned debtors appeared inadequate. Not only does the social work culture prepare its adherents for recognizing inadequacy, the prisoners themselves would seem unimpressive to an outsider. Unlike criminals, debtors were not officially denounced before they arrived in prison. Their deviant status was not confirmed by authority. Instead, they were provided with a distinctive brown uniform which emphasized how different they were from most prisoners, they were segregated and covered by special rules. The prison and legal systems combined to present the debtor as a particular type of inmate who was rather unimportant to the main business of Brixton. Whilst the criminal's pariah status is continually affirmed in prison, a debtor was shown to be marginal and exceptional. An observer might therefore conclude that the defaulter is not a true deviant.

Such an assumption would be reinforced by the debtor's own protestations and behaviour. Most debtors are unfamiliar with prison[11] and they are unlikely to be prepared for what they find there. Their place in prison has been described by Irwin and Cressey (1964, p. 233). They belong neither to the larger criminal culture outside prison (the 'thief' subculture) nor to the inmate community within the walls (the 'convict' subculture):

> The category of inmates we have characterized as oriented to 'legitimate' subcultures includes men who are not members of the thief subculture upon entering prison and who reject both the thief subculture and the convict subculture while in prison. These men present few problems to prison administrators. They make up a large percentage of the population of any prison, but they isolate themselves—or are isolated—from the thief and convict subcultures.

Debtors are isolated from another significant body. Prison staff regard them as nuisances who ought not to be in prison under their surveillance. In consequence, the debtors are poorly acquainted with the unofficial and official laws that govern conduct in penal institutions. Moreover, their sentences are so short that they are given almost no time in which to learn these laws. They are, in fact, clearly inadequate in the prison context. Their gauche behaviour in Brixton could be taken as a sign of greater lack of sophistication. In contrast to the convicted inmates, defaulters personify many of the traits which social workers designate as basic personality defects.

The debtors' attitudes towards themselves might provide further

[11] 24·9 per cent of the 1961 sample of Brixton debtors had been prisoners before.

support for the belief that they are inadequate. They have been persuaded by bailiffs that prison is a sensible solution to their problems. Not only are they rationally coping with their indebtedness, they can also claim that their imprisonment is a penance which offsets any offence they may have caused. They seem able to neutralize their anxiety about stigma by shunning other prisoners, condemning their condemners, appealing to the moral force of other goals, and so on. Whilst the debtors are convinced that they have taken a reasonable and mature stance, social workers do not credit them with intelligence or a capacity for 'realism'. It is possible that the defaulters' definition of their situation is not even known by outsiders. Instead, the extreme reluctance of debtors to pay and their protestation of innocence are taken as proof of an insensitivity to others and an inability to face 'reality'.

I have described some elements of the public, social control and social work conceptions of defaulters. The public reaction seems to be nascent and as yet inactive. There is no widespread clamour for action to be taken against defaulters. This public indifference allows the two polar cultures to engage in an unhampered contest for mastery over enforcement policies. The social control ethos argues that defaulters are culpable persons who should be exposed to deterrent and punitive methods of control. The social work ethos is based on hard determinism and points to treatment as the only model of social action. Lawyers and legislators appear to straddle both positions contending that there are innocent and dishonest debtors to whom different policies are appropriate.

The social services' belief in the inappropriateness of punishment stems as much from a professional interest in treatment as from a deterministic philosophy. It is possible that punishment could become just another causal factor in the determination of a person's actions. In this sense, prison and execution are new factors which affect a person's behaviour (Baier, 1968, p. 80):

> An agent's ability to do something does not depend on his ability to want to do it. An agent's inability to *want* to pay his taxes may or may not be an exculpatory explanation of his *refusal* to pay them, but it cannot prove his *inability* to pay them. Such a person may be exusably or justifiably *unwilling* to pay them, but he is not *unable* to pay them. Moreover, if it is desirable that he should pay them and so that he should want to pay them, and if making him liable to punishment will make him willing to pay them, then the fact that (if determinism is true) his wanting to pay them was ruled out, as things were, does not militate against his being held liable for not *paying*.

Whether or not one can properly describe a debtor as good or bad is irrelevant to whether one should hold out the threat of punishment. Collectors build their social types on the responses which debtors make to their tactics. They manipulate the debtor's environment so that it will force payment out of people who may or may not be absolutely determined in their actions. The two cultures could meet on this ground, but they do not do so.

By 1971, when the research for this book was completed, the treatment orientation had gained favour. One memorandum to the Payne Committee (Penal Affairs Committee, 1965) exemplified the stance which was urged on legislators:

> It is our view that civil courts should explore every alternative before a committal order is made and be given more positive methods than imprisonment (both as sanctions for non-adherence to the court orders, and as a preventive measure against repeated contravention) that take more account of the social factors. In many cases we suspect that prevention of further 'offences' would involve a great deal in the way of work-training and other 'social engineering', as well as social case work to improve the attitude of the debtor to his situation. Despite the obvious cost of such work we believe that the community is obliged (and it is economically to his advantage) to tackle this job as far as resources permit rather than deal merely with that isolated symptom of the social problem which shows itself in persistent refusal to pay a credit debt.

In the competition for providing authoritative definitions of default, the social control culture was structurally disadvantaged. I argued in Chapter 1 that creditors and debt-collectors seem to benefit from concealing their real practices. Public fear of collection methods depends on the continued existence of ossified beliefs about the brutality of collectors. Moreover, since most collection is privately financed and does not require public assistance, there is little need to elicit popular support for the agents that carry it out. Enforcement agencies have therefore been poor at communication. Despite its drive towards professionalism, it does not rest on a body of skills and knowledge which is generally regarded as esoteric and scientific. It cannot convince outsiders that its conceptions are as well-grounded intellectually as the ideas of social workers. In contrast, the occupation of social work contains many articulate spokesmen who propagate their views in periodicals, journals, books and broadcasts. It influences other pressure groups, such as the Society of Friends, which urge policies based on social casework themes. Most social work is accountable to public bodies and its growth is, in part, dependent on popular sympathy. Social workers are more effective in disseminating their opinions and are often officially consulted when government decisions are taken. As a result, legislation has increasingly reflected the view that debt collection should be organized around therapeutic notions. The Payne Committee (1969, p. 316), for instance, recommended that a 'Social Service Office for Debtors' should be incorporated in the structure of a county court. The Office would consist of trained social workers who

> . . . might be able to assist debtors heavily in debt to adjust their weekly budget to allow for necessary weekly outgoings as well as payments ordered to reduce their debts. . . . We think there is great need for social workers to perform, for financially incompetent or inadequate or irresponsible debtors, the functions which are discharged for more successful members of the community by bank managers, accountants and solicitors.

Such a recommendation clearly reflects the increasing influence of the social work culture. Although that provision was not incorporated in the Administration of Justice Act, 1970, much else that was permeated by similar themes did receive legislative expression. In the battle between social control and social work perspectives, the notion of 'inadequacy' is obviously supplanting the definition of debtors as 'Rogues and Spendthrifts' (anon., 1757). As Berger and Luckmann (1967, p. 126) argue, 'the confrontation of alternative symbolic universes implies a problem of power—which of the conflicting definitions of reality will be "made to stick" in . . . society.' It is clear that the social work perspective is the more powerful of the two. Indeed, it seems that the decline in authority of the punitive rhetoric is widespread throughout all areas of social control (Sutherland, 1950, p. 147):

> For a century or more two rival policies have been used in criminal justice. One is the punitive policy: the other is the treatment policy. The treatment policy is evidenced by probation, parole, the indeterminate sentence, the juvenile court, the court clinic. . . . The treatment policy has been gaining, and the punitive policy has been losing, ground. The trend toward treatment is consistent with a general trend toward scientific procedures in other fields, as illustrated by medicine, with its techniques of diagnosis and with treatment and prevention based on scientific knowledge of the causes of disease. The trend away from punishment toward treatment is not, however, based on a demonstration that treatment is more effective than punishment in protecting society against crime, for no such demonstration is available. . . . Not only

> has there been a trend toward individualization in treatment of offenders, but there has been a trend also toward psychiatric policies. Treatment tends to be organized on the assumption that the criminal is a socially sick person; deviant traits of personality, regarded as relatively permanent and generic, are regarded as the causes of crime.

Whilst the therapeutic culture seems to be in the ascendant, members of the punitive culture are firmly in control of the day-to-day workings of enforcement. They will probably remain in control as long as collectors are allowed to exercise discretion in their treatment of defaulters. Because the threefold typology is particularly appropriate to the decisions which have to be made in debt collection, the professional defaulter is unlikely to disappear for some time.

Debtors and the career

Finally, I shall discuss the general structure of the career and the manner in which it affects defaulters' self-conceptions. Enforcement is strongly influenced by economy because it almost always involves a creditor in loss. It leads to an inevitable diminution of profits and creditors seek to make this loss as small as possible. Their search for inexpensive remedies affects all collection policies. The enforcement machine is designed to act as a filter which exposes very few debtors to costly sanctions. Economy and the bureaucratization of control lead to the simplification of procedures. They also determine the creditor's means of manipulating defaulters.

Etzioni (1964, p. 59) argues that an organization can employ physical, material or symbolic types of control. Physical control rests on real or threatened assaults on the body; material control confers or withdraws the right to enjoy goods and services; and symbolic control relies on 'normative symbols, those of prestige and esteem; and social symbols, those of love and acceptance'. That is, symbolic control depends on the organization's ability to alter the way in which a person is regarded by himself and others. It is concerned, in part, with issues of status and self-definition. Debt collection is based on weak versions of all three types of control. Creditors threaten imprisonment but the realization of their threats depends on a court's co-operation. A minute proportion only of the threats actually result in a debtor being incarcerated. The threats do not always precede action, instead they are devised to make a debtor experience stress. Similarly, execution is a form of material control although it is unlikely to entail the sale of goods. Most enforcement is characterized by the threat rather than the imposition of physical and material sanctions. Creditors excite feelings of anxiety by informing debtors that they are advancing towards a dangerous position in which a new unpleasantness will be encountered.

Enforcement is also supported by covert and overt attacks on a debtor's status. The covert attacks stem from the use which is made of physical and material control. At each stage, a debtor is expected to learn that he is a normal person who will be treated as an abnormal person unless he complies with the creditor's wishes. At the end of the creditor's letter sequence, for instance, there is often the threat that debt-collectors will be employed. The threat suggests that the defaulter is in danger of being recognized as an unusually obstinate person who deserves unsympathetic handling. Although the threat refers to physical control, it also warns the debtor that he is almost worthy of the stigma that a debt-collector's attentions can inflict. Covert attacks are also made when, with each new phase of the career, there is an elaborate change of personnel, titles and tactics. Collection attempts to impress upon the debtor the fact that his position is rapidly changing and his decisions are becoming increasingly fateful. As Dewey (1922, pp. 216–17) pointed out, 'the thing actually at stake in any serious deliberation is . . . what sort of person is one to become, what sort of self is in the making.' It is in this sense that collection is a lengthy series of forced changes of status which collectors try to make as significant as possible. Enforcement is also organized around overt symbolic assaults on the debtor. He may be telephoned at his workplace or threatened with the Van. He may receive letters whose envelopes proclaim that he is being dunned. He may find that his neighbours and employer have been approached by collectors. In certain areas, bailiffs are recognized by outsiders and they are able to stigmatize the debtors they visit. Again, a person's default can become public knowledge when he is taken to court. Collection can thereby progressively undermine the debtor's social position.

However, the collectors' symbolic control is no more potent than their physical or material control techniques. They cannot afford to make full use of it because debtors are generally thought to be redeemable. When the personnel of one stage despair of a defaulter, they usually send him on to the next phase where he is defined as a person who *might* be unfortunate. Thus, instead of submitting him to a decisive degradation ceremony, they refuse to confirm his deviant status. They dare not affront him or make him too hostile because he is able to punish *them*. Few creditors can resort to the overt methods I have described above. Not only might they precipitate secondary deviation, they might also estrange present and future customers. Enforcement must therefore steer a course between the Scylla of too little action and the Charybdis of excessive action. It cannot really depend on symbolic control.

The damage which enforcement might cause to a debtor's self-esteem can often be neutralized. The debtor can appeal to a whole gamut of reasons why he should not be reproached. He can claim, for example, that the pressures applied by the collector were not morally compelling. He may invoke what I have termed the apologetic convention to explain why he was unable to continue his payments. Whatever justification he employs, it is almost never put to the test of a brutal crisis of identity. If he pays his debt, he can quietly pass back into the normal community because he has never been fully absent. Although the career may have been disquieting, it was not able to award him an unambiguously pariah status. If he persists in refusing to pay his debt, he must cope with more serious threats to his identity. Collectors will muster a greater range of weapons against which he must defend himself. Yet, ironically, it is precisely during the stages of execution and committal that expert help is at hand. Because a sudden change in status might provoke an uncontrollable reaction, bailiffs are concerned to reconcile the debtor to his fate. They do so by providing a new set of rationalization, definitions and interpretations which reassure the debtor that he is basically normal. Bailiffs are what Strauss (1959, pp. 110, 112) terms 'status coaches':

> A coaching relationship exists if someone seeks to move someone else along a series of steps, when those steps are not entirely institutionalized and invariant, and when the learner is not entirely clear about their sequences (although the coach is). . . . The general features of the coaching relationship flow from the learner's need for guidance as he moves along, step by step. He needs guidance not merely because in the conventional sense he needs someone to teach him skills, but because some very surprising things are happening to him that require explanation. The coach stands ready to interpret his responses, which may otherwise only have the status of ambiguous signs. . . . In malevolent kinds of coaching—as in seduction, or in conning by confidence men—the relationship is one of trapper and victim. . . . Abstractly stated, the coach not only works on current desires to get action directed along given paths, but seeks to create new desires and aims. He seeks to create a new identity for the pupil—or victim—and to do this involves him in a variety of canny maneuvers.

Debtors often assist the bailiff in this coaching relationship. Not only do they want to understand what is happening to them, they might also welcome new reasons for not repaying their debts. To the extent that they are troubled by guilt, they may be willing to accept the accounts which are offered to them. After all, a person who is not anxious to discharge his debt will find the bailiff's style of interpretation very helpful. Dishonest defaulters thus share much in common with the confidence trickster's victim (Maurer, 1940, p. 16):

> A confidence man prospers only because of the fundamental dishonesty of his victim. . . . As the lust for large and easy profits is fanned into a hot flame, the mark puts all his scruples behind him. . . . In the mad frenzy of cheating some-one else, he is unaware of the fact that he is the real victim, carefully selected and fatted for the kill. Thus arises the trite, but none the less sage maxim: 'You can't cheat an honest man'.

In some cases, it is possible that the bailiff–debtor relationship is almost identical to the one portrayed by Maurer. The bailiff (confidence man) makes the debtor (victim) believe that they are colluding together in order to cheat the creditor. Yet, although the relationship is likely to develop in the same way as the classic confidence game, it will seldom have the same outcome. The victim does not often learn that he has been made a victim. Instead, he is given a new, acceptable identity without any feeling of loss.

The identity provided by bailiffs in these trying stages will achieve a number of results. It will allow the debtor to assume his new status without undergoing too abrupt or painful a transition. It will explain his situation in such a way that he can keep his face, his pride and his belief that he can control what happens to him. It will also support the idea that the bailiff acted properly and in the debtor's own interests. That is, bailiffs coach debtors through critical periods which might bring about unwelcome changes of status. The bailiff is just as anxious as the debtor to avoid inflicting stigma. The debtors I interviewed in Brixton certainly classified themselves as ordinary albeit unfortunate people.

In conclusion, debt collection sets up a drawn-out career based on weak forms of social control. Collectors operate with a threefold classification of defaulters which is linked to two features of enforcement: the need to predict a defaulter's intentions; and the particular information that a process involving variable amounts of time and effort generates. The career is drawn out because it is subject to legal restraints which prevent precipitate action; it relies on bluster and the creation of impressions rather than direct sanctions; and it has to be both complicated and simple. It must be complicated enough to cater for a variety of types of default and response. It must differentiate between the feckless, the unfortunate and the professional. Having established a means of differentiation, it must further incorporate appropriate strategies for each type. Yet it must be simple enough to proceed smoothly, cheaply, rapidly and with little attention. In many cases, thousands of defaults must be efficiently handled at the same time. The result is that the career automatically applies a series of tests which probe the debtor's situation. The tests are strung together in sequence, each failure leading to another test. Complexity and simplicity can be united in a process which is both 'exhaustive' and mechanical. The career system routinely creates and then identifies the three social types of defaulter.

Such a system does not have the resources to control large numbers of hostile debtors. Because it cannot antagonize them, it relies instead on manipulating feelings of guilt and anxiety. It contrives to keep defaulters within the normal community and ostracizes very few of them. During those phases in which antagonism is most likely to arise, debtors are carefully coached into accepting a new identity which ensures their compliance. Inmate debtors, at least, are not seriously perturbed about the lengthy experiences which they have gone through. Whilst they define themselves as normal, and are defined as deviant by collectors, they are regarded by the social and welfare services as inadequate. These differences are allowed to flourish by a control system which does not award unambiguous identities to the people it processes. The 'real' nature of default and defaulters remains a matter of dispute.

13 Conclusion

Social control agencies can be classified by the kinds of technique which they employ. At one extreme, an agency can rely exclusively on persuasion. It is responsible for deviants who are thought to respect its authority and status. They accept its goals and interpretations as reasonable and legitimate. It can reform the wayward by invoking the common sentiments to which they both subscribe. In this case, the agency conceives its task to be clarifying complicated moral questions, urging the desirability of the proper path, and providing the facilities and instructions which can lead to reform. Such organizations as Alcoholics Anonymous, Synanon and Grendon Underwood Prison aim at what Gusfield calls 'assimilative reform'. When the deviants do not respect the authority of an agency, however, force may be used to compel obedience. Gusfield (1963, p. 77) describes the polar cases of assimilation and coercion in his history of the American temperance movement:

> The champion of assimilative reform viewed the drinker as part of a social system in which the reformer's culture was dominant. On this assumption, his invitation to the drinker to reform made sense. The champion of coercive reform cannot make this assumption. He sees the object of reform as someone who rejects the social dominance of the reformer and denies the legitimacy of his life style. Since the dominance of his culture and the social status of his group are denied, the coercive reformer turns to law and force as ways to affirm it.

There are therefore two radically different worlds of social control: assimilative reform with its compliant deviants, and coercive reform with its hostile deviants. If the control techniques are altered for some reason, it is likely that the behaviour of the deviants will also alter. At the very least, the situation which the deviants face has changed. They have to contend with new measures which present new problems. To the extent that their objective world has changed, they may experience subjective transformations which produce new identities. When an agency shifts from using persuasion to using force, one of the possible consequences is the generation of an antagonistic or devious secondary deviation (Lemert, 1951, p. 76):

> . . . if the deviant acts are repetitive and have a high visibility, and, if there is a severe societal reaction, which, through a process of identification is incorporated as part of the 'me' of the individual, the probability is greatly increased that the integration of existing roles will be disrupted and that reorganization based upon a new role will occur. (The 'me' in this context is simply the subjective aspect of the societal reaction.)

If an agency can shape deviants' responses to itself and the larger society, it follows that the two worlds of control tend to be relatively self-maintaining. Whilst assimilative reform encourages co-operation, coercive reform can engender antagonism. Each world has its own logic and set of accounts; agencies based on force need to use force, in part, because they create an opposition which cannot be easily conquered by pacific means. Hence many of the attributes which coercive reformers identify as *essential* parts of the deviant personality may, in fact, be nothing more than the products of coercion. The treatment of narcotic addiction provides a useful illustration. In America,

> the use of certain classes of dangerous drugs . . . are considered deviant. Because such use is labeled deviant, criminal, and outside legitimate medical practice, users develop a life style quite far removed from that of straight society. The roles, statuses, functioning, and self-concepts of the users are derived from this subculture (Dinitz, Dynes and Clarke, 1969, p. 277).

The behaviour of American drug addicts must thus be largely understood as a concomitant of enforcement practices:

> While certain patterns of addict life may have been in existence before the Harrison Act, the conversion of addiction into mass criminal activity appears to have given special form and meaning to addiction, so that we may speak reasonably about an addict culture operating as a system (Fiddle, 1963, p. 3156).

The coercive policies adopted by the Federal Bureau of Narcotics have produced a fairly stable situation: addicts acquire deviant identities in response to the problems posed by oppression and these identities, in turn, serve as justifications for further oppression.[1] The typification of the addict which is maintained by official agencies in the United States is a truly frightening one. His 'veins collapse and livid purplish scars remain. Boils and abscesses plague the skin; gnawing pain racks the body. Nerves snap; vicious twitching develops' (Kuh, 1961, p. 4). Not only is the addict physically rotted, he is also morally depraved. He has 'an increased dependence upon others and a marked aversion to work. . . . Drug addiction itself directly causes a cancerous invasion of the moral structures . . . with an absence of ethics, scruples, and even the minimum demand of human decency' (Richard, 1961, p. 87). The official definition of the addict thus supports the control structure, and the control structure contributes towards the realization of some of the features that make up the official definition. Coercive reform can flourish on self-fulfilling prophecies. As Lindesmith (1960, p. 222) argues:

> The fact that opium smoking became a fad in the American underworld probably provided the original grounds for the idea that there is an inherent connection between crime and addiction and provided the impetus for anti-narcotics legislation. This legislation in turn reinforced the notion that addicts are necessarily criminals by actually making them that. The agencies which enforce anti-narcotics legislation have become a vested interest in the status quo, and the fact that addicts in most of the other nations of the West are not nearly as criminal as those of the United States has been ignored.

In contrast, British policy towards addiction has been comparatively benign. Until quite recently, drug use was defined as a medical problem which should be handled by medical agencies.[2] Because addicts did not have to resort to a black market, and because they did not have to base their lives on deception and evasion, they had little need of subcultural support. It is obvious that the addict's situation has changed, but Schur's (1965, pp. 154–5) comments about drug-taking before 1965 are still illuminating. They show how assimilative reform can affect the nature of the addiction problem:

> The addict in Britain need not become a thief or a prostitute in order to support his habit. Very few addicts are imprisoned for any sort of offense. . . . Addiction and the underworld have not become intermeshed, and there has been no serious spread of narcotic addiction to juveniles. British policy has also inhibited the development of an addict subculture. The addict is not subjected to a continuous struggle for economic survival and

[1] Cf. Becker (1963) and Dickson (1968).

[2] Cf. Lindesmith (1957), Schur (1961a, 1961b, 1962).

> for drug supplies, nor need he constantly attempt to maximize his anonymity and mobility. There is relatively little need for group support and actual contact with other addicts may be slight.

Both as cause and consequence, the British are not so ready to believe in a dope fiend mythology. The recent legislation on drugs, however, has impressed a coercive stamp on control policies and the dope fiend is likely to grow as a figure in popular thought as well as in fact. With the increase of secondary deviation, the anomic and dangerous sick-role will inevitably become a prominent aspect of British addiction.

Of course, certain kinds of assimilative reform can also produce secondary deviation. When the reforming agency is held in great admiration or fear, it may well have dramatic effects on its deviants. The deviants may be so impressed by the goals of the agency that they will experience identity transformations. This is particularly likely to happen when a deviant believes that he is almost beyond redemption. His life may then become organized around penitence and good works. Something of this strain was surely suggested by Weber's description of the agonized Protestant who sought certain knowledge that he was a member of the Elect. It is also suggested by the example of the mental hospital patient who conspicuously demonstrates how normal he is by adopting a psychiatric standpoint from which to view himself and others. Similarly, the frightened Catholic may become a secondary deviant (Lea, 1896, p. 353):

> Confessions may be too perfect and minute, and the terror of the confessional is the overscrupulous penitent, who is constantly tormenting himself with the dread that he has not secured pardon for the sins which he has confessed; that he has not confessed them properly and must repeat them again and again; that things are sins which are no sins. It suggests what an infinite amount of misery the system has caused to timid and conscientious souls, surrounded by multitudinous observances on which they rely for salvation, ever afraid of failing in some minute particular and seeing hell yawning before them as the penalty for some trifling omission.

It is possible that the Brixton debtors' protestations of innocence can be explained in the same way. The prisoners did not feel estranged from normal society, and they clearly respected the bailiffs who had incarcerated them. None questioned the propriety of his punishment although they *did* question its rationality. To this extent, debt collection was an assimilative system and the defaulters' reactions were of the same order (but not the same magnitude) as the Catholic's.

It is clear that enforcement is neither wholly assimilative nor wholly coercive in its approach to defaulters. Whilst some stages rely on overt intimidation, others are organized around appeals to the debtor's conscience and reason. A creditor's letter stream, for example, is intended for the honest, feckless and unfortunate consumers who have not forfeited their right to be regarded as normal, moral people. The letters call upon a debtor to respond so that some new arrangement can be made. Later on, however, threats of force are offered and sometimes realized. Yet, even when they are realized, the debt-collector or bailiff typically urges the defaulter to respect the common norms that should bind them together.

One of the reasons why debt collection is neither wholly assimilative nor wholly coercive is that the debtor and the creditor enjoy a peculiarly symbiotic relationship. Very few control agencies attack deviants whom they have themselves consciously created. Creditors are the necessary, if not the sufficient, cause of default and they have an interest in increasing the demand for credit as well as ensuring that the credit will not be improperly used. Although the analogies cannot be pursued too far, a creditor acting out an enforcement role is not unlike a brewer attempting to cure alcoholics or the Mafia attempting to curb the immoderate use of heroin. Whilst it is obviously not in the interests of the creditor to encourage bad debt, it is not in his interests to restrain the demand for his services. He is not an altruistic reformer,[3] but a victim who knows that an efficient exploitation of the market must lead to some bad debt. Creditors have told me of their anxiety about the unhappiness caused by collection; they recognize that their enforcement role is a necessary consequence of their entrepreneurial role. Some moneylenders, for instance, said that they felt uncomfortable about the very high rates of interest (usually 48 per cent per annum) which they charge. One stated:

> Quite honestly, I think we try to treat [the debtor] so reasonably because we're charging a high rate of interest. There's no doubt about it, we feel *guilty*. There's no doubt about it at all. And we try therefore to be so reasonable with him that we can't understand if he doesn't go to meet us halfway on it. If he

3 Of course, altruistic reformers tend to have a vested interest in perpetuating the deviance which they claim to abhor. Control agencies give their members jobs, prestige, power and so on which would have to be relinquished if the agencies were too successful. Ironically, if the police managed to achieve the impossible by 'stamping out crime', they would probably stamp themselves out as well. All control agents have a symbiotic relationship with their deviants.

> made an offer of *any* sort, and it was reasonable, if he came to talk to us, he would *always* get what he wanted because we feel guilty about it (Creditor 27).

As a result, many creditors are reluctant to pursue completely coercive policies.

There are more important reasons why collection occupies a midway position between the two poles of assimilation and coercion. A purely assimilative policy is not viable because some defaulters undoubtedly prey on creditors; because the enforcement system is so structured that some defaulters must become professionals; and because creditors are often challenged by the edicts of a person-oriented culture. Such a culture exists outside the lower class areas of America. Hoggart's (1957) description of the traditional working class, and Mays' discussion of Liverpool youth, show that the culture influences behaviour in England. In its most naked form, the culture can legitimate predatory activity against strangers and impersonal institutions (Mays, 1964, p. 118):

> Larceny seems as a general rule to be confined to such business firms and other groups with whom boys have no experience of personal relationship to act as a restraining factor. The closer the person or group is to the boy the less the likelihood of him thieving at their expense. It is nearly always abhorrent to rob members of the family or personal friends. To a much lesser extent, it is not done to steal from small one-man shops or elderly people. But with strangers inhibitions are weaker and fellow sympathy reduced to a minimum. They are therefore the natural victims on whom to prey.

The neutralizing techniques made available by a person-oriented culture permit many consumers to deny the moral force of agreements made with hire purchase or mail order firms. Whilst most debtors eventually succumb to the intolerable anxiety manufactured by enforcement, it seems that creditors have to contend with a prevalent and, from their point of view, subversive perspective on relationships. Debt collection cannot therefore rest on assimilation alone.

On the other hand, enforcement cannot be entirely dependent on coercion. An exclusive resort to violence would be expensive, inefficient and detrimental to trade. It would also be curbed by lawyers, legislators and others who are often concerned about the plight of debtors. In other chapters, I have outlined numerous reasons why collection cannot make extensive use of its sanctions, but there is one major reason which deserves fuller attention. Default has a peculiarity which distinguishes it from many other forms of deviance. Creditors and collectors suffer from their inability to classify a debtor accurately whilst enforcement is going on. Any early classification may have to be revised or discarded because there is always the risk that behaviour which *appears* deviant is really something else. That is, default involves not one, but two separate instances of rule-breaking: there is the initial refusal to comply with the terms of a contract, and there is also the possibility of a final refusal to discharge the debt. Whilst most borrowers become rule-breakers in the first sense, few become deviants in the second. Any defaulter *may* repay his debt in the end and, if he does so, his actions will inevitably acquire a totally different significance from those of a permanent defaulter. A seeming professional may, in fact, be a feckless or unfortunate debtor. Indeed, newspapers sometimes contain reports about anguished debtors who return sums after decades of default.

Judgments made during the enforcement process must always be suspended because the defaulter's last action or inaction will alone decide what kind of person he has been all the time. However, whilst creditors cannot suspend their judgment indefinitely, they can never be sure that a debtor's action *is* his last. The unfortunate debtor might always make one more response which will reveal him as a fraud. Similarly, the professional might unexpectedly make a payment or furnish some proof of his integrity.

Enforcement is not the only control system which is plagued by such indeterminacy. What might be the onset of alcoholism could also be nothing more than a 'binge'. Similarly, what might be the first stage of a mental breakdown could also be a 'temporary depression'. Yet most control agents are usually able to make the comfortable assumption that deviant processes have natural histories, that in time it will become clear whether a person's drinking was an isolated episode or something more sinister. Collectors cannot make this assumption because default is a kind of inactivity which does not necessarily have a natural history. They cannot discern neat boundaries which separate one phase from another, nor can they predict the direction which phases will take. Indeed, most changes in the debtor's status are imposed by the collectors themselves.

Collection can be made manageable only when default is defined in a certain way. After all, enforcement would be incredibly difficult if there was no natural point at which the harassment of a seemingly intractable debtor must end. At some point, a collector must be able to decide that no more can or should be done. In consequence, each enforcement must be artificially treated as a distinct episode with a recognizable beginning, middle and end. When the episode draws to a close, the collector will feel that he is competent to perform the decisive, authoritative act of classification. He will then proclaim that, further evidence notwithstanding, the debtor is *really* professional, feckless or unfortunate and, furthermore, he has been so all along. The episode will then be complete.

A viable collection system must also divide its enforcement episodes into smaller stages, each stage being followed by its own tentative review of what has happened. Greig (1964, p. 141) states:

> We will . . . remark in passing upon the need for a most carefully-thought-out routine (to suit the particular class of business involved), designed to prevent the possibility of accounts 'drifting' into 'long past due'. Every efficient system must provide that at a certain stage (and that not too long delayed) a slow account shall be brought to the manager's notice so that his skill and experience may be utilized and trouble saved.

Having decided that a certain period of time is critical, collectors must project themselves forward in time and imagine what the debtor's behaviour in that period has meant. They search for a theme in the debtor's known past which will make sense of what has happened. Such a search is common to all attempts at defining the situation (McHugh, 1968, p. 37):

> Actors assume before the fact that a pattern of meaning will be discovered in the events they observe. They are *future oriented*, in that they take it for granted they will be able to make something of what is yet to occur. They are also past oriented, in that they take it for granted that what has already occurred will inform the future. Each of these orientations folds back as an actor's description of the present.

The collector's themes are based on interpretations which are made meaningful by his own benchmarks. They centre on a debtor's intentions which may be construed as honest, dishonest or muddled. It is apparent that creditors and collectors are seldom knowledgeable about their defaulters. As a result, their tentative reviews will often be rudely contradicted by unpredicted behaviour. It would be extremely foolish to take precipitate coercive action on the basis of these reviews alone. Expensive sanctions can be implemented only when a rare state of certainty is reached. Otherwise, undesirable consequences will probably flow from premature judgments.

Other agencies control deviants whose intentions are important to them, but the need to suspend judgment will be significant only when they have limited powers. A powerful agent does not have to concern himself about *predicting* a deviant's intentions because he can effectively *alter* those intentions. Whilst collectors face the risk of antagonizing debtors who are able to evade them, other agents have so complete a mastery over their deviants that any antagonism is inconsequential. Mao Tse-tung, for example, stated that the 'past errors' of people with 'unorthodox tendencies' . . . 'must be exposed with no thought for personal feelings or face'. (Mao Tse-tung, 1951, p. 392.) Such a lack of concern about the effects of status degradation stems from the strength of Chinese control agencies. A weak agency could never afford to be so unconcerned. A description of coercive thought reform (Lifton, 1961, p. 66) shows how intimidation could be used against two people whose intentions were of paramount interest to the reformers:

> Both Dr Vincent and Father Luca took part in an agonizing drama of death and rebirth. In each case, it was made clear that the 'reactionary spy' who entered the prison must perish, and that in his place must arise a 'new man', resurrected in the Communist mold. . . . Neither of these men had himself initiated the drama; indeed, at first both had resisted it, and tried to remain quite outside of it. But their environment did not permit any sidestepping: they were forced to participate, drawn into the forces around them until they themselves began to feel the need to confess and to reform. . . . The milieu brings to bear upon the prisoner a series of overwhelming pressures, at the same time allowing only a very limited set of alternatives for adapting to them.

Similarly, religious attempts to combat heresy were often distinguished by the great powers of the inquisitors. The Inquisition was another agency established to tackle deviants whose intentions were critically important. Heretics were forced to undergo status degradation ceremonies and emerge as penitents. The Spanish 'inquisitor was as much a father-confessor as a judge, aiming not at condemnation but at ending estrangement, at restoring erring lambs to the fold'. (Turberville, 1949, p. 98.) The inquisitor chose to employ coercion although he might have adopted a policy of assimilative reform. In so doing, he helped to maintain a deviance-amplification process which seemed to manufacture heretics as well as suppress them. Thus, Lea (1908, vol. 1, p. 104) observes 'it is not easy for us to realize what there was in the faith of the Cathari to inspire men with the enthusiastic zeal of martyrdom, but no religion can show a more unbroken roll of those who unshrinkingly and joyfully sought death in its most abhorrent form in preference to apostasy'. Indeed, Lea (1908, vol. 1, p. 107) argues that martyrdom promoted the growth of Catharism because the 'exaltation caused by persecution' kept 'it alive among the enthusiastic and the discontented'.

Duster (1970, p. 91) makes much the same point but his argument is based on slightly different foundations. He argues that, although 'the "deviant" in Protestant nations is viewed in terms of his total evil or total deviance', the outsider who is thought able to alter his intentions and beliefs may always return to the normal moral community (Duster, 1970, p. 95):

> In both the political and religious areas . . . , the nonbelieving deviant becomes a moral deviant to the extent that his identity as deviant is believed to be total. However, because conversion to the community of the normal and moral is possible because men can move back and forth between the communities, the political or religious deviant is not as intensely responded to as the *finally immoral man*. The final measure of total identity is when the violation of a community's moral dictation has as its result a cutting off of the pathway back to the 'normal and moral' community. Along a continuum of ways and methods of assessing the degree of moral strength and sanction, this is the most significant indicator. With those moral outsiders who simply believe differently . . . the community can choose to treat the deviance as something which the individual can himself control, and thereby can re-enter the community. Even though heretics are banned and political enemies are bombed, the community retains the hope or the ideal that the violence may be corrective. For those men who believe that homosexuality is (1) immoral, (2) totally identifying, and (3) nonconvertible, the violence against the homosexual has an entirely different meaning. . . . The addict, the prostitute, the bank-robber, the murderer; all are stained permanently as total identities. . . .

Coercive reform aimed at deviants whose intentions are significant must be able to change those intentions or, in some cases, override them. It cannot be effective if it is not strong enough to cope with the secondary deviants which it has created. Debt collection is dominated by the problem of how force should be applied. Defaulters are not cowed deviants who have to respond to a 'series of overwhelming pressures'. They are more akin to contestants who can punish a collector who makes a foolish move. Moreover, a collection system with weak sanctions cannot afford to estrange debtors who might still be amenable to assimilative reform. Casson (quoted in Greig, 1964, p. 160) argues that, even at the debt-collector stage, assimilation is preferable to coercion:

> It is wiser to employ a Trade Protection Society or a Collection Agency than a lawyer for the following reasons: (1) A Society

> or Agency is likely to be less dilatory than a lawyer. (2) Many lawyers encourage litigation. (3) Lawyers are likely to neglect small claims. (4) They are not specialists in debt collection as the people in a Trade Protection Society or Collection Agency are. (5) They do not use tact. They do not try to educate debtors. They use the hammer. They write war letters. They do not endeavour to protect goodwill of a firm. They do not consider future business. They use threats and peremptory demands. They deal in ultimatums. Once a debtor's account goes to a Solicitor he is destroyed as a customer.

It is this risk of 'destroying a debtor as a customer' (or creating secondary deviation) that inhibits the use of coercion. When a control agency is not powerful, its few weapons are as likely to be harmful to itself as to its deviants.[4] This contention is best supported by the behaviour of debt-collectors and bailiffs in face-to-face enforcement situations. Agents who are supposed to intimidate defaulters feel too weak to risk a direct trial of strength. Instead, they rely on overt techniques of assimilation or on their covert counterpart—'conning'. In either case, appeals are made to the morality of the person-oriented culture. Few coercive situations will therefore be presented by agents *as* coercive situations. It is only when collectors are unable to confront defaulters face-to-face that they will employ the inferior device of sending threatening letters which are pretences at coercion. Letters are poor substitutes for personal enforcement because they lack the immediate moral force of collection calls. When personal contact is impossible, collectors must fall back on techniques which are coercive in tone. These techniques are dangerous to the collector. When the deviant's

[4] Weak weapons may, indeed, strengthen the debtor's resolve not to pay. He may cite the collector's brutality as a reason why default is justifiable and not immoral. Berne (1966, pp. 82–3) puts this point well: 'the hard form of the game occurs if the creditor is determined to collect. In order to get his money he will have to resort to extreme measures. These usually have a coercive element. . . At this point there is a switch. [The debtor] now knows that he will probably have to pay. But because of the coercive element, . . . [he] feels peremptorily justified in getting angry; he now switches over to a variant of "Now I've Got You, You Son of a Bitch". In this case he wins by demonstrating that the creditor is greedy, ruthless and untrustworthy. The two most obvious advantages of this are (1) it strengthens [his] existential position, which is a disguised form of "All creditors are grasping", and (2) it offers a large external gain, since he is now in a position to abuse the creditor openly to his friends without losing his status as a "Good Joe". . . . In addition, it vindicates his taking advantage of the credit system: if that is the way creditors are, as he has now shown, why pay anybody?' If creditors are strong enough to act in a way which permits debtors to 'condemn their condemnors', but are not strong enough to defeat the now self-righteous defaulter, there is nothing to be gained from coercion.

attitude determines the outcome of enforcement, any resort to unambiguously coercive sanctions can imperil the agent's chance of success. Hence debt collection is often assimilative in form, if not in substance.

Contemporary enforcement resembles the world of assimilative reform. Its methods rely on attempts to persuade (coupled with vague threats) rather than on direct, persistent intimidation. Its deviants are seldom moral outcasts; instead, they are 'inadequate', 'feckless', or 'unfortunate'. It could be argued that enforcement is necessarily assimilative because debtors are the innocent victims of poverty, incompetence or exploitative marketing techniques. I believe that such an argument is ingenuous. Collection has not always been assimilative. When it *was* coercive, there is some evidence that debtors were forced into roles which justified coercion.

I shall describe a few features of the world of coercive enforcement that existed in the late eighteenth and early nineteenth centuries. I intend only to illustrate my contention that debtors can become secondary deviants. I shall not pretend to provide anything like a scholarly or detailed account of the law and institutions that prevailed before assimilation became the chief mode of collection.

In the late eighteenth and early nineteenth centuries, creditors were given almost total control over a limited area of their debtors' lives. They could execute on 'moveable' goods and deprive a debtor of his liberty until the debt was paid. They could not, however, seize any of the debtor's immoveable assets.[5] Thus, whilst a creditor had 'a right to the body of his debtor every hour till the debt is paid' (Plank *v*. Anderton (1792), 5 T.R., p. 40), the defaulter, in turn, enjoyed considerable invulnerability. If he chose to do so, an imprisoned debtor could steadfastly resist all his creditor's attacks. Unparalleled strength in one area of the law was balanced by extraordinary weakness in another. Romily (1842, vol. 2, p. 326) stated in 1813:

> . . . the law respecting the enforcing the payment of debts required, in my opinion, great amendment; that, while our laws were very severe as far as they gave a remedy against the person of the debtor, they were very relaxed as they supplied remedies against his property; and . . . there was no reason why a debtor's freehold and copyhold estates should not be taken in execution and sold for the payment of his debts, or why money in the public funds, and other property of the same kind, should not be made applicable to pay the demands of the creditors who sued him.

[5] That is, there were no equivalents to garnishee and charging orders.

Prolonged imprisonment was the sole sanction which creditors could use against debtors who refused to surrender these protected items of property. Although defaulters were under no obligation to liquidate their assets and pay their creditors, 'the creditor was enabled to deprive the debtor of his liberty, upon a simple swearing of the debt'. (Rawdon, 1793, p. 648.) Furthermore, provided some elementary rules were observed (such as paying the prisoner a trifling allowance), the creditor was empowered to decide when, if ever, his debtor was to be released. Neild observed in 1802 (p. 17), 'as the law now stands, the remission of punishment is only in the creditor's power, who too often, regardless of clemency, becomes a monstrous species of despot. . . .' Thus the law allowed the two parties to engage in a bitter and lengthy conflict; the debtor hoped that his creditor would despair and release him, whilst the creditor hoped that he would be repaid. Creditors occasionally acted out of caprice, refusing to free their prisoners even when it was evident that they could never be repaid.

During the early 1800s there were some eight debtors' prisons in London,[6] although convict establishments would receive debtors when numbers grew too great. The debtors' prisons were attached to the courts which fed them prisoners: the Fleet was, in its later life, the prison of the Courts of Chancery; and the Marshalsea and Queen's Bench belonged to the courts of the same names. Unlike the convict prisons, they were ultimately administered by the judges of their courts and this control led to a great diversity of structure and policy. They were also coloured by the type of debtors that their courts dealt with. Newgate, for instance, received much poorer debtors than the Fleet or the Queen's Bench. One small prison, Ludgate, housed only clergymen, attorneys, proctors and Freemen of London.

A consequence of this system of control was the differential effects which some legislation had upon the debtors' prisons. In 1815, for example, an official report (Report, 1815) condemned the extortion which was practised in four of the prisons. In the same year, the exacting of fees was made a penal offence, but these four prisons were excluded by the Act (55 Geo. III, c. 50) because there were no central funds to reimburse the gaolers.

The prisons differed greatly in size; some contained as many as six hundred inmates whilst others housed as few as fifteen. Again, there was great diversity in the accommodation which was offered debtors. The prisons which received wealthy people could afford to

[6] The prisons included the Marshalsea, the Fleet, the Queen's Bench; Poultry, Giltspur Street and Borough Compters; Newgate, Ludgate and Whitecross Street Prisons, and so on. Their numbers fluctuated: some were merged, some abolished, and others were founded during the period under discussion.

offer expensive and elegant rooms, but the poorest prisons were totally squalid. The Borough Compter was described in 1802 as having:

> . . . no bedding, or even straw to lie upon. No mops, brooms or pails, to keep the prison clean. No fire in the winter; the casements rotting off their hinges, and scarce a whole pane of glass in the windows. Out of the nine poor wretches who were confined, seven of them were scarce half-cloathed, three were very ill, and without any medical assistance whatever. . . . The men debtors live below stairs totally in ruins. . . . (Neild, 1802, p. 63).

By contrast, the Queen's Bench could offer 'several good apartments which . . . usually let at five guineas a week'. (Neild, 1802.)

It was recognized by Parliament and the prisons' administrators that the prisons must generate profits. In 1701, a bill which proposed that the overcrowding in the Fleet and Queen's Bench should be halted was rejected on the grounds that if there were a decrease in the number of prisoners 'the profits thereby accruing will not be a proportional recompence to the officers to attend the Courts, so that the king's four Courts at Westminster will be without prisons and without officers to assist them'. (*House of Commons Journals*, 15 May 1701.)

The private means of a debtor were paramount in determining his life-style within prison. Any goods or services available outside prison could be bought inside it and, as a result, the more prosperous institutions resembled market places. Thus Smollett (quoted in Thornbury, vol. 6, p. 66) stated of the Queen's Bench:

> . . . except the entrance, where the turnkeys keep watch and ward, there is nothing in the place that looks like a gaol, or bears the least colour of restraint. The street is crowded with passengers; hawkers of all sorts are admitted to call and vend their wares, as in any open street in London. There are butchers' stands, chandlers' shops, a surgery, a tap-house, well-frequented, and a public kitchen, in which provisions are dressed for all the prisoners gratis, at the expense of the publican. Here the voice of misery never complains, and, indeed, little else is to be heard but the sound of mirth and jollity.

The rents of all such enterprises went to the prison's administrator, and it seems that no profitable business was forbidden whilst it remained profitable. Running a prison was regarded as an entrepreneurial activity. In 1718, for instance, the office of Marshal of the Queen's Bench was sold for £10,500 to a Company of Proprietors who farmed it out for a yearly rent of £800. A hundred years later, the Marshal received more than £5,000 a year from his prison. This conception of the administrator's role meant that only a bare minimum of free services were provided. Very few prisons had hospitals or surgeons, and many of the poorer debtors had to beg or rely on charity for their food.

Control within the prison could be erratic and extremely punitive. As an extension of his entrepreneurial role, the administrator often used the system of rewards and punishments as another means of making profit (Webb and Webb, 1922, p. 21):

> Mere parsimony could not, however, make the gaol yield a profit, and many eighteenth century gaolers accordingly varied the squalid misery of prison life by deliberate torture for the purpose of extortion, and the systematic encouragement of drunkenness and vice.

The Webbs indicate how the amenities of prison life could be compatible with its deliberately contrived privations. It seems that the 'encouragement of drunkenness and vice' established an ethical system which neither rewarded normal virtue nor punished normal vice. The pursuit of profit led to a corruption of the mechanisms of social control within prison, such that sanctions were related to the status and wealth of the inmates rather than their moral qualities (Howard, 1780, pp. 31–2):

> . . . the gaoler's interest in the sale of liquors may prompt him to be partial in his behaviour to his prisoners; to treat at least with neglect those who are poor and have nothing to spend, which is the case of the greater number; while he may caress dishonest debtors who take shelter in prison, in order to live there in riot, upon the property of their creditors.

There was social differentiation between the prisons, and there was also social differentiation within them. Inmates were stratified on the basis of their wealth: the richest paid high rents for attractive accommodation in the 'master's side' of a prison; the moderately wealthy paid lower rents for less pleasant rooms in the 'common side'; and the destitute or poor lived in the 'charity wards'. Some prisons were able to offer affluent debtors complete freedom. The Fleet and Queen's Bench were surrounded by areas known as the 'rules' in which prisoners could live on a permanent or daily basis, unmolested by their creditors. The inhabitants of the rules were unaffected by their nominal imprisonment (Select Committee Report, 1730, p. 809):

> The prisoners make large presents to the Marshal . . . for the liberty of these rules, and live in a very easy manner; whilst the

> poor honest debtor, who hath paid away all his substance to satisfy his creditor, is a close prisoner within the prison; thus the debtor who will not pay his creditors, lives at ease, and he who cannot pay suffers.
>
> The King's Bench is in Southwark, its rules are more extensive than the Fleet, having all St. George's Fields to walk in, but the prison house is not so good. By a Habeas Corpus you may remove yourself from one prison to the other; and some of the gentlemen that are in for vast sums, and probably for life, choose the one for the summer, and the other for their winter habitation; and, indeed, both are but the show and name of prisons. (Defoe, 1772, vol. 2, p. 3.)

The administrator's overriding interest in profits completely undermined the effectiveness of coercive reform. If a debtor was wealthy, he could adopt one of the three courses: he could pay his debt, he could attempt to outwit his creditor, or he could enter prison. Imprisonment was anything but coercive because all his wants could be satisfied. Indeed, by purchasing the liberty of the rules, he could live out a perfectly normal life and keep his resources intact. As Burges (1790, p. 383) argued:

> A day rule was not now obtained as a favour to the hard case of any individual debtor, but was an indulgence bought for money, without pretence of any ground for its being granted to one debtor more than to another. The only purchase was its price, and he who had money enough in his pocket was sure to obtain it. When the House knew that the emoluments of the marshal of the King's-bench were not less than £5000 a year for day rules, they would, perhaps, think that the matter deserved some inquiry. He reminded the House of the extent of the rules of the different prisons, and the opportunities they afforded for fraud and iniquity. The rules of the Fleet extended up a part of the Fleet market and of Ludgate-hill, and to various adjoining places. . . . Every man had it in his power to procure his being arrested, and he might say, 'I like to live on Ludgate-hill; I think it is the pleasantest part of London'; or he might carry on any trade in St. George's Fields, to the amount of many thousands of pounds, and set his creditors at utter defiance, by being able to tell them, 'I am in prison already; I choose to live there, and you may do your worst, I won't pay you a shilling'.

Even if he was forced to live in prison, the wealthy debtor could have a comfortable room. He was able to share his bed with a wife, mistress or prostitute.[7] Indeed, from the administrator's point of view, he was the most desirable of all inmates because he was a source of considerable revenue. Instead of suffering, therefore, the debtor was attentively pampered.

There were two alternatives for the poor debtor: evasion or imprisonment. If he did undergo incarceration, it was likely that his ability to repay his creditor would decline steadily. The cruder the conditions that he experienced, the more tempting it must have been to soften them a little (Neild, 1802, p. 16):

> . . . if the first offers of a compromise are refused, the debtor has seldom any opportunity to repeat them; because, from confinement a decrease of property ensues immediately, and his ability to do is lessened in proportion . . . and hence it is obvious, that a prison, so far from leading to a recovery of the debt, becomes the whirlpool . . . of the debtor's remaining property.

Debtors' prisons were supposed not only to create profits, but also to aid creditors. They were remarkably efficient at prising money out of debtors, but the money typically passed to the administrator rather than the creditor. One of the prisons' functions was completely subordinated to the other. After all, profitability was sought by those who actually controlled the prison, whilst coercion was demanded by those who had little influence. The two types of prisoner, the rich and poor, were equally unlikely to respond in a manner desired by their creditors; the one did not do so by choice, the other through inability.

The impact of coercive reform was further lessened by successive Insolvency Acts which released debtors when there were problems of undermanning in the armed forces. The Acts allowed defaulters to discharge their obligations by enlisting. The debtor must have viewed the passing of such Acts as erratic and unpredictable events. Moreover, the creditors' actions must also have appeared irrational and incomprehensible at times. All imprisoned debtors had to plan their lives on the basis of their understanding of the world. This understanding was surely confused and incomplete because relationships between cause and effect were often problematic. The desired effect (release) might have come about without action on the part of the debtor. Similarly, the wrong effect (prolonged incarceration) might have been produced despite the 'right' causal action (a willingness to compromise). Coercion inevitably loses much of its effectiveness in such a situation.

Although enforcement during its coercive phase was thoroughly

[7] See, for example, the First Report of the Select Committee on the Gaols and Houses of Correction in England and Wales, 1835, p. 228.

inefficient, it *was* able to pose acute problems for debtors. They faced the ever-present threat of arbitrary and cruel punishment. Many defaulters took evasive or retaliatory action and, by so doing, justified the repression to which they were exposed. Defaulters were able to flout their creditors by acquiring the liberty of the Fleet or Queen's Bench rules. They were also able to make enforcement so complicated that many creditors gave up pursuit. For example, Romilly (1820, vol. 2, p. 67) complained of the 'Sham Pleas, Writs of Error, and the various other artifices by which the profligate and unprincipled are in the habit of protracting the proceedings, and increasing the expenses of their Creditors'. In 1817, he produced evidence before the House of Commons which demonstrated that secondary deviation was encouraged by lawyers (Hansard, 28 April 1817, vol. 36, p. 26):

> Sir *Samuel Romilly* presented a Petition from certain inhabitants in the county of Gloucester, complaining of the difficulties which had been so disgracefully and so successfully thrown in the way of creditors in recovering small debts. He was satisfied that the evil was more generally to be traced to the interested and unprincipled interference of legal advisers, than to a want of principle upon the part of debtors generally; but never . . . had he learned that the heedlessness of the legislature had left open so wide a door to an abuse which operated completely as a fraud upon nine-tenths of creditors for small sums. . . . He had derived this information . . . from a letter which came into his possession, in consequence of its having been directed generally to the persons confined for debt in the gaol of Gloucester, by an attorney. . . . The primary object of the writer, was to obtain for himself the business, as agent, to the prisoners for debt in that gaol. The letter enjoined such as were confined there to sue out an Habeas, and move themselves to the King's-bench, there advising them how to file sham and dilatory pleas, and upon proceeding to get judgment, to have the office at the Temple searched by their attorney, who, beforehand, should be armed with a writ of error to be filed, recommending them, however, in case they were desirous to be particularly troublesome, to make the writ of error returnable in parliament, the additional expense of which would cost the defendant not more than £1 while the plaintiff would thereby be put to an expense of £100; that by these and similar proceedings of a dilatory nature, they might, at the moderate expense of £24 9s. put their several plaintiffs to an expense of £343.

Such was the ease with which people could be imprisoned for debt, that debtors themselves sometimes contrived to send their creditors to prison. Burges (1790, p. 381) cited:

> . . . The case of Mr. Miller, a merchant of undoubted character and credit. Mr. Miller felt himself obliged to arrest a tradesman, his debtor for £700; that debtor found means, in revenge, to cause Mr. Miller to be arrested for £40,000, not one shilling of which he owed: and as the practice was to require double bail, although an express act of parliament forbad the taking larger bail than the amount of the original debt, Mr. Miller was to find bail for £80,000, the enormous amount of which rendered it impossible for him to procure bail, and he was obliged to go to the King's-bench prison, where he continued six weeks, before he could obtain relief from the court, which he was enabled to obtain, by the humanity of the marshal of the King's-bench. . . . No sooner was he at liberty, than the debtor contrived to have him arrested again, by a writ from the court of Common pleas, for £20,000, and he was kept in the Fleet 191 days, before he was able to obtain relief.

Although it is impossible to know how widespread such practices were, they do show that the response to repression could be both organized and ingenious. It is also clear that the debtors' prisons deliberately encouraged wealthier debtors to adopt a deviant life-style. Few contemporary professionals can ever have been so blatant or extravagant in their behaviour as the inhabitants of the rules. Indeed, secondary deviation must have been peculiarly attractive to defaulters who had money enough to enjoy it. Debtors of substance often chose to spend their lives in the rules so that they could pass their undiminished estates on to their heirs. Grant (1838, p. 78), for instance, observed, 'there are generally a fair sprinkling of the nobility in the Queen's Bench. Considering the proportion which the aristocracy bears to the other inhabitants of the country, their relative number in the Bench is strikingly great.'

As a result, coercive control measures were justified by the contention that debtors were so deviant that force was essential. Lord Thurlow (1793, p. 650), for example, stated he 'was fully persuaded that the check of imprisonment was necessary to restrain unprincipled adventurers from incurring debts which they had not the intention nor the means of discharging'. An observation of greater significance was made by the writer (Anon., 1757, p. 5) of a pamphlet which urged that debtors should be released from prison. He felt compelled to defend himself against the 'Imputation of pleading for Rogues and Spendthrifts, the trite, stale, Reproach that, in this Case, used to be thrown out against all Arguments for common Compassion'. The brutality of the law was frequently condemned, but it is apparent that debt collection in this period was based on a coercion which created, and was justified by the secondary deviation of defaulters.[8]

Of course, enforcement in the period which I have described was not a pure case of coercive reform. Yet the extent to which defaulters were thrust into a deviant status at that time was truly remarkable. In Chapter 12, I suggested that many of the factors which affect enmity towards debtors are independent of the enforcement system. If the checks that now prevent the stigmatization of defaulters were effective then, the scale of secondary deviation was even more remarkable.

Similarly, contemporary enforcement does not represent a pure case of assimilative reform, but its structure *does* permit primary deviation to retain its primary form. Mere rule-breaking does not lead to a process which forces a change of identity on the rule-breaker.[9] Debt collection has evolved into a system which elaborately tries to minimize its impact on defaulters and the wider society. It is probable that the current tendency to label defaulters as 'inadequates' and deplore the coercive features of the system that processes them[10] is itself largely a consequence of the assimilative

8 It is possible that the shift towards a more sympathetic definition of debtors (which was always present, but not always authoritative) was permitted by legislation which enabled creditors to seize immovable assets. (1 and 2 Vict., c. 110 (1838).) When imprisonment was not the sole sanction against defaulters of means, secondary deviation was not so attractive.

9 There may be a significant exception to this structural inhibition of secondary deviation. Interestingly, the exception does not appear to be connected with the world of enforcers and defaulters as I have described it. Instead, the London hippy 'underground' encourages the growth of sophisticated default techniques as a part of its propagation of a more general deviant role-style. In an underground manual, there is the following advice:

> *ACCOUNTS* Smith Bros: complete department store; ... Listen to people giving their names for their account. They don't use cards there.
> Go into a big tool shop where they do credit. Stand about, and make sure you catch the name of a cat getting credit. Then return two weeks later and give his name (preferably a big firm).
>
> *BANKRUPTCY* A little handbook called *A Debtor's Guide* is in underground circulation.
> 'If you have nothing you have nothing to lose'. Order something, then let them repossess it; keep being out, and they can't break in; keep moving, you don't have to see them.

This handbook, *Project Free London*, contains abundant information about a great many other kinds of phenomena. Default and related practices were only a slight part. I have been unable to obtain a copy of the *Debtor's Guide*.

10 Cf. Payne Committee, 1969, p. 95: 'The majority of the Committee think the the word "court" should not be used as part of the name of the new body charged with the enforcement of judgment debts . . . [One reason] is that the word "office" more closely describes the functions of the enforce-

character of enforcement. The Payne Committee's (1969, pp. 246–61) recommendation that the 1869 Debtors Act be repealed has accelerated this movement towards an assimilative system.[11] It will, in turn, reinforce the popular conception that debtors are not really deviant.[12] Creditors and collectors will, of course, be the last people to accept this change of definition.

ment of judgment debts than the word "court". On the other hand, some members of the Committee urged that the word "court" should be part of the title, in order to emphasize its possession of coercive powers in the service of enforcement. The majority held that this lays undue emphasis upon the coercive rather than the administrative side of the enforcement of judgments and orders of the court. . . .'

11 In some marginal cases, however, it is possible that a weakening of sanctions will lead to an increased use of violence. Nevertheless, I believe that violent enforcement is unlikely to grow in the world of routine enforcement. What is more likely to happen is that the large bureaucratic creditors will couple more stringent credit sanctioning with a greater reliance on person-oriented collection techniques.

12 The Payne Committee's recommendation that a Social Service Officer for Debtors should be established is clear evidence of this change of definition.

Bibliography

ABEL-SMITH, B., and STEVENS, R. (1967) *Lawyers and the Courts*, Heinemann, London.

A.L.L. (1962) 'The bailiff's job: "Z" Cars episode in Chesterfield', *County Court Officer*, vol. 37, no. 16, 14 December.

AMERICAN ASSOCIATION OF SOCIAL WORKERS (1929) *Social Casework Generic and Specific*, American Association of Social Workers, New York.

ANDERTON (1831) Quoted in *Parliamentary Papers*, 1831, XX, Appendix E.

ANON (1757) *Considerations upon the present increase of civil prisoners and debtors in England*, Kinnersly, London.

ANSLINGER, H. and TOMPKINS, W. (1953) *The Traffic in Narcotics*, Funk & Wagnall, New York.

AUSUBEL, D. (1958) *Drug Addiction*, Random House, New York.

BAIER, K. (1968) 'Responsibility and freedom', in R. de George (ed.), *Ethics and Society*, Macmillan, London.

BANTON, M. (1964) *The Policeman in the Community*, Tavistock, London.

BAYLEY, D. and MENDELSOHN, H. (1969) *Minorities and the Police*, Free Press, New York.

BAYNE-POWELL, R. (1937) *Eighteenth-Century London Life*, Murray, London.

BECCARIA, C. (1963) *On Crimes and Punishments*, Bobbs-Merrill, Indianapolis.

BECKER, H. (1963) 'Becoming a marihuana user', in *Outsiders*, Free Press, New York.

BECKER, H. (1967) 'Whose side are we on?', *Social Problems*, vol. 14, no. 3, Winter.

BERGER, P. and LUCKMANN, T. (1967) *The Social Construction of Reality*, Penguin, London.

BERNE, E. (1966) *Games People Play*, Deutsch, London.

BITTNER, E. (1967) 'The police on skid-row', *American Sociological Review*, vol. 32, no. 5, October.

BLACK, H. (1962) *Buy Now, Pay Later*, Pocket Books, New York.

BLUMBERG, A. (1967) 'The practice of law as confidence game: organizational cooptation of a profession', *Law and Society Review*, vol. 1, June.

BURGES, J. B. (1790) Speech made in the Commons debate on the Debtors Relief Bill, 1790. Hansard, vol. 28. pp. 381–2.

CAMERON, M. (1968) 'Identity and the shoplifter', in E. Rubington and M. Weinberg (eds) *Deviance*, Macmillan, New York.

CAPLOVITZ, D. (1963) *The Poor Pay More*, Free Press, New York.

CAPLOVITZ, D. (1968) 'Consumer credit in the affluent society', *Law and Contemporary Problems*, vol. 33, no. 4, Autumn.

CHAMBLISS, W. (ed.) (1969) *Crime and the Legal Process*, McGraw-Hill, New York.

CICOUREL, A. (1968) *The Social Organization of Juvenile Justice*, Wiley, New York.

CICOUREL, A. and KITSUSE, J. (1968) 'The social organization of the high school and deviant adolescent careers', in E. Rubington and M. Weinberg (eds), *Deviance*, Macmillan, New York.

CLAYTON, T. (1967) *The Protectors*, Oldbourne, London.

CLEMENTS (1969) 'I am the only one in the family who has ever had a carpet', in K. Martin, 'The sad society', *Observer*, 24 August.

COHEN, S. (1967) 'Mods, rockers and the rest', *Howard Journal*, vol. 12, no. 2.

COMMITTEE ON COUNTY COURT PROCEDURE (1949) *Final Report*, London, HMSO, Cmnd 7668.

COUNTY COURT OFFICERS ASSOCIATION Memorandum to the Payne Committee (q.v.).

CRESSEY, P. (1932) *The Taxi Dance Hall*, University of Chicago Press.

CRESSEY, D. (1953) *Other People's Money*, Free Press, New York.

CRESSEY, D. (1967) Foreword to E. Sutherland, *White Collar Crime*, Holt, Rinehart and Winston, New York.

CROWTHER, G. (1971) *Report of the Committee on Consumer Credit*, HMSO, London.

CUMMING, E., CUMMING, I. and EDELL, L. (1965) 'Policeman as philosopher, friend and guide', *Social Problems*, vol. 12, no. 3, Winter.

DAHL, R. (1968) 'On entering a mental hospital', in C. McCaghy, J. Skipper and M. Leyton (eds), *In Their Own Behalf*, Appleton-Century-Crofts, New York.

DAVIS, F. (1959) 'The cabdriver and his fare', *American Journal of Sociology*, vol. 64.

DAVIS, F. (1963) *Passage Through Crisis*, Bobbs-Merrill, Indianapolis.

DAVIS, K. (1964) 'Illegitimacy and the social structure', in W. Goode (ed.), *Readings on the Family and Society*, Prentice-Hall, New Jersey.

DE BERKER, P. (1965) 'Impressions of civil debtors in Brixton', *British Journal of Criminology*, vol. 5, no. 3, July.

DEFOE, D. (1772) *Tour Through the Whole Island of Great Britain*, London.

DEWEY, J. (1922) *Human Nature and Conduct*, Holt, New York.

DICKSON, D. (1968) 'Bureaucracy and morality', *Social Problems*, vol. 16, no. 2, Fall.

DINITZ, S., DYNES, R. and CLARKE, A. (1969) *Deviance*, Oxford University Press, New York.

'DOBB'S DILEMMAS' (1965) *County Court Officer*, vol. 39, no. 7, 29 October.

DONNISON, D. (1955) 'Observations on university training for social work in Great Britain and North America', *Social Science Review*, December.

DUSTER, T. (1970) *The Legislation of Morality*, Free Press, New York.

EDWARDS, L. (1958) *Shoplifting and Shrinkage Protection for Stores*, C. C. Thomas, Illinois.

EGAN, B. (1968) 'The debt merchants', *Focus*, vol. 3, no. 10, 14 October.

ERIKSON, K. (1964) 'Notes on the sociology of deviance', in H. Becker (ed.), *The Other Side*, Free Press, New York.

ETZIONI, A. (1964) *Modern Organizations*, Prentice-Hall, New Jersey.

EVERSHED COMMITTEE (1953) *Final Report of the Committee on Supreme Court Practice and Procedure*, HMSO, London, Cmnd 8878.

FIDDLE, S. (1963) 'The addict culture and movement into and out of hospitals', in U.S. Senate, Committee on the Judiciary, Sub-Committee to Investigate Juvenile Delinquency, *Hearings*, Part 13, United States Government Printing Office, Washington.

FIELD, X. (1963) *Under Lock and Key*, Parrish, London.

FISHER, J. (1950) 'Income, spending and saving patterns of consumer units in different age groups', in *Studies in Income and Wealth*, Washington, National Bureau of Economic Research, vol. 15.

FOSTER J. and BLOM-COOPER, L. (1969) *Joint Memorandum on Imprisonment for Debt*, submitted to the Payne Committee (q.v.).

FREIDSON, E. (1968) 'Disability as social deviance', in E. Rubington and M. Weinberg (eds), *Deviance*, Macmillan, New York.

FULLER, R. and MYERS, R. (1941) 'The natural history of a social problem', *American Sociological Review*, vol. 6, June.

'GAIUS' (1965) 'County court image', *County Court Officer*, vol. 39, no. 6, 10 September.

GANS, H. (1962) *The Urban Villagers*, Free Press, New York.

GARVY, G. (1948) 'The role of dissaving in economic analysis', *Journal of Political Economy*, vol. 56, no. 5, October.

GIBBONS, D. (1968) *Society, Crime and Criminal Careers*, Prentice-Hall, New Jersey.

GLASER, B. and STRAUSS, A. (1971) *Status Passage*, Routledge & Kegan Paul, London.

GLASSER, C. Undated and untitled paper on the county courts.

GOFFMAN, E. (1952) 'On cooling the mark out', *Psychiatry*, vol. 15, no. 4, November.

GOFFMAN, E. (1961) *Asylums*, Anchor, New York.

GOFFMAN, E. (1963) *Stigma*, Prentice-Hall, New Jersey.

GOFFMAN, E. (1968a) 'The staff world', *New Society*, 21 November.

GOFFMAN, E. (1968b) 'The moral career of the mental patient', in S. Spitzer and N. Denzin (eds), *The Mental Patient*, McGraw-Hill, New York.

GOFFMAN, E. (1969) 'On face-work', in *Where The Action Is*, Penguin, London.

GOLD, R. (1952) 'Janitors vs. tenants: a status-income dilemma', *American Journal of Sociology*, vol. 57, March.

GOVERNOR OF BRIXTON (1969) Information sent to the Society of Civil Servants (Prison and Borstal Governors) for their Memorandum to the Payne Committee (q.v.).

GRANT, J. (1838) *Sketches in London*, London.

GREGORY, R. (1962) *County Court Manual*, HMSO, London.

GREIG, C. (1964) *Commercial Credits and Accounts Collection*, Institute of Credit Management, London.

GRIGG, M. (1965) *The Challenor Case*, Penguin, London.

GUSFIELD, J. (1963) *Symbolic Crusade*, University of Illinois Press, Urbana.

HALSBURY, LORD (1957) *The Laws of England*, vol. 20, Butterworth, London.

HEYNEN, J. (1970) *Imprisonment for Debt*, Unpublished paper delivered at a seminar at the University of London, 16 February.

HOGGART, R. (1957) *The Uses of Literacy*, Chatto & Windus, London.

HOME OFFICE (1960) *Prisons and Borstals*, HMSO, London.

HOPKINS, G. (1964) 'How much are your receivables really worth?', *Merit News*, IAC, Montreal, vol. 16, no. 9, November-December.

HOWARD, J. (1780) *The State of the Prisons*, Warrington, London.

HUGHES, E. (1958) *Men and Their Work*, Free Press, New York.

IRWIN, J. and CRESSEY, D. (1964) 'Thieves, convicts and the inmate culture', in H. Becker (ed.), *The Other Side*, Free Press, New York.

JAMES, W. (1963) *Psychology*, Fawcett, New York.

JENKINS, L. J. (1953) 'in Re a Judgment Summons', in H. Christie *et al.* (eds), *All England Law Reports*, vol. 1, Butterworth, London; and [1953], Ch. 195.

JOINT WORKING PARTY (1963) *Report on the Enforcement of Judgments and Decrees of the Courts in Northern Ireland*, HMSO, Belfast.

JONES, W. (1964) 'Exciting city!', *County Court Officer*, vol. 38, no. 9, 31 January.

KATONA, G. (1949a) 'Analysis of dissaving', *American Economic Review*, vol. 39, no. 3.

KATONA, G. (1949b) 'Effect of income changes on the rate of saving', *Review of Economics and Statistics*, vol. 31, no. 2.

KLAPP, O. (1962) *Heroes, Villains and Fools*, Prentice-Hall, New Jersey.

KUH, R. (1961) 'Dealing with narcotic addiction', *New York Law Journal*, 8 June.

LAW COMMISSION (1966) *Landlord and Tenant: Interim Report on Distress for Rent*, HMSO, London.

LAW SOCIETY (1969) Memorandum to the Payne Committee (q.v.).

LEA, H. (1896) *Auricular Confessions and Indulgences*, Swan, Sonnenschein, London.

LEA, H. (1908) *A History of the Inquisition in the Middle Ages*, Macmillan, London.

LEIGHTON, N. (1965) 'Two cultures in social work', *Case Conference*, vol. 11, no. 9, March.

LEMERT, E. (1948) 'Some aspects of a general theory of sociopathic behavior', *Proceedings of the Pacific Sociological Society*, Research Studies, State College of Washington, 16, no. 1.

LEMERT, E. (1951) *Social Pathology*, McGraw-Hill, New York.

LEMERT, E. (1967) 'Is there a natural history of social problems?', in *Human Deviance, Social Problems and Social Control*, Prentice-Hall, New Jersey.

LIEBOW, E. (1967) *Tally's Corner*, Routledge & Kegan Paul, London.

LIFTON, R. (1961) *Thought Reform and the Psychology of Totalism*, Norton, New York.

LINDESMITH, A. (1957) 'The British system of narcotics control', *Law and Contemporary Problems*, vol. 23, Winter.

LINDESMITH, A. (1968) *Addiction and Opiates*, Aldine, Chicago.

LLOYD DAVIES, A. (1963) 'Psychotherapy and social casework', in *Relation in Casework*, Association of Psychiatric Social Workers, London.

LYMAN, S. and SCOTT, M. (1968) 'Coolness in everyday life', in M. Truzzi (ed.), *Sociology and Everyday Life*, Prentice-Hall, New Jersey.

McCORMICK, M. (1965) 'Human values and the poor', *Social Casework*, vol. 46, no. 3, March.

McCORMICK, M. (1966) 'Professional responsibility and the professional image', *Social Casework*, vol. 47, no. 10, December.

McHUGH, P. (1968) *Defining the Situation*, Bobbs-Merrill, Indianapolis.

McINTOSH, M. (1968) 'The homosexual role', *Social Problems*, vol. 16, no. 2, Fall.

MACIVER, R. (1942) *Social Causation*, Ginn, Boston.

McNAMARA, J. (1967) 'Uncertainties in police work', in D. Bordua (ed.), *The Police*, Wiley, New York.

MAO TSE-TUNG (1951) 'Correcting unorthodox tendencies in learning, the Party, and literature and arts', in C. Brandt *et al.*, *A Documentary History of Chinese Communism*, Harvard University Press, Cambridge, Mass.

MARSDEN-SMEDLEY, S. (1969) 'Is the legal system any use to consumers?', *Focus*, July.

MATZA, D. (1964) *Delinquency and Drift*, Wiley, New York.

MAURER, D. (1940) *The Big Con*, Bobbs-Merrill, Indianapolis.

MAYS, J. (1964) *Growing Up in the City*, Wiley, New York.

MEAD, G. (1918) 'The psychology of punitive justice', *American Journal of Sociology*, vol. 23.

MEAD, G. (1963) *Mind, Self and Society*, University of Chicago Press.

MESSINGER, S. *et al.* (1968) 'Life as theater', in M. Truzzi (ed.), *Sociology and Everyday Life*, Prentice-Hall, New Jersey.

MEYER, C. (1966) 'The changing concept of individualized services', *Social Casework*, vol. 47, no. 5, May.

MILES, A. (1954) *American Social Work Theory*, Harper, New York.

MILLER, W. (1958) 'Lower class culture as a generating milieu of gang delinquency', *Journal of Social Issues*, vol. 14, no. 3.

MOFFETT, J. (1968) *Concepts in Casework Treatment*, Routledge & Kegan Paul, London.

MORRIS, P. (1962) 'Debtor's prison still exists', *New Society*, 29 November.

MORRIS, P. (1965) *Prisoners and their Families*, Allen & Unwin, London.

NEILD, J. (1802) *An Account of the Society for the Relief and Discharge of Persons Imprisoned for Small Debts*, Nichols, London.

PARK, R. (1927) 'The American newspaper', *American Journal of Sociology*, vol. 32, March.

PARK, R. (1936) 'Succession: An ecological concept', *American Sociological Review*, vol. 1, April.

PARK, R. (1937) Introduction to *Interracial Marriage in Hawaii*, by R. Adams, Macmillan, New York.

PARK, R. (1967) 'The natural history of the newspaper', in *On Social Control and Collective Behavior*, University of Chicago Press.

PAYNE COMMITTEE (1969) *Report of the Committee on the Enforcement of Judgment Debts*, HMSO, London, Cmnd 3909.

PENAL AFFAIRS COMMITTEE OF THE SOCIETY OF FRIENDS (1965) *Committal to Prison for Failure to Pay Civil Debts*, memorandum to the Payne Committee, London.

PERLMAN, H. (1963) *Social Casework*, University of Chicago Press.

PINSON, B. (1968) *Revenue Law*, Sweet & Maxwell, London.

POLSKY, N. (1967) *Hustlers, Beats and Others*, Aldine, Chicago.

PRESIDENT'S COMMISSION ON LAW ENFORCEMENT (1967) *The Police (Task Force Report)*, United States Government Printing Office, Washington.

'PROTEUS' (1965) Letter to *County Court Officer*, vol. 39, no. 6, 10 September.

RAWDON, LORD (1793) Speech delivered in the Lords Debate on the Insolvent Debtors Bill, 27 March 1793, *Hansard*, vol. 30.

REGISTRAR OF E COURT (1969) Memoranda to the Payne Committee (q.v.).

REISS, A. and BORDUA, D. (1967) 'Environment and organization', in D. Bordua (ed.), *The Police*, Wiley, New York.

REPORT (1815) *Report of the Committee on the State of the King's Bench, Fleet, and Marshalsea Prisons, and on the New London Prison for Debtors*, London.

RICHARD, R. (1961) In M. Harney and J. Cross, *The Narcotic Officer's Handbook*, C. C. Thomas, Illinois.

ROBERTS, J. (1961) 'Opening of new court at Harlow', *County Court Officer*, vol. 37, no. 3, 14 April.

ROCK, P. (1968) 'Observations on debt collection', *British Journal of Sociology*, vol. 19, no. 2, June.

ROGLER, L. and HOLLINGSHEAD, A. (1965) *Trapped: Families and Schizophrenia*, Wiley, New York.

ROMILLY, S. (1820) *The Speeches of Sir Samuel Romilly in the House of Commons*, vol. 2, Ridgway, London.

ROMILLY, S. (1842) *The Life of Sir Samuel Romilly, Written by Himself*, Murray, London.

ROSE, A. (ed.) (1962) *Human Behavior and Social Processes*, Routledge & Kegan Paul, London.

ROSE, A. (1968) 'Law and the causation of social problems', *Social Problems*, vol. 16, no. 1, Summer.

ROTH, J. (1963) *Timetables*, Bobbs-Merrill, Indianapolis.

RUBINGTON, E. and WEINBERG, M. (eds) (1968) *Deviance*, Macmillan, New York.

SCHEFF, T. (1966a) *Being Mentally Ill*, Weidenfeld & Nicolson, London.

SCHEFF, T. (1966b) 'Typification in the diagnostic practices of rehabilitation agencies', in M. Sussman (ed.), *Sociology and Rehabilitation*, American Sociological Association, Cleveland.

SCHEFF, T. (1967) *Mental Illness and Social Processes*, Harper & Row, New York.

SCHUR, E. (1961a) 'British narcotics policies', *Journal of Criminal Law, Criminology and Police Science*, March-April.

SCHUR, E. (1961b) 'Drug addiction under British policy', *Social Problems*, vol. 9, Fall.

SCHUR, E. (1962) *Narcotic Addiction in Britain and America*, Indiana University Press.

SCHUR, E. (1965) *Crimes Without Victims*, Prentice-Hall, New Jersey.

SCHUTZ, A. (1962) *Collected Papers*, vol. 1, Martinus Nijhoff, The Hague.

SCOTT, M. (1968) *The Racing Game*, Aldine, Chicago.

SELECT COMMITTEE (1730) *Report of the Select Committee of the House of Commons*, 1730, Parl. Hist., 8.

SHIBUTANI, T. (1966) *Improvised News*, Bobbs-Merrill, Indianapolis.

SIMMONS, J. (1965) 'Public stereotypes of deviants', *Social Problems*, vol. 13, no. 2, Fall.

SKOLNICK, J. (1966) *Justice Without Trial*, Wiley, New York.

SMIGEL, E. and ROSS, H. (eds) (1970) *Crimes Against Bureaucracy*, Van Nostrand-Reinhold, New York.

SMILES, S. (1877) *Character*, John Murray, London.

SOMMER, R. and OSMOND, H. (1961) 'Symptoms of institutional care', *Social Problems*, vol. 8, Winter.

'STALWARTS, THE' (1966) Letter to the *County Court Officer*, vol. 39, no. 11, 22 April.

STANTON, A. and SCHWARTZ, M. (1954) *The Mental Hospital*, Basic Books, New York.

STEPHENSON, O. (1961) 'Integration of theory and practice in professional training', *Case Conference*, vol. 8, no. 2, June.

STINCHCOMBE, A. (1963) 'Institutions of privacy in the determination of police administrative practice', *American Journal of Sociology*, vol. 69, September.

STORY, J. (1966) *Something for Nothing*, Penguin, London.

STRAUSS, A. (1959) *Mirrors and Masks*, Free Press, New York.

SUDNOW, D. (1965) 'Normal crimes', *Social Problems*, vol. 12, Winter.

SUTHERLAND, E. (1950) 'The diffusion of sexual psychopath laws', *American Journal of Sociology*, vol. 56, September.

SUTTLES, G. (1968) *The Social Order of the Slum*, University of Chicago Press.

SYKES, G. and MATZA, D. (1967) 'Techniques of neutralization', in R. Giallombardo (ed.), *Juvenile Delinquency*, Wiley, New York.

SYKES, G. and MESSINGER, S. (1960) 'The inmate social system', in *Theoretical Studies in Social Organization of the Prison*, Social Science Research Council, New York.

TANNENBAUM, F. (1938) *Crime and the Community*, Columbia University Press, New York.

TAYLOR, A. (1966) 'This scandal of the lawyers' closed shop', *Sunday Express*, 1 May.

TAYLOR, L. and BENTHAM, J. (1965) 'Britain's national credit reference bureau', *ACB of A Management*, January.

THOMPSON, E. (1971) 'The moral economy of the crowd in the eighteenth century', *Past and Present*, no. 50, February.

THORNBURY, W. (n.d.) *Old and New London*, Cassell, Potter & Galpin, London.

THURLOW, LORD (1793) Speech delivered at the Lords Debate on the Insolvent Debtors Bill, 27 March 1793, Hansard, vol. 30.

TROLLOPE, A. (1947) *Framley Parsonage*, Harrap, London.

TURBERVILLE, A. (1949) *The Spanish Inquisition*, Oxford University Press, London.

VERNON, M. (1962) *The Psychology of Perception*, Penguin, London.

WALLACE, S. (1968) *Skid Row as a Way of Life*, Harper Torchbooks, New York.

WEBB, S. and WEBB, B. (1922) *English Prisons Under Local Government*, Longmans, London.

WESTLEY, W. (1967) 'The police', in E. Burgess and D. Bogue (eds), *Urban Sociology*, University of Chicago Press.

WILKINS, L. (1964) *Social Deviance*, Tavistock, London.

WOODSIDE, M. (1962) 'Profile of a prison population', *Prison Service Journal*, July.

WOOTTON, B. (1963) *Social Science and Social Pathology*, Allen & Unwin, New York.

WORKING PARTY (1956) *Report on the County Courts*, London.

YEOMAN, F. (1965) 'Imprisonment for debt', *County Court Officer*, vol. 39, no. 7, 29 October.

ZANDER, M. and GLASSER, C. (1967) 'A study in representation', *New Law Journal*, 27 July.

Index

For Product Safety Concerns and Information please contact our EU representative GPSR@taylorandfrancis.com
Taylor & Francis Verlag GmbH, Kaufingerstraße 24, 80331 München, Germany

www.ingramcontent.com/pod-product-compliance
Lightning Source LLC
LaVergne TN
LVHW011112300926
849160LV00008B/353

* 9 7 8 0 4 1 5 8 2 8 3 2 1 *